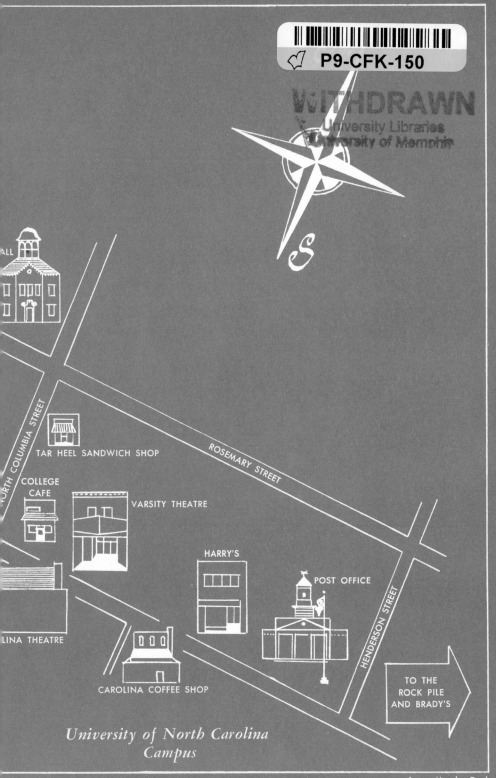

ALL

NORTH COLUMBIA STREET

TAR HEEL SANDWICH SHOP

COLLEGE
CAFE

VARSITY THEATRE

ROSEMARY STREET

HARRY'S

POST OFFICE

HENDERSON STREET

LINA THEATRE

CAROLINA COFFEE SHOP

TO THE
ROCK PILE
AND BRADY'S

*University of North Carolina
Campus*

Lynn Moody Deal

THE
FREE
MEN

Books by John Ehle

Nonfiction

THE FREE MEN

SHEPHERD OF THE STREETS

THE SURVIVOR

Fiction

THE LAND BREAKERS

LION ON THE HEARTH

KINGSTREE ISLAND

MOVE OVER, MOUNTAIN

THE

FREE

MEN

by John Ehle

 Harper & Row, Publishers

NEW YORK, EVANSTON,

AND LONDON

FIRST EDITION

LIBRARY OF CONGRESS CATALOG CARD NUMBER: 64-7829

C-P

"Sometimes you feel so bad you
want to go out into a cabin
in the woods and just forget
about freedom."

JAMES FOUSHEE,
in conversation, 1964

A section of illustrations follows page 116.

Foreword

        In the summer of 1964, visiting us in Vermont, John Ehle held many long telephone conversations with North Carolina prison and parole officials, seeking to persuade them to release a number of North Carolina students who had been imprisoned for civil rights demonstrations in Chapel Hill, the site of the University of North Carolina. A resident of Chapel Hill, Ehle had come to know the young leaders of the movement—John Dunne, Pat Cusick, Quinton Baker, and others; he was writing a book about their unsuccessful efforts to desegregate the restaurants and retail stores in the town, of the arrests, trials, and sentencings that had followed; and now he was helping to arrange parole, Northern jobs and schooling, hoping that the young people would be allowed and would allow themselves to complete their educations before plunging back into full commitment to a struggle that had been altered by passage of the Federal Civil Rights bill.

On the telephone he shamelessly had turned on all his Southern powers of persuasion and jocularity. When he hung up he said, shaking his head, "Sheer plagiarism, but I had to do it."

Ehle's ability, like that of some other Southerners, to establish direct, warm personal relations, whether face to face or on the telephone, reflects a society where people maintain strong ties to kin and place, and where people in a poor and sparsely settled country have for generations been thrown upon each other. Beyond that, Ehle has an eloquence hardly to be found today except in the regional and ethnic pockets of America.

These qualities, plus a ready but not uncritical sympathy, were among those that made it possible for him to become so deeply involved, so fully the confidante of the determined young militants whose chronicle this book is. Unlike Howard Zinn, whose book *SNCC, The New Abolitionists* gives historical perspective to this civil rights movement, Ehle was not the inspirer, mentor, or public defender of a SNCC or CORE. Nor is he the older faculty member taking vicarious pleasure in the assaults by irreverent students on an established order toward which he himself is ambivalent. On the contrary, Ehle's involvement began by accident and continued by escalation; he remains an interested and helpful interpreter and sometime mediator. The result is that he is not cut off from the officials nor from the unhappily bigoted townswoman with whom he still takes Sunday dinners, nor from the newsmen, lawmen, aldermen, and university officials of Chapel Hill who in various complicated ways let the students and the community down. Thus, in *The Free Men* we ourselves share the perspectives not only of the student activists but of their often reluctant white and Negro supporters, their many different opponents, and those who stood by.

The result is the most rounded picture I know of how a single community experienced an effort at integration. Professor Russell Barrett's *Integration at Ole Miss* is a circumstantial and dramatic book on the Meredith case, presenting in addition to what the national spotlight picked up the many aspects of intra-university maneuvering and the dedication of a few members of the faculty to Meredith's cause. Ehle's story, on the other hand, is almost entirely unknown to us: as he says at the end, the national press gave the Chapel Hill struggles virtually no publicity, and while I had read a bit about them in publications of Methodist Social Action groups at Duke and had heard of Floyd McKissick, the brave, scathing, Negro civil rights lawyer of Durham, most of *The Free Men* was news to me. I had thought of the University of North Carolina not only as among the most fearless of the great state universities but also as one of those (like Wisconsin or Minnesota) most concerned with and responsible to its region. But in the crisis created by student agitation, its leaders did not lead, though some of its faculty did; and most of its students, though not Rebel-yell-prone, were indifferent if not hostile. The momentum of John Dunne, Pat Cusick, and the other activists, and the lack of early response from the adult communities of university and town, drove the students not only to drop out of school but also to a point of increasing polarization from the rest of their society. John Ehle remained one of their few ties to the older ongoing world. This book is in part an effort to hitch them up again to the progress of America by interpreting them to us.

To the students, in their passionate, uncompromising idealism, the timid university officials and the ever-damned white liberals seemed at first part of a general conspiracy of those in power. But for those of the students who are Gandhian and deeply Christian, no Americans can be considered unredeemable, not even the sadistic hoods and lawless officials who, as Ehle rightly points out, our country throws up without even having to train them in brutality. I am less hopeful than are the students about such redemptions.

At the end Ehle quotes some of the students as realizing their naïveté about society and about how people would react to the spur and irritant of demonstrations. Some of the demonstrators had second thoughts in 1964, for example, when a segregationist candidate defeated a moderate in a run-off for the North Carolina Democratic gubernatorial nomination, partly because of backlash against their demonstrations and the Federal action which many such demonstrations helped to make timely. Until then the students had been sheltered from the most bigoted elements of a state with a reputation for moderation by the climate of relative toleration in Chapel Hill itself.

But just as the reaction of North Carolina voters reflected the impact of the national Civil Rights Act on many Southern states, so the students at Chapel Hill are part of a larger current. It was at North Carolina Agricultural and Technical College at Greensboro that the first sit-ins had occurred in 1960. The quartet of Negro students who began this were non-ideological, daring each other, but they were beginning something that was more than they could possibly have known. By the time of the Chapel Hill events, which led to fifteen hundred arrests, students and their older partisans had discovered many other ways of evoking what Arthur Waskow has termed "creative disorder," ways which often add up to brilliant guerrilla harrassment, more inventive than the malign counter-guerrillas who bomb churches, fire guns at night at interracial parties or make equally unbrave obscene telephone calls. Furthermore, the students have become steadily more ideological, and, last summer in Mississippi as presently at Berkeley, a few have determined that only revolution will allow the Negro to claim his full equality. (It is, paradoxically, a revolution designed to bring about what the Constitution already ordains.) Some of the Northern students I myself know, and who have worked in the Deep South, do not quite fit the delineation Ehle presents in his last chapter; they are as brave and dedicated, but a bit more cynical and corrosive; somewhat less committed to nonviolence, save as a tactic of the weak; and perhaps a bit less apt to be broke or late.

Like John Ehle, I see these young people, and others of analogous temper who have gone into the Peace Corps and other overseas agencies or into Vista and other domestic programs, as among the finest people to be found in our history or anywhere on earth. Like him, I feel that these young people do not know their strength, and that their understandable despair may give rise to destructiveness toward themselves if not toward others. Their refusal to compromise has been one of their strengths, as is their insistence that equality come now, this moment, not tomorrow. Yet militancy, like any other means, can become an end in itself; and militants can and do compete in intransigence. For many, the race issue has absorbed all priorities, blotting out, for example, what are for me the even more urgent issues of foreign policy which determine whether there will be a world in which to struggle. Students at Chapel Hill might have felt Vietnam beyond them, while Mr. Watts, manager of a segregated café, was the enemy right there, as he is right there in less blatant fashion in our larger cities. Now that Mr. Watts must and does comply, no doubt with a certain relief, I hope the students do not drift back into indifference and privatism. I hope so for the country's sake, which needs their criticism, their energetic, at times gay sense of commitment, and their inventiveness. I hope so for their particular sakes, as well as my own, for, thanks to John Ehle in person and to this book, I myself have become engaged with these free men I have never met, with Dunne, Cusick, Quinton Baker, Rosemary Ezra, Lou Calhoun, Charliese Cotton, Buddy Tieger, and the others; I have been caught up in their ethical and tactical dilemmas and dangers. I hope so also in a more general way, for it seems to me that the experiences young people are gaining in the civil rights movement serve to extend their competence, as war also does, but in many instances with a less parochial and transient sense of human solidarity and significance. As a parent and teacher, I wish such competence and scope could be gained in a less cruel and abrasive school than John

Ehle's friends endured, which I suppose is a way of saying that I hope that the chasm between these, our best young people, and even our rather decent, unfanatical majority may someday be less grave.

DAVID RIESMAN

University of Sussex
Brighton, Sussex
January 30, 1965

PART I

THE CONFRONTATIONS

Chapter One

To reach sandy ridge prison in a car, one cuts off U.S. 40 west of Greensboro and east of Winston-Salem; the overpass is marked "Sandy Ridge." One follows a twisty country road for three miles to a small general store, where a pot-bellied stove and several benches are patient reminders of the way many old people still live and think and are in North Carolina. From the store, one can see the prison, its tall steel fences and barbed wire, its old-fashioned wooden guardhouses and a sign announcing visiting hours—one Sunday afternoon for whites and another for Negroes.

The storekeeper told me there were about 120 prisoners in there now. They had been sent up for murder, assault with a deadly weapon, seducing children, theft, forgery and the other assorted crimes of want and passion. About a third were Negroes, and the rest, except for four Indians, were white men.

I had come here to visit John Dunne and Pat Cusick, both white prisoners, and both of them until recently students at the University of North Carolina in Chapel Hill. I didn't know Pat Cusick. I did know John. I had first met him when he came to my home in Chapel Hill, where I was a professor, and asked to rent a room. He was a freshman at the university, and the only room in town he had been able to find to live in was a home in the Negro section; his advisers at the Morehead Foundation, which supplied his college expenses, wouldn't allow him to live there.

My wife showed him a room we had recently fixed up for students, and he rented it for thirty dollars a month, utilities furnished. Our house is three-story on the back, and this room had a sliding glass door which opened onto the back lawn. It had a pleasantness about it, and there were enough places to put his many books. Together we moved into it a battered record player whose knobs kept falling off and which, when touched, emitted tiny electric shocks from time to time. Music seemed to be important to John. He allowed himself only

3

one dollar a day for food, in order to have money to buy records. Some of them were opera recordings, and it was not unusual to hear him downstairs singing along with them, in an unsure voice. I suppose neither of us could have known then that we were starting an association that would lead us both to the State Prison at Sandy Ridge, he as a prisoner and I as a visitor who wondered why in the world he had ended up there.

John had been nineteen when he came to my house. He was twenty-one now. He had been born in the Massachusetts General Hospital in Boston, and when he was two years of age, his parents had moved to Pittsburgh, where in good time he was entered in the public schools. When he was in the fourth grade, they moved to Centerville, Ohio, which is near Dayton. When he finished elementary school, they moved to Brecksville, Ohio, a residential town south of Cleveland, but they didn't take John with them. By then it was clear to his teachers that he had a truly exceptional mind, and, at the suggestion of Eleanor Roosevelt, an acquaintance of his mother, he was entered at the Choate School, the boarding school in Connecticut, where he was given an alumni scholarship. In his freshman year he did so well that he was given the Joseph P. Kennedy Memorial Scholarship, which had been established by the Kennedy family in memory of the eldest son, a graduate of Choate, who had died in the war.

John was at Choate three years, and graduated with a number of honors, including the School Seal Prize for the most outstanding contribution in leadership, scholarship and character. He also was voted by the senior class "the straightest arrow," an award which goes each year to the senior who disobeys the fewest rules, who is willing to be of most help to others, who is ready to go the second mile and so forth. He was fullback on the football team, first violinist in the orchestra, and was voted the outstanding musician in his class.

He was offered college scholarships at Harvard and at the University of North Carolina, and he chose the University of North Carolina, where the Morehead Foundation, which awards fifty to seventy-five scholarships in each undergraduate class there, offered to pay his tuition, fees, room, board and other expenses for his four undergraduate years. The Morehead Foundation is respected generally for its ability to discover potential leaders and felt secure in its judgment of John Dunne. During his two years at Chapel Hill, John did three years of college work and took part in many extracurricular activities.

John came south partly for financial reasons; it would have cost his family more for him to attend Harvard. Also, he wanted to know the South. While at Choate he had become interested in the problems of the American people, and it seemed that many of them focused most intensely in the Southern region. They were problems of poverty, of politics and government, of racial unrest and misunderstanding, of economic development. In a sense John Dunne was chosen by the South, and he in turn chose the South because the South was America's greatest challenge. He came south to meet the Southerners; if he could find a way, he would cast his lot permanently among them.

Captain C. E. Muncy is head of Prison Unit 074. He is a husky, friendly man of about sixty years. Some people say he runs the best prison in the best prison system in the country. During the day the gates are unlocked. Most of the prisoners are on work-release, which means that they are driven each morning in busses to nearby communities where they work in factories, in construction companies and the like. They are brought back to the prison at night. John Dunne and Pat Cusick had been driving the busses, and cleaning up the barracks and yards between bus trips; also, they spent part of each day slopping the hogs.

I met with John in the dayroom of the prison, a concrete-block place with flowered curtains at the windows. It is furnished with a plastic-covered sofa, eight chairs, a set of drums, a guitar and a bookcase in which there were thirty copies of the Bible and four battered Westerns. John Dunne was as pleased to see me, and as relaxed and confident, as he had been when, almost three years before, I had first met him at my house. I had not seen much of him for the past two years, for he had rented an apartment uptown and our ways had taken quite different paths. It was a friendly, casual time of reacquaintance, and I liked him as much then as I had earlier. He seemed to me, even there in the prison, dressed in the faded blue work clothes of the prison system, to be the same confident, youthful, almost adolescent, black-haired, dark-eyed boy whom I had known in happier circumstances.

Pat Cusick came into the room, and John introduced me to him. I had read about him in the local papers, and I expected to see a man of considerable toughness, a leader capable of commando-like action. He is not quite that. He is, in fact, moderately overweight, and his general attitude and appearance are rumpled. There is a warm friendliness about him and a mature, cautious gentleness. He is a round-faced, blond man, thirty-two years of age, a Southerner born and reared in Gadsden, Alabama. His great-grandfather on his mother's side was a Confederate major and was the founder of the Ku Klux Klan in Etowah County. Pat grew up hearing Civil War and Klan stories. He attended school in his home town; however, a year before he was to enter high school, the local high school lost its accreditation, so his parents packed him off to private school, a Benedictine boarding school in Alabama named the St. Bernard High School.

During his first year there his father died. That distressed him greatly, and he wanted to return home; his mother refused firmly, so he lingered over his books and listened to his scholarly tutors. The one who made the deepest impression on him was a priest who taught the religion class. The priest irritated the boy, in that he maintained that the South was unfair in its practices affecting Negroes. Pat objected with the fury of his grandfather and found himself arguing openly in class. Pat told me, "The priest was saying that segregation is wrong, and the students were all arguing that it was right. I led the revolt, but when I graduated from there, I was changed; I was convinced in my mind that segregation was wrong. I don't think emotionally I was convinced, but I knew I had lost a four-year-long argument."

Young Pat Cusick went home to stay. His mother had moved to Rome, Georgia, and had married again, so really he went to a different town, to a different house and to a different family. He got a job selling haberdashery and settled down to a life of dating the local girls. Then the Korean War came along. He joined the Air Force and became at the age of twenty the air traffic control supervisor at Tempelhof Air Force Base in West Germany.

"When I got out, I went to work as an assistant chemical engineer in Rome, Georgia, for General Electric. They had a new plant, and there was a dearth of semitechnical people. I was having to work to support my mother and stepfather, so I couldn't go to college, and here was this brand-new plant which didn't have anybody right below the professional men, the chemists and engineers. I didn't know a thing in the world about chemistry, but most of the other hired people didn't either, and before the chemists caught on that I didn't know anything, I had learned enough to hold the job."

He worked there for over two years, then went to Belmont Abbey, a college near Charlotte, for two years. In 1961 he came as a junior to Chapel Hill, where he majored in math and took a job at the computation center. When his stepfather fell ill from cancer, he dropped out of school to work full time as a programer in the computation center, but even so he continued to take a course or two a semester. At Sandy Ridge he told me he had only one course left to earn his bachelor's degree.

He said his mother was a Catholic, and that he had been a Catholic most of his life. "When I first came to the university I went to Mass every Sunday. It was just a matter of course, and it worried me that it meant no more than that. It seemed to me that there were a lot of things I didn't believe any longer, and it was sort of with a sense of regret that I stopped going and stopped considering myself a Catholic. I went through a period of being an atheist, then an agnostic, and I don't know just where I am now. I do believe in God, and who knows, I might start going to Mass again every Sunday sometime in the future. I don't know."

I talked with the two of them there in the dayroom, and got to know John once again and Pat for the first time. At eleven o'clock, or even before, the lunch bell rang, and I was invited by one of the guards to eat, which I did, paying a small fee for the meal. Each of us was given a paper bag, "a poke," as one of the prisoners called it, which had four sandwiches in it. One of them had a slice of baloney between two pieces of bread, another had preserves between two pieces of bread, and the other two I didn't get around to eating. We drank water with the meal.

I went outdoors to smoke and to wander about the place. It is certainly the least restricted prison I've ever visited. The main building is the barracks, or cell block, where the men sleep; here there are long rows of cots in one big room, and latrines with facilities for eight or ten men. I noticed that there were no seats on the toilet bowls. There was a wood or coal stove at the end of the room.

I started back toward the dayroom and ran into somebody, a guard or another visitor, who kindly asked me what the two men I had eaten lunch with had been "sent up" for. I told him, and he seemed to be quite surprised. "Why, they wouldn't send men to jail for that, would they? Send white men to jail a year each for helping get them niggers off the streets?"

I tried to smile, for I meant no offense to him. "They were helping the Negroes who were on the streets," I said.

He became flustered, as I had known he would, and I felt embarrassed for him. He turned away, and I heard him murmur, "I don't know what to say."

That afternoon Pat, John and I continued our conversation, and I visited them in prison often later and tried to set down those aspects of this story which only they could tell. They wanted to talk about it, about what they had been part of; they wanted to try to figure it out and evaluate it, to have it set down, all of it, so that they could see it, too. They had been condemned by a court, and they knew they were in a sense guilty of breaking laws, but they were moralists essentially, and what they were trying to determine now was the nature of their deeper crime, whether they had violated not only laws but also justice.

During January of 1963, Pat Cusick had tried to start a campus chapter of the Student Peace Union. He needed five students to get a charter from the national office, and he had only three when he sought out John Dunne. They went to a coffee shop and talked about the national organization and about the need on the campus for a discussion group to deal with the subjects of world peace and personal responsibility. John agreed to be the fourth student member, and this talk was the first of many he and Pat had during the winter. Often, they would talk late into the night about the individual's responsibility in the American society.

Seven students organized the local chapter. They reviewed books and led discussions in the dormitories and local clubs, their aim being to focus attention on ways to achieve world peace. This got them into questions of the relationship of world peace to local peace, and the obligation of the individual to his own town. The group, which came to number about twenty members, decided one Sunday afternoon to go ahead and do something to help improve Chapel Hill. Since civil rights matters were on everybody's mind at the time, they decided to put their talents to work in this area. Their decision was just that casual; they were, in fact, as casual as they were confident of being able to make a contribution.

Their first act had been to visit many of the restaurants and beer halls of town, asking if the establishments were segregated and, if they were, trying to discuss the problem with the managers. This resulted in their being evicted from several places. They mimeographed a list of sixteen businesses, by no means all the segregated ones in town, and mailed the list to the mayor, to the managers of these sixteen places, to ministers, to leaders of other organizations they thought might support the SPU, and they enclosed with each copy a request that everybody boycott segregated businesses.

They were confident that this action would result in immediate improvement. No pressure had been put on most of these managers up to this point, and the students believed that here in a liberal community the response would have to be progressive. They were quite surprised when the only response they got was a cry of alarm and anger from the businesses named. They had gained nothing.

So the SPU decided upon a second form of action. They would picket somebody. More specifically, they decided to picket the College Café, a comfortable, informal eating place in town, owned and operated by Max Yarborough and Jesse West, both members of well-established Chapel Hill families. The restaurant, located on the main street, in the main block, seated about thirty customers, most of them in booths placed in line along the west wall. Mr. Yarborough and Mr. West evidently made a living out of the breakfast and lunch trade; at any rate, they always locked up the shop at two or two-thirty and went home, leaving the dinner customers to fare elsewhere. The restaurant was segregated. The year before, at the time a citizens group began picketing the two movie houses, the other restaurants on the main block had decided along with the two movie houses to integrate.

Mr. Yarborough and Mr. West did not so decide, and they still did not serve Negroes—either the Negro residents of Chapel Hill and its suburbs, of whom there were about two thousand, or the Negro students attending the integrated university across the street, of whom there were about sixty.

The first civil rights picketing signs that Pat Cusick and John Dunne ever made were painted in the Alumni Building on the campus of the university on the night of April 4, 1963, only a year before they entered prison. John had bought the paint at Huggins Hardware and the paper at Ledbetter-Pickard Stationers on Franklin Street, the main street of the college town, and Pat had driven out to the city dump near the airport and had collected poles, which were broomsticks and the like. Both men were novices at racial demonstrations and didn't know that it is better not to use poles, that they can become clubs, or at least people can claim in court that they were struck by them.

The two men brought their materials to the campus building, to an assembly room where other members of the campus chapter of the Student Peace Union met with them and helped out. About midnight, the signs were painted. John Dunne had taken elaborate pains on one which read: "1863-1963—How Long Must Americans Wait for a Cup of Coffee?" He remembers lettering it in vertical letters, an act of protest against Pat Cusick's preference for slanted lettering. Pat worked on his own sign: "Land of the Free—for Whom?"

After midnight Pat did two signs over as he and John talked about the next morning's work, which they were to begin at 6 A.M. They were by now alone, the others having gone to the dormitories, and they talked idly, passing the night away. John was worried about the Morehead Foundation, which very likely would be unhappy when it saw him picketing. Pat was more concerned about how one picketed, how one went about it.

Just before 6 A.M., they selected two signs for use on this first day. Because of a town ordinance prohibiting one picket from following another picket closer than fifteen feet, only two people could picket the narrow little College Café at a time. They took the two signs and quietly crossed the old south quad of the university, which borders on Franklin Street. On the opposite side of the street, not far at all from the Alumni Building, are the shops, restaurants and stores which cater to the ten thousand students. Pat and John crossed the street at the post office and walked along the sidewalk. Near the west end of the block, the College Café had just opened for the day. Max Yarborough had just admitted the few townspeople and students who had been waiting, and he had put bacon on to fry. The customers were seated at the counter, drinking coffee and talking, as the two young men arrived outside the plate-glass window a few feet away.

"We felt pretty foolish," Pat says. "We didn't quite know how to go about it. Of course, there really isn't any one way to go about it; like falling off a log, it's hard to do the first time, at least to do it confidently. Each of us took a sign. We went to opposite sides of the restaurant and started walking toward each other, and I could see that John felt pretty silly."

So doubtless did Max Yarborough. He stared through the window in disbelief. There had never been any picketing of his restaurant, or any other restaurant in Chapel Hill, except that in 1960, soon after Greensboro students began sit-ins in Greensboro, a group of Negro Chapel Hill high school students had picketed the Long Meadow Dairy Bar four blocks away, down near the Negro section of town. Whether picketing was an infringement of his constitutional rights, Max didn't know, but certainly he was licensed to have a public business and this ought to mean he could run it without public interference.

A customer came in, huffing and puffing, closing the door with a bang. "Max, what the hell's going on?" he said.

"Land of the free—for whom?" Max murmured, reading Pat's picket sign. "Must not be free for me."

The customer shouted through the plate-glass window, "You boys better get away from here."

Neither John nor Pat answered. One of the rules of picketing, they knew, was not to reply to anybody except policemen. And they saw a policeman approaching now from down the block, casually walking along, aware of their presence but not revealing any concern. He stopped nearby. "Captain Blake said you'd be here," he said, "said a dark-haired boy talked with him yesterday. Was it you?"

John said that it was.

"I told him if I knew students, you'd most likely stay in bed at six o'clock in the morning." He watched to see if they saw any humor in that remark. Evidently they were too intent on their labor. "You boys planning to picket long?"

"Only until he integrates," Pat said grimly.

The officer got no further conversation from them, so he moved on down the block. Two workmen arrived, stopped on seeing the signs and scowled at them. "Damn them," one of the men said, "damn you all. What are you trying to do, make us eat with the niggers?"

That was the first comment of real anger that Pat and John had heard, and it went through them sharply. There were several other like comments, as the workmen came to realize and to resent that the two pickets wouldn't answer, wouldn't argue. They began to ask questions which, if left unanswered, would be embarrassing. "You don't need to reply to this if it's so, for we know you wouldn't want to talk about things like this out here on the main street; if your sister sleeps with niggers, don't say a word."

Silence. Not a word as John and Pat walked eight steps down the street, turned, walked eight steps up the street.

"Long pricks with signs on 'em, that's what they got in their hands. Like to hold them poles, boys?" The men were flushed with anger, their features were contorted with it. It was a revelation to see them, to see in faces the depth of hatred that these men held for white men who would represent Negroes. John Dunne shivered with anger, but he held his peace as the two workmen went on inside the café and began to talk to Max Yarborough, shaking their fists at the demonstrators on the other side of the big window.

It was dawn now. On Franklin Street nothing moved except the two pickets, and now and then a car, which drove slowly past as the driver stared at the picket signs. The only exceptions to the customary, orderly day were Pat Cusick and John Dunne walking slowly back and forth in front of the restaurant, seeking the town's notice.

That day the two pickets were spat upon and cursed by one person or another, but most of the town's citizens responded sanely and with the sophistication of people who have learned not to be surprised at anything that happens in a college town. A few of them, Mrs.

Charlotte Adams, the wife of a university professor, among them, spoke a word of encouragement.

But rather than bring about the goal they sought, the pickets seemed to increase Max Yarborough's business. Any number of new customers sought out the College Café to say that they thought a businessman ought to be allowed to shut his door on any race or on anybody. It was, they said, as sacred an American right as—well, as picketing. So many people came to the restaurant for lunch that Max had to go across the street to buy more bread. Not since a college football weekend the previous fall had he run out of bread. Max's boom, as it was called, caused a competing restaurant manager to mention to the pickets that he wouldn't mind them coming to his place, for his business had been pretty bad of late.

Another matter distressing to the pickets was that people didn't flock out to serve on the picket lines, as John and Pat had hoped they would. Only three members of the SPU seemed to be able to free themselves from classes, and John had to picket five hours that first day. When at two-thirty Max Yarborough closed up and went home, John was more thankful the day was done than Max was, and he walked wearily, sleepily down Franklin Street to Harry's Grill, where he could sit quietly, munching a sandwich, and think the matter over. How in the world, he wondered, did demonstrators manage when they had to handle something larger than a two-man picket line?

The next day, and the day after and the day after that, John and Pat began picketing at six in the morning, and for two hungry early-morning hours they smelled Max Yarborough's bacon and eggs frying, smelled his good coffee brewing, while their stomachs growled. Regularly each morning at seven, Mr. E. A. Brown, an elderly, tall businessman, crossed the picket line complaining about the picketing. Soon after him, an employee of the the telephone company crossed the line, wondering out loud if a man shouldn't have a right to run his own business as he pleased. And at various times each morning a Tar Heel Cab driver would pause at the cab stand across the street and shout insults.

At eight Pat would go to work, but he would be back at lunchtime to see if John Dunne was successfully holding the line together. It was up to John to see to it that somebody always was on hand to carry each poster. It might be Mary Lindsay Spearman, the blond daughter of a local university journalism professor, or Katherine Strong, a pretty, shy, brown-eyed sculptress from Georgia, or a member of the SPU. Whenever pickets didn't show up, it was John's task to find substitutes to fill the gap or to fill it himself.

One morning he talked Wayne King, a past editor of the *Daily Tar Heel,* the university student newspaper, into picketing for half an hour. Wayne was reluctant to agree to more than that, and he began his tour of duty with a sense of aggravation at the whole idea. When a man came along and said something mildly insulting, Wayne swung toward him. "Just a minute there," he said, "I'm not nonviolent."

John took him off the picket line.

John says he got tired walking up and down in front of that little store. He learned every single limb on the leafless tree overhead, every crack in the cold, concrete sidewalk below. He began to tabulate the looks of passers-by, to catalogue them under such headings as hurt, angry, encouraging, complacent, annoyed, surprised, glad-to-see-you-out-there. The picket signs became as worn and weary as the pickets. The wind and weather had damaged them; they had begun to fade, and during a rainstorm two of the signs had dripped paint on the demonstrators, to the amusement of the customers inside the dry café.

It might have been that John and Pat would have got out of the whole affair right then if they had been able to do so gracefully. John was in the advance section of every course he took, and he had registered this semester, as he had in semesters past, for more than the customary maximum load. He was really having trouble keeping up, as were the others, and there was no prospect of a letup. So Pat relinquished his dream that the SPU could lead the way to the integration of Chapel Hill, and he appealed to the Wesley Foundation, a Methodist youth organization, to join in the effort. The president of the Methodist group was a student named Lou Calhoun, who had a part-time job waiting on tables at Harry's Grill.

I talked with Lou Calhoun in May, 1964, after he was sentenced to prison. He is a tall, blond, slender young man with a narrow, quizzical face, which always seems to be on the verge of smiling. One senses about him a gift for comedy, and there is a keen alertness about the way he moves and speaks. I found out later he had been a Golden Gloves boxing champion in Tennessee.

He told me that Pat Cusick had come up to him one night, a very fateful night, he said, when he was taking a coffee break in the Carolina Coffee Shop on Franklin Street. "Pat asked me what I thought would be the possibility of the Wesley Foundation supporting the picketing. He asked me if he should come talk to the Foundation or what. I told him I would talk to them because I knew we had on the council several anti-SPU people. It was no sense having him come and have to defend the Student Peace Union; if I talked with them, we could keep that issue out."

Lou had no trouble getting the council to agree. "Everybody had been saying it would be nice if we could find something to do, something that wouldn't take too much of our time. Integration had not been something we had discussed doing anything about. We had talked about helping with the local recreation program. But we were interested in both."

Lou's parents were Southerners. He had been reared in Alabama, Tennessee and North Carolina; now his father lived in Shelby, North Carolina, where he was the public recreation director. The only contact Lou had ever had with Negroes was in recreation programs in towns where his father had worked. He had never thought much about segregation, although the previous year he had been irritated by certain activities in the South, when Negroes had been dragged off busses and beaten.

"It was just the most horrible thing I had ever heard of," he told me. "We had segregation in Tennessee and North Carolina, but I had never seen any real hatred between whites and Negroes as such. It was just inconceivable. You don't pull people out of busses and beat them. This sort of thing—it was quite a shock. It was just bewildering." But he had not joined the freedom rides, and he hadn't known what to do about it and had done nothing. He had never taken part in any civil rights activity at all, or even joined any organizations on the campus, except the Wesley Foundation.

"The first time I picketed, I was very nervous, but after ten minutes I felt pretty good. I was supposed to picket an hour, but the relief didn't show up. This got to be sort of a standard thing, which messed up my grades. I got to picketing two, three hours a day, and suddenly it wasn't fun. A few members of the Wesley Foundation helped out, but in the Wesley Foundation, as well as in the SPU, it seemed that the leaders had to carry the signs most of the time, and so it was Pat, John and me hour after hour. It got pretty tiring, I can tell you."

Meanwhile, Max Yarborough's business continued to boom right along. Some of the fraternities now required their pledges to eat at least one meal a day there, and some of the students from the campus unit of the NROTC, assuming that a peace organization was not in favor of soldiers, began to march through the picket line each day on their way to morning coffee or to lunch.

Chapter Two

IN A SENSE the wave of civil disobedience tactics in the South had started three years earlier, on February 1, 1960, in Greensboro, North Carolina, when four Negro students at A & T (Agricultural and Technical) College walked into a five-and-ten-cent store, sat down at the lunch counter and began reading books. At least they started reading books when they found out they weren't going to get anything to eat from the waitresses. A tremendous commotion began, and other students from A & T College and the Women's College of the University of North Carolina joined in the sit-ins, which created consternation in Greensboro and excitement everywhere, and resulted in the integration of many public eating facilities in the South. In the spring of 1961 Greensboro began street marches and traffic-blocking tactics, and this activity also sent ripples of activity throughout the country.

Now, in the spring of 1963, the biggest activity was not in Greensboro, but in Birmingham, Alabama. Street marches were daily occurrences, and the police were locking up hundreds of Negro demonstrators. While the Chapel Hill students were quietly walking back and forth in front of the little restaurant, mass action was taking place a few hundred miles to the south.

Mike Putzel of the *Daily Tar Heel* asked John Dunne if he would drive down there with him and see what was going on. Pat Cusick and Lou Calhoun said he ought to go, and he and Mike and one or two other *Daily Tar Heel* reporters left at 11 P.M. in a Volkswagen bus and drove all night. As they came into Birmingham, the first thing they noticed was a replica of the Statue of Liberty standing atop the highest building with a real flame coming out of the torch, and groups of police and armed white civilians on the street below.

They found that daily mass meetings of Negroes began in Birmingham at eight-thirty each morning in the churches and lasted until five, when there was a break for dinner; the meetings resumed at seven-thirty and lasted till ten. The daytime meetings were orientation sessions and lectures; the street marches were planned there. The evening services were rousingly inspirational. The people would fill up first one church and then another, pouring from one to another till all were filled. The Negro ministers of Birmingham would preach, and there would be singing, with a slow beat, much slower than in the North Carolina churches. The music evidently washed away the worries of the people, and the last song sung each night, "We Shall Overcome," was the victory sound in Birmingham these nights, with thousands of people, some of whom had that day been beaten, singing along with thousands of others who believed that on the next day they would be beaten.

White people couldn't get into the meetings. Those who tried were stopped by the police and arrested. (Three days earlier Miss Mary Hamilton, a Negro CORE field secretary with very light skin, was dragged from a mass meeting and taken to jail by policemen who thought she was white.) Quite obviously, the better part of wisdom was to let the matter be, but the first night he was there, John Dunne, along with Hugh Danaseau, a commentator for a Cleveland broadcasting station, approached the police and showed them their press cards—John using a press card of the *Daily Tar Heel*. "The niggers won't let reporters inside there," they were told. John said he thought it wouldn't hurt to try, if the police didn't mind. The police shrugged and let them through.

When they got to the door of the church, John took out membership cards in the SPU and the NAACP; he had joined the campus
chapter of the NAACP after the College Café picketing had started.
He was welcomed and passed through, and he managed to get
Danaseau admitted with him.

For a while they stood at the back of the hall, watching and listening to Rev. James Bevel, a Baptist, as he talked about freedom and
about the jails being full and maybe people dying in them. Birmingham was a besieged city, he said, and would stay troubled as long
as the Negro was not given his full rights as a citizen and a human
being. He talked a good deal about nonviolence. "If you can't conduct yourself nonviolently, go up into the balcony," he said. He
insisted on the Negro's responsibility "to love your white brothers"
regardless of his condition and suffering. The Negro had learned
suffering, he said, and would go on suffering. The Negro had suffered
many generations, not knowing why, he said; now he had a reason, he
knew the reason.

There were about two thousand people there, all Negroes except
for John and Hugh Danaseau. The Negroes had been instructed to
wear old clothes and to bring raincoats and galoshes, so that the
water from the police fire hoses wouldn't do too much damage. They
had also brought toothbrushes and toothpaste with them, so that they
would have them if they were sent to jail that night. It was hot and
stuffy inside the building, and the place was packed. As Rev. Bevel
talked, the people swayed and their murmuring voices responded.
"Tell the truth," they said. "Amen," they said. "Say on, Preacher."
John watched the people, all of them ordinary people, accept what
the pastor said, yielding so fully to the group response that death
itself, or the promise of death, did not seem to discourage them.
"Creative suffering is redemptive," the pastor said. "Love your
enemies, love those who spitefully use you."

John says he was deeply affected by the talk and the response of
the audience, and Danaseau began to sense that John wasn't going to
be standing at the back of the place with him much longer. He
advised John not to lose his objectivity, and certainly not to become
involved in the meeting. "Somebody has to tell the story as a reporter," he said.

The sermon ended and the congregation began to sing "Which Side Are You On, Boy?"

> Over there in Mississippi,
> No neutrals have I met.
> They either join the freedom fight
> Or "Tom" for Ross Barnett.
> Which side are you on, boy,
> Which side are you on?

John told Danaseau he didn't see how he was going to remain neutral in this emotion-filled situation. Danaseau intensified his arguments in favor of neutrality. He didn't see any police in the building, but he knew there was danger if a white man expressed a commitment.

> Come, all you freedom lovers,
> Good news to you I tell,
> About that good old freedom fight
> That's coming here to dwell.
> Which side are *you* on, boy,
> Which side are *you* on?

John told Danaseau that he had lost his objectivity, and he walked down the aisle of the church and sat down in a seat a woman had just vacated.

He sat there for ten or fifteen minutes before he was invited forward and given a seat on the platform. They were now singing another song, "I Woke up This Morning with My Mind Stayed on Freedom." In the course of the singing, the song leader motioned for John to come forward to the microphone and sing a verse. John had never heard the song before, except on a Pete Seeger record, but he made up a verse and sang it as best he could.

The next day, and each day after that, John went to the meetings. He listened to two-hour sermons from the Reverends Bevel, Martin Luther King, Jr., A. D. King, Ralph Abernathy and others of the top leaders of the nonviolent civil rights movement in the South. The meetings were evangelistic in style, and the doctrines preached involved nonviolence not as a tactic or a philosophy, but as a way of life, essentially a religion, which combined the teachings of Jesus, Gandhi and Thoreau. Actually, Gandhi had first brought together this fusion of doctrines and views, and now it was being adapted to the conditions and needs of the Negro in the South. The nonviolent philosophy goes beyond the "turn the other cheek" admonition and insists that the person who is wronged love the person who has wronged him.

John had been brought up a Methodist, but his commitment had lacked meaning in his life; in the meetings in Birmingham he underwent an emotional conversion, here in an old-fashioned evangelical atmosphere, listening to the sermons of Southern ministers, sitting in the congregation of Southern Negroes, listening to them respond and responding with them.

He was soon made an honorary member of the student committee of the Alabama Christian Movement for Human Rights, and he spent many hours near the Birmingham jail.

"The second Monday afternoon I was in Birmingham," he says, "I was walking around outside the jail talking with parents of those kids. There would be hundreds of parents there in the square. They had heard the rumors that kids were being killed inside, so they were worried sick. I tried to raise their spirits. At that time prisoners were being bonded out at the rate of about sixteen an hour, and I tried to help them find their parents and get a bus back to town. Several jail wardens saw me and got very irritated. I guess I wasn't hard to see, for I was the only white person there. They told me to leave. I said I would be happy to leave if they would tell me what I was doing wrong. They said, 'Get out of here, kid. We don't want any trouble.' I didn't want any trouble, either, but I didn't want to leave and didn't. They asked me for identification, so I showed them my press card and driver's license and so forth.

"Then they said, 'All right, let's go, you're arrested.' The main one of them, the most angry one, got in a police car and for some reason got his gears wrong and backed his car into the chief's, into Bull Connor's car, knocking it about six feet, and he got so angry he told the wardens to book me not only for loitering, but also for resisting arrest, which was sort of silly.

"They took me inside and booked me on both counts. Then they pushed me around and hit me a little. This was at the place where they were checking and taking my name. We also had some discus-

sion about what my race was. They put me down as black. I noticed
that and called attention to it. The guard got very angry, as if I had
challenged his veracity, so I decided not to press the point. I thought I
might get put into the cell with a lot of demonstrators anyway, and
that would be great, for I was kind of scared to be put in with the
whites. Most whites in jail are poor whites, and in Alabama most of
the poor whites are opposed to the Negro, and most of all to white
people who help Negroes. They were livid because of the street demonstrations.

"The guards took me into jail and down a hallway to a long,
narrow cell. The prisoners were white. There were about forty of
them, some lying on cots, but most of them standing around, idly
waiting for something to happen in that place. The guard unlocked
the door and pushed me inside. I heard him say, 'All right, men,
here's a nigger for you.' "

A while later one of the prisoners spoke to him, asking what he
was in for.

"Loitering," John said. "They said I was loitering."

"They said, they said," the prisoner said sympathetically. Then, as
if that settled it, as if somebody arrested for loitering was not guilty
of anything, for indeed most of them had often been arrested for
loitering, they appeared to stop caring about John Dunne or what he
did.

But the climate inside a jail keeps changing. John says a cellful of
prisoners takes on an attitude during any hour which tends to reverse
the attitude and compensate for the failures of the hour before. Somebody makes a claim; somebody challenges it. Somebody tells a joke;
somebody doesn't laugh, and they turn to look at the man who
doesn't laugh and wonder why. Or they hear his accent, an accent
unlike theirs, and they ask where he's from.

At dusk a man came in, swaggering, talking loud about being
arrested on a charge of "shooting at niggers." That was the wording
of the charge, he said. "The cops told me to start doing it at night
when they did it," he said.

Everybody laughed except John Dunne, so the other prisoners
began to consider him with new interest. Nobody said anything, but

the evidence was entered in the unwritten record of the jail cell. They knew now that he had been called a nigger by the jailer, that he didn't laugh at jokes about niggers, and that he had an accent unlike theirs.

Among the reprobates, bums and castoffs of the world are many who like to have somebody to punch and poke at, to push down once in a while, hopefully to make as ignoble as they are, more ignoble if they can, some young person if they can find one. They had found one there in the cell; they had been provided one by the jailors and had been given free license to use him. They began to contemplate the coming event, relishing it, hesitating to enter into the event itself and use too soon the pleasure of it. A group gathered at the far end of the cell. They murmured among themselves, saying a little something aloud now and then, asking the same questions, simplifying their questions as if purifying their thoughts, until certain words were heard from the group in a broken cadence, repeated often: "nigger lover," "white man," "kill him."

After a while, slowly, patiently, for time was what they had too much of, they began to move toward him. They stopped before him, and John says he knew two things clearly. He knew that there was no use calling for help and that now he had to prove to himself that there was strength in the nonviolent code which he had been taught in Birmingham and earlier by Pat Cusick in Chapel Hill.

"I want you to know," he said, "that I wish you no harm, and that you can't make me hate you, and you can't make me fight you." He said that, perhaps none too surely, as they moved in on him and began to beat him.

Some time later John called for a key boy and asked him if he might be put on the Negro side of the prison. He pointed out that he had been registered into the jail as a Negro, and his presence in the "white" cell had become a point of contention with the white prisoners. The key boy called a warden, who came to the cell bar and looked John over. "What color is you, boy?" he asked.

"I proceeded to try to analyze my color," John says. "I have black hair and brown eyes, and I explained to him very seriously that I didn't know what my ancestry was beyond my grandparents."

The warden reached through the bars and felt John's hair, which is straight and didn't seem to him to be "nigger hair." He wasn't certain, however, for he had to weigh in the fact that the prisoner did want to be considered as a Negro, which was strange, was perhaps unique in the warden's experience.

He called the jail nurse, "a short, fat and frumpy woman," John says, "with hard lines in her face, a tough woman. She examined my fingernails. Apparently there's a myth that you can tell from the color of the half moons whether a person is white or Negro. It seems she couldn't tell anything by this method, so I was removed from the cell and placed in an isolation cell, about four by four feet in size, where I stayed for about an hour and a half. During that time I sat there and tried to keep down tears. I was very scared. I sang freedom songs to myself. I kept telling myself, 'We shall overcome.' "

The warden evidently decided that John was not a Negro. At any rate, he returned him to the first cell.

There were more prisoners in the cell now. The antagonism toward John had intensified, and it wasn't long before the men had backed him the length of the cell block, pushing and poking at him. They backed him up against a sink in the latrine. One Irishman who was drunk punched him in the stomach and in the face.

"It wasn't a bad thing," John says. "It was more of an effort to get me to fight him. But then they began to talk about killing me, and that really scared me. They said nobody would ever know, that the guards would never tell. I kept telling them the oft-repeated line that there was nothing they could do to make me hit back, that I was in Birmingham out of concern for them. One person would say something to me, then another, then another; their anger was building up and quite a crowd was gathering. Then a big man, a native of Birmingham, came in, and he decided a group of men was picking on this kid. He was slightly intoxicated, and he came up and grabbed the drunk Irishman and started to beat him up. I stepped in between them to try and stop the fight, and the big Alabaman heard my accent and asked me where I was from. I got the 'North' in 'North Carolina' out and he said, 'Forget it,' and walked off. The others left with him, explaining the situation to him.

"I went back into the cell and began talking with a very old, sick man about his illnesses. Soon the big Alabaman came up behind me and got a hold around my neck, picked me up and took me into the latrine. I pulled his hand away from my neck, enough so I could explain to him that I was in Birmingham as much out of concern for him as for the Negroes. I had already kissed good-bye to the world. I told him he was stronger than I was, but that he couldn't make me hate him. Suddenly he stopped, he released me; he just stepped back and stared at me with a really awful look of bewilderment and fear. I never will forget it. Then he turned around and walked off swearing."

A group had gathered to watch the fight, and now they went back into the cell, too.

"I was scared to death; I had decided I was going to die sometime that night," John says. "Yet only twenty or so feet from me, outside the jail, were my friends. I went to a window. They were high windows, but I stood on a radiator at a place where the glass had been broken out. I could barely see the people in the yard outside. I began to hum and whistle freedom songs. I told myself this would help them keep up their spirits, but really I was trying to keep up my own and establish contact with them."

He saw his friend, the Negro pastor, Rev. Harold Middlebrook, going back and forth from the jail. Rev. Middlebrook was the one in charge of bailing people out. He saw John and said he was going to get him out as soon as he could.

"At that point," John says, "I felt very guilty, for some of the other people had been jailed for fourteen days and I had been locked up only that afternoon. I told him to make sure everybody else had been bonded out before he bonded me out. By thinking in these terms, you know, you can make yourself feel stronger than you really are."

John was standing at the window when suddenly, off somewhere, maybe fifteen city blocks away, two bombs exploded in succession. At once a solemn response, an angry sigh, went up from the Negroes below. There was a rumble from within the prison, followed by the clanging of the jail doors, an almost deafening sound, which John knew came from the cells where the Negroes were crowded in.

Where had the bombs gone off? he wondered. He supposed they

had been intended for one of the Negro leaders. He wondered about the prisoner who had been arrested for "shooting at niggers." He had been bonded out by a policeman, the prisoner had claimed as he left; he and others were out there now.

"I told myself not to hate them. I told myself that these people were suffering as much from the hatred and from the system as we were, and were just as much victims of the society."

He wondered how it was that he was different from the men doing the bombing, what pattern of life had been set up in him that had made him a friend and not an enemy of the Negro. He remembered a story about his little sister, that when she was five she had been asked by a neighbor if she wanted a piece of candy called a "nigger baby," and the sister had replied, "In my family we would call it a Negro baby." What had his parents done so that even by the age of five a child had begun to sense and dislike what amounted to disrespect for others, even when the disrespect had been jokingly intended? John couldn't remember any instruction he had received, any inference that he ought to accept one pattern of thought and reject another, yet he and his two sisters had grown up together as members of a liberal family.

Even so, he had never known many Negroes. In his neighborhoods there were never many around; there was one family, and in that family one Negro boy whom he remembered. The boy had been accepted into the local groups without prejudice. At Choate when John arrived there were no Negroes. In his fifth form, which means his junior year, the administration had asked him if he would object to rooming with a Japanese boy, and he had found even the question strange, much less the assumption that anybody would object. He had roomed with the boy and had liked him very well. In his sixth form the son of Ralph Bunche had been admitted to Choate, and he and John had become friends. And during the spring vacation period he had been sent, along with other debaters, athletes and musicians from Choate, on a friendship tour of the Caribbean. On this, his first extensive contact with Negroes, he made three friends with whom he corresponded later on. During the tour there had been little discrimination in evidence, and he concluded that a color-blind society is possible, that one can associate with Negroes without awareness of race and racial differences.

Another bomb went off, and the window glass in the Birmingham jail rattled. No doubt the white men out there bombing Negroes, John thought, were expressing instincts and convictions that they had formed in early youth, that they had been taught, yet what strange and unChristian convictions they seemed to him to be, how out of sorts with the concepts of fairness he had learned. How could one in America, he wondered, rear a son in such a way that, when he reached the age of his maturity, he could be counted on in a moment of crisis to go out and bomb the homes of Negroes?

He wondered about all this and stood there at the broken window whistling and humming freedom songs.

He was there when the big Alabaman came up to him again. This time the big man said a few kind words, awkwardly, tentatively approaching the idea of a conversation, not being certain yet whether he wanted to talk with John or not. He asked about civil rights, and John quickly got off that subject and asked what the man was in jail for. His family had turned him in for being drunk in his own house, he said. John asked what he did for a living, and the big man told him, but soon he started talking about Negroes. John tried to change the subject, to find some common bond, one that hopefully would relieve the tenseness of the situation and lessen the danger.

The Alabaman, as if resenting the idea of friendship with John, left, but soon he returned. He did this several times until finally, deep in the morning hours, about four o'clock, he began to talk freely about himself. He told John he had only gone through the sixth grade in school, but he had, as an adult, taught himself to read well. In the course of his reading, he had come upon an anthropology book, and this book had stirred up questions in him. For example, he had read that the first man on earth was probably a black man. He accepted that as scientific truth, yet he also accepted the Bible's teaching that God made man in his own image, so he was left with the inference that God was black. The Alabaman had asked his friends and relatives about the matter, and as a consequence had been ostracized. Nobody had been able satisfactorily to explain the problem away.

He was also worried about how in heaven God was going to tell the spirits of the white people from those of the Negroes, since the bodies of the two would not be present as evidence.

John wasn't of much help in answering his questions, but his attitude was sympathetic, and they began to feel at ease, the two of them sitting there calmly talking in the midst of a hostile jail. The big Alabaman didn't apologize for his actions earlier in the evening, and perhaps he didn't regret them, but he did welcome the opportunity to respond to friendship. He was not converted from segregation to integration, but the change in him did indicate to John that love could win out over hate, that the philosophy of the Birmingham pastors was not merely an abstract theory.

The rest of the night was spent in conversation, and the other prisoners, although they grumbled and criticized, did John no further damage.

In the morning John was bailed out by Rev. Middlebrook. He was a little bit sick, and his legs trembled when he walked. Rev. Middlebrook and another Negro helped him down to the square, where hundreds of parents, some of them dew-dampened, still waited.

They started walking toward Martin Luther King's brother's house, one of the places that had been bombed the night before. The streets were empty, except that at every corner a group of policemen and deputies waited. The deputies were armed farmers and mill workers who had been given badges.

"Last night, after the bombing, there were riots down here," Rev. Middlebrook said. "They have hundreds of police down here now."

As they approached each group, the policemen would discuss what their attitude ought to be—a white man walking with two "niggers." Each group would hold a session, discuss the matter as John approached and be waiting indecisively when he arrived. But when they saw his face and realized that already he was emotionally exhausted, they let him go by. Each group for fifteen blocks let him go by.

At Rev. King's house, the men washed and rested, then went together to a Baptist Church nearby, arriving while the early-service singing was going on. John slumped down in a pew near the aisle, about halfway down the church, and let the slow music wash through his mind. It was swelling music; he was in the middle of the church, and the sound engulfed him and seemed with every beat and measure to release him from the knotted muscles and fears inside.

"So much tension had built up that I had to let go of it," he told me at Sandy Ridge. "I had cried very little during the night, but I felt very lonely, and it had to come out. I really had to let it out, so I sat there and cried. It was a fantastic experience. I had been so moved by what had happened in jail I had to cry now that I was released.

"I became aware that the preacher had noticed me and had called on me to speak. He invited me to speak or testify, or whatever they call it at these fundamentalist churches. I had never spoken in a church before, but I stood up and talked a little, and I began to talk about finding something stronger than hate, which was love, the love that forgives and is able to transcend hate and violence. Never before in my life—and I had given an awful lot of speeches in Chapel Hill about peace—never at any other time had the words just come. I felt completely as one with these people, so completely accepted by them. They understood me very well. We had existed through something. We had lived through it together and would go on living through it together. I told them that in the jail I had actually seen, had tested, the power of love. I had seen the way it affected men, penetrating deeper than hate could. I told them that when morning came, several prisoners had come to where I was and, some of them with words and others wordlessly, had said they didn't understand what they had seen, but they knew that there was something to what I stood for. And they were sorry and ashamed and ready to talk. And they listened, too.

"So I am pretty deeply committed now to the power of love."

Reports of the Birmingham demonstration went out over the country and set into motion other forces. John Dunne heard that demonstrations had begun in Raleigh, the capital of North Carolina, even while the General Assembly was in session, and that demonstrators were ready to march in Durham, which is near Raleigh and is only ten miles from Chapel Hill. Finally, word came that a march was being planned in Chapel Hill itself, to go right down the main street of town.

John wanted to talk with Pat Cusick and Lou, for he believed now that Chapel Hill needed a massive march, a demonstration far bigger than the picketing of the College Café. Chapel Hill, as a symbol of the enlightened South, was different from and perhaps more important than Birmingham. If a dozen pickets went out on the streets in Birmingham, there was a riot and forty arrests and all sorts of angry, hateful confusion. That would not be the way in Chapel Hill, or in most towns and cities of the country. Chapel Hill was representative of the well-administered, decent town which must begin to wrestle with these tough problems, and its leaders, with a sense of fairness and with the resources available in a university community, ought to be able to move the town forward and to show other towns the way.

Chapel Hill, John saw, more than Birmingham or other such explosive places, held the key to the solution of the Southern problem. Where more likely than in Chapel Hill would the solution be found?

And where better than in Chapel Hill, John thought, could a college man take an active part in helping to break the barriers down?

On Wednesday, May 1, he wrote a letter from Birmingham to his family, which went as follows:

DEAREST FOLKS:

It is nearly 4:30 A.M. and the sun is reluctantly beginning to rise over Birmingham. I'm sitting in the front yard of Rev. A. D. King's house where I have been on guard duty for the last two nights.

Yesterday I talked with Floyd Patterson, Jackie Robinson, Sen. Brown from Denver, Rev. Epps from Staten Island, etc., with many pix, etc. The compelling factor in my staying here has been the fact that I am, to my knowledge, the only white man actively in the movement. The effect of my presence, helping lead mass meetings, speaking in church, consoling the families of violence victims and helping (outside the jail gates) the parents to understand that their kids would be out eventually, helping kids get food when out, and finally, going to jail myself for the movement— the effect of this on the movement has been awfully rewarding. It somehow renews their faith that perhaps, someday, blacks and whites can truly overcome these strange and tragic barriers of irrationality, fear and hate.

Nearly every adult and child in the movement knows me by name —you can't imagine how glorious it is to step from the street where perhaps 20 policemen are gathered on one corner alone, threatening, scaring, etc., into a church where only love and trusting brotherhood greet you. And it's not the old Uncle Tom type revering of the benevolent white—rather it is the complete acceptance of another man into the fellowship of all men who have let themselves love.

My trial is at 9:00 this morning. I'll probably be convicted and sentenced to a jail term, and the decision will be appealed to a higher court. The movement will bond me out, probably by Thursday morning. I'll have someone call you if this is the case (my being in jail and thus unable to call myself).

Mrs. A. D. King is a delightful lady. Rev. Fred Shuttlesworth, president of the movement, is improving, but will be in bed a while longer. Must run. Your telegraph was a source of great, great joy—to know those whom I love are behind me.

Much love,

JOHN

John's trial actually was held in the afternoon, at about 2 P.M., and an Alabama lawyer, Orzell Billingsley, Jr., represented him. One of the officers who had arrested him was the first to testify. John's lawyer, who was a Negro, asked the officers what had caused the arrest, what had John done.

As John recalls, the entire trial went as follows:

"He was causing a disturbance," the policeman said.

"What disturbance was he causing?"

"He was talking with them niggers, so I went out and arrested him."

"But what disturbance was he causing?"

The policeman, stressing each word as if talking to a dumb child, repeated, "He was talking with them niggers, so I went out and arrested him."

The lawyer turned to the judge and objected to the use of the word "nigger" in the court. The judge called the lawyer a nigger and told him if he didn't shut up he would be thrown out of court. Then to John Dunne the judge said, "Step forward for sentencing." And, in a singsong voice, as if he were weary to death of justice, he disposed quickly of both the loitering and resisting-arrest charges. "A hundred eighty days for each, and for each a hundred dollars."

John spent two more days in jail before he was bonded out on an appeal. His friends in Birmingham and Chapel Hill decided he wouldn't be safe on a bus, so they bought a plane ticket for him and flew him back to North Carolina, where his experiences were already known.

When I talked with him at Sandy Ridge Prison, he told me the charges against him in Birmingham had since been dropped.

John was a changed person when he returned from Birmingham. Anne Queen, an official of the YMCA-YWCA on the Chapel Hill campus, recalls that he bought a briefcase and filled it with material pertaining to civil rights. He had the zeal of a new convert to an important mission, she says. His idealism and tendency toward martyrdom had found a cause.

In the briefcase, John says, were all sorts of letters and papers, including a copy of Martin Luther King's famous letter from the Birmingham jail, which has become a prime document of the civil rights movement. Several pastors had written Rev. King and told him they approved of his cause but not his methods of going about attaining the goals he wanted, and from the same jail in which John had been imprisoned, Rev. King had replied as follows:

I guess it is easy for those who have never felt the stinging darts of segregation to say "wait." But . . . when you see the vast majority of your twenty million Negro brothers smothering in an airtight cage of poverty in the midst of an affluent society, when you suddenly find your tongue twisted and your speech stammering as you seek to explain to your six-year-old daughter why she can't go to the public amusement park that has just been advertised on television, and see tears welling up in her eyes when she is told that Funtown is closed to colored children, and see the depressing clouds of inferiority begin to form in her little mental sky, and see her begin to distort her little personality by unconsciously developing a bitterness toward white people; when you have to concoct an answer for a five-year-old son asking in agonizing pathos, "Dad, why do white people treat colored people so mean?"; when you take a cross-country drive and find it necessary to sleep night after night in the uncomfortable corners of your automobile because no motel will accept you; when you are humiliated day in and day out by nagging signs reading "white" men and "colored"; when your first name becomes "nigger" and your middle name becomes "boy" (however old you are) and your last name becomes "John," and when your wife and mother are never given the respected title "Mrs."; when you are harried by day and haunted by night by the fact that you are a Negro, living constantly at tiptoe stance never quite knowing what to expect next, and plagued with inner fears and outer resentments; when you are forever fighting a degenerating sense of nobodiness . . . then you will understand why we find it difficult to wait. There comes a time when the cup of endurance runs over, and men are no longer willing to be plunged into an abyss of injustice where they experience the bleakness of corroding despair."

John understood this now, sensed deeply the pain of the Negro, and the cause of the Negro became the central thought and purpose of his own life.

Chapter Three

CHAPEL HILL first became important as a place in 1792 when a group of state leaders headed by Revolutionary War General William R. Davie decided on it as a suitable spot to locate the proposed state university. It was about thirty miles, a day's horseback ride, from Raleigh, and it was centrally located in the state, with a substantial growth of young hardwoods and a pleasing prospect of hills all around.

The university opened its doors, the first state university in America to do so, in 1795. By the time of the Civil War, it was one of the two largest universities in the country and was considered proudly to be the best in the South. During the war Union General Sherman took care to spare both town and campus, and after the war Union General Smith Atkins, whose troops occupied the town, became so infatuated with the place that he married a Southern girl, the daughter of the university's president.

Chapel Hill always has had a way about it; it's a winning spot, secluded and friendly. It has no factories, or even a railroad station. It rests in a luxurious woods, isolated by twisty highways from other places. It manages to have plenty of dogwood and redbud trees in bloom every spring, and maple, oak and sweet gum trees in color every fall. The weather is perhaps too warm in the summer, and a few days each winter are bitingly cold, but on the whole Chapel Hill has close to ideal weather.

For these and other reasons, it is able to accept gracefully the title illustrator William Meade Prince once gave it, "The Southern Part of Heaven."

Being the home of the university has given the small town a lively spirit. There always are students who aren't satisfied with the way things are and who set out to change them. Some of them, to be sure, are merely pranksters. In the old days, the village reports say, the pranksters might take a cow to the top floor of a building and tie its tail to a bell rope, a situation which results in a lot of racket in a hurry and gets everybody up at the same time in the morning. Such pranks were frequent and were tolerantly received. There was a prevailing attitude of friendliness, in spite of all.

Once geologist Collier Cobb saw several students stealing his scuppernong grapes. As they scampered away, trying to escape identification, he noticed that one of the boys dropped a letter. Professor Cobb retrieved it, and when he next saw the boy on Franklin Street, he stopped him. "Mr. Jones," he said to the trembling student, "several boys came to my house the other day to steal my grapes, and before they came to steal my grapes, I judge they must have stolen this letter from you." Evidently the attitude of the faculty, like that of the place, was conducive to pleasant living.

Historically, the university has encouraged student and faculty participation in events of the day. It was the philosophy of Edward Kidder Graham, president during the early part of the present century, that the boundaries of the university campus were coexistent with the borders of the state. His cousin, Frank Porter Graham, president from 1930 to 1949, approved this concept and encouraged students and faculty members to exert their influence by right action, each individual being free to work out his own definition of what that meant.

Starting in the 1920's, Howard Odum, Paul Green and other major writers released from Chapel Hill appraisals of the condition of the Southern Negro, the plight of the tenant farmer, the cruelty of the prison system and other controversial topics. Angry replies came from the public at large, and the university quivered often as a consequence, but it grew stronger, not weaker, and won a national reputation as one of the nation's freest and most valuable centers of thought.

After World War II, the Communists had their representatives on the campus, and, much to the distress of the state as a whole, they were afforded free speech. Even in that period the university was able to maintain its status as a free society, where ideas could compete in the marketplace.

When the Beat Generation arrived in the 1950's, the new president, William C. Friday, and his staff, and the town as a whole, tried to grin and bear it. There were not very many of the Beats, and I believe they were not deeply committed. I remember talking with one of them who had read *On the Road* and was so much taken with the idea of a life of travel and despair that he sold his texts and hitchhiked out of town. The next day he was back, trying to get his books again. He told me he had stopped in Durham to say good-bye to his mother, and she hadn't wanted him to go.

By the start of the 1960's, the Beat Generation began to fade and civil rights activities came to the fore. The high school students from the Negro community revolted first. Later there was picketing of theaters and restaurants involving both high school and college students. Now, in May of 1963, the university and the university town watched the formation by Pat Cusick and a few others of a new organization, one evidently designed to lead street marches, carry on picketing and generally to direct a more massive effort than any that had gone before, which was called the Committee for Open Business.

The new organization was Pat's idea. He had talked with Lou Calhoun and a young Negro named Harold Foster about it. Harold had been born and reared in Chapel Hill, and although he now attended North Carolina College, a state Negro college in Durham, he continued to live at home. He was a bright, nineteen-year-old, good-looking fellow who wore sports clothes well and spoke in a soft, in fact a mellow yet clipped speech, with a Beat tinge to his choice of words.

Pat's idea had no immediate appeal for him; Harold knew very well the rigorous work that would be involved. In 1960, when he had been in high school, he had picketed the Dairy Bar and the Colonial Drug Store; in 1960 and 1961 he had picketed the movie houses. So he knew what Pat was getting into. "Man, this town is hard to crack," he said. "It's called a liberal place, but that's a mirage, man. When you go to get water, you just get a mouthful of sand."

Pat didn't think so. The whole South was alive now to the need for change, and Chapel Hill ought to be the hub of it, as it always had been before. He persevered, and it was decided one night at Harry's Grill to start the new organization. Harold Foster phoned a Negro minister, Rev. W. R. Foushee, and asked if the group could have the first meeting in his church on May 3, a Sunday, in the afternoon. Rev. Foushee agreed. Lou Calhoun phoned all the white ministers he knew in town, inviting them to attend, and Harold called several adults in the Negro community. There was little planning involved. They simply wanted to gather a group together and get rid of some of the burden they carried.

On May 3 the organizational meeting, attended by about sixty people, was held at the church. On May 10 a second meeting, attended by only fifty people, was held, and an executive committee of twelve people was appointed. Harold Foster and Father Clarence Parker, a retired, eighty-year-old Episcopal pastor who lived in Chapel Hill, were made co-chairmen. On the executive committee were Pat Cusick; Lou Calhoun; the Rev. W. R. Foushee; Hilliard Caldwell, a Negro technician at the hospital; Lester Carson, a Negro student at the university; James Foushee, a Chapel Hill Negro of twenty-two, not related to Rev. Foushee; James Clotfelter and Bill Hicks, students at the university; one university instructor, James Gardner of the English department; and Anne Queen and Tom Davis of the campus YWCA and YMCA. Anne told me she and Tom were walking into the building and as soon as they appeared they were appointed, to what she didn't know until later.

All except one member of the executive committee were Southerners, and all had lived in the South for many years. With them, perhaps to balance the group, was appointed a New York native, Robert V. N. Brown, who had lived for five or six years in Chapel Hill.

In his undergraduate days Bob Brown and two other men had operated a coffee house named Pandora's Box on Sheridan Square in New York City. While thus gainfully and pleasantly employed, Bob had completed his A.B. degree work at Columbia University. He had moved south and applied himself to the goal of acquiring a Southern accent, which he succeeded in doing to an exaggerated degree. He completed work for a master's degree in history at the university, then, deciding against getting a doctorate, started a magazine named *Reflections,* a journal which carried short stories and poetry, as well as essays which Bob wrote commenting on the Southern scene. The magazine had excellent writing and beautiful artwork by Miss Katherine Strong, the sculptress, who also helped Bob with the typing, printing and binding.

Bob put copies of the first issue of the magazine in stands all over town. He also sent copies throughout the country. He sold one thousand copies at sixty cents a copy, but since the printing costs were forty cents a copy and the sales commission on each copy was twenty cents, he gained nothing at all, and actually was the loser. Nevertheless, he managed in a six-month period to publish a second issue, which was even better than the first; it sold 2,500 copies and lost him even more money. Still he proceeded to get out a third issue, which sold 3,500 copies.

Bob lived in an apartment near the campus, which also served as his office, and he learned to live on next to nothing. His car got more and more bedraggled. It's a 1954 Sunbeam convertible, an English make that isn't manufactured any more. It's quite a fast machine, and Bob used to race it. He has had it up to 110 miles an hour in professional auto races, but it's a safe bet that he'll never get it up there again. It was blue at the start, but now it's a bleak, flaky gray with black blotches. The canvas top, once tan, flies tattered blue patches. The windows have got cracked somehow. The stuffing has begun coming out of the upholstery. But the car, like the apartment Bob lives in, is spotlessly clean; it is made of first-class materials, and usually it gets to where it is going, though it's very likely to arrive late. So, in a way, the car and Bob suit each other.

Bob's initial involvement with the Chapel Hill civil rights movement began with the picketing of the movie theaters in 1960. "I wasn't on the executive committee or in any leadership capacity," he told me recently, "but I participated in the picketing."

I asked him if the movie managers were furious when the picketing started.

"Yeah, more or less, but not exactly. I wouldn't say that there was that much—yeah. A number of things tended to sort of equalize the fury on either side."

I'm afraid that's the way he talks sometimes.

The picketing of the movies began because of *Porgy and Bess,* which had an all-Negro cast. A teacher at the Negro high school wanted to take her class to see it. Her request to the manager of the Carolina Theatre was rejected. She appealed to the Ministerial Association, which tried to arrange permission for her students to see it, but they didn't get anywhere, either. Paul Green, the dramatist who many years ago wrote *In Abraham's Bosom,* a play about Negroes for which he was awarded the Pulitzer Prize, took an interest in the matter. Mr. Green, who has lived most of his life in Chapel Hill, went to the manager of the theater and asked that a special showing of the film be held for Negroes. When his efforts failed, too, picket signs were made and Rev. Charlie Jones of the Community Church and others organized the picketing. They agreed on six rules, the fifth and sixth being the most important:

5. Conduct yourself nonviolently in word and action.
6. If your relief does not come, keep walking.

According to Bob Brown, there wasn't much antagonism shown toward the pickets at either of the two movie houses in Chapel Hill. Rev. Jones would often talk with the theater managers, and would go to Raleigh and talk with Mayor W. G. Enloe, who owned the Carolina Theatre. Conferences were held over a period of many months. "Charlie Jones would go back and forth to Raleigh," Bob says, "and would call on the guy who is the manager here, and there would be another meeting, and Charlie would report. And this went on and on, on and on, without bringing any results. At the same time you had full-page advertisements in the *Daily Tar Heel* and other newspapers, with signatures of the faculty and students. I don't know how many hundreds and hundreds of faculty and students signed."

Each theater had fourteen pickets each night, so there were twenty-eight people to be scheduled daily. On the lists of pickets were faculty members, among them Joe Straley and Wayne Bowers; there were townspeople, among them Marian Davis and Mary Gilson; there were university and high school students. The pickets, of whom half were Negro and half were white, formed a committee called the Committee for Open Movies.

Now, on the new Committee for Open Business, Bob Brown was head of the action subcommittee. One of his tasks was to organize the picketing at the College Café. He prepared new posters and launched a full-scale attack on the beleaguered little restaurant.

"We had no problems with getting pickets," Bob Brown says. "We had students out there early in the morning; we had women on from nine to ten or eleven; we had people coming off the lunch hour, taking their swing on the picket lines from eleven to about two, when they closed. We had townspeople and students, white and Negro. As a matter of fact, the students began to become more interested, now that it wasn't connected with the SPU."

Pat Cusick watched all this with pleasure. He was interested to see, for example, that business began to fall off at the College Café, and to hear businessmen complaining to Max Yarborough about this continuing sidewalk exercise. "Integrate," they advised him. "The Negroes don't use restaurants uptown anyway." They said the picketing hurt the reputation of the town.

Sometimes John, Pat and Harold Foster would go to dinner at Harry's or to the Chicken Box Number Two, which was in the Negro part of town. They would talk with Harold about the predicament of the Negro in a white world, and the problem they had as whites in a Negro world, such as at the Chicken Box, where they were stared at by everybody and suspected. Around them were people who supposedly had inferior educations, inferior home life, inferior opportunities, inferior cultural backgrounds, yet John, having had every cultural advantage, felt inferior in the Chicken Box.

"I wasn't any more a free individual there than the Negro was a free individual in the larger society," John told me at Sandy Ridge. "As a matter of fact, I was painfully conscious of the fact that I was white. I was being looked down upon. That I was white was all they were seeing. The others were thinking, 'That damn white man, he doesn't know, doesn't have any idea that these people in here hate him.' I had come into this place where there was all this hostility toward me, and it wasn't because I was John Dunne, but because I was white, or, to go beyond that, it was because the situation of segregation existed and had for some time, one I didn't make, but damn it, I was stuck with it, and the situation dictated the attitudes. I wasn't free as a white man in Chapel Hill. Even walking down the street, I wasn't free. I wasn't free in the white section whenever I passed a colored man or a colored child and realized the chasm which separated us and had separated us for all our lives. I wasn't free in Harry's whenever a Negro sat down nearby or sat down at my table, for I was conscious of the chasm between us. Neither was Harold Foster free. Or Pat. Or anybody in that town, not in a meaningful sense. At least, not in a sense meaningful to me in the spring of 1963."

While John and Pat and some others discussed the emotional problems, of which they were becoming more conscious and with which they were becoming more involved, the Committee for Open Business began making plans for the first street march. The town looked on defensively, and some citizens shuddered. Why Chapel Hill? any number of them asked. Didn't Chapel Hill have an excellent record in race matters? The university had admitted the first Negro graduate student in 1951. The public schools were partially integrated. One member of the school board, elected in 1958, was J. R. Manley, a Negro minister. One member of the six-person Board of Aldermen of the town, elected in 1953 with the largest number of votes cast for any alderman that year, was Hubert Robinson, a Negro. Two of the policemen were Negroes, and thirty-five other Negroes worked for the city, a few of them in what might be termed supervisory jobs. The university and the hospital hired almost a thousand Negroes, and some of them worked in "nontraditional jobs."

So why Chapel Hill?

The answer came in the general murmur of discontent, rising from the Negroes, but also from many liberal white citizens. The integration of both the university and the schools had come about only by reason of court action. In the town itself Negro income was pitifully low. Almost half the Negroes lived in white-owned houses which did not meet the minimum requirement of the town's housing code, which everybody admitted was a lax code, even so. The schools from which Negroes graduated seemed to be poor; only one graduate had been able to satisfy the academic entrance requirements of the university. Negro visitors to the town had to be severely oriented to what a Negro could do, where he could go and where he couldn't, where he could eat and where he couldn't, and whether he could sit down when he ate or was required to stand up. And what could the Negroes aspire to? What jobs? What businesses? What chance for success? What sense of dignity and opportunity?

The debate began to generate a fair amount of anger, and on Wednesday night, May 22, there was an open meeting of the Committee for Open Business, about fifty people attending, and the question was raised whether or not to hold the march in spite of the increasing criticism. There was, Pat Cusick told me, a lengthy floor discussion. On May 19, only three days before, twenty ministers had asked Mayor Roland McClamroch to appoint a committee to work toward desegregation of the town's public facilities, and the mayor had indicated that he would do so. He already had a Human Relations Committee to work generally for development of better understanding between the races. Nobody present wanted to hamper these efforts, and it was feared by some of the white members of the new Committee for Open Business that a march might do so. However, other members felt that the best encouragement that could be given the mayor would be the demonstration, an appeal for action. A vote was taken, and it was decided to have a march on the following Saturday at two o'clock.

A number of freedom songs were rehearsed during the meeting. Pat says the Negroes sang with a different beat from the white members and that the singing was no better than it needed to be, even though words to the songs had been printed. The group rehearsed "Give Me That Old Freedom Spirit," "Hold On" and "We Shall Overcome."

The meeting ended on a passive note, and Pat admits he was apprehensive. He had learned not to count on people showing up for public demonstrations. How many of these people and their friends were going to put in an appearance on Saturday? The Negro adults at the meeting had said little. Were they going to stay with this program? Many of the white members had spoken up for caution. Would many of them appear on Saturday for a parade which presented them publicly to the town as avowed friends of the Negroes' cause?

The next day, Thursday, the Merchants Association passed a resolution calling on all segregated businesses to stop discriminatory practices. That evening the Board of Aldermen listened in town hall to Professor Don Irish of the university sociology department, a member of the Mayor's Human Relations Committee, who advised them to pass a public accommodations ordinance for Chapel Hill, a law which would assure reasonable service to all citizens in all public places. He told them that if they had the power to regulate the use of property through zoning and to decide even the size limit of a business' signs and awnings, they had authority for this, too. The aldermen, who had spent much of the past year hearing bitter complaints about zoning and awnings, smiled grimly at this. There were, however, indications that they were willing to consider any reasonable action, and that they did not exclude a public accommodations ordinance as a possibility. Most, perhaps all, of the members were against public facilities being segregated.

The next morning, Friday, Robert V. N. Brown called on the chief of police, William Blake, and introduced himself. There is no Chapel Hill ordinance having to do with street marches, but Bob said it was the policy of the COB to give notice, hopefully twenty-four hours before any march was to take place. The chief, a large, hefty, balding man of about forty-five, who had grown up in Chapel Hill, accepted the news warily. Chief Blake said he didn't know whether he could assure order and safety, that he had a small police department of only twenty-five men, and on a round-the-clock, seven-day-a-week schedule that wasn't very many.

I have talked with Bob Brown about this early meeting. "He didn't want the street," Bob says. "He wanted us to use the sidewalk. I said we were going in the street anyway. We were going to have a parade, and it was reasonable. He said that he didn't know that he could assure order, and if he had to call in the Sheriff's Department and the Highway Patrol, he couldn't necessarily be sure what some officer would do. I told him that if one of the officers struck one of the marchers, that would be fine. 'You know as well as I do, Chief, that if

one of our people gets hit on the head with nothing harder than a
wool sock, it will appear the next morning in all the newspapers in
the state.' We had these minor differences. Hell, he was doing his
job."

Word about the march quickly went out to every home in the
community. As a resident of Chapel Hill, I remember that it was a
matter of general, friendly speculation wherever one went; at least
this was so among the white residents. No doubt the Negroes were
more anxious about it. I'm sure that many Negro men wondered if
they would lose their jobs if they took part. Negro children doubtless
became aware of rekindled resentments their parents held against
white people; there was the fanning of old fires. Ministers, both white
and Negro, discussed their parishioners' and their own and their families' obligations to participate. And the managers of segregated establishments considered integrating. One of them, the manager of the
bowling alley, All-Star Lanes, said he had heard that the march was
going to be extended out to his place of business. "You needn't do
that," he told the mediation subcommittee. "We plan to integrate in
the fall."

"That's fine," they said. "We won't need to march out there *in
the fall.*"

The manager of the Oh Boy Drive In had heard a rumor that his
entrances and exits were going to be blocked by the marchers. He
phoned to say he had been thinking about integrating.

In general, there was a flurry of phone calls, of questioning and
wondering, of jockeying for positions before a storm, a new kind of
storm which nobody knew much about yet, but which was popularly
believed to be not dangerous.

James Foushee, the young Negro member of the executive committee of the COB, watched all the friendly dealings suspiciously. The
planning was going very well, but he knew Chapel Hill and was leery
of it. It was pretty as a garden, but had a lot of bees that could sting.
He had had his first fight with a white man when he was eleven. He
had been working in the kitchen of a restaurant on Franklin Street.
When he told me about it, I noticed that his slender body was held
taut, his dark eyes were glistening.

"The man called me a nigger and told me to get out. I said, 'Who you talking to? If you can't talk any better than that, we both better get out together.' I wasn't but eleven years of age, a little pup was all, but I told this big man that, and we began to fight there in the kitchen. We knocked down all the pots and pans in the place before we were done. The fight wasn't much of a success for either person, but I lost my job. So I went to work at the Porthole as a waiter and bus boy, and there I didn't get in a fight with a white man until I was fourteen. This time he was the one got fired, and I was left on."

Now Jim, who had a job as a cook at the Porthole, didn't get into fights. "I learned pacifism when I went to a conference in Atlanta when I was around sixteen. I had heard Mr. Floyd McKissick talk in Durham a few times, and he took me. Dr. King and Roy Wilkins spoke at the meetings. They talked about Gandhi and what he went through with, and they tried to get us to see that it was the best way. It was hard convincing myself. I said to myself, 'I can't stand up and let a man beat me.' But I've found that I can."

He knew Chapel Hill because of the fights and his lifetime of living as a Negro there, and he watched the development of the march, wondering when the pleasantness would give way and reveal the ugliness underneath. He was ready for it himself; being a pacifist was hard, but it gave a man freedom from fear. He wasn't afraid of anybody or of anything that anyone could do to him, and he wasn't afraid, either, that he would lose self-control and harm another person. The only thing he didn't trust himself to do was make a speech. He had tried it, but he got emotional, he got to talking too plain, his feelings began to break through his restraint. Nobody could really know what kind of fire he had inside unless he tried to make a speech, so he had sworn off that.

On Friday Pat Cusick had new reasons for optimism. That morning the manager of the bowling alley had once more phoned. The marchers need not come out to his place, he said, for he planned to integrate in about a month.

"Fine," he was told, "we won't march out to your place *in about a month.*"

The manager had rung off, but he was giving in, and Pat suspected other segregated places would, too.

Also that morning the mayor had appointed his special committee, the Mayor's Committee on Integration, and on it were two members of the Board of Aldermen and the mayor himself. If they could agree on an action in the Committee on Integration, they ought to be able to carry it through the Board of Aldermen easily enough.

So progress was ahead, Pat thought. The start he and John Dunne had made was amounting to something. All that concerned him was that the tidal wave was carrying him along with it. The movement had become to him a keystone in his own life, so that he spent every moment thinking about what more could be done.

He talked that day with Lou Calhoun and Harold Foster, who estimated that a hundred people would show up for the march. Both of them had been telephoning friends, inviting them to attend. Pat said he believed there would be two hundred.

Bob Brown concluded that fifty posters would be enough in either case. He sped around in his convertible, picking up poles, scraps at Fitch Lumber Yard, things like that. Katherine Strong helped him, and she agreed to help with the lettering that needed to be done. She had been a Phi Beta Kappa undergraduate student at the university. She now was working at the university on her sculpture. Some of the art department professors wanted her to work toward a master's degree, but she wasn't interested in taking the academic courses; she registered each term only for Professor Robert Howard's sculpture class, paid her tuition, scraping together money from typing and part-time secretarial jobs, and used the class's studio day after day, working with clay and stone.

On Friday afternoon, when they were ready to begin painting the posters, nobody was around to help, not a soul. Pat and John Dunne were off in Durham, where John was making a talk; Lou Calhoun wasn't present; James Foushee and Harold Foster were in the Negro community, stirring up interest in the next day's march. So Bob did as he and Katherine had often done when they had encountered trouble getting out the magazine; they went to find friends, a writer named Leon Rooke, a tall, lanky, quiet-mannered North Carolinian, and his wife, a native of New Orleans.

"All night we painted posters out there in Leon's house," Bob says.

"We would fasten them on the poles and paint them, then take the posters out into Leon's front yard and lay them on the ground. When morning come, man, they were all over the yard. We had fifty, sixty of those bastards out there, and the neighbors were looking out their windows like crazy and shaking their heads. Later the landlady called up Leon and told him to move out of there. We had that whole front yard full of freedom signs, and the neighborhood was about dead."

At one o'clock the young people moved the signs down to St. Joseph's Church and laid them on the ground.

At about this time, Charliese Cotton, a sixteen-year-old Negro girl, was at home. "My mama told me to go up there and march, and I didn't know nothin' about it," she told me later.

At the same time, Rev. Charlie Jones was preparing to leave his home on Purefoy Road. Rev. Jones had a long history in civil rights work in Chapel Hill. In 1944 he had invited the Negro members of a military band, then playing in Chapel Hill, to attend his Sunday morning church service; several of them came and this created a storm of criticism. In 1947, when Bayard Rustin, George Houser, Jim Peck and one other man had visited Chapel Hill, evaluating public transportation facilities available to Negroes in the South, Rev. Jones found out that the group had been arrested and that several taxicab drivers, armed with clubs and stones, were waiting at the police station for them to come out. He went to the station and walked out with them, put them in his car, drove them to his home, and later drove them out of town to safety. He then, at the request of the police, sent his family away from Chapel Hill for a week, but he remained at home and was in the house when a group of white men gathered and stoned the doors and windows. In May, 1954, soon after the school desegregation decision of the U.S. Supreme Court, he had organized a group to help implement the Court's ruling. Over six years of work followed.

In 1960 he had been out of town when he read in the newspaper that a group of Negro students had held a sit-in at the Colonial Drug Store and had swarmed up the street to the bus station, where they had been turned away at the door to the lunch counter. There had been no violence, but the activities had taken on something of the nature of a disorganized mob, and the night's work had ended with the thwarted, dissatisfied students throwing snowballs at each other. He returned to Chapel Hill and met with the students, at their request, in the Negro recreation center.

He arrived a few minutes after the meeting started and found that Harold Foster had taken over the chairmanship, had literally taken it away from Rev. Manley, who had started the meeting. The students asked Rev. Jones if he would help them, and he said that he had found that student groups asked adults to help them when they wanted an adult who would serve as a yes-man, and that he didn't plan to serve as a yes-man, but that he would advise them, for he thought they were doing right and not to let anybody tell them otherwise. He was surprised to find that he was applauded and cheered for this, and later he found out that the Negro pastors present had, before his arrival, refused to serve in any way and had told the students they were doing wrong.

He went ahead with his promise, however, and arranged for a CORE official to come to Chapel Hill and train the young people in the tactics of nonviolence. One of the training techniques was to have half the students picket while the other half tried to make them angry; the climax of one session came when one of the hecklers spit in one of the pickets' faces.

In 1961 Rev. Jones had helped organize the picketing of the local theaters. Now, in 1963, he was to speak at the first march. For the first time publicly in the town, he would mention the need for a public accommodations ordinance. He believed the Committee for Open Business ought to focus attention on that as a specific goal. It seemed to him that a public businessman had many rights, but among them was not the right to invite the public into his place of business and then routinely to insult and to refuse to serve a portion of that public.

When he arrived at the Negro church, the starting point for the march, only twenty-five people were there. They were looking at the signs, selecting the ones they wanted to carry. There was a show of jubilation, in spite of the small crowd, for word had leaked out that the bowling alley had capitulated that morning. The manager had phoned, saying the marchers needn't come by his place at all, that he had integrated. A similar call had come from the Oh Boy Drive In.

By one-thirty over a hundred people had gathered at St. Joseph's

Church. Harold Foster invited everybody inside and gave out the printed texts of the freedom songs. There was a rehearsal of the singing.

By 1:45 the church was pretty well filled. One of the reporters of the Chapel Hill *Weekly,* J. A. C. Dunn, approached Bob Brown. "How many imports did you bring in for this?" he asked.

"Imports?" Bob said indignantly. "What's the matter with you? There ain't an import around. There's a man from the history department. There's sociology. There's public health." He went down the list of university departments and other divisions of Chapel Hill life represented. "There ain't an import in the place."

Professors and students, townspeople of both races, young people of both races, rich and poor, pastors and the not-very-religious were sitting there together. It was as varied a group as ever assembled, and they were singing together, a spirit of elation taking hold of them, Bob says.

At two o'clock the throng of people moved out of the church onto the lawn. Police motorcycles and cars were standing by. Many hundreds of onlookers had gathered on the main street and were waiting to see what sort of parade this would turn out to be. Harold Foster took his place at the front. Pat Cusick, John Dunne, Bob Brown, Father Parker, Lou Calhoun and the others found their places. A signal was given, and 350 citizens of the town, about half of them white and half of them colored, began what was perhaps the first fully integrated public march in support of integration that the South had seen.

They walked down Franklin Street, Father Parker beside his wife, other Protestant and Catholic priests and pastors walking nearby. There were Negro high school and college students, many university students, all of them following a police motorcycle escort. They stopped the parade in front of the College Café, and a big cheer went up and they waved their signs at the place, which now seemed small and vulnerable indeed. Pat Cusick and John Dunne recalled that here, only a few weeks before, they had had trouble manning a two-man picket line.

They marched down the street singing:

We shall overcome.
We shall overcome.
We shall overcome someday.
Deep in my heart,
I do believe,
We shall overcome someday.

Max Yarborough could still hear them singing as they came up Rosemary Street behind the restaurant. He stood there behind the counter, no doubt impressed in spite of himself. The weeks of picketing had been the work of a few scattered people, but this was a major uprising.

His Negro cook, who had worked for him for years, who had nailed the nails and hung up the pans in that place, was standing nearby watching him. The cook said he was going to leave his job, that his minister and friends were out there, and he didn't think he could continue to work in a segregated place. It was then that Max decided to integrate.

I watched that parade that day, as did everybody else, it seemed, in Chapel Hill. Like many others I took pictures of it, as I would of any parade. It was a festive occasion; it was a deeply serious effort which had been decked out with color and had a victorious sound to it. I remember feeling at the time, as the hundreds of singing people walked by, that they would surely win, that in a democratic society one can't very often stop people who have the dedication they were showing.

I had also seen the Raleigh marches and could compare the two. At this time, I was working in the office of the governor, Terry Sanford, as his special assistant, and I had had occasion to see three or four Raleigh demonstrations. I remember one evening I was in the State Capitol working when I heard a heavy-beated, pulsating song sung by a large group of men and women. I was alone in the building, yet the music was coming from all around me, it seemed, and was drawing closer. "It's nothing more than the ghosts of past legislatures," I remember thinking.

Then, through a window, I saw them, hundreds of them, almost all of them Negro young people. They carried torches. Their cadence was the beat of threatening men and women, of natives in the streets. Here and there among them was a white face. I recognized Allard Lowenstein, a professor at North Carolina State in Raleigh, for one; I very likely would have noticed Pat Cusick, for another, if I had known him back then. They moved around the Capitol; the Capitol for that moment was their prisoner, was their possession. My office was the only lighted room in the place, and I was the only person there, but as I stood there at the window I felt no fear at all. They were not menacing, but they did represent protest and power and a plea for help.

I got my camera and went running after them. When I reached the new State Legislative Building, they were walking up and down before it, on the marble front terrace before the low spotlights which threw their shadows on the long row of white columns and the hundreds of sheets of glass. The building reflected them; their bodily comments were on the building, billowing in exaggerated, distorted forms, swaying to the cadenced, challenging beat of their own music.

The Chapel Hill march was not so overwhelming; it was more of a holiday excursion. In Raleigh the police watched with cold, hard stares as the Negroes moved on the sidewalks; the demonstrators did not use the streets at all, and they didn't dare block traffic at the intersections. In Chapel Hill the marchers had a motorcycle escort; policemen stopped traffic at all side streets. In Raleigh there was the attitude: "We will die for our cause." In Chapel Hill there was the attitude: "We would like you to join us so that we can improve the community."

I left the main block, once the marchers had passed, and walked the two short blocks to the town hall, a small-steepled colonial building which seems to me to be bound by the telephone lines that converge at that corner. I arrived just before the marchers did, they having gone around the long way. I saw Mayor McClamroch looking out from behind the screen door; as the marchers approached, he bounded back inside, then returned. But when they reached the corner, he drew back inside and wasn't seen again. He had been invited to speak to the group, and he still hadn't made up his mind as to whether he should do so.

Rev. Charlie Jones came forward, went up two or three steps of the town hall and stood before the screen door. In his customarily calm, reasoned way, he gave a talk. One heckler, standing behind the marchers, challenged him a time or two. The group continued to listen to Charlie Jones. It was very much the marchers' day.

Chapter Four

NOBODY COULD SAY how many segregated places would yield to the pressure of such marches. There was even a discussion during the next two weeks about how many segregated public places there were in Chapel Hill, with Joe Augustine, director of the Merchants Association claiming 95 percent integration, and the Committee for Open Business suggesting that it was much less.

Negotiations were one of the principal activities of the Committee for Open Business these days. The more influential members of the executive committee talked with restaurant and motel managers, and the Mayor's Committee on Integration began to do the same.

Some of the Negroes found pressure put on them. One Negro man who had for years worked at a fraternity house was advised by the fraternity to have his son stop marching; the man did so. Another Negro man, an employee at a sorority, was told to stop demonstrating or lose his job, but the other Negro employees of the sorority said they would leave with him, so a truce was declared. White employees of several businesses, including the Hospital Savings Association, the second largest employer in the town, were told to stop supporting demonstrations and to see to it that members of their families did, too.

All over town, personal crises were being met in one way or another, and much of the worry came to fall on Pat Cusick, Harold Foster and the others involved, who were almost buried under the burden of planning other marches, as well as meeting with the Committee for Open Business, the Mayor's Integration Committee, the

Mayor's Human Relations Committee, and with distraught individuals, people who were afraid of losing their jobs, or people who were beginning to see in this public testimony a meaningful use of their time. The young Negroes particularly, elated by evidence of success on every side, believing that now perhaps the world was going to change and that they could begin to aspire to higher rungs of the social ladder, were anxious to see more marches carried out, and quickly.

Involved as a peripheral figure at this time was John Dunne, the only one in town who had been thrown into jail for civil rights action, and the only one who had been involved in Birmingham. Birmingham was still the angry word which stirred up feeling on both sides of the civil rights struggle.

John's apartment, which at his request I had helped him rent the previous September, was located on the main street near the post office. It was a convenient place to drop by, and John was visited by students and townspeople alike, by Negroes and whites from the civil rights movement in Chapel Hill and Durham. The pressure from all this, and from his schoolwork at the close of the semester, brought him pretty close to the breaking point. Also, he was out of money and was in debt a few hundred dollars, a sum which loomed like a mountain before him.

One evening in early June, he phoned me and asked if he could come by the house for a visit. When he arrived I was startled at the way he looked, for he was very tired and nearly worn out. He came into the living room and sat down, slumped down really, and suddenly he smiled in the boyish way he has. He said he was leaving Chapel Hill for the summer. His parents said he had to work to pay off his debts. He agreed that this was fair. They were debts he had made because of all the people coming by and because of money he had loaned friends; his new friends never seemed to have money, even for the necessities of life. He had passed his schoolwork by cramming for the exams, he said; he had been in the "A" sections, which were programmed for the intellectually gifted students and which the students called the "suicide sections." Overloaded in courses, picketing the College Café, working in Birmingham for about two weeks, working with the Committee for Open Business since then, being in Durham and

Raleigh marching night after night, he had come to the last of his strength. Yet there he was, he had come through, and what was ahead for him was a summer which would be spent away from Chapel Hill.

"How are you and the Morehead Foundation coming along?" I asked him.

"Some of them want to take away the scholarship," he said.

"It would be a prominent news story, if they did," I said, "and they won't."

He said he might give it up anyway. "They think they own me body and soul." He said they had tried to make him leave the SPU. "There were three Morehead Scholars in it, and they tried to get all of them to leave. Then when I started picketing, they became furious. They had warned me that if I got into any controversial activity, they would take the scholarship away."

I told him the university ought to give him a replacement scholarship in that case, since it was shaky educational policy to interfere with a student's moral convictions like that. I believed then, and believe now, that such attitudes only push a willful student toward the position the adults try to guard against, and I suspect that the authoritarian attitude of this private foundation had much to do with pushing John to an open break with authority itself.

I asked him about the demonstrations in Durham. Durham is not only the home of one of the state's largest Negro colleges, North Carolina College; it also is the home of an educated Negro community, which operates the largest Negro-owned insurance company in the world, as well as a bank with several branch offices in the state and a savings and loan association. The total assets of these three companies in 1963 were about ninety million dollars.

John told me that demonstrations had started in Durham on a recent Saturday at 4 P.M. This was the day of city elections, and some two hundred Negro youth leaders staged sit-ins at segregated restaurants; 132 of them were arrested and put in the Durham County jail. On Sunday night 759 students went to a Howard Johnson restaurant between Chapel Hill and Durham and staged a sit-in; all were arrested and were carried in busses to the Durham County jail, where the police worked until 4 A.M. booking them. The leader of the sit-ins was Quinton Baker, head of the NAACP chapter at

North Carolina College. These were his first demonstrations since taking the post, and his control of the Howard Johnson demonstrators was such that not a demonstrator would move unless told to do so, even though in some cases cars backed into them. All were arrested except Quinton, who returned to the campus and organized a mass street march for the same night. He led over a thousand people through the streets of Durham and to the town hall.

A new mayor, Wensell Grabarek, was inaugurated on Monday morning, and he spent the early part of the afternoon meeting with Quinton and other Negro leaders. The Negroes agreed to call a moratorium on demonstrations once the mayor brought evidence that negotiations with the segregated establishmens in Durham would be successful. Quinton staged a mass demonstration that same afternoon, marching through the streets to the courthouse, where he read a statement urging the city leaders to take action at once. That evening another mass meeting was held at St. Joseph's Church, and this time Pat and John were among the congregation.

They were also present on Tuesday night when the mayor came alone to the meeting and reported that he had that day got the managers of five restaurants to agree to integrate, and that he believed others would integrate soon. The meeting was broken up by a bomb scare and the people at the church were urged to go on home. Quickly they filed out into the dark streets.

John said he felt awkward and frightened, for there were only a few white people in the neighborhood. His and Pat's fears were considerably relieved when Quinton Baker, whom they had met for the first time that night, invited them to come with him to the North Carolina College campus.

When they arrived there, they heard that Floyd McKissick's daughter Joycelyn and a small test team had been surrounded by a mob at the courthouse. The report was that the police would not assure them protection. Quinton, John and Pat drove downtown, where they found the white crowd dispersing. They drove at once to Mr. McKissick's house, where they found that everybody was all right. Joycelyn said the mob had been armed with pipes. Also, they had apples from which the cores had been removed, and which had been packed with broken glass.

Quinton, Pat and John drove back to the college, and arrived as the male students were pouring out of the dormitories, armed with bricks and pipes. Quinton moved to try to stop them. The students said groups of white men had been seen around the women's dormitories. Quinton said he thought the students had, in that case, better deploy themselves on the campus and protect the dormitories. He began assigning students to various strategic posts, and in this way broke up the mob.

That had been Tuesday night. On Wednesday night John spoke at the mass meeting and Mayor Grabarek made another report, after which a moratorium was called. That was the situation now, John told me. He said Duke as well as North Carolina College students had been involved, and there had been grave danger until the mayor took a firm hand in negotiations.

He asked me if the situation in the state as a whole looked dangerous, and I told him that the governor was handling the racial matters himself and that my impression was that he was deeply worried about the prospects of violence. My own work for the governor, I told John, had to do with a poverty program and new educational programs. I talked for a few minutes about these projects, and John listened with interest, but the programs I described were long-range processes, and he was more concerned with this week's battle. In mild criticism I asked him what would happen if he managed to knock the segregation walls down, and there was no work for the Negro to do, and if the Negro wasn't trained to do anything on his own, and if his leaders and institutions were not competent.

But the long view only cut off his vision. He was a leader, anxious to get to work now, willing to risk danger. He had come into the South to get to know the South, and now he was held by the South; but what he had not learned was the ponderableness of the South, the evolutionary way the South has of yielding finally to a pastor with the controlled planning of Charlie Jones, but of resenting even more than most sections of the country anything which seems to make demands or to involve coercion. The instinct of the South was not part of him yet. As is the case in any revolution taking place, the need for immediate action was inside him and was what he breathed.

I suggested that he visit my farm one day before he left, believing that might calm him down somewhat, and he did come by later for the key. When next I saw him, he told me that he had had a great time out there. The farm is isolated and deserted, and he had been able to strip off his clothes and take long runs along the timber trails. He was away from machines and from society, which is a form of machine, and away from the university, which also is a form of machine. He was able to flop down by a creek and lap water, and to go wearily back to the old house to sit on the porch and read until dusk, then to read by candlelight and firelight. Even the snakes were friends, he said. He honored them and every living thing.

And I remembered as he talked that when he had lived in my house in Chapel Hill he had spent so much time in the garden smelling the flowers, burying his nose in the flowers to get the full scent of them, that I had come to think of him in terms of Ferdinand the Bull, an amiable fellow with the same tendency. No doubt at the farm he was a friend of the wildflowers, too, as well as of the creeks and candles and the hearth fire. Nature clothed him with calmness. She is the soothing mother, after all, not of the institutions we have made, not of the Committee for Open Business or the Board of Aldermen or the Chicken Box Number Two, but of us, of all the creatures of this earth who bleed if cut.

The meeting of John and Pat with Quinton Baker, the young Durham leader, was important because Quinton became one of the three chief leaders of the Chapel Hill demonstrations. Quinton, twenty, had grown up in Greenville, a tobacco town in eastern North Carolina, where as a youngster he worked as a shoeshine boy and later as a gang hand in the tobacco finishing plants. He spent his spare time down by the river, where he would go to read. During his junior year in high school, he says he became sick of the lifeless ways of his school and virtually took control of student activites; he organized special events, clubs, lectures, parties, and in his senior year was elected president of the student body and was given five other offices. He graduated with honors, one of the top three students in his class.

Quinton, the only member of his family who has involved himself in civil rights activities, says he has done so partly because of an incident in Greenville at East Carolina College, when he was refused permission to attend a performance of Fred Waring and his Penn-sylvanians. Quinton, a member of his high school glee club, tried for weeks to get permission to attend, and when he was finally rejected by the college, he became furious.

"My reaction was to determine to develop and prepare myself so thoroughly that the white man would have no other choice but to respect and accept me as equal," he says. "When I entered North Carolina College, my one ambition was to finish my education so that I could return to Greenville and live a most proper life, only to make myself look good in the eyes of the whites. How foolish I was!"

At North Carolina College his ability as a leader quickly got him involved in civil rights activities, and in his junior year he organized the Durham sit-ins and marches. He was soon to be elected state president of the Youth Chapters of the NAACP, and as one of his first actions he was going to assign himself to Chapel Hill, where with John Dunne and Pat Cusick he would pit his strength against the crusty walls of the university community. He, like John and Pat, would be sent from there to prison.

I remember that Governor Sanford, early in January, before there was picketing at the College Café or any street marches in Raleigh or Birmingham, called a breakfast meeting at the governor's mansion. He sent out twenty-five invitations to people in various parts of the state.

I was invited, and since the breakfast was to be at 8 A.M., I decided to spend the night in Raleigh, in a room I had rented for $25 a month in a rooming house for such occasions. I ate dinner at a nearby restaurant, then returned to my office at the Capitol. About nine-thirty, Joel Fleishman, the governor's legal assistant, came upstairs and asked me to come to the governor's mansion.

We found Governor Sanford in the library. He greeted us in a relaxed and friendly way. During the two years I worked in his office, I often wondered how he could exist in a world in which he was forever being petitioned or advised or pestered or telephoned or ques-tioned or challenged or charged with something, and still remain as casual as if he had just come in off the golf links. Nor was he ever hurried or distressed. Perhaps beneath the exterior was a sea of worries, but, if so, they were not permitted to affect anybody else.

He is blond, about forty-eight, and was born in Laurinburg, North Carolina. He is an alumnus of the University of North Carolina and served in World War II as a paratrooper. He had run hard for the governorship, emphasizing education and trying to avoid the race issue. Since boyhood he had wanted to be governor, and since he could not by state law succeed himself in the governorship, he had only four years to do all that he wanted to accomplish for the state.

On this particular night he handed me a statement he had written in longhand on a large yellow pad. It was entitled "Observations for a Second Century," and in it he discussed his views concerning racial intolerance. He said that this document was to be the topic at the breakfast meeting the next morning; we were to decide at breakfast whether the statement was a good one and if it ought to be released at all. I remember thinking that this would be the first time in history that a Southerner while governor of a state had taken a stand openly, avowedly in favor of Negro rights.

The breakfast was to be in the mansion, a three-story, wood and brick structure, the upper floors of which are used by the governor's family, the main floor being reserved for the entertainment of their guests. The house is an excellent example of gingerbread architecture. It has many towers and porches and doodads and the like. It really is festooned, yet it has a stately attitude. The builders made it large enough to serve purposes of state, set it in a grove of trees on a square city block near the center of Raleigh, and filled it with high-ceilinged, cheerful rooms which open outside onto large porches and inside onto wide hallways dominated by a great central stairway.

At the back of the main floor of the house are three rooms: the library, which will seat about twenty people comfortably and which usually has a fire burning in the fireplace; the dining room, which always is decorated with large bowls of flowers; and the kitchen, where the chief housekeeper, Mrs. Byrd, is in charge of the meals, which are excellently cooked and served by prisoners from the prison system.

To this remarkable house, the governor had invited twenty-five of us. We ate breakfast at the long table, and, as I recall now, we had fried slices of country ham, which in North Carolina is a distin-

guished product, indeed, cured for about ten weeks in salt, then usually smoked and hung for several months before cutting. We also had
scrambled eggs, candied pieces of apple, biscuits, grits, gravy and
much else, no doubt, which I've forgotten. When we finished eating,
the coffee cups were filled again and cigars were passed around to the
men. The governor, at the head of the table, rose to speak.

I looked around at the people present. Among them were some of
the most influential citizens of the state: Hugh Cannon, director of
the Department of Administration; Bert Bennett, chairman of the
North Carolina Democratic Party; Hargrove Bowles, chairman of the
Department of Conservation and Development; Martha McKay, a
member of the National Democratic Committee; and John Wheeler
and John Stewart, two Negro leaders, both from Durham. Four other
Negroes were present, among them Albert Best of Greenville and
John Larkins of Raleigh. Joel Fleishman, the governor's legal assist-
ant, was present. So was Alex Schenck, a foundation executive of
Charlotte, and other men of influence.

"Most of you don't know why you were invited here this morning,"
Governor Sanford said, "and when you leave, you doubtless will be
asked by reporters why you were here. We won't make any public
announcements about it ourselves, and I hope you won't, either. We
have sessions at the mansion often, and we try to keep them off the
record. It's a game we play with the Raleigh *News and Observer,* and
we like to win." There was just a hint of firmness in his voice, and in
the context of the informality of his manner it stood out effectively.

He began to talk about what he had in mind. He said he was
thinking about saying something publicly about the race problem. No
doubt some of his visitors could not have been more surprised if he
had said he was going to open the doors of the sixty state prisons at
noon.

I had known for months that he was fretting about this issue,
considering whether to tackle it or leave it alone. The issue had kept
coming up more and more persistently. He had told me once that one
trouble he had with the race question had occurred when he made his
early tour of the state schools. He used the same basic talk in all of
them, varying it as he wanted to, and as he looked down at the Negro
children, what he had been saying to the white children about the

promise of America simply didn't realistically apply. He decided he would have to change his speech or change the state. The previous summer, I recalled, he had asked me to draw up a paper on what the state might do to help the Negro. I had done so, and later he had mentioned the paper to me briefly, but there was no evidence of commitment to it on his part. Since then, I had sent along to him papers I thought were pertinent, but he had never returned any of them or mentioned having seen them.

Now, here in the dining room, he took up his handwritten statement and read it aloud. It was only two pages long, so it took only a few minutes to read. I have no copy of it, and so far as I know the original copy, like much else of historic importance, ended up in the wastebasket. I do, however, have the notes I made that morning, and it's apparent to me both from them and from my memory that the one who had the most criticism of the statement was John Wheeler, the Negro banker. Mr. Wheeler favored the statement, but he wondered if the governor shouldn't modify his reliance on goodwill and persuasion as the ways to handle the problem, and lean somewhat more heavily on the law, particularly new laws. The governor didn't seem to think so. There was a lengthy discussion, and I realized somewhere during it that John Wheeler, by attacking the statement for being too moderate, had got the group past the point of debating whether a statement ought to be released, and on to the question of whether the statement went far enough. I suspect that he realized this, and that the governor realized it, too, and let him take this road.

The result was a statement only slightly modified by the governor. "Even if I were a firm believer in passing some laws," he said, "I couldn't get them through."

As the meeting broke up, along about ten o'clock, I overheard Martha McKay ask the governor if he would consider adding equal rights for women to his declaration, which was an apt question, one which the governor, by means of some distraction or other, managed to avoid answering.

The governor sent the statement to a hundred leaders of the state, with a request for their opinion of it. In the week to follow, he received many responses, most of them favorable, many of them from people one would not expect to be favorably inclined toward it—for example, political leaders in the eastern part of the state, the old plantation belt of North Carolina. Only a few leaders felt that the statement should not be released. One of them, a politician, arrived at the governor's office for a routine conference a week or so later. The governor, smiling disarmingly, asked him if he had read the statement. "Yes," the man said grumpily. He sat down and shook his head sadly. Then, noticing that the governor was still smiling, he blurted out, "My God, you're not going to release it, are you?"

The governor prepared the statement for release at a meeting of the North Carolina Press Association in Chapel Hill on January 18, 1963. I recall this very well, partly because this event overlapped another, the visit to the state of seven officials of the Ford Foundation who had accepted the governor's invitation to see the Southern situation firsthand and give him their advice, particularly about possible ways of breaking what he had termed the cycle of poverty.

I had taken the Ford officials to an all-day meeting in the mountains, then one in the coastal plain, and on the third day of their visit, which was the seventeenth, they were in Raleigh, where they spent the day in the governor's office talking with him and representatives of the state agencies and schools. Foundation officials Clarence Faust, Paul Ylvisaker and their associates pried into matters with considerable interest and with appreciation for the willingness of Governor Sanford and the others to discuss basic issues frankly. They had dinner with the governor that night, then on the fourth day came to Chapel Hill, where they talked with editors and several other people.

That afternoon, after the Foundation officials were on their way home, the governor met with about two hundred editors in the ballroom of the Carolina Inn. He told them he had a statement to read. There was, of course, nothing unusual about that; governors read proclamations all the time, sometimes more than one a day, about every conceivable subject, the announcement of fire prevention week being about average in importance.

The governor began reading: "The American Negro was freed from slavery one hundred years ago. In this century he has made much progress, educating his children, building churches, entering into the community and civic life of the nation. Now is a time not merely to look back to freedom, but forward to the fulfillment of its meaning."

I saw one of the deans of the university look up, startled; the Negro waiters stopped in place at the back of the room.

"The time has come for American citizens to give up their reluctance, to quit unfair discrimination, and to give the Negro a full chance to earn a decent living for his family and to contribute to higher standards for himself and all men. We cannot rely on law alone in this matter because much depends upon its administration and upon each individual's sense of fair play."

Many television film cameras were turned on, of course, and now reporters began snapping pictures. The governor read with a calmness and simplicity that seemed to be unrelated to the importance of what he said.

"North Carolina and its people have come to the point of recognizing the urgent need for opening new economic opportunities for Negro citizens. We also recognize that in doing so we shall be adding new economic growth for everybody. We can do this. We should do this. We will do it because we are concerned with the problems and the welfare of our neighbors. We will do it because our economy cannot afford to have so many people fully or partially unproductive. We will do it because it is honest and fair for us to give all men and women their best chance in life."

The governor said he was that day appointing a Good Neighbor Council for the state, twenty-four people, to be headed by David Coltrane, a past director of the Department of Administration who knew state government and North Carolina politics thoroughly. The Council would seek to establish voluntary nondiscriminatory hiring practices in the state and would help establish training programs. The Council would work with local committees to be established by mayors and chairmen of County Commissioners. Heads of all state agencies were being asked immediately to formulate nondiscriminatory policies. A conference of the business and industrial leaders of the state would be called in the spring. All church and civic leaders were called upon to support the objectives of the Council.

The talk lasted less than five minutes. The governor folded his papers and sat down. There was a smattering of applause; then, as the editors began to respond to the importance of the occasion, they stood and gave the governor what can only be termed an ovation. They applauded what might prove to be one of the greatest political errors, yet one of the finest achievements, of Terry Sanford's life.

Governor Sanford had made his announcement in the most public forum he could find, and in the town he must have known was best able to lead the way.

Chapter Five

THE COMMITTEE FOR OPEN BUSINESS had three marches a week all that summer," Pat Cusick told me at Sandy Ridge, "and we held them on a regular schedule, which was probably a mistake. It meant that the town was able to get accustomed to them, to fit them into the summer's routine. On Sunday afternoons we marched from St. Joseph's Church to the Colonial Drug Store, where we sang freedom songs. Every Wednesday and Saturday we had a street march all the way downtown."

Picketing was started at several places, and the COB began to meet often with the mayor.

Mayor Roland (Sandy) McClamroch, in his late thirties, is a Chapel Hillian by birth and a graduate of the university. He is a descendant of Buck Duke, the tobacco capitalist, and owns the local radio station, WCHL, which he personally manages. He is a public-spirited and charitable person, an ideal mayor for a pleasant, contented village, one which has solved most of its problems and has set itself in a genteel, friendly routine. That essentially is what Chapel Hill was, or thought it was, when he was elected in 1961.

Of late, however, the mayor's job had become crowded with activity and animosity which spilled over into his social and business relationships. Mayor McClamroch likes to play golf; he has a beach house and a boat; he has an attractive wife and children and a small greenhouse attached to his comfortable home; he has enough money to get along well, to travel if he wants to travel, to have dinner with his friends and to sit at the country club afterward and sip brandy. Instead, he found himself worrying about the COB, the Mayor's Committee on Integration, the Human Relations Committee, the governor, and taking calls from citizens who had suggestions on one side or the other. Early in his administration, he had set a policy of not taking a drink before dinner on nights when he had official duties to perform, and the point had come where he couldn't seem to take a drink before dinner at all, not on any night of the week.

Soon after the first march, he had gone alone to the COB executive committee and had asked them to stop their efforts for two weeks. He said he would rather see the town go without social change for a year than have another march, an opinion which infuriated Lou Calhoun. However, the mayor also said that he believed Chapel Hill could be integrated by negotiation, and if after two weeks it couldn't be, they could go ahead and march and he wouldn't blame them.

Well, he had been given his two weeks, but he had not integrated anything, not one of the fourteen prime targets that had been agreed on. So this had left him looking either to a long period of demonstrations and public antagonism or to a public accommodations law. Since it would be the first public accommodations ordinance in the state, and for that matter in the South, it would doubtless be an expensive thing to enforce.

Whether such an ordinance could be passed remained a question. The newspaper might not support it. The editor, James Shumaker, was a liberal man; he had published an editorial following that first big march, calling for the voluntary desegregation of public facilities, and it was reported that he had also been attending the public meetings of COB and could be heard singing "We Shall Overcome" with them. But Mayor McClamroch had heard that back when the theaters were being picketed, Jim Shumaker had written the defense statements for the theaters, had edited the news stories reporting on the issuance of the statements, and had written the editorials criticizing the statements, so evidently nobody could know quite what he was up to.

In mid-June the Mayor's Committee on Integration reported that a public accommodations ordinance was the best solution. On June 19 the Merchants Association stated its strong opposition to such a law. "Businessmen should not be picketed, coerced or threatened by any means," it said.

On the same day a possible way of escape from the entire dilemma came in the form of an official statement by Governor Sanford, which asked for a cessation of all demonstrations in the state and called for a more intensive campaign of negotiations. The governor's statement came, of course, in answer to a great deal of public and private pressure, and in response to his fears, which now accompanied him day and night, that several places in the state might break out into riots and suffer bloodshed. He had taken the action in spite of the pleas of John Wheeler and other Negro leaders, who said that the street demonstrations were the most effective tool the Negro had found.

In an editorial a few weeks earlier, the Chapel Hill *Weekly* had quoted from a nationwide survey of businessmen who had been polled concerning desegregation. "Time and time again they said they would yield only so much as was necessary to avoid violence and serious dislocation of commerce." The editorial commented: "This fact alone would be enough to convince those now demonstrating, if they needed convincing, that they are on the right road."

On the same day as the governor's appeal, however, the *Weekly* called for a cessation of demonstrations.

It was uncomfortable for the demonstrators in Chapel Hill to find that the press and the governor had taken stands against them, for often they had expressed confidence in the judgment of both. It was apparent that society was now turning a darker frown on them, and the demonstrators, at least those in Chapel Hill, were not willing to frown back. They had never believed their protest was against the town or the state; it was against the segregated places, which were actually in the minority in the town itself.

The executive committee of COB held an uncomfortable meeting. Some of the members thought the governor's announcement had, in the light of conditions elsewhere, been advisable, but only one member, Anne Queen, felt it ought to apply to Chapel Hill.

As for the newspaper, a member contended that the paper had had three stages in its history. It had been a friendly letter home in the old days when Louis Graves had owned and edited it; it presented Chapel Hill as a woodsy place full of tall trees and contented people. The second phase began when George Watts Hill and Orville Campbell had bought it, modernized its format and hired Jim Shumaker to come to Chapel Hill to edit it.. Shumaker was a gifted journalist who understood the town and offered it a modern, streamlined newspaper ready to support community groups which sought to improve the place. The third phase was appearing now, when the business-oriented, moderate views of Mr. Hill and Mr. Campbell would begin to predominate in spite of Mr. Shumaker, and the newspaper would become a voice for the business interests in the community. They said that this three-stage development was not an unusual development in a newspaper. All the more reason, therefore, to be cautious about accepting what the paper had to say at face value, or bowing to its advice.

Members pointed out that Mr. Hill had interests all over town; he was a capitalist of immense wealth who was rarely seen in meetings, who did not appear at functions, who did not often announce his participation in business of any sort, but who held the biggest vote in Chapel Hill commerce; further, he was a member of the executive committee of the Board of Trustees of the university, and was a frequent adviser to the governor. In Durham he was working to bring about integration, but in Chapel Hill his position seemed to be more moderate.

Mr. Campbell also had many business connections in town. He had graduated from the university, where he had been editor of the *Daily Tar Heel,* winning out by a few votes over Lou Harris, who later went into the profession of predicting election outcomes and who attributed to this experience his belief that a candidate should always be eager to shake a few more hands. As editor, Orville was chosen for special attention by the late Billy Carmichael, the conservative vice-president of the university, who encouraged him to start a print shop. Orville, with many protestations and repeated predictions of failure, started a small, modest shop in a concrete-block building which was barely large enough for Orville and one printer. He got orders from the university and local businesses, and, still insisting that he would go down to financial doom, he expanded year by year, spawning rooms at the back and side of his shop. Now he pretty well did all the printing that was done in town, and he was involved in other businesses as well. He was energetic, immensely public-spirited and painfully proud of Chapel Hill's standing nationally as a progressive, liberal town; he was also rather conservative.

It was believed by the COB that behind the scenes Watts Hill and Orville Campbell were opposing the passage of a public accommodations ordinance, and it was apparent that their newspaper had reversed its earlier position and no longer supported the demonstrations.

If one alienates the press in a small town, he is in trouble. In Chapel Hill the radio station, which was popular with the townspeople and students, was owned by the mayor. The *Daily Tar Heel,* although it was responsibly edited by two seniors, Gary Blanchard and David Ethridge, elected by the student body for a one-year term, was not widely read off campus. There was, finally, the *News of Orange County,* which came out twice a week and which was edited by Roland Giduz, a member of the Board of Aldermen.

At the COB meeting Harold Foster and James Foushee were in favor of continuing the demonstrations. Pat Cusick supported that position, too, as did Bob Brown. One by one the majority of the executive committee came around to that position, but by no means all. "If we lose the support of the community," they said, "not much can be done; the community can't be integrated by a minority faction which is alienated from the community itself." Even so, they agreed, except for Anne Queen, who resigned that night, to continue the demonstrations, and made this recommendation to the full Committee for Open Business, where it was approved. They held a street demonstration and continued with their plans.

Among these was the picketing of the Colonial Drug Store, a small store located near the Negro community, which had become a symbol of segregation to the Negroes. A few years earlier, Harold Foster, James Foushee and others had decided to try to integrate it. One afternoon, six Negro high school students went into the drugstore, as they often did. They were welcomed, as they always were, by the owner, John Carswell, and his wife. The high school students bought a few candy bars and a newspaper, then moved to the soda fountain, where they ordered milk shakes and were promptly served. Mr. Carswell was happy to serve them at the soda fountain.

When they began to ease over toward the three booths, Mr. Carswell became wary. When they sat down, all hell broke loose. John Carswell was not going to have Negroes sitting down in his soda fountain booths.

The students went home, made picket signs and picketed the place for eight months, rain and shine and even in the snow, and got nowhere.

Now the COB, reasoning that success with that little drugstore would arouse support for the COB throughout the Negro community, and believing John Carswell had had ample time to solve this problem in some way, prepared for a new round of action.

"For a week before we started picketing," Bob Brown says, "we clocked him every day to see what his trade was. For seven days we counted everyone who went into the place. We found that 30 percent of his business was Negro trade.

"Well, our picketing managed to turn off completely his Negro trade. I mean completely. And we turned off about 15 percent of his white trade. In all, we took away almost half of his trade, and therefore we cut his profit even more, for he still had as much upkeep cost as before."

The picketing started in June. It was evident the first day that Mr. Carswell had a camera. He was in and out of the store every time the pickets changed off, snapping pictures, getting close-ups of the demonstrators, for what reason nobody could say. The pickets slowly went back and forth and tried to pay no attention.

It next became apparent that Mr. Carswell had a pistol. He would take it apart and clean it, and on his way to the bank to deposit his money, he would carry it with him in plain view, which is legally permissible in Chapel Hill.

It also became apparent that Mr. Carswell had a temper and that he was angry at the demonstrators, as one would expect him to be. He denounced them, he gave them orders, and at one point he swore out a warrant against Bob Brown, saying that Bob had assaulted his son with a picket sign, which was, he maintained, a deadly weapon.

"The charge was changed from struck to grazed to touched," Bob says. "To the best of my knowledge, this never happened, but I had to get a lawyer. As a matter of fact, the bill is still outstanding. I owe the lawyer seventy-five dollars for defending me. The case was thrown out, of course, since in an assault violation with a deadly weapon one had to prove intent, and that was impossible. It was all insane."

Bob was particularly worried because of Mr. Carswell's attitude. He complained to Chief Blake, who went to the drugstore and talked with Carswell. "Carswell called him a pig and wouldn't discuss the matter," Bob says. Chief Blake says Carswell "didn't call me a pig, but it was something as bad, or worse."

"He was threatening people," Bob says about Carswell. "He told the pickets, 'I'm going to get you.' He tells me, 'I'm going to get you, I'm going to get you.' His wife was the same way, and his boys were even worse. It's really a disgrace, I mean it's a shame to see kids be this way, the hate, just full of hate. They're only eight years old, you know, and one is thirteen. Well, we told the pickets, 'You're running a decided risk here, your life is at stake,' and I pointed out that the chief was worried and so forth, but that we would maintain picketing, and we did."

The COB constantly attempted to negotiate, and once a week a negotiation team would come by or would phone Mr. Carswell for an appointment, but apparently he wouldn't negotiate. So they picketed, day after day, week after week, right there on the concrete slab outside his store.

Picket lines were also maintained at Leo's Restaurant. Leo, a fifty-some-year-old Greek immigrant, would stare at the pickets in bewilderment. Picket lines were maintained at Brady's Restaurant, one of the oldest places in town. Brady, a really huge man with an amiable disposition, evidently would tell the negotiation team that integration wouldn't bother him in the least. Let them pass a public accommodations ordinance or the Civil Rights Bill in Congress, he said; then he would integrate and have an excuse for doing so. But he couldn't do it now, for he would lose business. "His position was identical to that of several other businessmen contacted by the COB during these weeks," Bob says.

On June 25 the vote on the Chapel Hill public accommodations ordinance was to come before the Board of Aldermen. Pat Cusick had tried to find out how each of the seven members was likely to vote.

One of the aldermen was Hubert Robinson, a Negro. He was seventy years of age, a retired janitor of the university. He had been born in Hogansville, Georgia, and had moved to Chapel Hill in 1930. When he was elected alderman in 1953, he became the first Negro ever to serve on the board. He was re-elected in 1957 and in 1961. He undoubtedly was in favor of the public accommodations ordinance.

A second member, Adelaide Walters, was in her fifties, had been born in Gouverneur, New York. She had lived in Chapel Hill with her husband, who was retired from business, since 1939. She had a master's degree in history and government from Radcliffe College. She had helped organize the Fellowship for School Integration, the local and state unit of the League of Women Voters, and had worked in the Adlai Stevenson campaign. She favored passing the public accommodations ordinance.

Joe Page, in his late forties, was the manager of Ledbetter-Pickard Stationers on Franklin Street. He had lived in Chapel Hill since boyhood, except for service with the Air Force during World War II. He graduated from the University of North Carolina in business administration, was a Democrat, though he didn't always vote Democratic, he says. He was a Kiwanian, a Mason, a member of the Merchants Association. He believed that agitation for social change often was Communist-inspired, and almost certainly would vote against the public accommodations ordinance.

F. Eugene Strowd was in his fifties. He had been born in Chapel Hill and had attended Duke University for two and a half years. He was part owner of a furniture store on Franklin Street. He was a Kiwanian. He was on the board of a local bank and his position on the ordinance was unknown, though he probably would vote against it.

The fifth member of the board was Paul Wager, seventy years of age. Born in New York State, he had been a professor of political science at the university for many years. He was in his third term on the Board of Aldermen. He was on the board of directors of a local savings and loan association. He once described himself, according to Gary Blanchard of the *Daily Tar Heel* as a "moderate, liberal, Independent Democrat." He was a member of the Mayor's Committee on Integration, which had recommended the public accommodations ordinance as the best solution to the problem, and it was quite possible that he would favor the ordinance.

Roland Giduz, the sixth member, was in his late thirties. He was editor of the *News of Orange County* and of the *Triangle Pointer*, which is published weekly and carries tourist hints about the Raleigh–Durham–Chapel Hill area. He was born in Massachusetts, but he had lived in Chapel Hill almost all his life. He graduated from the university with a major in journalism, received his master's degree from Columbia and had spent a year at Harvard on a fellowship. He was in his second term on the board. In 1963, he had become mayor pro tem, a two-year designation which revolves among the aldermen. He was an active Democrat, describing himself as a "national Democrat, as opposed to an ADA Democrat, which I wouldn't always oppose, either." He was one of the more liberal members of the board and usually voted along with Mr. Robinson and Mrs. Walters. Many people believed he would vote for the passage of the ordinance.

If either Giduz or Wager voted against it, the board would be tied three to three, in which case the mayor would need to break the tie one way or the other. Since both of the mayor's committees dealing with civil rights had highly recommended passage, Pat Cusick believed he would vote in favor of it.

All the aldermen had been put under considerable pressure through visits, telephone calls and letters. Some of the calls had been threatening in nature; most of them were simply efforts to persuade aldermen to vote for or against the measure. George Watts Hill, for example, phoned Mrs. Walters and perhaps other aldermen, simply to say he was against passage of the ordinance and hoped the vote would be against it. Mrs. Walters told him she favored the ordinance, but that she doubted it would pass. Mr. Hill repeated that he was against it. Mrs. Walters said she hoped he would consider that Chapel Hill was different from most places, in that the town didn't have many enlightened businessmen to work for integration of local businesses, as did Durham and some other places Mr. Hill was helping to integrate; that Chapel Hill's only large business was the university, and the university had decided not to use its influence in the current struggle, so the town government itself would need to substitute as best it could. The passage of the ordinance was therefore necessary, she said.

The meeting itself was open to the public. The public came. It filled the town hall courtroom and flooded over into the jury box and the judge's stand, and people stood along the walls. More than one hundred people were asked to leave the stairway outside, and others couldn't get into the building. Reporters said it was the largest crowd in memory to attend a meeting of the Board of Aldermen.

Sandy McClamroch recognized first of all Dr. Robert Phillips, chairman of the Human Relations Committee, who presented the public accommodations ordinance to the aldermen. There was not a distracting sound in that big room. Pat Cusick remembered football games, when the last few seconds seemed to be ticking away and the fate of the game hadn't been decided; for him the suspense here was the same. He saw Harold Foster leaning forward in his seat, and Charliese Cotton, the pretty young girl who had been told by her mother to join the first march, was sitting there on one of the benches, holding a younger sister's hand and listening to every word, trying to follow all of it.

I talked with Charliese Cotton about that meeting. Dr. Phillips spoke for what seemed to her to be a long while; then he sat down and there was quiet in the place. The mayor asked if members of the board wanted to speak. Charliese saw Alderman Robinson move in his chair, the old man she had seen so often in her own neighborhood, and she heard him speak there in that big hall before all those people, and without a tremble in his voice.

"About fifty years ago an old preacher told me that some of these days Negroes are going to have to stand up for their rights," he said. "Well, little did he know that they would have to sit down and march for their rights, too. I hope the board will pass this ordinance." He spoke on about the law, which was all merely words to Charliese, but the idea was meaningful to her in so many ways, for she had been one of the students, back when she was only thirteen, who had tried to sit down in Big John's soda fountain booth and had been thrown out of the place. This whole meeting had started that day for her, and whatever they were talking about meant the booths in Big John Carswell's drugstore. It meant all the walking in the picket lines in the snow at the Long Meadow Dairy Bar, too, and picketing the Carolina Theatre the time two boys came along with a big black dog and tried to scare her.

Now Mr. Robinson was through, and people in the audience were rising and talking, too. Charliese wanted more than anything to stand up and say something about Big John, but she wasn't sure she should. She couldn't very well talk about the soda fountain booths.

"We recognize Mrs. Charlotte Adams," the mayor said.

Mrs. Adams spoke. She was in favor of it, of the law, Charliese realized, with wonder that such a fine white woman would talk that way. Charliese said it made her almost weep to hear her talk so well.

When she sat down, the mayor said he had a letter from an assistant attorney general in Raleigh, in which he said the question of the legality of this ordinance hadn't been settled by any North Carolina court, and in his opinion the courts would find that the necessary municipal authority to pass it had not been delegated to Chapel Hill.

Then Charliese fidgeted while there was more talk. Some of it, I find now, was about a law professor, Daniel Pollitt, and his views. Professor Pollitt's field was constitutional law, and he believed the law could be passed, that thirty states outside the South had enacted such ordinances, that they had been sustained by the supreme courts of a number of states and by the United States Supreme Court.

Another man rose to speak and he spoke in favor of the law. He was a white man, an English instructor, James Gardner, and he appealed for an end to segregation in Chapel Hill. Charliese remembers that Lou Calhoun stared at the man so intently she thought he must be in a trance. Lou had been a boxer in Tennessee, she had heard, and she wondered what would happen if Big John Carswell got hold of him. She had almost wished it had happened that time she and Lou had been picketing together. She guessed he wouldn't do a thing in the world to strike back, but maybe he would. Maybe he would forget, even if only for a blow or two.

A Mr. George Coxhead stood, a businessman, he said. He said he

was for freedom, Charliese told me, but it was the freedom of the
businessman to run his own place of business.

Another businessman, who said he was from the Merchants Association, stood, and he said the nation was founded on the principle of
free enterprise. He said the law wouldn't give a person a choice. Oh,
she knew about not having a choice, all right, and was in favor of
choices.

Another man rose, and on and on they spoke, some for freedom
and yet against the law, some for freedom and in favor of the law.
She saw that Pat Cusick would be angry one minute, then pleased the
next.

A man said, "This is how Nazism started in Germany, on the
principle that the end justifies the means. The minute you try to
legislate in this fashion, you open a Pandora's box. Let's solve these
problems as rational people, not as Mussolini did by passing a law to
make the trains run on time. This must be solved with goodwill."

"I believe a man has a constitutional right to discriminate," another man said.

A professor stood and talked about the child labor laws. He talked
about smoke abatement ordinances, about health and sanitation laws.
"You have the authority to help in this further extension of human
rights over property rights," he said.

Then it seemed to be all over. Was it over? Charliese wondered. If
it was over, what had been done? She wasn't too sure, and she felt her
sister tug at her hand. "I don't know nothing," she said, and quieted
her.

A man up front at the big table said something about a substitute,
a substitute motion. Somewhere in all the words, she supposed, was
the thing she wanted, which was the thing she had never had, so that
she didn't know exactly what it was yet.

Alderman Wager was speaking now, and slowly what he was saying filtered through. He was proposing a substitute motion. He was
not in favor of the ordinance.

Alderman Walters spoke up. "It's later than we think," she said.
"We have complained about passing our responsibilities on to the
Federal Government. It's time we acted responsibly on our own."

Alderman Giduz asked to be recognized, and the mayor nodded to him. Pat Cusick remembers straining to hear every word, listening as Mr. Giduz talked on, until it was clear he was going to take his stand for the substitute motion, that he was against passing the ordinance. Almost without knowing it, Pat realized that it was over. He knew what the vote was going to be: four to two for tabling the ordinance itself.

Pat stumbled from the building, deeply hurt. As he saw it, the town had come close to solving its segregation problem, but in a brief moment, almost in a shudder, it had drawn back. If the aldermen had passed the ordinance that night, what a different world the Negroes of Chapel Hill would have awakened to the next morning, he thought. A million other Negroes throughout the state would have taken heart, too; so would millions of others in the rest of the South.

Maybe it had been too much to ask. Yes, of course it had been too much to ask, he decided. But it had been asked. Now the issue was thrown back onto the streets, where the marches and picketing would resume.

Charliese came out of the town hall, asking what had happened.

"It's all over," he told her.

Other Negroes came out. They stood around, as if waiting for the next meeting to start. Soon a large group of integrationists had assembled there in front of the town hall, all of them disappointed and sad. Charliese said, "Pat, can we sing something?"

Pat smiled. "Yes, you sing something."

She did. And she sang like an angel, Pat says, but she wasn't able to make him feel better about the meeting. She did make Alderman Walters feel a good deal worse, however, Adelaide Walters says, for upstairs the Board of Aldermen had now got around to talking about more routine matters of business, while outside she heard the Negro girl singing, and later she listened as the other people out on the street joined in. They sang "We Shall Overcome," the words floating in through the open window of the Chapel Hill town hall.

The frustration which affected the demonstrators was shared, though perhaps to a less extent, by some members of the Board of Aldermen. Adelaide Walters and Mr. Robinson were clear in their own minds concerning their support of the ordinance, and Mr. Page and Mr. Strowd were clear in their own minds concerning their opposition to it. Paul Wager and Roland Giduz, however, apparently suffered the qualms of conscientious public officials faced with a measure they accept idealistically but reject on practical grounds.

Professor Wager was sympathetic to the Negro's objectives. His friend, D. Dudley Carroll, the retired dean of the School of Business Administration and a past chairman of the Human Relations Committee, had advised him to vote for the measure, and so had Professor Frederic Cleaveland of the political science department and Professor Guy Johnson of the sociology department, who got from Wager the idea that he would vote for the law. But Professor Wager also had advice from local businessmen whom he respected, who thought he ought to leave this ordinance alone and see if a voluntary system wouldn't work better in Chapel Hill. Also, he had been told that some of the segregationists in town had begun to carry weapons, and that segregationists from other towns had begun to visit Chapel Hill in small groups and make threatening phone calls and do petty mischief. The prospect of turning the town into a battlefield disturbed him greatly.

In his mind, too, was an obligation he felt to the university, which is necessarily involved in anything that takes place in Chapel Hill, for which it is held accountable in the minds of most North Carolinians. He was afraid this was potentially a complicated and damaging situation. He had talked the matter over with one of the university administrators, who felt that in the light of growing animosity against the university and intellectualism in general, his worries on this score were justified. At the age of seventy, serving his last term on the Board of Aldermen, he had weighed the situation, knowing that he more than some of the others was free to make a decision, and he had decided at the meeting itself that he would propose a substitute motion and put the vote off until he was better able to make a clear decision in his own mind.

Roland Giduz had talked with only one other member of the board about the matter; Mr. Robinson had approached him in his office and had asked him to vote for it. He was in favor of advancing Negro rights in the community, but he wondered if this could not best be done by persuasion, by community action through individuals and committees. He was not free from influence by the business community, and the influence was not simply from Chapel Hill, either, but from Durham and Raleigh, where businessmen took substantial advertising in his *Triangle Pointer;* however, his decision seems to have been based on his confidence in the community's ability to work out its problems without a law being passed.

Chapter Six

THE EXECUTIVE COMMITTEE, and in fact the entire Committee for Open Business, kept changing membership, and since there was no paid staff, or office, or rules of procedure, the organization's only stability came from its sense of mission. It had gone into action believing that it wouldn't take long to desegregate the town, and there had been no effort made to establish a permanent organization. There were no by-laws used at the meetings. Anybody could attend and take a part. If a member stopped coming, it was apparent that he was no longer a member. For one reason or another, members would resign from the executive committee and at a later open meeting somebody else would be appointed to fill the vacant place.

Some of the newcomers were university students, but most of them were Negroes, high school students or high school dropouts, young people who had little influence in the community but were anxious to take part. Pat Cusick gathered them in. He and Quinton Baker, who by now spent much of his time in Chapel Hill, were responsible for training them in nonviolent philosophy and tactics. There were to be no knives in anybody's pocket, Quinton said, and no razors, either. There was to be no rough stuff with the police. He said he knew some of them didn't like police officers, but they had to learn nonviolence as a way of thought and a way of life. He told them that when the Southern youth movement started in 1960 the pickets were required to wear ties when they picketed. There had been many strict rules regulating conduct then, and most of them would still apply, he said.

Quinton and Pat taught the students about Gandhi. It was an intriguing sight to visit the field outside the Negro recreation center on Roberson Street and see twenty or thirty Negro and white young people sitting together on the ground seriously listening to the big, rumpled white man and the medium-built Negro tell them about Gandhi.

Pat and Quinton also taught the boys how to go limp when arrested, so that they offered neither resistance nor help to the police. They showed them how to protect themselves in a fight. They divided them into two teams, one of which was the bad guys and one the good guys, and they had the bad guys throw around the good guys and punch them a little bit, and they showed the good guys how to protect themselves. Whenever one of the good guys forgot about the nonviolence and started punching back, Pat and Quinton would pull him out of the group, and later would talk with him about the superior nature of the nonviolent man. Or, for that matter, woman, for women also took part in the training program.

The police were astounded by the whole exhibition. Patrolmen would come to the fence which bounded the playing field and lean against it for hours, watching all this, asking each other what Pat Cusick thought he was doing, what sort of army he was training, and for what action in Chapel Hill.

While Pat and Quinton were busy with the training program, other COB members were busy with meetings, which were held with church and civic groups and with interested individuals. Also, there were many meetings with the mayor, with some of the aldermen, with Joe Augustine of the Merchants Association, with one or another of the mayor's special committees, with the managers of segregated businesses and so on.

Then there were the street marches, three of them each week, now carried off as regularly and expertly as clockwork. On July 4 the march was the largest yet, with over four hundred, perhaps five hundred, people taking part. Half of them were Negroes and the other half whites. The COB for all its changes of membership and informality, was a vigorous organization.

Nobody knew this better than the mayor, who at the next meeting of the Board of Aldermen recognized the need for further action on his part. He admitted that the Committee on Integration had proved less than effective and said it might be replaced by a secret committee of businessmen, who would try to integrate the holdout establishments. He called on Chief Blake, who reported that his men had put in a total of 777 unpaid hours of overtime during the past month, at considerable personal inconvenience to them and their vacation plans, and that there was no money in the Police Department budget to pay for this extra work. There was no money in the town budget, either, the aldermen admitted.

The student newspaper during this period was sympathetic to the demonstrators; the radio station was neutral; the Chapel Hill *Weekly* was now quite critical. Its editorial page maintained that the plans of the Committee for Open Business to continue demonstrations constituted "gross irresponsibility," and it urged an end to demonstrations in favor of further efforts at voluntary desegregation. The paper called on town officials to "take whatever steps are necessary to end downtown marches. The convenience and safety of the public . . . now demand it."

The issue which contained this advice also carried an interview with John Carswell, the Colonial Drug Store proprietor, who said he did not hate Negroes and had served them for a long time. "We serve Negroes just like white people," he said, "except we don't allow them to sit in the booths."

Mayor McClamroch, holding to his hope of voluntary desegregation, asked the executive committee if it would grant another moratorium, so that his secret committee of businessmen could have a better atmosphere in which to work. He undoubtedly made the request in good faith, and he undoubtedly was startled to be told that his request had, by a unanimous vote of the committee, been rejected.

I have talked with Bob Brown about this decision and what it meant. He said that all summer long the mayor or his committees had asked for moratoriums so that they could negotiate, and sometimes the COB would grant one and sometimes it would not. In either case they couldn't find evidence that much negotiation was going on.

"I know Leo personally," Bob said. "Leo was willing to be talked into integrating. I know Percy, the man who runs the Tar Heel Sandwich Shop. Percy is not a nasty man, and besides that, on two occasions he had served Negroes in his place, once at the counter and once in a booth. If the mayor had guaranteed to support those places once they integrated, I believe they would'a integrated. They wanted to do it because he asked them to, so they would have a good reason when their customers asked them."

Bob admitted COB's mediation committee had tried and had not succeeded. "We told Leo we would guarantee him trade. 'We'll all come to eat,' we told him. 'Everybody'll come.' Father Parker—do you know he and his wife don't have any bread at all, they're extremely poor people, but you know still to this day twice a week they eat at the College Café? They're people who can't afford to eat out anywhere. But they go and eat in the College Café. They do things like that. And there are hordes of people in this community who would do that, who would drive all the way up to Leo's and eat Leo's food, have a God damn bacon, lettuce and tomato sandwich, in order that he not lose money when he integrated. But Leo wasn't sure of that. All summer he was saying, 'What am I going to do? I don't want the picketing, but I'm going to lose my trade if I integrate.' "

Leo once had operated the bus station's restaurant, and when he realized the bus station, due to Federal requirements affecting interstate travel, would have to integrate, he declared his place integrated. His customers complained, and within a week he had to let all his help go, except for a single waitress. He finally closed up shop there and opened a restaurant of his own about a block up Franklin Street. In the change he lost a great deal of money, for not only did he have to furnish a new restaurant, but the fixtures and counter in the old place were built in and couldn't be salvaged, so most of his investment was a total loss.

Now the crises had followed him, and at a poor time, too. The university was building an addition to the football stadium; the construction workers had gone uptown to eat, only to find that uptown was integrated, so they had gone around town until they found places that were not. Leo was doing a nice business.

It's a trait of our country, as David Riesman has pointed out, that we sometimes will catch a moral fever which causes us to sweep away all other considerations. In the days of the Civil War we swept away slavery, but the economic loss was suffered by those who opposed the moral fever and its effects, even though, before that fever struck, they maintained a legal position in the society.

Leo, an immigrant from Greece who was trying to build a business, was now being asked to make an economic sacrifice because of a moral change in the community, a community which had existed much as it now was since it was founded, and which Leo had nothing to do with creating. Evidently nobody was going to suffer economically except Leo. Mayor McClamroch says he talked with Leo for two hours, and he honestly didn't know what to advise him to do. This indecision on the mayor's part in a sense bears out the criticism Bob Brown was making of him; at the same time, it indicates the complexity of the situation itself.

"Leo said he would do it for the mayor," Bob tells me, "if the mayor asked him. So we knew what sort of negotiations were going on. I don't mind reactionary sentiment, but I believe in truth and honesty, and much that was going on with this secret committee of businessmen and all that wasn't honest, because they weren't really negotiating. Before three ministers on our executive committee, the mayor and some of these others would come in and promise they were going to do so and so, but they wouldn't. I'm not a religious man. I don't go to church or anything of the kind, but you either tell the truth or you get off, man.

"The Tar Heel Sandwich Shop, for example, was willing to integrate if the mayor would agree to one thing. Percy, the manager, was afraid of a little trouble the first few days, so he wanted a policeman there, not inside the place, but outside, late at night, for a few hours. The mayor wouldn't agree. Why wouldn't he agree? The place is practically across the street from the town hall, and the police sit there all the time anyway. You can go by the shop any night and there's a God damn patrol car there. The desk sergeant always is coming over for a cup of coffee. The lieutenant stops by. They leave the patrol car door open, and they can hear the machine when it comes on a call. They turn the volume up, you know."

Clarence's Beer Hall is right next to Bob's house on Franklin Street, and he believed Clarence and his wife Sally would integrate their place, too. They had lost much business because of the picketing, he says. Other members of the COB felt, as Bob did, that the mayor and the Merchants Association could have convinced Clarence's, or Leo's or some other places to integrate if they had really been convinced themselves that they should and if they had asked them to do so as a service to the community. Mayor Grabarek had integrated many of the restaurants in Durham, for example. The COB, rightly or wrongly, was convinced that at least three places could be integrated any time Mayor McClamroch decided really to try to integrate them. So they turned down his request for a moratorium.

At the same meeting the committee took one further action. It discussed the possible use of civil disobedience tactics. As one would expect, this caused long and serious discussion, for the willful breaking of the law was out of keeping with the lifelong habits of all the members present.

Civil disobedience was practiced extensively in India by Gandhi, Nehru and their followers. Some say it was practiced by Jesus, who was arrested for disturbing the peace and teaching people to do acts which were unlawful. The early Christians broke the law when their consciences dictated to them that they should, and they accepted punishment for it in accordance with the law they had willfully broken. In the Old Testament, Shadrach, Meschach and Abednego were heroes, as Rev. Charlie Jones pointed out to his congregration, because they practiced civil disobedience in refusing to obey the king's order to worship his idol. Rev. Jones also points out that Martin Luther defied the constituted authority of his day because his conscience, which he claimed was instructed by God, would allow him to do nothing else.

Martin Luther King, one of our country's chief exponents of non-violence and civil disobedience, wrote in 1958:

We will take direct action against injustice without waiting for other agencies to act. We will not obey unjust laws or submit to unjust practices. We will do this peacefully, openly, cheerfully because our aim is to persuade. We adopt the means of non-violence because our end is a community at peace with itself. We will try to persuade with our words, but if our words fail, we will try to persuade with our acts. The way of non-violence means a willingness to suffer and sacrifice. It may mean going to jail. If such is the case the register must be willing to fill the jail houses of the South. It may even mean physical death. But if physical death is the price a man must pay to free his children and his white brethren from a permanent death of the spirit, then nothing could be more redemptive.

Of course, nobody at the COB was talking about going as far as Rev. King seemed to be willing to go. Their worry was over civil matters of trespass and the like, and over whether one could properly abandon the basic community structure, which was based on law. Could one responsibly go about breaking the law in order to try to persuade the town to pass or change a law?

Pat Cusick said one could and should, provided he was willing to accept the penalty, and this view was finally carried in the meeting that night in Chapel Hill. The group, including several of the leading people in town, voted to authorize civil disobedience tactics and to leave up to the executive committee the selection of targets and tactics. Only six of over 150 people present voted against the motion.

This action and the rejection of the mayor's request for a moratorium dramatized the determination of the Committee for Open Business. They appeared to be confident of themselves, and they were, in truth, the largest civil rights group anywhere around. Mayor McClamroch, understandably worried, went to the COB executive committee and asked them what terms they wanted for the granting of a moratorium. The committee replied that they would like to see three businesses integrated during the coming week, and to have efforts to integrate the remaining eleven on the main target list continue unabated.

Mayor McClamroch called in his secret committee of businessmen and asked them what he ought to do. Their advice was that he should not comply. He took their advice, and the competing forces were left to work it out for themselves.

Roland Giduz, worried more than ever, invited Negro leaders Hilliard Caldwell and Harold Foster to his home, and they talked about what might be done. Mr. Giduz felt the main problem was not integration but elevation, helping the Negro improve his lot; if that were done, through education and better jobs and better standards all around, the segregation matter would take care of itself. He did not feel that full integration was needed at the start, although he recognized that it would give added motivation to the Negro people.

After about four and a half hours of talking, the Negro leaders went home. This was the very night before the first sit-in. They had not told Giduz that. But implicit in his and their concern had been the realization that the demonstrators were about to move into a tougher, rougher tactic in demanding social change.

When young people get ready to go to jail, they do a lot of wondering about little things, such as whether they ought to take a toothbrush with them. They also like to get their hair cut and their shoes shined, and they want to wear their best clothes, in spite of their parents' protestations. Particularly is this true of young people who have never been to jail before.

The first act of civil disobedience was to be a sit-in. It was planned by the entire executive committee, though Pat Cusick, more than any other individual, was in charge of it. The university professors on the executive committee, as well as most of the other adults, didn't want to get arrested, so the sit-iners were to be the young people whom Pat had trained. The young people wanted to do it.

The place the committee chose was the Merchants Association, which now was more of a concern to them than the segregated restaurants in town.

While at Sandy Ridge talking with Pat, I asked him about this first sit-in. I remembered the upheaval it had caused in Chapel Hill at the time and the attention it brought to Chapel Hill nationally. As I recalled, a group of young people had gone into the office of the Merchants Association, on the main street of Chapel Hill about two blocks west of the center of town, and had sat down on the floor and stayed there until they were dragged out.

Pat told me that the group definitely wanted to be arrested. "At least, we wanted to make a suitable witness to the community of our beliefs, and we knew we would be arrested. There were twenty-one of us. Some of the young people didn't want to go, and others were too young. No juveniles were permitted on this first one."

Peter Van Riper was the only University of North Carolina student among them, Pat told me. There were a number of high school students from the Negro community, Charliese Cotton being one of them.

The Merchants Association office fronts on the sidewalk. Between the side wall and the counter is a six-foot-wide area. The demonstrators sat in this area, blocking the passageway to the office beyond. Then they began to sing. They had not planned to sing, Pat says, but they felt foolish sitting there on the floor doing nothing at all, so they sang to hide their uneasiness.

Mr. Augustine, the manager, came forward. "Mr. Cusick," he said, "you can stay in here all day so far as I'm concerned if you'll just stop singing. We can't do our work." About this time the police arrived outside. They had an electric bull horn, and Joe Augustine began speaking through that.

"The thing was making an awful lot of racket," Pat told me, "and so was our music. The testimony in court was that we were ordered to leave. We didn't hear anybody order us to leave. We were singing and this thing was out on the street squealing."

Bob Brown's house is directly across the street from the Merchants Association office. It's an old, two-story, wooden structure, thus far by-passed in the commercial development of West Franklin Street. He and two university students who had been helping him prepare copy for the next issue of *Reflections* went out on his upstairs porch, where they could see what took place.

They had watched the demonstrators arrive and go inside. They also saw eight or ten other young people arrive and wait around outside, among them the ones who were too young to sit in or who didn't want to get arrested.

"The newspaper reporters, including Shumaker, commented to me later about the relish the police had in making the arrests," Bob told me. "It was one of the most effective jobs I ever saw. The police must have been waiting for just this chance. They stacked the limp bodies up at the curb, which was completely unnecessary. They did it because they were out for Cusick. They believed Cusick had started all this and they knew he had trained these young people, so they stacked the bodies up on the sidewalk on top of Cusick. They laid them out just like you lay out dead bodies. It's like when the decontamination team comes along in trucks. I hadn't seen anything like it since I was in Korea.

"As the police cars arrived, they would pull bodies off, drag them along the street, throw them into the police cars. It was so bad that the other people there, the children and other ones who hadn't been scheduled to be arrested, sat down on the sidewalk in protest. So they were arrested. They went limp, as they'd been trained to do, and the cars came and carried them off, too. They carried about thirty people off.

"I went inside my house and sat down in the kitchen at the table. I sat there for half an hour, for three-quarters—I dunno. I decided I had to make a protest. I went into the front room where there were a few picket signs, and I took one poster from there. I walked two blocks up the street to the main intersection of town, at Columbia and Franklin Street. I went out into the middle of those two streets, hung the sign around my neck and sat down."

Bob doesn't remember much about the cars or the pedestrians or the startled or angry looks of the astounded men and women who stared at him from along the street and who gathered around him as finally the police car came to a stop and policemen got out.

"I went limp, so they dragged me along," he says. "They threw me in the car. Very nasty, very nasty. When they got me down to the station house, they pulled me out of the car. This officer was pulling me along, and he said, 'Kick him, kick him.' I had had fair relations with the police. I don't like police of any nature. My attitude toward them is much like a Negro's is. I don't see them as law and order; I see them as suppressors, men out there to do something antagonistic. But I will say that I had thus far had fair relations with the police. And one of the cops who is a segregationist, who had opposed everything we had done, said to the officer, 'No, let's pick him up.' That's what he said. I looked up at him. He said, 'No, let's pick him up.' It was the officer who said, 'Let's kick him,' and wanted to drag me inside. Those are bad stairs in that building; you can really get hurt on them. But two cops picked me up and put me in the hall, and the chief came out and said, 'Bob, come on, get up.' He was very kind; he's a kind man, a good man.

"And I said I couldn't, you know, because all the kids went in this way and that's the way I had to go."

The Chapel Hill jail has cots for twelve prisoners. Perhaps some of the cells were already occupied that day. At any rate, the four-man cell where Pat Cusick was put was occupied by fifteen men. It was a hot July day and the cell was like an oven, Pat says. The prisoners were relieved to be through the ordeal which for days had worried them, and at the same time they were angry because of the handling they had received from the police. One of them broke the window glass, another somehow managed to stop up the toilet. They turned the shower on to get water, and the shower water flowed out over the floor. The police began raising hell about the mess and the broken window, and the prisoners began to shout and sing and shake the prison bars in a spasm of frustration and wrath and emotional release.

At last they quieted down, but not before about forty dollars' worth of damage had been done, Chief Blake says.

Something happens inside a person, Pat Cusick says, when he is arrested for the first time. He crosses a barrier. It's an emotional experience which jars and confuses him; later, after the emotional impact has worn thin, he is left with a new sense of himself as a citizen. Pat sensed this, at least, and suspected that it was true of the others. They had all broken a law. They had contended that they were obeying a higher law. Be that as it may, they had broken a law of society, of the town. In doing so, they had crossed a barrier. Now that they had a police record they were freer than ever to follow the dictates of their consciences.

All during the summer activities in Chapel Hill, John Dunne had been away. He had painted greenhouses near Cleveland and after a month had enough money to pay off his bills, which he did. He wrote Pat Cusick to this effect in late July, and said he was moving to Connecticut, to the home of the medical doctor of Choate, Harold Anderson, and that he would do some work helping organize the March on Washington. "Predictions are that we will antagonize the Congress and irritate the President," he wrote, "but without pressure nothing gets done in the civil rights movement; at least, that's the contention here."

Pat Cusick replied on August 2:

DEAR JOHN:

I wish you would come back here and let somebody else do the March on Washington. We are in a real stew here.

Twenty-one of us went downtown two weeks ago and sat-in at the Merchants Association. Maybe you read about it in the newspapers up there. The police came after us and we ended up in jail. The town leaders were distraught, not so much because of the issues involved, but because of the image of the town. They were certainly concerned. The Mayor's Human Relations Committee called a meeting at the Town Hall of seventeen organizations, the Merchants Association, the Junior Chamber of Commerce, the Ministers Association, the Police Department, the civic clubs, the press, the COB, etc.

I was in jail. So was Harold Foster. So was Bob Brown. Bob and Harold weren't scheduled to be in jail at this time and could have done more good at those meetings, but they were cooped up with me. When we got out, we were told that a two-week moratorium had been arranged so that the town could simmer down; in return for this concession, the mayor's secret committee of businessmen and the Merchants Association (which are just about the same group of men, I suspect) are to try diligently to integrate some of the holdout businesses, and the police and the Merchants Association have agreed to recommend that all charges against us be dropped.

We accepted all of this hopefully, but we were on hand the week following when all these organizations came together again, this time to hear the report of the businessmen. The businessmen didn't even come. Representatives from all these organizations sat there, but there was no report. The businessmen didn't show up at all.

To make matters even more distasteful, the charges against us, in spite of the urging of Chief Blake, Roland Giduz and others, aren't being dropped by the town solicitor. Floyd McKissick is so distressed that he is serving as our counsel. The solicitor's unwillingness to let the charges be dropped irritated Rev. Loren Meade so much that he told me he was thinking about staging a sit-in himself, at the main intersection, to show his personal objection, but I believe he has gone to England for some reason.

We have resumed our civil disobedience workshops. The full committee voted to do this, but by the narrow margin of 33 to 31, so you see that some of our members are fearful now. I moved the workshops indoors so that the police can't watch everything; they don't know what we're doing and are suspicious. We have started street marches again, too. When we first went into street marches, that stirred up criticism, but now the marches are pretty much accepted as the summer way of life. No place on earth has ever had as many street demonstrations as Chapel Hill.

When we staged this first sit-in, the town's lid flew off literally and completely. Each time we do something new, the cry of alarm goes up and we are denounced, in large part by people who tell us: We believe in your goal, but not your method.

After we staged our sit-in, the Chapel Hill *Weekly* in a front-page editorial said the leaders of the COB had "a lust for power, for revenge, or a neurotic need for martyrdom." The executive committee of the COB tried to figure out who among us had the lust for power and against whom we had the desire for revenge. Somebody suggested we cast lots for the privilege of being the first martyr, but I think the pastors on the committee thought this wasn't the way martyrs ought to be chosen. We agreed to follow historic precedent concerning that selection process.

Bickering inside COB has set in heavier now than ever. Maybe the summer heat is to blame. At any rate, we need you here. Can you leave this other thing, this March on Washington?

PAT CUSICK

John could not. At least, he did not. John had determined to try to stay clear of the Chapel Hill situation, to return to the campus in September and finish his degree. He and his parents had talked about his involvement in civil rights work in Chapel Hill, and he and they now felt his first obligation was to give a fair return for the scholarship money he was accepting. His father was particularly anxious about this; he had dropped out of school in his junior year in college, and later he had had to spend two years grubbing to support himself, his wife and daughter while he finished at New York University. For those two years he had lived day after day on five-cent candy bars, and he could see the same pattern shaping up for John. So did John, for that matter, and he knew if he got into the civil rights situation in Chapel Hill that summer, he would become engulfed in it once more, not only for the summer, but for the year.

Pat also was worried about his involvement in civil rights. He tells me he thought often, and fondly, of his trip the previous summer to an isolated island, Ocracoke, near Cape Hatteras. He lived on the beach, stationing his tent about seven miles from the small fishing town of Ocracoke. He would walk into town occasionally to buy what he needed at the store and to sit around talking with the residents. He spent his time this way, as well as reading books he had brought with him and thinking.

He was not committed to peace or nonviolence or civil rights or any other special cause back then. He made his living in a computation center, and he was worried about that commitment, for it seemed to him that computors were helping in the development of nuclear warfare. He thought about this and his own responsibility, but it was merely a casual, summer study of his sense of values.

The study of his values continued when he returned to Chapel Hill. In the fall he attended a few meetings of a liberal group, the New Left Club, but he didn't care for it. "They try to use people," he told Anne Queen. In the winter he formed the university chapter of the Student Peace Union, a national organization which, he says, "felt that, because of nuclear weapons, military means could no longer be used to settle international disputes, that other ways would have to be found; also, the SPU felt that no nation or group of people had the right to suppress another nation or group."

A few months later, he began picketing the College Café.

A few months after that, he became a founder of the COB and a leader of the street marches. Also, he had resigned his job at the computation center. Now he was without a job, without money and without a completely developed view of his philosophy.

Yet he saw that his efforts to be a free man were taking him into a commitment which was demanding all his time and energies. It was, of course, the same form of bondage John Dunne was struggling to avoid, once he returned to Chapel Hill.

Chapter Seven

THE DEATH OF THE COB was brought about only in small part by forces outside the organization; the tear which later became the ripped seam of the organization was started from within. The COB consisted of a group of mature white adults on the one hand and a group of young Negroes on the other. The adults were well educated; the Negroes were not. The meetings that featured informational reports and lengthy discussions of issues were pleasing to the white adults but were boring to the Negroes, most of whom would go home. The meetings that were devoted to the singing of freedom songs and to the pep-rally type of speeches were inspirational to the Negro members but were embarrassing to the white adults. Whenever the time came for picketing or for the sit-in, the white members clung to their seats, the young Negroes jumped to their feet and volunteered for action. Many of the adult white members found it inconvenient to come to three street marches and one or more meetings every week; many of the Negroes were present at every one. Moratoriums were acceptable to the whites; direct action was pleaded for by the Negroes.

One way to help bridge the chasm between the two groups was to bring into membership more middle-aged Negroes. However, Chapel Hill's middle-aged Negro leaders were ministers, and although they supported the COB, they had not been the ones to start it and didn't feel like accepting positions under young men such as Harold Foster and James Foushee. One or two of the ministers were even antagonistic to Harold, who had said openly in a meeting that the churches had failed to lead in this struggle and who had implied privately that the Negro ministers were not satisfactory leaders. Rather than be of increasing help to the COB, the ministers were now listening sympathetically to rumors intended to hurt the COB, including the rumor that the training workshops merely existed for sex orgies. The sessions were held in a church, adults from the COB were in charge, and always visitors from the COB were present, among them Father Parker, the retired Episcopal priest. Even so, the rumors persisted and were dignified by a secret meeting of parents with Rev. Manley.

The workshops were a source of embarrassment to many of the white members of the committee, too, though not for that reason; they were not even aware of the rumors in the Negro community. Their complaint was that the nonviolent workshops seemed to feature protection against violence more than they featured moral commitment to nonviolence. Bob Brown was extremely critical of the workshops on this score. "The important thing, Pat, is what goes on inside the person, not how to fall like a paratrooper," he would say.

But Pat had found that the young people liked to fall like paratroopers, and much preferred that to lengthy discussions. By emphasizing action, he could get them to listen when he taught them the theories of nonviolence. "You can't get kids to sit around talking all the time like college people," he would explain.

"Some of the white members would come to me," Bob says, "and they would express all sorts of apprehensions. Were we training an army? they would ask me. My answer was, 'Go up there, it's open.' So they'd go up there, and they'd be throwing them around on the floor and all that kind of stuff. They'd say, 'What the hell is this, is this nonviolence?' I didn't have any answer. I talked with Pat, and Pat had this business about he wouldn't let any newsmen or police in for some crazy reason. Some sneaky business was going on up there, people were concluding."

Pat says there were about eighteen workshops, and that newsmen were admitted to all except one of them, but he does agree that there was a lot of dissatisfaction.

It was the conclusion of the dissatisfied members that much of the problem was Harold Foster. The co-chairman of the committee, Father Parker, never served as chairman and didn't want to; Harold had taken full charge, and Harold was one of the most aggressive leaders of the whole lot. If Harold could be replaced, both the Negro ministers who weren't happy and the white leaders who were insecure would feel better. Then, too, if Harold would resign and a new leader go in, a person eminently qualified to represent the committee before the public, the charges of irresponsible leadership would have to be re-examined by the community at large.

They made the case against Harold sound imposing, and the solution might have worked out very well, except for the fact that Harold didn't want to give up the chairmanship. He and his supporters, among them Pat and Quinton, felt that a Negro, one of their own age group, ought to be chairman, and they were not going to allow the more conservative members to turn the COB into a discussion society.

This debate developed much bickering. "They started rumors about me," Bob says, "because I was wavering, I was thinking we ought to get rid of Foster. They said that when we were all in jail after the sit-in, I had a cigarette and wouldn't give anybody a smoke. Now I know it don't sound like much, but it hurt me, it hurt me bad.

The Negro kids believed it. So I would talk with Pat about that and other things so petty I don't even like to think about them now. I would say, 'God damn it, Pat, you've got to put a stop to this.' But he wouldn't or he couldn't. Pat wanted to be liked, he wanted to be liked by both sides."

Most of these little arguments didn't amount to a serious threat, but the COB was now in trouble with the mayor, in trouble with the businessmen, in trouble with the main newspaper, even in trouble with the governor. They were in trouble with everybody, so they began to get in trouble with themselves, and Harold Foster, who was only nineteen, wasn't representative of the total organization and couldn't hold the disjointed group together.

So he resigned. The executive committee then agreed on a new slate of officers to take before the full committee at its next meeting.

The next meeting was well attended. Present were well over one hundred people, most of whom didn't know about the dissension. The executive committee assumed, Bob tells me, that Harold would get up, gracefully announce his resignation, and then the new slate of officers would be presented. But Harold didn't do this.

"It was incredible what happened," Bob says. "Harold came walking in, in overalls. In overalls like they wear down there in Birmingham, Alabama. It was disgusting. He had gone out and bought them for the occasion. And as he entered, fifty or sixty eight- and ten-year-old Negro children stood up in the balcony and started yelling, 'We want Harold, we want Harold.' It was astonishing. And Harold got up there with a prepared speech. He sounded like Martin Luther King with all those words thrown together. He got up there and tore those white people apart. They were going to have to vote, they were going to have to stand up and vote against that colored boy. It was terrible. Oh, it was just awful, the whole thing was terrible. I didn't want nothin' to do with it.

"I stood up, and, man, all those questions and everything, I wanted to say Pontius Pilate, I wanted to wash my hands of the whole God damned affair. I wanted to go home. It was really bad. And the whites burned, and the Negroes, the old people, not knowing what was up, except they were going to vote against one of their own up there. You have no idea.

"So the vote was taken, and Harold's group won. What happened was, they had these fifty, sixty kids up in the balcony, and when the time came to count votes, Harold had his men do the counting, and they counted those little eight- and ten-year-old children. But we had no constitution, we had no by-laws, so anybody could vote. So those little eight- and ten-year-olds got up and voted for Harold, and he defeated our new slate of officers. So we had no officers. Then somebody gets up and says to Harold, how about adopting a constitution for this outfit? There's a lot of talk about that, and then, lo and behold, Harold resigns from the executive committee, then others resign."

The remaining members of the executive committee evidently appointed a nominating committee to try to find a suitable compromise slate of officers. On the committee were Mrs. Van Darity, a Negro housewife; Father Parker; Rev. Foushee; and Bob Brown, chairman.

Bob, at a meeting of the executive committee, did the only thing he says he could have done: he invited Harold Foster and his supporters to the meeting, and he asked them to help decide on a suitable slate of officers. One of them immediately nominated Harold Foster for chairman. A vote was taken and Harold won; he was to be the person recommended to the COB as their new chairman, to replace himself.

Bob resigned. "I was hurt. I really was hurt. God damn it, the boy was going back to college in September, he couldn't serve but one more month anyway. He could at least resign and let the organization hold together. I believed we had almost won out uptown. I really believe if the people who were in charge while Pat and Harold and I were in jail, right after that first sit-in, if they had gone ahead with a march that night, gone down to the jail, as we had planned—but they canceled it. Chief Blake came up to the church and told them he couldn't guarantee safety. Well, he always said that, don't you see? That's what he's paid for, to discourage things like that. I knew that, but I was in jail.

"Then next they accepted a moratorium. At a critical time we sat on our hands and did nothing, while the mayor and the businessmen acted like they were doing something. And now this bickering and dissension, and this Harold Foster thing. So I resigned. I said, 'There you are. You got it. The posters are all painted. You got it all,

Harold. And I'm going to support you, I'm going to support whatever you decide to do. But I'm off this committee. I'm tired of all this mess. We're killing ourselves around this place. So it's yours.' "

Joe Straley, physics professor at the university, who had put up bond for the sit-in demonstrators, and Charlie Jones, the pastor, who had just returned from a summer out of town, sought to bring about an adjustment. They met with the various factions, and out of the discussions came the concept that a new organization ought to be formed to be called Citizens United for Racial Equality and Dignity, which abbreviates to the word CURED. Harold Foster and his group would write a constitution and present it to an open meeting, and after the constitution was agreed upon, the full committee would elect officers and continue the work. Also, in order to lend assurance to the white liberal element, not only was the new group to administer the marches and sit-ins; but it would conduct studies of housing, health and other conditions in the Negro community, would work toward voter registration, would seek ways to improve the schools, and generally would let the white members contribute in constructive ways. The organization would also try to penetrate more deeply into the adult Negro community and win the full support of the older leaders of Chapel Hill, white and Negro.

Everybody agreed and a large open meeting was held at St. Joseph's Church, attended by about one hundred people. At the meeting the proposed constitution was presented. Joe Straley and T. Franklin Williams had written a two-page draft, and Harold Foster and Pat had worked on it for a week, rewriting it while they drank coffee at Harry's Grill.

"It was really an incredible document," Bob says. "It was eight, ten pages long. It barred Communists and all that sort of thing, so we discussed all the prohibitions. Then we came to voting rights. Harold's faction wanted to permit eight-year-olds to vote. That's right. He wanted the voting age to be eight years of age. So all those mature people sat there and debated whether eight-year-old children ought to vote. For hours. I mean for hours. Professors of the university sitting there talking about that.

"So we had three meetings on it, and finally it got adopted by somebody jumping up and saying, 'To hell with this, man. I move we take the whole God damn thing, lock, stock and barrel!' We were on page two. We had been talking for three weeks about the first two pages. So somebody else said, 'I second that,' and then there was a vote and everybody said, 'Aye, take this son of a bitch and forget it!' It was just ridiculous."

Pat Cusick, when I talked with him later, could see a good deal of humor in the whole situation. "But I think it really had to happen," he says. "I was working with the young Negroes, and I knew the sentiment. There had to be some Negro control of the Negro's protest movement, or it was all off. That control brought with it annoyances at times, but Harold Foster didn't cause them and wasn't, in my judgment, at fault. The white members, Bob Brown included, were no longer really in control of the actual work being done by the organization they had helped found; they were, in fact, more a drag than a help in the action that the young Negroes now felt had to be taken. The Negroes wanted to go ahead, right down the middle of the civil rights road, and the white people on the whole weren't ready."

Meanwhile the work in the streets continued, as did the work in the conference rooms. The mayor's committee had told the civil rights leaders that they had support from every member of the Board of Aldermen for an ordinance prohibiting any new segregated public businesses from being established; on the basis of that, they asked for a respite, which was granted. The ordinance was then opposed by the Merchants Association and died without a vote. A street march was held, but only fifty people showed up. The picketing of the Colonial Drug Store stopped when John Carswell closed the store for a two-week family vacation, and was not resumed after he opened again. And so it went as the activities gradually wound down.

Pat Cusick himself was put out of his house, where he had lived for two and a half years. His landlord, an employee of the university, had the town constable summon Pat to appear before the Chapel Hill justice of the peace, and there Pat was told to leave the house within four days. The action was taken because "the rent was five days overdue" and because of "the mess" that was entering Pat's house.

The mess evidently was Quinton Baker. By now he spent most of his time in Chapel Hill, only going to Durham in the mornings to his college classes, and he had been staying at Pat's house. Now both of them were without a place in Chapel Hill to live, and they were unable to find one. Finally, in desperation, they asked a fraternity manager for permission to live in a fraternity house, since the fraternity, St. Anthony's Hall, was closed until the start of the fall semester. The manager agreèd, and they stayed there temporarily.

Quinton, as NAACP commando, made about $12.50 a week. The two men used this as their food money. This was, of course, too little money, barely enough to sustain themselves. For entertainment they would take long walks in the evening and would discuss the local civil rights movement. They discussed how their street marches had caused hate, which they decided had been buried for many years under the surface in Chapel Hill. Now many people who had been friends of Pat's hated him intensely. Quinton, who had previously been respected in Chapel Hill for what he had done in Durham, felt he was hated for what he was doing in Chapel Hill.

In late August, Quinton was asked by Floyd McKissick to go to Goldsboro, North Carolina, where there had been racial violence for two nights. While there Quinton trained a group of demonstrators and went with them to a restaurant, where they were arrested. On August 22, he celebrated his twenty-first birthday in the county jail. He says it was the day when legally, and in terms of his own personal declaration of rights, he became a man.

He was released from jail barely in time to attend the March on Washington. John Dunne was already there, working at the March on Washington office, and Pat Cusick and a group from Chapel Hill arrived on two busses. In all sixty people arrived from Chapel Hill. Pat says it was ironical to him that in Washington the Chapel Hillians were the ones best able to sing the freedom songs and do the marching. They had done more marching than any other group in Washington that day. Yet, as Pat told John Dunne, the end had come to the COB, to the whole way the movement had started in Chapel Hill. Not a single place had been desegregated in that long, hot summer, and a whole new start would have to be made by a group willing to take more chances.

Chapter Eight

IN NATURE, as everybody knows, spring is a time of birth, summer a time of bearing, fall a time of flouting and then accepting the winter dying. In a university, however, and in a university town, the seasons get turned around, so that spring is the time of finishing things up, summer is a lull for catching up or resting or filling in, and fall is the time of birth, of starting again. The professors meet their new classes, the lecture notes are flipped back to the beginning, and there is plenty of hope and ambition.

This September Franklin Street came alive with hellos and what did you do this summers and don't we come from the same towns. The students drenched themselves in the coffee, beer and atmosphere of their favorite meeting places. The revolving tubs in the automatic laundry machines tumbled and spun continuously, and realtors were in their heyday, smiling in spite of their sleepiness, pretending assurance in the midst of chaos, giving the wrong keys to everybody. The dormitories filled to overflowing; the fraternity house doors were propped open.

Some of the students were veterans of Chapel Hill terms; others were new students, arriving hopefully and fearfully, having been warned by novels and uncles that college is a dangerous time of life and Chapel Hill a dangerous place, a seedbed of new ideas, some of them lethal on impact, and do be careful and don't fall in love while so young. Students arrived in cars and busses, protecting their luggage, their raincoats, their family ideals and their personal virginity and integrity. They were the outpouring of the best talent from the schools of the state, and they were the mass of raw material from which would come many of the state's future legislators, judges, mayors, writers, thinkers, doers, professors. Generation after generation, since the days of the American Revolution, Chapel Hill has been extremely productive of talent. As a state university, it is uniquely successful, and almost every phase of enlightenment and

97

progress in the state, and to some extent in the South, can trace its birth to this small town.

John Dunne was back, but he had no place to stay. He had written me during the summer and asked me to stop at the realtors and cancel his lease on his apartment. He had rented a room by mail, but once the landlady realized who he was, that he was the one who had been locked up in Birmingham, she wouldn't let him in the house. She said she didn't rent to people with racial dispositions.

One day John phoned me and asked if he and Quinton Baker, whom I'd not met, and a professor's daughter could go out to my farm. There were several small trees near the old house which I had meant that day to cut down, so it suited me very well for them to go, and almost at once the three of them appeared at the front door. I got the Jeep started. I keep a 1948 Jeep, which somebody long years ago painted red; it has a cab over the front two seats and the back part is open.

By now all four of us were standing out front where the Jeep was, and it had occurred to me that seating this group was going to be a problem. There were two seats up front and two out back, and we had one Negro and one attractive blond young lady. I knew John well enough to know that he was perfectly aware of the problem, and that he was waiting to see how I would handle it. If I put Quinton up front, it would be supposed that I was trying to hide him in the cab. If I put the girl up front, I would have to drive about Chapel Hill with my integrated group clearly on display. That didn't bother me, however, and it was clearly the best solution. "Well, where shall we sit?" I said.

There was an awkward moment as everybody realized what I was asking was: Where shall we put Quinton? A Negro must get awfully tired of finding himself isolated in these subtle ways. I expected to offer my suggestion, but John spoke up first. "Quinton, you two get in the back and I'll ride up front with John."

This was an arrangement I had not counted on. To go through town in a red Jeep with a white boy and a Negro boy in the open back part was one thing; to do the same thing with Quinton and a beautiful blond girl on display was quite another. John knew all this, mind you. He is much too clever a person not to. "That will do very well," I said, for there was nothing else to say at this point, unless I wanted to make an open issue of the fact that Quinton was a Negro.

I had mentioned in the house that perhaps we could stop somewhere and buy a watermelon. If I took the back way to my farm, avoiding downtown, I could buy a watermelon at Merritt's Service Station and Grocery. However, Mr. Merritt was not an integrationist, and my hunch was that my party would not be welcome there. The stark truth was that I would need to drive through the very middle of Chapel Hill, which I proceeded to do, being no doubt the first person ever to work in a Southern governor's office who has driven a red Jeep down Main Street with a Negro and a blond on display.

The minute we stopped at Fowler's Food Store, John and I hurried inside for the watermelon. When we got back, Quinton mentioned that two cab drivers had thought it best to stop and say a few delicate words of warning to our group. John scowled at this. "I don't care," he said. "I simply don't believe in segregation in any way."

I think Quinton would have understood perfectly if at this time I had suggested a swapping of seats, but John would not have understood at all. Really, the challenge he was making was to me, and I accepted it as such and let everybody stay where he was, for I believed it was more important to keep the confidence of John Dunne than to discard it in favor of expediency, no matter how much I would have preferred expediency at the moment.

Fortunately, the cab drivers didn't bother us and we got out to the farm all right. We cut down only one tree. John cut it down himself, literally beat it down with the ax in a sweep of energy and strength that was remarkable to see. But one tree was all. There were other trees which ought to come down, but John argued resourcefully on their behalf, pointing out their assets to the place, being totally unable to see why I would want to part with them. In his tendency to support the underdog, he now identified himself with the scrubby trees brushing against my cabin, and I was being persuaded to see in these perfectly worthless and uninspiring creations so much charm that my yard began to take on the aspects of a garden.

He has tremendous energy and was active every minute. He saw everything the farm had to show, every log in the barn, every stone in the fireplaces. Finally, I came back to the house and sat down in a rocking chair and made myself at home. He sat down for about a minute, then asked if he might drive the Jeep. That was all right, of course, and the three of them went tearing out of the house and soon had the Jeep going. A while later I heard them shifting gears and backing up. This was down at a bad creek crossing. Then they were off, up the deserted, old road which once had been the main thoroughfare of this part of the county and, like so much that gets lost in the sweep of change, is now almost never used at all.

They were gone for over an hour and returned by a different route entirely. They had got lost back in the woods somewhere and had passed several farmhouses, they said, which baffled me, for there were few farmhouses within miles. They had gone through a dairy farm, they said, opening the pasture gates and closing them. All of this had no doubt been seen by the farmers, whoever they were, and most farmers in Orange County are not accustomed to seeing integrated groups of young people riding past at all, much less so festively. None of these young people seemed to me to understand the dangers they were courting, to understand that the mores of Southerners are not to be flouted safely, and indeed I saw no use in flouting them at all in this particular type of rural demonstration.

I felt as old people must feel when they realize the thinking of the young has put them out of reach. So I said nothing. We ate the watermelon and I talked with John, asking what his plans were for the school year just ahead, advising him to spend his time in the classrooms rather than on the streets, advice he listened to without comment. He brought up the subject of the March on Washington, of which he was proud. I told him I had been to Washington that day, conferring at the Office of Education about a state school the governor wanted to start, and when the offices all closed down, I had gone by to watch part of the march.

John then began to talk about my farm and how much he liked it, the isolation and the quiet. When he had spent a day or so out there earlier, he said he had managed to get tremendous amounts of studying done. He wondered, since he had no place to stay, if I would permit him to rent the farmhouse for the year.

I rejected the idea at once, and it must have hurt his feelings. I remember his putting his hand on my arm and turning me around to face him, and I saw in his eyes the hurt and question he had, which was no doubt the question he had wanted to ask the landlady, too, and which he was trying to ask now of everybody in the whole world—the cab drivers and the farmers and everybody: Was it because he had friends who were Negroes? His gaze was starkly honest and intense, so I asked myself if it was that, and I had to admit that I didn't want to see my farmhouse burned down because of interracial gatherings or because a leader of the Chapel Hill civil rights movement lived there. Also involved was my belief that John should return to the campus, live and study there and be part of that established community. But the race matter was involved, too, I admitted to myself.

I said nothing to John, however, and turned away. A man who knows the South can sense the feelings of it, can sense danger when the ways of the South are challenged, can sense how far one can go safely, and I realized that John didn't know, perhaps couldn't know, and that almost certainly he was going to find himself in a place dangerous to him and maybe to the South before this year was out. It was not the best thing for John, I thought, and I wasn't sure it was going to be the best thing for the South.

"I'm sorry, John," I said, and I know he felt that I had failed him, as had all the others, and he balled his fist and struck me slightly, a glancing, friendly blow, as a man who is hurt by a friend will do at times to say it didn't matter anyway.

When we got back into town, he had an apartment waiting, one which a friend had found for him, and he was instantly elated. It was located in a pleasant residential section and was what he needed, he said. It was what I thought he needed, too, exactly. I was therefore disappointed to find on the next day that he had lost the use of the place. He had shown up with Quinton, or one of his other Negro associates, and the lady of the house had sensed what her year in that neighborhood was going to be like.

John also was having trouble with some of his friends. One Durham lady invited him and, if he liked, Quinton to have dinner with her family, a gesture of confidence in her liberalism perhaps, and a way to put John at ease. John accepted for the two. The lady was known for her excellent Southern cooking, particularly her biscuits. The two men arrived at the appointed time, neatly dressed and anxious to be pleasant. Unfortunately, the hostess took one drink more than she meant to, and once her tongue was free, her social instincts were relaxed, too. At one point, leaning close to Quinton and staring hard at him, she said, "You know where you belong, don't you?"

Quinton shook his head.

"Africa," she said.

Quinton smiled. He has an easy way with white people and takes no offense, even at insults; his tendency is to sympathize with others.

"What part of Africa are you from?" she asked.

"West Africa," Quinton said simply.

John and the host asked Quinton if he wanted to see the backyard with them. They were much more in need of escape than he was, but the three of them went outdoors and looked at the shrubbery. They discussed the size of the lot, as one tends to do in suburban back yards when there is no other topic of conversation, and the host guardedly assured Quinton that no affront had been intended. When they returned to the house, however, the host had no sooner opened the door from the porch to the living room than he was greeted by a sight which quite electrified all of them. The hostess, her hands matted with biscuit dough, struck the piano a discordant chord and began pounding out a rendition of "Old Black Joe."

On the campus, too, John was encountering problems. Those professors who cared most about him recognized his ability and wanted him to settle down to serious academic work. Once he had his degrees, they thought he might want to enter some sort of public service, but not now. The students, too, were disposed to give the same advice. University of North Carolina students are not, of course, liberally inclined, as a group. About ninety percent of them come from the South, most of them from North Carolina, and they represent the attitudes of thousands of Southern families. In 1959, as a teacher at the university, I polled a class of about fifty students, asking them if they felt segregation by law ought to be enforced in schools, churches, movie theaters, restaurants and housing. The response was about fifty-fifty to all questions. Other, recent polls show similar results. I found a master's thesis in the library, done for the sociology department twenty-five years earlier, asking on the same campus the same questions, and at that time the results were about one-third liberal and two-thirds conservative. So the change hadn't been so great as many people would have predicted, and the contemporary group wasn't basically liberal by disposition, wasn't sympathetic to John Dunne's full commitment.

Wherever John went these days, seeking a place to live, seeking a leisurely evening with his friends, meeting with his instructors or his fellow students, he was advised to stay out of the movement and spend his time on his books; yet the attitudes shown all around him toward the Negro could not have been better designed to push him further into the social problem itself.

On September 16, in the wake of new outbreaks in Birmingham, he wrote his parents:

The bombings and shootings in B'ham, as well as the fires that broke out during the night have affected me deeply. If the Negroes do not retaliate after this, it will be only because of the most courageous self-restraint. How can anyone ask them to sit by, after all these years of frustration and fear, with no real tangible indication that it is ever going to stop, and with the federal gov't avoiding comment and so far removed in their carpeted offices on Capitol Hill, with Pres. Kennedy spending the weekend at a nice resort, celebrating his anniversary, so out of touch with this, the B'ham Negroes' only reality, so unable to understand that these flare-ups are only the occasional burstings through the shield of ignorance which covers the everyday life of that city, and keeps its secrets hidden from all but those who must live these hideous secrets.

He told of an event which had occurred the previous spring in Birmingham, about a

little Negro girl who had her head beaten in with a brick behind the Motel while her crippled older sister on crutches stood by helpless and watched the child thrown into a car and carried away to be dumped somewhere along a lonely Alabama road—this was never reported, no one but the girl, the killer, myself and five or six others at the Motel and several neighbors who heard the screaming and the car, plus the two policemen who were dispatched to "investigate," and left without even asking questions of those of us involved. But I will never forget the face of the girl, hysterical, sobbing uncontrollably, "They've killed my sister," nor can I ever forget the strange look of helplessness (or was it a look of sad awareness that I'd never learn, that the white boy from the suburban North was too innocent to understand why they didn't move, why they just stared at the sobbing girl with an acceptance of this fact of their existence, a fatalism almost inhuman, like that of the war-crazed soldier who has seen too many people die?) which crossed the faces of the others when I urged, "Why doesn't someone call the police?"

He wrote further: "So much hate and self-destruction—WHY?" The question came out of his heart at the time when he was trying to go to school and pay attention to the work of his courses, and at the same time was becoming more and more busily engaged with the local problems.

He wrote his parents about a trip he had made to Danville, Virginia:

It also is a tragic situation and is about to blow up. They have had some of the worst police brutality there of anywhere. I can't understand such depravity and hatred. I was going to say that it wasn't human, but I guess that's one of our great problems, that we don't face the fact that this is human, that man is a cowering, frightened animal before the unspeaking mysteries and cruelty of the universe, and when he transcends this state and attains true dignity and love it is one of the most significant days in the history of the cosmos. The wonderful thing is that man CAN attain this state, if only for brief moments, and for this we should rejoice and praise Love and smell the richness of the earth and know that it is good. Perhaps this is the real justification for humanitarian goals—that in the struggle itself we have just the barest chance of purifying ourselves, not by our deeds but by the state of mind from which they emanate.

He tried in his courses to bury his commitment to the civil rights movement. For a week or two, he would do this successfully, but then the wall of exclusion would cave in. At last, in November, he decided he must face the decision itself. He talked with Walter Spearman, the journalism professor, with Kenneth Reckford, the Greek professor, in whose home John finally had found a room, and with others, and on December 4 he wrote his parents:

I have just returned home from a most long and exhausting day. A fire is in the fireplace. Bloch's *Sacred Service* is playing, and I feel like writing a long-overdue letter home. Both of you wrote me such wonderful and deeply moving letters, that I want to answer each separately, but I feel that it is important that I let you know the facts of my situation at least, to avoid more worry on your part. I am in the process of withdrawing honorably from the school.

He said that Floyd McKissick of Durham, now the national chairman of CORE, had offered him a job as task force member of CORE for the State of North Carolina at a salary of $25 a week, that he was going to accept it, and that later he would return to school and finish his work.

There is so much more to say—I don't have the time right now, as it's been a long and hectic day, ending with a community-wide adult meeting to organize an all-out voter registration campaign for the town, which meeting I was asked to chair. . . . I'll keep you posted as developments come in. Meanwhile, I want to thank you both from the depths of my heart for your encouraging letters, your love and your faith. Occasionally a man needs someone to say, "I have faith in you." Must go to bed. Much love, as always.

His decision was perhaps inevitable, but the delay in leaving school was inevitable, too, for he had a full-expense scholarship and his lifetime ambitions were very much involved with completing his college courses.

One might interpret his decision in terms of a letter written to him almost exactly five years earlier by the headmaster of Choate, Seymour St. John. The letter is dated November 26, 1958.

Dear John:

It is fitting at Thanksgiving time that I should have the privilege of telling you that you have been awarded the Joseph P. Kennedy Memorial Scholarship. The scholarship which you now hold, to which the income from Joe's Fund will be applied, becomes herewith one of Choate's marks of distinction, awarded after careful consideration to those whom we particularly delight to honor. I congratulate you upon being one of them.

You will want to look at the Choate Memorial Volume in the Library and see Joe's picture and the brief account of his life and death. You will recognize at once the quality of his character, and understand what it means to have your name linked with his. The first sentence about Joe says it all: "With his warm heart, his instinct for friendship, and his native zeal to work for the best and make it better, Joe was at Choate a leader in all good things." Words like that are a challenge for a whole lifetime, and I know of no one, John, whom I count on more than you to fulfill them.

You will want to have in mind those words of MacLeish:

They say:

> "Our deaths are not ours;
> They are yours;
> They will mean what *you*
> make them."

*   *   *

A local chapter of CORE had been started in Chapel Hill in
late summer. Floyd McKissick came over from Durham one night
and talked about the difference between CORE and the NAACP, of
which he was also an influential member. The former is more aggressive, takes more chances, sometimes gets into trouble, and does not
believe the way will be opened by court action predominantly—that
sometimes such demonstrations as the CORE freedom rides bring
new rights for the Negro more quickly. Professor Joe Straley, Professor Al Amon and most other people present that night did not believe
in civil disobedience tactics, except perhaps as a personal, individual
testimony, and they could not quite come to grips with massive civil
disobedience, such as large-scale sit-ins constitute.

Floyd McKissick is capable at one moment of expressing a gentle
sincerity, a deep compassion for people; at another moment he might
be forcefully, loudly berating the white liberals for not giving him the
support he wants. He tells me he decided to be a lawyer while he was
a freshman in high school. Until then he didn't know whether to be a
lawyer or a doctor, and the decision was made for him by a white
policeman in his hometown, Asheville, North Carolina. Floyd and
another Negro boy scout were directing traffic at a meeting place.

"A white cop came up to us," McKissick says, "and told us to move
on. We told him that the scoutmaster had assigned us to this place.
He said, 'Don't talk to me, nigger.' He had a big glove. You remember how policemen used to wear big gloves with red and green reflec-
tors on them, like motorcyclists sometimes wear. He had one, and he
slapped me across the face with it. He proceeded to beat me, and I
was bloody. I remember the black asphalt of the street and the blood
pouring on it. There was no sense in the world to what he did."

Young Floyd McKissick, the son of a hotel bellhop, decided then
to be a lawyer. "I was going to protect myself," he says, "so that

nobody would ever be able to do that to me again." He started working his way through North Carolina College. When he got back from four years of service with the army in the war, during which he was wounded in action in Europe, he worked as a waiter in a segregated restaurant and finished his degree. He had a wife and three children by then, and even though the GI Bill helped, the days were lean, indeed. He became headwaiter at the Bartlett House in Durham —also segregated. "Everything was segregated in those days," he says.

One summer he took courses, not for credit, at the Law School in Chapel Hill, the first time a Negro had been admitted there, and began his practice.

The Chapel Hill chapter of CORE which McKissick helped start didn't really do much of anything until John Dunne joined it. John took offices for it in what had up until then been the Negro Odd Fellows Hall. Pat and Quinton were not members of CORE, and Pat was spending most of his time these days in Danville, Virginia, but they helped John get the place in order. The office was over a Negro funeral parlor, about a block from the Chicken Box Number Two.

There were two other civil rights groups in town, CURED and the Mayor's Human Relations Committee, and the leaders of both were trying diligently to get something accomplished. Mrs. Margaret Taylor, wife of History Professor George Taylor, was now chairman of the Human Relations Committee. She tells me she went to Mayor McClamroch and others and pleaded with them to move ahead, now that the pressure was off and the way was clear. Nothing was done. Her committee consisted of six Negro leaders and six white leaders; all the white leaders except one were connected with the university, and she tried to find members of the business community who would accept appointments to it. She could find none.

CURED, meanwhile, was trying to decide on a program, one involving voter registration and the improvement of employment opportunities, and its white and Negro leaders were having trouble, too. There was simply not much interest in doing anything, Professor Straley said later. "We couldn't stir up interest in civil rights in this town to save our lives. People had an open field, but they wouldn't move. White liberals are only going to move when the heat is on."

He, Rev. Charlie Jones and Rev. Tom Davis among the white leaders, and Hilliard Caldwell and Harold Foster among the Negro leaders, made little headway.

CORE, meanwhile, offering to introduce new techniques, was beginning to become the center of civil rights interest, and some of the leaders of the two other organizations suspected that National CORE was selecting Chapel Hill for special attention. What, they reasoned, could be more natural for Floyd McKissick to do? He lived nearby, he had attended the university Law School, he had represented the Merchants Association demonstrators in the Recorders Court, and he had appealed their cases to the Superior Court, so he was their counsel to this day.

The possible use of massive civil disobedience worried the established leaders of the liberal community, and they noticed that John, Pat and the others were prone to see issues in terms either of black or white; they seemed unwilling to accept the lesser of two evils in a situation. It appeared to Rev. Charlie Jones and some others of the CURED organization that the young leaders were talking about using peace as if it were a missile, of using love as it if were a weapon—admittedly a nonviolent weapon, but a weapon of coercion, nonetheless—and there was an impracticality about the timetables they seemed to be setting for the town. But the CURED organization, embarrassed by its own inability to get anything started except a single street march, one that was poorly attended at that, could only fret.

Bob Brown was out of it; he would not help with CORE. Most of the town's white liberals had little influence over the young people now. Of perhaps even more consequence, the established leaders of the Negro community had not been asked to join. There were few local Negro leaders involved in any central way, and naturally there was much jealousy and antagonism as a consequence.

CURED managed to formulate a program of action, but it had to call four meetings before it could get a quorum, though only five members constituted a quorum of the executive committee. They voted approval of the voter registration project and asked John Dunne, interestingly enough, to head it.

Chief Blake was aware of much of this. He had set up intelligence procedures, charging every member of the Police Department to find informers and to be alert for any rumors or statements, to secure copies of leaflets, to make lists of license numbers of cars seen around integrationist meetings, and generally to gather pertinent information. In late November and early December he began to receive word that civil rights leaders were coming to Chapel Hill: J. V. Henry, a white field worker for SNCC; Arthur Tracy, a Negro co-worker of Henry's; Avon Rollings, a Negro who had been a leader of the Danville, Virginia, movement; Joseph Tieger, a white field worker for CORE; John Salter, a white worker for the Southern Conference Education Fund; LaVert Taylor, a Negro minister and one of Martin Luther King's representatives. He was well aware of activity above the Negro funeral home, in what had been the meeting place of the Odd Fellows Lodge.

Most other people in town, however, were slumbering along, unaware of the significance of the changes, partly because nothing much was being done on the streets. The picketing and marches had stopped, and so, therefore, had the various efforts to negotiate desegregation. The great giants, the town and the university, had settled back into their established niches. But in the Negro section young leaders were going from door to door, passing out leaflets and seeking supporters, young and middle-aged and old.

They were, as often as not, unconsciously creating severe reactions of relief, hope, fear and hostility, depending on the ability of the Negro citizens to relate to the changes they were advocating. The basic social and economic pattern in Chapel Hill, as elsewhere in the South, required that there be two major, different masses of people living in the town: the white people and the Negroes. The Negro was supposed to be inferior overall, with less ability to think and learn, with an almost uncontrollable interest in sex, and with a tendency toward violence which he could not be expected always to contain. He was said to be somewhat childish, irresponsible, and that what he most wanted in life was a good time, which he had to excess on Saturday nights, when he got drunk, and on Sunday morning, when he prepared himself for life in heaven.

Many white people in Chapel Hill no longer accepted as valid this image of the Negro; they had been exposed to the various sociological, psychological, anthropological and other reports on the matter over the past twenty years, which have disproved just about every myth the white man long ago created about the differences which separate him from the Negro race. But the image was held generally in the white community, to one degree or another, and it was held in the Negro community as well.

A Negro child of four or five years of age begins to understand that he is a member of a disadvantaged group. From that time on, his parents begin preparing him to accept his role as such, for to do otherwise would be to expose him to the full avalanche of social, economic and political consequences, which are sufficiently massive in any Southern or Northern town to crush an individual Negro. Since it is expected of the child that he fit into a pattern, he is instructed along those lines; since it is expected that the Negro will repress his drives toward self-realization and development, the child is carefully confined; since Negroes are not expected to take part in the affairs of government, except in occasional and nominal ways, the child is not encouraged to consider himself as part of the political institutions of the town or state or country; since it is assumed that a Negro will take a job working at physical labor and will not aspire to a profession or do anything requiring mental ability, the child is encouraged along those lines.

This type of training produces a citizen which in the South, and even in Chapel Hill, is known as a "good Negro." The good Negro can expect paternalistic guidance from the whites who know him, can be assured of their interest in him and his family, can get small loans from them, and can rely on them to bail him out of jail should he get into trouble. They do not particularly resent his getting into trouble, for they have been expecting that, and some of them have a real need that he do so, in order to support their image of him and their own image of themselves.

John Dunne, Pat Cusick and their associates understood some of this, but they were basically college English majors, and they knew little about the underlying social and psychological matters involved. They were asking for a major change in the attitudes the Negro people had toward being a Negro, toward being a worker, toward being a political being in Chapel Hill. Stark fear, even antagonism, met their ideas when they were first presented in some homes. Negro parents weren't convinced that they could aspire to a situation of full equality, and they were unfamiliar with what such a situation would require of them in the daily habits of child-rearing, job-hunting and growing older.

Day after day, the young white people, and the young Negro people who accepted the challenges of this new way of life, knocked on doors and sat on porches and porch steps and stood on the sidewalks and talked to Negroes. Meanwhile, the Odd Fellows Hall was being partitioned and made into an office and assembly room for CORE.

John Dunne, when I talked with him at Sandy Ridge five months later, said that the office had been contributed by the Odd Fellows after a long evening of talk. Only five Odd Fellows had come to the meeting, held in the hall itself, which, among other furniture, had a Coke machine, a Nabs machine and the battered, delinquent chair of the dentist who had used the place years earlier. The five members of the Odd Fellows listened to John and other leaders explain what CORE planned to do. They discussed Negro rights, voter registration and equal employment opportunities with them. Every now and then an elderly Odd Fellow would drop off to sleep and begin to snore, and one of his fellow members would gently awaken him. Three of the members were sleeping and had to be awakened for the vote, which went very well. John then began the second phase of the request; he asked if they would permit the CORE chapter to partition off the back one-quarter of the room for an office. The members again selflessly voted aye and were done with it.

So the wall was built and had to be rebuilt, for it was none too secure the first time, and tables and chairs were scrounged from this place and that. Bob Brown contributed a swivel chair with a broken back, for example; Joe Straley brought a table. The office had space for eight or ten people to work at a time, and a phone was installed.

They were located there in November, when President Kennedy was shot in Dallas. Quinton, as president of the NAACP Youth Chapters of the state, had invited John Dunne to help him set up a statewide voter registration conference, and the two of them were on their way to Rocky Mount, where the conference was to be held, when the news of the President's injury reached them. They were badly shaken and broke into tears from time to time as they followed the radio reports.

Pat Cusick was in Danville, working in the office of the Danville Christian Progressive Association, one of Martin Luther King's outfits. The grief, he says, was profound, and all activities of the organization came to a stop and a prayer meeting was started. The violent death of the President was particularly shocking to the sensitivities of the men and women dedicated to nonviolence.

In the CORE headquarters in Chapel Hill, the young people huddled around the radio and listened to every last report, until their hope for President Kennedy's survival was extinguished. The Negroes fell into deep mourning, and in the schools the Negro children broke out in tears and went out of their classrooms, seeking the toilets, the most private place they could find, and there tried to get control of their trembling bodies. President Kennedy had meant more to them than any idea they had ever had, for somehow his compassion for them had got through to them, and it was as if their parents had been struck down and they were left alone in an unfriendly world.

No doubt everybody reading this has his own memories of that day. My own revolve not so much around the death of the man as around an incident early that same morning. I was in Washington to have meetings about one phase of the governor's ever-expanding poverty program, and I awoke before dawn. Out the window of my room I could see the dome of the Capitol, and I was so attracted by it that I got up at once and caught a cab and asked the driver to take me to it. The building was closed at that hour, of course, but writers learn to get into places, and it so happened that, after walking almost around the building, I came to a place where workmen later on that day would resume the construction of an addition. A door of the Capitol was unlocked, and I went inside.

The hallways were deserted. Far off I saw a Negro janitor sweeping. I opened a door and looked down at the House Chamber of the United States. Its color and dignity seeped into my mind, then I went on down the hallway, anxious for some reason or calling to go into the rotunda itself, to stand beneath the dome. I walked for what seemed to me to be a long time, down this corridor and that, this stairway and another, this passage way and that hallway, nodding confidently to Negro janitors and dusters and the like, afraid I would be apprehended and put out.

I found it. I stood in it. There I saw dawn come. One can hear a marvelous lot of birds by standing inside the rotunda at dawn, and can see the light from the clerestory windows fall on the high carvings near the dome's top, and move softly over the paintings of battles and discoveries on the lower walls, and come to cover the marble statues of the founders of the nation. And with the light, and as softly as the light, came the sounds of Negro voices talking, chattering as the workers cleaned and swept and prepared the other rooms for the day's work.

A Negro woman, young and humming some tune, came into the rotunda and began dusting the feet of a statue.

I left there, not knowing quite where I was going now, or caring, for I had seen dawn in the best place I had found thus far. I left the building, ushered out by an aggravated guard, just as the first white people began to arrive, to take over the place from the Negroes, who own it early in the morning. I cannot think of President Kennedy's death now without thinking of that incident.

Joe Straley tells me that on the day of President Kennedy's death he had been on the way to the post office to mail announcements of a meeting of CURED; when he heard the news, he went back to his office, talked on the phone with three or four other members of the executive committee and decided to cancel the meeting. For months he and others had been laying the groundwork for their organization, and he says they had at long last aroused enough interest to make it possible to call a sizable group together.

Hilliard Caldwell says that he posted a notice of the cancellation on the church doors, phoned the radio station and tried to stop the announcement in the newspaper. John Dunne and Quinton, when they got back to town that night, were unhappy that the meeting had been canceled.

Joe Straley, Hilliard Caldwell and others wonder to this day what would have happened had the meeting been held, had CURED been able to establish itself. But they did not meet, they did not effectively re-form, and the field was left open to the young people.

By December, CORE had their physical offices and their meeting place, and John was working full time. Pat was still spending much of his time in Danville, but he was consulted on plans as they developed. Developing the plans were John and Quinton, who, still not a member of CORE, represented the Youth Chapters of the NAACP. They had managed to find many supporters in town, some of them high school and some of them university students, and there were others they could call on in Durham, particularly at Duke and North Carolina College. What they did not yet have was a plan of action.

Quinton, John, Pat and the others talked this over and tried to decide on what they ought first to do. They had gathered information about segregation in business employment practices in town, including the university hospital, and they had been unable to negotiate satisfactorily with the hospital or university officials. They decided that a sit-in in the office of the university president, William Friday, would be a suitable start. Some of them were not satisfied with that, but the decision was tentatively made.

The solution to their problem came when it was apparent that the Merchants Association demonstrators were, in fact, going to be tried. Pat Cusick expected an outcry from the town, a reminder from the mayor, the Board of Aldermen, the police, the Merchants Association or the Committee on Human Relations that the Merchants Association and the Police Department had wanted to drop the charges if the demonstrators ceased sit-ins. The demonstrators had cooperated, as requested. Even so, Pat and three others had been scheduled for trial in the Superior Court in Hillsboro. It seemed probable that fines, or even prison terms, awaited them.

The four defendants discussed going to jail rather than pay fines. It was Pat's feeling that one who for moral reasons broke a law ought willingly to pay the penalty provided by the law. Mrs. Hope Van Riper, the wife of Peter Van Riper, said she was going to serve her term. Miss Charliese Cotton, Mrs. Christine Glover, who is a Negro housewife, and Pat agreed to do the same. They discussed this with Floyd McKissick, their attorney, when the five of them went to lunch at the local Negro high school in Hillsboro (they requested service there since they didn't know of any integrated restaurants in town).

At this luncheon they decided that the four would choose jail sentences rather than pay fines, and it was their hope that the publicity of four civil rights demonstrators spending Christmas in jail would excite community sympathy on behalf of the Negro cause.

The trials opened on December 12. Mr. McKissick, representing the defendants, first asked that the cases be continued to a later session of court, since the United States Supreme Court had before it a test case and would soon decide on the legality or illegality of this type of civil rights action. The judge, Leo Carr, seemed to favor this, Pat says, but the solicitor, Thomas D. Cooper, Jr., insisted that the trials be held.

Mr. McKissick then made a motion to quash the indictments on the grounds that they violated rights protected by the Fourteenth Amendment to the U.S. Constitution. The motion was denied.

Since the four cases had been grouped, Mr. McKissick had six preemptory challenges of jurymen for each defendant, or a total of twenty-four. The judge for one reason or another excluded one or two, and Solicitor Cooper excused two who, on questioning, indicated there might at times be justification for breaking the law. Attorney McKissick's chief line of inquiry was whether each prospective juror felt that all persons were entitled to equal rights under the law, regardless of race. He excused fifteen jurors. Judge Carr, recognizing the need for other prospective jurors, had a child draw forty names and suspended the trial until nine-thirty the next morning.

On that day, which was Thursday, a jury of seven white men, two white women and three Negro men was found acceptable and was sworn in.

Attorney McKissick was determined to put up the best possible defense, hoping to establish no unseemly civil rights precedents in the courts of the state. The trial, therefore, lasted most of the day, although only two witnesses took the stand, Joe Augustine of the Merchants Association and Chief of Police William Blake.

Mr. Augustine testified that over twenty people came into his place of business at about one-thirty on July 19 and sat down all over the floor and started singing loudly. He said he asked Mr. Cusick, who had his head down at the time, whether he was the leader of the group, and Mr. Cusick had indicated with a nod that he was. Once the police arrived, Mr. Augustine, with an electric bull horn provided by Chief Blake, told the group that they could stay if they wanted to, but that they would have to stop that singing because they were interfering with business.

Mr. Augustine testified that this only brought louder singing, so he gave the group thirty seconds to stop singing or he would have them removed. He admitted that there was a great deal of confusion in the office at the time, with all these people on the floor, their arms interlocked, braying out freedom songs, and with photographers and television cameras taking their pictures. He said Chief Blake took the bull horn and asked them to stop all that racket, but they would not.

Mr. Augustine said they hadn't asked him for anything, and he had never refused them anything, and he didn't know why the group was in his place at all, though he had his own ideas.

Solicitor Cooper introduced a photograph of the scene, and Mr. McKissick objected repeatedly to its use, but was overruled by the judge. Mr. Cooper then introduced Chapel Hill's bull horn as evidence, and Mr. McKissick objected, saying that time had expired since the incident and nobody could possibly say at what level the bull horn had been set or if this were the actual bull horn. The judge said he wondered himself if the bull horn could be set at the same volume, and Mr. Augustine took the bull horn outdoors to adjust it. Mr. McKissick continued to object, but was overruled.

Mr. Augustine in due time came back indoors with the bull horn and said he would now speak through it. Solicitor Cooper advised everybody to hold his ears. Mr. McKissick objected to that remark, and the judge told the jury to disregard Mr. Cooper's instructions and to do whatever they pleased with their ears.

Mr. Augustine, speaking through the electric bull horn, told the courtroom, and for that matter much of East Hillsboro, what he had told the demonstrators that day at his office.

Once the courtroom had regained its composure after Mr. Augustine had unplugged the thing, Mr. McKissick said, "You told the defendants they could stay if they quit singing. In other words, their physical presence didn't bother you, but the singing did."

Mr. Augustine said he was at first concerned with the noise they

Sherry Sitton, Ruby Farrington and other demonstrators block Franklin Street, February 1, 1964. (*Al Amon, for the Chapel Hill Freedom Committee*)

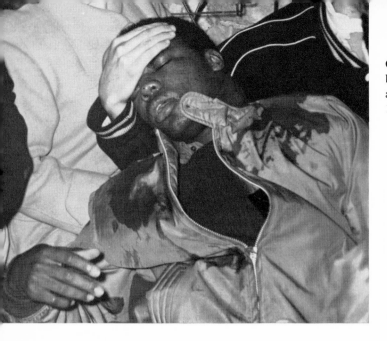

Quinton Baker after being doused with ammonia, December 1, 1964. (*Al Amon*)

James Brittain of Lincoln High School being thrown from a segregated store. (*Al Amon*)

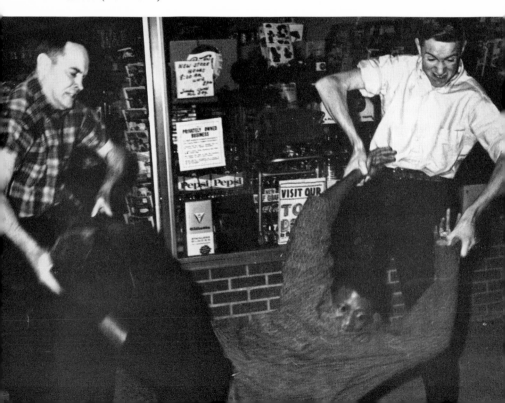

James Foushee holds Jerdine Alston after a sit-in at Watts Restaurant. (*Al Amon*)

Jo Anne Johnson being arrested at the Pines Restaurant. (*Jimmy Wallace, for the* Daily Tar Heel)

Sit-inners stacked up by police, awaiting patrol cars. (*Jimmy Wallace*)

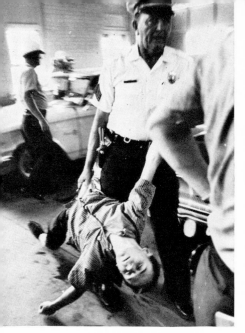

gt. Hester hauls away a limp demonstra-
or, Terry Chapin. (*Jimmy Wallace*)

A local housewife being carried off to
jail. (*Jimmy Wallace*)

Peter Van Riper pulled past Pat Cusick and into the back seat of a patrol
car. (*Jimmy Wallace*)

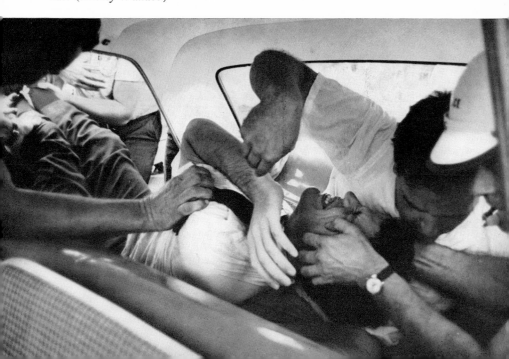

Opposing views on the same question. (*Jimmy Wallace*)

The Easter fast on the lawn of the post office, showing, left to right, Pat Cusick, LaVert Taylor, John Dunne and James Foushee. (*Al Amon*)

A sidewalk march along Franklin Street, led by Father Parker, LaVert Taylor, and John Dunne. The standard bearers are Ben Spaulding and Hilliard Caldwell. (*Al Amon*)

Demonstrators preparing for a street march. Albert Amon is at the extreme right. (*Jimmy Wallace*)

Hilliard Caldwell and a police officer during a march. (*Jimmy Wallace*)

were making, but that he became more and more concerned with their presence.

They were indicted for trespass, not singing, Mr. McKissick pointed out.

But they wouldn't leave when he told them to, Mr. Augustine pointed out. When they are in a place of business, they have to leave when they are told to.

Chief Blake took the stand next and said this was the very same bull horn. He said the singers had been asked to leave and hadn't done so, which caused him to tell the policemen to take them out. He said the singers had simply locked their arms tighter and had made no move to leave. When finally they were picked up, they went limp, but he said he knew very well they could all walk, for later he had seen them walk in the jail cells.

The state rested its case and Mr. McKissick moved for nonsuit. The jury left the room, and he discussed the state's case, saying that evidently Mr. Augustine's objection seemed to be the loud and bois-terous language, that there was no testimony that Mr. Augustine had talked with anybody except Pat Cusick, that there was no evidence that the defendants had entered upon the property after having been forbidden to do so, and that no conclusive evidence had been pre-sented that the foghorn or bull horn or whatever it was had been heard over the noise of the singing.

Judge Carr said he didn't see how Mr. Augustine could have called on each person individually to leave, when he couldn't be heard at all without the use of a bull horn. It would have been a "vain attempt," he said.

After lunch, when the court convened again, Judge Carr said that in spite of Mr. McKissick's argument there was cause for the jury to continue hearing the case. Mr. McKissick renewed his motion for nonsuit, which was denied.

Solicitor Cooper rose to speak and concluded his arguments. He said it was apparent to him, and he trusted to others, that the defend-ants had broken the law and had wanted to get arrested, that they were seeking publicity for their civil rights cause. He said that was their business, but that breaking the law did carry with it penalties. "Mr. McKissick will, I suppose, cite to you the example of the

118

Boston Tea Party," he said. He said that despite the fact that the trespassers at Boston that night were considered patriots, they nonetheless violated the law in that they stole the tea. "Christians have faced lions and gone to jail for publicity before. . . . It is admirable to make this sacrifice. . . . But where I disagree with them is where they come in and try to get out of it. I urge that they be given their right to be tried and found guilty so they can go on to other courts and get more publicity. I think they should be accommodated."

Mr. McKissick summarized his case by saying that he didn't think the solicitor had proved a violation of the trespass law. He said he had never advocated that a person break the law without paying the penalty, but that Joe Augustine had never said, "Do not come upon my property. I forbid you." Mr. McKissick read court opinions given in two other cases and discussed the differences in degrees of privacy represented by private homes and public businesses. "Public property is not the same kind of privacy," he said. He charged discrepancies in the warrants and repeated that Joe Augustine had never said, "You are on my property, get off," but had made the departure conditional on his request that they stop all their singing.

The jury retired and considered its verdict. After about forty minutes, they returned and said the defendants were guilty. Judge Carr gave the four defendants the maximum sentence possible under the Chapel Hill trespass ordinance: thirty days in jail or a fine of fifty dollars and court costs. The court costs amounted to $52.80 each.

Mr. McKissick rose once more to speak. "Mrs. Glover will pay the fine," he said. "She has a sick boy at home and she wants to go home and tend to him. Mr. Cusick and the two other women will go to jail."

There was quiet in the courtroom. "Well, all right then," the judge said after a long pause.

Following the sentencing, the Chapel Hill chapter of CORE issued a statement. It said the three people would serve the jail terms at the Christmas season "as a reminder of the continuing inhumanity tolerated with indifference in this town."

CORE then asked the other civil rights organizations to join with it in forming a coordinating organization, the Chapel Hill Freedom

Committee, to speak with a single voice for all of them. That week the new committee was formed, with John Dunne as chairman and Quinton Baker as vice-chairman. On the Freedom Committee were representatives of CORE, NAACP, SNCC, the Southern Christian Leadership Conference and SPU, each having equal representation. Several days later the Southern Conference Education Fund also joined.

The three young defendants were at first locked up in Hillsboro jail, which according to Pat Cusick is a dive, a stinking place with black mattresses, lice in the blankets and a jailor who goes by whims and extremes, being kind and considerate one minute and cantankerous the next. The two women were to stay there for the month's sentence, but Pat was taken off to the road camp in Durham County. Those who had been watching Pat closely for the past few days were aware of a nervousness which could be attributed to going off to prison, but actually was not due to that alone, for he had another idea in mind now.

The Durham Road Camp looks, in physical appearance, very much like Sandy Ridge Prison. That is, it has corner guardhouses, elevated from the ground and set outside a steel-fence and barbed-wire enclosure. Inside are the cell blocks and dining hall. At one corner is the guards' residence and office. The significant difference is that the camp is segregated. On arrival Pat told the captain he wanted to be transferred to an integrated camp, if there was one, or to a Negro camp. He said he believed that segregation was wrong and that he would not eat or work unless this were done.

The guards were a long way from being favorably impressed by this attitude. They gave him his blue prison suit and took him into the fenced enclosure. They walked him to a cell block where seventy-five other men were resting, and the guard announced: "Here's one of those nigger-loving sons of bitches. He says he's not going to eat or work, because he'd rather be with niggers than with you guys."

"To be perfectly honest, I was scared to death," Pat told me later. "One of the men told me that the guards had been working on the prisoners, that they would like to see something happen to me. He told me I would probably get killed during the night and advised me not to go to sleep. Well, believe you me, I didn't go to sleep. I pulled

my blanket up to my nose and I felt like burying my head under it.
My knees were literally shaking. But that night there was no physical
violence. Maybe what saved me from trouble was I had promised to
go on a hunger fast, and I think the prisoners wanted to see this done.
I had come to be a symbol of revolt against the prison."

The next morning they were all watching him when the time came
for breakfast. He made up his bed, then lay down on it, and when the
bell rang to go eat, he lay there. The guards came in. "Don't you hear
that, Cusick?" they said.

Pat said he heard it.

"Don't you want to eat?"

Pat said he did not.

"All right, nobody eats until you eat."

The seventy-five other prisoners froze in place, and there was a
long wait. Pat slowly got up from the cot and went to the door. He
walked across the prison yard to the mess hall and went inside.

An attendant gave him a metal tray and a spoon. Before him were
the serving benches. "What do I do?" he said.

"You just take your tray along that line."

Pat did so, but he took no food on his tray. He moved to one of the
wooden tables, aware that the other men were moving through the
line, getting their food. He set his tray down on the table, then sat
down with his back to the tray. He was through with breakfast, he
told the guard who questioned him.

Each meal was the same with him; he went through the line, took
his empty tray to his place at the table and sat down with his back to
it. This went on for two days, and every time he went through the
line, the other prisoners would watch him sullenly.

A major of the North Carolina Prison Department came to the
prison and held a hearing. He told Pat that he was sentenced to the
hole for the remainder of his prison term. He also told him he doubted
if he could change the whole State of North Carolina.

Pat was locked up in solitary confinement, in a bare cell, and he
lay there for days, headaches troubling him so much he could
scarcely stand to be awake and he could not sleep. He told himself he
was doubtless a fool, that he had certainly got himself into a corner
on this thing, for the prison guards were not going to relent and

neither was he. He wondered why he was willing to undergo such suffering. Was there inside him some need for punishment which dictated that he accept it? His notions about segregation had in high school been intellectual concepts; that had been true when he had picketed the College Café, too. At what point along the way since then had he gathered the convictions that now left him prone and weak and starving in a segregated prison?

There, in the utterly private room, imprisoned and longing to be fed and free, he contemplated the remarkable example of himself, a single being in revolt against the world, an Alabaman starving because of an issue that would have been repulsive to his ancestors and that would have been repulsive to him when as a child he first came to know what people were and believed. Yet by the God he no longer quite understood or formally accepted, he would not eat.

On the sixth day word came that he was to be transferred to the State Penitentiary in Raleigh for medical observation. He got to his feet, little caring now, not knowing what Raleigh would mean. He was too weak to wonder or acutely to be aware of thoughts of fear. He came out from the cell, and the guards said for him to go on down to the gate, and he started that way. He could see the gate, but he could not walk straight. He walked as best he could. He saw other prisoners watching him, their gazes intense and wondering. Once they had been antagonistic, but not now. They were impressed by the spectacle, more than anything else, and humbled by it.

"How many days?" Pat asked one of them.

"Six," the man said.

Chapter Nine

IN MAY I borrowed from Albert Amon of the university psychometric lab his scrapbooks of the civil rights activities in Chapel Hill. You would be amazed to see the stacks of material, but not very much of it consists of newspaper accounts of the action part of the story which happened about this time, the sit-ins. Evidently the Chapel Hill *Weekly* had imposed self-restraint on its efforts; it carried pleasant accounts of the fierce action, and no pictures, for pictures would have told of the desperateness of what was going on. One judges that the editor sent somebody down to the police station every day or two to see if he could learn from the police blotter what had been happening in Chapel Hill. The *News of Orange County* did about as well, which is to say it did no better.

Even living in Chapel Hill, spending about half my evenings at home during the period, I was unaware of the dangerous action going on all around me, and I'm sure, after talking with friends who live there, that they didn't know about it, either. One can read in a newspaper that so many people have been arrested, but it all goes by the board if the item seems to attach little excitement or significance to the event, or if the reader does not manage to capture any of the essence of the thing itself. It's silly to think we trust reporters to do our thinking for us, for most of the ones I've known aren't the type of people I would have think for me ordinarily; yet we do, or most of us do, and the general thought and temper of a town are often ordered by the general attitude the newspaper and other communications media suggest.

Only the student newspaper, which unfortunately because of the Christmas holidays was not published during much of this period, and which doesn't have a professional staff or much of a budget, and whose reporters and editors have to go to class and do homework as well as carry on their newspaper—only the *Daily Tar Heel* did a creditable job, and its work is so far superior to the other newspapers that it gives one greater respect for amateur effort. But most people in town don't read it, and didn't really know what was going on.

What was going on started modestly. On the night Pat Cusick was put into prison, a wave of visits to segregated restaurants was to start. Plans for these were made that afternoon at a meeting of the Freedom Committee. Three small teams were to go to three restaurants and seek service, leaving when asked by the police to do so. It happened that David McReynolds, a leading white liberal, who was an adviser of the SPU and frequently a writer for New York City's

Village Voice, was in Chapel Hill for speaking engagements, and John invited him to go with one of the integrated teams.

About seven o'clock this group drove out to the Pines. Present were David Dansby, twenty-four, a Negro, who was head of the campus chapter of the NAACP; Phyllis Timberlake, eighteen, a Negro girl who lived in Chapel Hill; John Dunne; and David McReynolds, who later described the occurrence for the readers of the *Village Voice:*

> We drove out to the Pines, Chapel Hill's only elegant eatery, and walked in. The hostess dashed over as soon as we got in the door and asked us to leave. Dunne didn't refuse, but he didn't leave. The manager, a Mr. Leroy Merritt, came on the scene. He exploded almost immediately: "We're segregated! Everybody in Chapel Hill knows we're segregated! You got to leave right now!" Dunne spoke quietly about how he had made a reservation by phone and hadn't been told Negroes wouldn't be served, and, pointing to me, said I was a visiting speaker and he had planned to have me out for dinner at the best place in town, and now he was terribly embarrassed, etc.
>
> All this time the moral elite of Chapel Hill continued to come into the restaurant, walk by, and sit down to their dinners. And all this time Mr. Leroy Merritt got redder in the face and kept yelling, "You gotta get out of here!" Then he called the police. They arrived almost at once, with poor Mr. Leroy by now almost inarticulate and on the verge of apoplexy. (One of the police went over to him and suggested he stop shouting.) The four of us were ushered out and, to our dismay, notified we would be arrested as soon as Mr. Leroy Merritt could get down to the station to sign the warrants. Would we be so kind as to come down to the station at 8 P.M. for arrest, by which time the warrants would be ready? Yes, we would.

John arranged bond for all four, then went to the police station, where the four of them waited until their bond, delivered by a singing group of demonstrators, was delivered. Then all of them went back to the CORE headquarters and sang songs and talked until 2 A.M. These were the first civil rights arrests made in the Chapel Hill–Durham –Raleigh area since fall.

On December 14, Saturday, Lou Calhoun led a contingent of two whites and two Negroes to Clarence's Beer Hall, where Clarence met them at the door and ordered them to stay out of his place of business. Lou Calhoun managed to get inside and, when Clarence grabbed him, went limp. Clarence called to some of his customers to help throw him out, and they did so. Lou hit the sidewalk with a thud and suffered bruises, but he was all right; he got up, shook himself, and the demonstrators went away.

Nearby at the Shack, which is another beer hall, four other demonstrators sat down in a booth. They ordered sodas. When the manager asked whether they were going to go outside to drink them, they replied that they would prefer to stay inside. He told them to leave, and when they didn't go, he walked up the street half a block to the police station. The group waited for a few minutes, then left, feeling dissatisfied about the whole affair.

At the same time, three people entered Leo's Restaurant and asked to be served. They were Rosemary Ezra, who is white, Karen Parker, a Negro junior at the university, and James Foushee. The hostess called the police. When the police arrived, the young people went limp, were dragged from the café and shoved into police cars. They were taken to the Chapel Hill jail.

On December 15 seventy people, forty of whom were Negroes, marched silently through Chapel Hill, some of them carrying signs which said, "Give Freedom for Christmas." That night twenty of them, of whom thirteen were Negroes, were briefed by Quinton at a local church on tactics, then were driven to Brady's Restaurant, where they asked to be served. Among them were Lou Calhoun, Quinton and two minors. Brady refused to seat them and phoned the police. All twenty demonstrators went limp and were dragged to the police cars.

Seven of these demonstrators were university students, and Dean of Men Bill Long and Dean of Women Katherine Carmichael came down to the jail to see what could be done. They told the university students that bail would be arranged for them on condition that they cease further trespass violations and further participation in the demonstrations, which only one of them would agree to do. The deans phoned the parents, and the parents pleaded with the other students, but to no avail. The students sat on the bunks and floors of their cells and sang freedom songs.

On December 16, Monday, the Mayor's Human Relations Committee asked several of the young leaders to meet with them. The

125   :   THE FREE MEN

young people assumed that the committee wanted to talk about the sit-ins, but Margaret Taylor, the chairman, says the meeting really was intended to decide what disposition to make of the cases remaining from the Merchants Association sit-in. John Dunne, Hilliard Caldwell, Peter Van Riper, Lou Calhoun and James Gardner left a mass meeting to attend the committee's meeting, leaving word that they doubt-less would return with an offer of some sort.

Mrs. Taylor says John that evening was "absolutely impossible, rude, brash and dirty." Henry Brandis, dean of the Law School, who is a member of the committee, says he found John to be "not at all rude, not in the sense of being boorish. I have never seen him come anywhere close to losing his temper, and he is very courteous, though rather adamant."

The meeting got off to a poor start when John, after finding out what the committee's purpose was, said that his group really ought to get back to their mass meeting. The committee told him, as Dean Brandis recalls, "that he could spend as much time as could we in examining the situation." The discussion then became involved with the current rash of sit-ins, and so far as Dean Brandis could deter-mine, "The demonstrators had no understanding of the consequences of organized lawbreaking. Without question, John Dunne was the real leader of the local group. Certainly the impression was that he could control what his group did. That was the supposition on which I was operating that evening."

Dean Brandis, using what some other members of the committee recall as forceful language, sought to discuss the implications of breaking the law. So far as he could tell, John's position was that unless the town gave in the sit-ins would continue.

"I tried to urge that the ballot and legislative processes had in no way been closed," Dean Brandis says, "that I realized they had not got the aldermen to do what they wanted, any more than I had got them to do what I wanted, but as long as the legislative processes were open, they had not been denied their fundamental rights. I urged them to consider the alternatives, which, though less dramatic, left the way open for peaceful change. All I could get out of John and his group were Martin Luther King's views, which I have always believed were wrong. They seemed to be saying that there are two kinds of lawbreaking, and that their kind was right and the other kind was wrong."

Dean Brandis himself is not a prejudiced man. In 1959 he resigned from the Chapel Hill School Board because it was not, in his view, working within the law as defined by the United States Supreme Court. He is personally hopeful that people will come someday "to realize that skin color comes without any merit or demerit." But he couldn't make his point with John Dunne, and this annoyed him. Perhaps he was further annoyed by recognizing in John the same sort of tendencies which he had had as a college student in Chapel Hill himself when he had spoken to a mass meeting in the auditorium and called for the ousting of the president of the university, and had edited a student publication called *The Yellow Sheet,* which he says resulted in his being expelled from school. Before him now stood another brilliant young person, as adamant as he had been, but now the young man was going quite beyond his own youthful position. John Dunne apparently was advocating the massive breaking of the laws of the community.

The Negroes are in the minority, Dean Brandis pointed out; the only hope they have is through legal processes. Unless they take up force of arms, a minority group must work through law, he said, or they will undermine their moral case, to say nothing of their legal case. John replied with the opinions of Gandhi, Jesus, Thoreau and the leaders of the nonviolent civil rights movement.

Other members of the committee also spoke that night, and John admits he was personally hurt by much of what was said. These were some of the most influential white and Negro liberals in the town, and much of what they had to say he interpreted as being an attack on him personally, attributing to him full control of the unrest in Chapel Hill and responsibility for it. Finally Professor T. Franklin Williams, a medical doctor at the university and chairman of the State Human Relations Committee, told John he would like to return with him and address the mass meeting. His offer was accepted.

At the church Dr. Williams was introduced, and he began explaining the nature of civic responsibility as he viewed it. Soon, John says, "nobody was listening except a few of us on the platform. The other demonstrators were talking among themselves or were idly studying the walls of the room. It became clear just how far removed from real understanding were the two liberal forces in the town."

That same night nine demonstrators, four of them Negroes, went to the Pines Restaurant and asked to be served. Mr. Merritt phoned the police and asked for protection. The demonstrators were arrested, among them Joseph Tieger, Duke CORE representative; Ben Spaulding of the University of North Carolina student body; and Father Clarence Parker, the eighty-year-old retired Episcopal rector, who was gingerly carried out by four officers. They asked him if he would mind walking, since he was old and they were worried about him.

"I can't do different from the others," he said.

"Well, can't you help us in some way?" an officer said.

"I can take a deep breath," Father Parker said quietly.

Also arrested at the Pines that night was Mrs. Kenneth Reckford. This was the first time a wife of a university professor had been arrested. It was in her and Professor Reckford's home that John Dunne was now living.

The next morning, a picture of one university coed being dragged on her belly across the concrete appeared in the student newspaper, much to Chief Blake's dismay. "Carry them," he ordered his weary patrolmen.

Next day, December 17, a Tuesday, thirty-two demonstrators went to Clarence's Beer Hall and asked to be served. When Chief Blake arrived, one of the Negro demonstrators was sitting at the bar asking for a beer, and Sally Gray, Clarence's wife, who helps run the place, was telling him, "I'll give it to you over the head."

Chief Blake said the demonstrator had been drinking, and it took four or five officers to pull him out of the place. "He wrapped his legs around the bar stool, and when we finally got him free and outside, we began to slip on the ice along the edges of the sidewalk and in the gutter. The boy's glasses fell off and broke, and J. V. Henry was out there exciting the crowd, saying we were inside beating people. I went back into the crowd and found John Dunne, and I said, 'John, are these the tactics you plan to use?' And he said no, that he didn't know what had gone wrong. Then he did what he could. That was the last and only time that demonstrator was allowed by the Freedom Committee to take part in a demonstration of this sort."

Chief Blake said his men tried to load all the demonstrators into the police cars, and the police were slipping all over each other. Meanwhile, the crowd was singing freedom songs.

Among those arrested were seven students from Duke University in Durham, a forty-one-year-old Negro housewife and one student from North Carolina State in Raleigh.

Chief Blake, baffled and beleaguered, reported that there was standing room only in the jail, and hardly that in one cell.

On December 18 the *Daily Tar Heel* called the activity "testimony to the failure of our town's political leaders to lead, whether through abdication or inability." They have "hemmed and hawed over the false issue of property rights vs. human rights, and have ended up doing nothing, which amounts to condoning the evil. As a result, humiliated Negroes and indignant whites have taken recourse to their only remaining weapon, the sit-in."

The newspaper carried an interview with leaders of the Freedom Committee. Quinton Baker said, "CURED encompasses all those who are willing to make certain contributions, but not go so far as to go to jail. The Freedom Committee's members are ready for anything." John Dunne said, "You might find a small element that feels we are stressing the wrong things now. That element is referred to as the 'white liberals.' There are very few Negroes, if any, included." Father Clarence Parker was quoted as saying, "It all goes into one basket. I'm behind anything subject to the principles upon which CORE is based." The Chapel Hill *Weekly*, which is only published on Wednesdays and Saturdays, came out loaded down with letters to the editor supporting the demonstrators.

That night, about 8:45, a group of demonstrators held a rally outside the Chapel Hill town hall, while at the same time six demonstrators went to Brady's and sat down on the floor, the only place available to them. They were arrested and carted off to jail. At the same time, eighteen demonstrators entered the Tar Heel Sandwich Shop and sat down at the counter and in the booths. Percy Quinlan asked them to leave, but they wanted to order sandwiches, they said. Percy phoned the police station. Now the demonstrators at the town hall moved up to stand in front of the restaurant and sang songs while two police cars arrived. When the full force of policemen had asssembled, the eighteen demonstrators left their seats and placed themselves in the aisle. Each was picked up and carted out, two policemen carrying each limp demonstrator.

On December 19, Thursday, the *Daily Tar Heel* said: "It must be nice for the Mayor and the Board of Aldermen to go home every night to a warm house while the underpaid Police Department has to pay the price for their default. . . . We are not sure what it will take, but if demonstrations will get the city fathers off their butts, then go to it." The co-editors of the paper, Gary Blanchard of Maine, who had served in the Navy and had lived for a while in the South, and David Ethridge, son of the Kentucky editor, Mark Ethridge, also took Solicitor Roy Cole to task for insisting on the trials which had given impetus to this whole affair. They dug out of the morgue the story that eighteen months before Roy Cole had disbanded the local Little League because a young Negro boy wouldn't resign from one of the baseball teams.

That afternoon at five-thirty, in perfect precision, fourteen young people went to Leo's Restaurant for dinner. Leo barred the door, so they sat down on the sidewalk, where they were arrested.

That night at nine-thirty at the Tar Heel Sandwich Shop, a mass of freedom singers raised their voices while seventeen of their silent peers went inside to be seated. The doors were barred and locked, so the students sat down on the sidewalk, and sang "We Shall Not Be Moved," while a smaller group of UNC students tried to sing "Dixie." An instant pang of tension shot through everything when a Negro boy of eighteen was kicked in the head; other Negroes were kicked by white men. The Negro boy was driven to the university hospital, seventeen demonstrators were arrested, and the police went looking for the white attackers. A house painter and an off-duty Hillsboro policeman were later charged by Lieutenant Graham Creel with assault.

On December 20, Friday, a crowd again assembled outside the Tar Heel Sandwich Shop. Ten, including John Dunne and Lou Calhoun, were arrested for obstructing the sidewalk and were taken to jail, while seventy other demonstrators stood on the sidewalk and sang freedom songs.

In this week leading up to the university Christmas holidays, 123 people had been arrested.

Next day, on December 21, Saturday, the Raleigh *News and Observer,* edited by Jonathan Daniels, took notice of the stormy Chapel Hill situation and concluded: "The owners of private facilities which hold themselves open to the public, and police who support them could damage the town if they failed to deal with the situation in the University community with less than real university enlightenment."

There were other editorials and letters to the editor in various papers. One was from Professor Reckford:

It is hard to explain to my young children why their mother spent a night in jail—and may feel obligated to go again. They thought, poor things, that only "bad people" went to jail. I wish to teach them to respect and even love the law, as I do, and to know, as I know, that without law and order no real personal freedom would be possible. I appeal to all the owners of still segregated businesses to choose, without compulsion, to help me in this process of education.

Charlotte Adams wrote, sharing with the public a statement of the late President Kennedy: "The true democracy [has faith] that the people will not condemn those whose devotion to principle leads them to unpopular courses, but will reward courage, respect honor and ultimately recognize right." Hilliard Caldwell, who had been a Negro leader of CURED and the COB, wrote expressing extreme dissatisfaction with the mayor and closed with this pledge:

We shall win our rights; God is on our side; we shall walk hand in hand; Black and White together; we shall not be moved; we will go to jail for our freedom; we will spend thirty days on the chain-gang for our freedom; the only thing that we did wrong was to let segregation stand so long. We ain't going to let Mayor, Board of Aldermen, or anyone stand in our way. We shall overcome and win our fight.

On Sunday afternoon, December 22, a prayer march was led by Father Parker from one of the Negro churches to the jail. That evening seventeen demonstrators sat in at Brady's Restaurant and were arrested. Eight of them were visitors to Chapel Hill from Sanford, North Carolina, where racial strife had recently broken out.

Next day, December 23, Monday, four demonstrators sat in at the

University Motel. When the police arrived, the four people were sitting quietly in the motel lobby. They were arrested.

On the twenty-fourth, the day before Christmas, the Freedom Committee called a stop to all demonstrations until after Christmas, to allow the policemen to spend Christmas Day with their families. A total of 150 people had, since Pat Cusick entered prison, been arrested. Eleven were still in jail and elected to see Christmas from behind bars. For their reading hours they had such sprightly material as Alderman Giduz' newspaper, the *News of Orange County:*

It is probable that by this time, even the misguided youths who have been nightly violating the law with acts of civil disobedience realize that they cannot reasonably expect to attain success for their goal in Chapel Hill by either their acts or examples.

If this realization has not yet become apparent, it will, through all of the agony and bitter frustration that will so unfortunately envelop them and their cause.

But although the responsible citizenry of this community disdains the unsanctionable acts of this group, Chapel Hill cannot question the fact that racial discrimination does exist in this supposedly enlightened town, and that it cannot simply be wished away.

In New York City the *Village Voice* was publishing its opinion, or at least the opinion of David McReynolds:

Chapel Hill is smug and self-righteous and so proud of the past that it has not really kept pace with the current situation. It has been so willing to live on the moral capital of men like Odum and Graham that it is now fearfully close to being morally bankrupt.

He closed his essay with the comment that "One also knows that towns and cities and whole cultures are changed, transformed, and saved through the willingness of the few to suffer and to endure."

Lou Calhoun spent Christmas in Chapel Hill. He slept late. He wondered how his father and stepmother in Shelby were spending the day. He had sent them gifts, and they had sent him gifts, but there was much antagonism between them now because of the sit-ins and jailings.

Lou tells me he had intended to stay out of the civil rights activities this year. He came back to school in September, registered for his courses and took a job working thirty hours a week at Harry's. He was a member of the Wesley Foundation still, and he had accepted the chairmanship of the SPU. Those activities were enough to keep him occupied, he knew, and his chief hope was to make good grades. By Thanksgiving the job in the restaurant had interfered with his schoolwork to such a degree that he stopped most of the work there and borrowed money from the bank to pay his bills. It was his senior year, and he had planned to do well.

When Pat Cusick went to prison, however, he couldn't see himself doing so little for the cause, in which he believed as strongly as did Pat, so he accepted John Dunne's invitation to attend a meeting at the CORE headquarters on December 13. There he agreed to be an active member of the new Chapel Hill Freedom Committee and to take charge of obtaining the use of churches for meetings and, since he had access to a mimeograph machine, of publicity.

He had not been scheduled to take part in sit-ins, but he had gone to watch the one at Leo's, with the idea that if the demonstrators got into trouble, he might be of help to them. He was surprised to see about fifteen other people there with the same idea, and he tried to shoo the younger ones off. They retreated half a block and watched fearfully from behind parked cars, he says. The next Sunday night, he went out on a sit-in himself and for the first time in his life ended up in jail. He spent the night there, and when he got back to his apartment the next day, his phone was ringing. It was his father calling, disturbed and bewildered. The night before, Dean Long had phoned to tell him about Lou's arrest. Later in the night he had received a telegram from Dean Long, which he didn't appreciate for he said a telegram simply informed others in the small town that his son had been arrested. "Why did he want to let everybody in Shelby know it?"

Lou, of course, had no information on that score. He did regret his father's dismay, however, and for the first time he realized his arrest had put his father in a disadvantageous position in Shelby, where he worked for the town government. His father drove to Chapel Hill and told Lou to come home or get out of the movement.

"It was the first time since I'd been in college he had told me I'd have to do this or I'd have to do that," Lou says. "I'm sure he realizes now, and I think he knew then, that this wasn't a fair thing to say. I told him I wouldn't leave. I told him I understood his anxiety, but that the people of Shelby would have to come to terms with the situation, that I was working as my own agent."

Lou's father went home unsatisfied, and for the first time in his life Lou spent Christmas away from home.

Charles Thompson, also a student at the university, went home for Christmas. His mother says she waited for him with a speech she had pretty well rehearsed in her mind. She wanted to explain to him what it meant to his parents to get a call at midnight from an official of the university telling of his arrest, and all because of some Negro trouble or other. She had not known what to say to the university man, who stated he neither condemned nor condoned the action, but did feel that she would want to know. She did, indeed, and she went back to the bedroom and told Charles' father that his son was imprisoned. Neither of them knew what to think or do.

She had known about the Negro unrest in Greensboro, where she lived; she had heard about the demonstrations there, and she had vaguely followed news accounts, which were sparse and lean, about Chapel Hill having trouble, but what had any of it to do with her son Charles? He was not a Negro. He could eat wherever he pleased, go wherever he pleased. She was a liberal and so was Charles' father; but sitting in, marching, picketing, boycotting all appeared to be sensational and dramatic, with the singing, clapping, chanting and praying in the streets. It was not at all dignified. Why should Charles get involved in a mess like that?

That very night she had phoned the Chapel Hill Police Department and asked how Charles could be got out of jail. They said he needed $175 bail, part for trespassing and part for going limp, which technically they called resisting arrest. "Well, I will pay that," she said. She didn't know how to put up bail for anybody; nobody she knew had ever gone to jail. "He won't accept the bail, ma'am," the desk sergeant said.

"Won't accept bail? Wants to stay in jail?" It was so foreign to her. "Well, is the cell warm?" she asked, and then asked all sorts of questions which she knew the sergeant must have thought were perfectly silly, but they were matters which worried her. "I even asked him if Charles had a pillow," she said.

So when Charles arrived home for Christmas she was ready to talk to him, all right. "I wanted to tell him to pursue his studies and forget the cause. To educate a son is an expensive process and we just cannot finance 'the cause.' I wanted to tell him he would lose friends by participating in the movement. I wanted to tell him he should take the middle of the road as we have done.

"But when it came time I couldn't say anything.

"I was very sad and very proud. And I thought maybe I am just beginning to understand."

Charliese Cotton spent the day at home, in her mother's concrete-block house in one of the poorer Negro neighborhoods. She listened to her sisters scream and holler, and she worried most about having left the Hillsboro jail. She had planned to stay in jail thirty days, as Mrs. Van Riper and Pat Cusick were doing, but the jail got on her nerves, with all those metal parts clanging and Jailor Jack creeping about. She didn't have any trouble with him, except that one night she had been awakened by a woman crying out in the jail somewhere: "Help me, help me, help me." The woman had cried as piteously as a caught hen. "I've been in here for two months and haven't had a drop of water to drink."

Charliese and Mrs. Van Riper were out of bed at once and shaking their jail doors. "Who are you?" they yelled back.

"I'm an old lady, and they won't give me any water, and I'm dying in here."

It was a chill to end her life almost, Charliese said. It went through her bones and blood vessels, and she got into bed and pulled the covers up over her head, while Mrs. Van Riper yelled for the jailer, but he wouldn't answer her.

The next day they told him about it, and he said there was no woman in the place except them, and to forget it.

The next night, the old lady yelled out again, and Charliese just pulled the blanket over her head and clamped her hands over her ears, but even so she could hear the horrible voice begging for water. Mrs. Van Riper was beside herself with fear and wonder.

"We did hear that woman again last night," Charliese told Jailor

Jack the next morning. He shook his head. "Prisoners sometimes hear strange sounds," he said and gave them their breakfast, which was always served in an ice cube tray, one slim enough to pass through the bars.

That day it happened again. They heard the old lady beg for water, and this time Charliese caught a glimpse of a man's shoe and part of his leg as he went out of a corner cell nearby and down the steps. So when Jailor Jack came upstairs with their supper, she said, "Did you make that noise like that old woman?"

"I told you there weren't no old woman," he said.

"I know there's not," Charliese said.

It was things like that that had done it to her, made her want to get out of there.

And Jailor Jack saying a man had hanged himself in the cell she was using and unless she stopped singing and talking so much that the man's ghost would take care of her. Charliese believes in ghosts, and she did her best to keep as quiet as she could after that.

She had finally said she wanted to leave the jail, and the Freedom Committee had paid her fine and court costs and she went on home, where she spent Christmas.

She felt John Dunne and Quinton were not entirely pleased with her. But what did they know about jailors and being a woman, being afraid in a cell, and not having any sanitary napkins or rags or anything in there, and the jailor not being willing to bring her any, and the coldness of the place, and being cooped up, away from everybody else and from all the loud singing.

She had rather be home at Christmas.

Quinton and John Dunne spent most of Christmas Day in staff meetings and visiting the Chapel Hill jail, where they took a Christmas tree and a pineapple cake Quinton had baked. At four-thirty they drove to Durham, borrowing Rosemary Ezra's car, and had dinner with Floyd McKissick, in his large house, which is always full of people—sometimes as many as ten or fifteen relatives and civil rights workers spending the night there. He has a son and three daughters; every one of the children has integrated a different Durham school. The family has lived on the front line of the civil rights movement for more than ten years. Partly as a consequence they have a warm dedication to each other and to others, such as Quinton and John, who participate with them.

They spent the evening talking and laughing together. They listened to a recording of the SNCC Freedom Singers singing freedom songs, which to them seemed somehow as appropriate as carols at this particular Christmas season. They talked about a gift of $200 to the Chapel Hill Police Department, made anonymously by two members of the Freedom Committee, a university professor and his wife, and about the way people who find themselves at opposite ends of an issue can still remain friends, even in the midst of general antagonism.

Dinner in the Chapel Hill jail was brought to the prisoners by Mrs. Leigh Gall, Mrs. Carter Williams, the wife of Dr. T. Franklin Williams, and others. The prisoners had learned, on being locked up, that the jail food was prepared by Leo's Restaurant, which they found particularly amusing. None of them, as a matter of principle, would eat it, and the Police Department tried to find another restaurant, an integrated restaurant, to supply food for them. The integrated restaurants weren't interested in the jail's contract, however, so the Freedom Committee had the Chicken Box Number Two serve the prisoners each day, until its money gave out. Then Mrs. Gall organized a group of women who brought better meals to the jail than the students had been eating when they were free.

There was a good deal of singing that day in the jail. Both Christmas carols and freedom songs were rehearsed in loud voices. And there was much talk about both civil rights and Christmas. Somebody said he wondered if Christ would have been a demonstrator if he had been alive in Chapel Hill, and most of them thought so. Somebody else said, "Why aren't there more ministers in the jail?" And nobody knew how to answer the question or why it had been asked, except that Christmas had arrived and they were trying to relate it to Chapel Hill and what was going on these days in the town.

Pat Cusick lay in his cell in the penitentiary in Raleigh, in the massive stone building which had been made by convicts and which had walls many feet thick and armed guards looking down at the compounds. There were row on row of cells, layer on layer of cells.

He had not eaten since December 13—twelve days now. He had been ordered to eat, he had been requested to eat, he had been presented with food many times, and he had always turned it down. Twice he had been hauled up before the head of the State Prison Department, George Randall, who had told him that there was no place to send him. Pat Cusick held firm to his own views. The prison director sent him back to spend Christmas in the same cell, to think it over and report his decision.

Pat had one cellmate, a Southerner who had a single big hope in life: that General Walker would lead an armed revolt and free the South of all liberal influences. Pat lay on his bunk, listening to him talk about niggers, niggers, niggers, which was all he ever talked about.

A man walked swiftly along the line of cells, tossing two envelopes into each one, looking neither to the right nor left as he hurried by. "Who's that?" Pat asked.

"The chaplain," his cellmate said.

Pat opened one of the envelopes. Inside was a Christmas card.

A guard came to the cell. "Cusick, you want to eat?" he asked.

"Want to eat," Pat thought. "Yes, I want to eat."

"Christmas dinner's not bad here," the guard said. "You want to eat?"

"I want to eat more than anything," Pat thought.

He lay there listening to the cell doors open and close, clanking all down the long row, as men went to eat. But he ate nothing.

"Where are you, John Dunne?" he thought. "Quinton, where are you? James Foushee, are you out of jail? What are you doing?"

He lay in jail praying, but he realized it wasn't to the God he used to believe in and he didn't know to which God it was.

"How far are you going, Cusick?" he thought. "Will you go through with this thing if it kills you?"

He began to write. He addressed a letter to George Randall, Director of Prisons. He would set down his answer to the question Randall wanted answered.

In my previous letter I stated the reasons for my hunger fast and refusal to work. I, too, am a believer in law. A society without law is anarchy. However, I believe that it is sometimes necessary to break a law for a higher good. . . .

I think that I understand and appreciate your position, although I have a divergent position. You by nature of your position must act for the best interests of the State of North Carolina, for the Prison Department and the goals which you have for that department. . . . I appreciate the validity of your point that if one man accomplished his desire by pressure, then a precedent would be set for others, of whatever motive, to do likewise. However, in the final analysis there is a difference, and, to my mind, a vast one. Our society functions in this manner. However, the goals or motives of the person are judged in accordance with whether or not they are in line with the good of the State. Obviously, a desire of a Black Muslim would be rejected on this ground. Hence I must continue my fast (today is the 12th in which I have only taken water) and refusal to work—and repeat my request that I be transferred to (1) a Negro work camp or (2) an integrated prison. . . . I must apologize for this letter—ordinarily I am more lucid than this. . . . If I am not transferred, I would like to talk with Rev. Finlator.

He dated the letter December 25, 1963, signed it and gave it to a guard.

Bob Brown spent Christmas in his apartment. Katherine Strong and a few others who worked on the magazine came by, and they ate what little bit of dinner they could get together. None of them had any money to speak of. Bob had not been part of the sit-ins, but he had decided the hero of them all was Father Clarence Parker, who had gone limp in a highly professional manner at the Pines. In the course of action, however, somebody had stolen his overcoat and hat. Father Parker wouldn't bring any charges against anybody, contending that perhaps the thief needed them worse than he.

A few days later Bob had seen Father Parker at the A & P food store, where he and his wife were shopping. "I couldn't believe my eyes to see what he was wearing," he told Kathy. "He had on a coat, a woman's coat, which fanned out just below the armpits, one that had great big buttons on the front. It had three big buttons, and he was standing there in the A & P in that thing. It was astonishing, it was wild. And I said 'Hello, Father,' and he said hello and blessed me and so forth, and I couldn't stop looking at that woman's coat. It was the most outrageous getup I ever saw."

Chief Blake spent his Christmas Day working on the series of problems, many of them involving personnel, which the demonstrations had caused. He would invite an officer to come for a ride with him; he would drive out into the country and go up and down the back roads, away from telephones and interruptions, and talk about how much the town needed the service the police were now providing, and how important it was for each officer to conduct himself in the best manner, in keeping with the excellent reputation of Chapel Hill.

Lieutenant Graham Creel talked with the men, too, urging competent, nonviolent enforcement of the law. A friend of mine who dropped by the town hall during the Christmas season says he saw Lieutenant Creel in an office poring over the police books, and heard him unconsciously humming "We Shall Overcome."

Chapter Ten

THE CHAPEL HILL *Weekly,* which had held its own counsel about the matter since the restaurant sit-ins began, printed on December 29 an editorial titled "If a Meaningful Victory Ever Comes, It Must Be Won in Our Hearts."

"Trampling on another's rights, even when hungering for your own, isn't the way to do it," it said.

I have a copy of the piece here before me, and it all reminds me for some reason that *Weekly* publisher Orville Campbell also prints and records popular songs. He recorded "All the Way, Choo Choo," the theme song for the university's star quarterback, Charlie Justice. Orville also recorded a reading record; he found a young man named Andy Griffith, who was entertaining civic clubs with a program titled "What It Was Was Football." Andy recorded it for Orville. Orville had other successes. He had a knack for the popular vernacular, and every now and then his songs, which he recorded with local artists in Chapel Hill, would appear on the best-seller lists. At one time he was running quite a large local operation and, like many other business-men, he began encountering unions and their rules and the pay demands of musicians, much of which is likely to be annoying to a person who feels that a businessman ought to be allowed to run his own business in his own way.

In addition to the criticism of the *Weekly,* the Mayor's Human Relations Committee met and said it deplored the activities of people "moved by the ardor of youth." Considering these two post-Christmas reports, it's apparent that the business community had used the Christmas respite to take inventory and that they felt secure enough to close up battle lines again, that the town had decided not to surrender its customary prerogative to the revolutionary forces operating from the vicinity of the Chicken Box Number Two.

The demonstrators, therefore, had no choice but to continue or else admit defeat and accept humiliation. A young people's group will rarely admit defeat, so they were, of course, destined to continue. They began to make ready for their next major effort by urging members to find professors at Duke and the university in Chapel Hill who would take part in the sit-ins, realizing that so long as young people were protesting pretty much alone the authorities would try to ignore them. In their new series of sit-ins they would use more mature people whenever they could. This second series of actions was to begin on Sunday, December 29, and on the same day there was to be a meeting at the uptown Episcopal Church to discuss the problems of segregation. John, who at this point had little confidence in being listened to, and who was deeply hurt by the white liberal criticism of him, was invited to speak. He accepted and asked that Quinton Baker be invited, too, since no Negro was scheduled to appear.

About 250 people attended, and there was a lively discussion of the issues and the need for a public accommodations ordinance. Alderman Giduz took note of this and said, "The people of this community are rightly concerned about a matter that's been before them for six months. They deserve a reply at this time, inasmuch as certainly adequate facts will be at hand by this next meeting. I'm perfectly willing at this time and with the assumption that we will be able to have the report that we've requested by then—I would like to get the advice we've asked for before reaching a final decision, but assuming that we have that, I'd be perfectly willing to discuss it and to reach a decision at this time."

The report he referred to was being prepared by the University Institute of Government for the Board of Aldermen, to advise them as to whether they had authority to pass a public accommodations ordinance. The meeting he referred to was the next meeting of the Board of Aldermen, which was to be held early in January.

At the point where the newspapers and other responsible community agencies turn bitterly against a group, real danger sets in for members of the group who continue to oppose the public will. It was now evident that the demonstrators had been rejected sternly by the community, that maltreating them would not result in public scorn or retaliation. The demonstrators had become fair game, and their pledge of nonviolence plus their intention not to bring charges against assailants opened up this danger all the way.

During the next week or so, they visited some of the old standby places—the Colonial Drug Store and the Pines, where they were not assaulted. However, they also decided to visit a few places they had not gone to previously, both inside and outside the town limits. One of them was a segregated grocery store. Six demonstrators went out there one evening, and returned with the report that the manager had thrown Clorox and ammonia on them. Fifteen young people at once volunteered to go back on the next day. John Dunne, Quinton Baker and Lou Calhoun were to lead the party, which they divided into two parts. The three leaders and three others would go into the store first; the second group would arrive ten minutes later and, if there was trouble inside, they would come in and accept their share of it.

When the six members of the first team entered the grocery store that evening, Quinton picked up a box of cookies and said to the manager, who was the only person tending the store, "I'd like to buy this box of cookies." He hoped, as he admitted later, that the manager would say okay and then everybody could leave. Most of them, they admit now, were scared to death.

The manager, as they remember, said, "I don't serve niggers, and that goes for white niggers, too, so all of you get out of here."

They didn't leave. The manager then said, as they recall, "Well, I guess I'll have to take care of you. I'll have to sweep the floor down." He got a broom and began to make threatening gestures at the six of them, but still they didn't leave. "I'll have to mop the floor, I guess," he said. He got a mop and filled a mop bucket. The six said "Uh-oh," and sat down on the floor, preparing for the ordeal ahead.

"I don't know what the concentration of ammonia in the bucket was," Lou Calhoun told me later, "but it was enough to keep me from breathing." The manager brought the bucket and mop to the nearest of the six demonstrators. He soaked the mop in the bucket, then placed it on the demonstrator's head and squeezed, pushing it down. Then he got another mopload, put it on a demonstrator's head and squeezed. He moved the bucket from time to time.

Evidently one of the six bolted for the door after the first round and tried to hold it open to let out the fumes. The manager got rid of him and locked the door. This meant that the nine young people scheduled to arrive any minute couldn't get in, and that the five people inside might have trouble getting out.

The manager filled up the mop and went to the next demonstrator, put the mop on his head, pushed down and squeezed. The ammonia-laden liquid flowed into the boy's hair and down his face and body.

Two other demonstrators couldn't take any more of this and, coughing and gagging, sought the door. The manager went to the door, unlocked it, let them out, then locked the door after them. He came back and looked down at the three remaining demonstrators. They were John Dunne, Quinton Baker and Lou Calhoun.

He moved the bucket nearer, striking John Dunne on the head with it, and began to mop their heads as before.

"The ammonia water was flowing all over us," Lou says. "I kept my face down in the sleeve of my coat, and I suspect the others did, too, and as long as you keep your nose buried, it doesn't choke you. You think you can't breathe. You think you're not getting enough air to live, but you are. But after fifteen minutes, it got a little bit worse. Finally it was so bad, I came out of my sleeve to see what was up, and when I looked up, Quinton looked up, and we both got licked right across the face with the mop, and this is very bad. Once you ever open up, once you ever look up to take a breath, you're in bad."

John Dunne looked up at one point, he says, and saw the manager pouring ammonia directly from the bottle onto Lou, and saw him tilt Quinton's head back and pour ammonia into Quinton's mouth, so that it ran down his throat.

Lou and Quinton got up and started for the door. They assumed John Dunne was behind them. The manager opened the door and they fell outside. As they tried to fill their lungs with fresh air, they saw that John Dunne hadn't moved, that he was still sitting on the floor inside. "When we realized John was still in there, I would have given that much of my arm to be back inside," Lou says.

John at one point did start for the door, he says. He characterizes this as "a moment of real weakness." But he heard the manager say, "Oh, so you've had enough, have you?" Something snapped inside him, he says, and he sat back down on the floor.

John says the manager began to pour ammonia from the bottle all over his body; he pulled out the top of John's pants, stuck the neck of the bottle in under the belt and let the ammonia flow over him. He poured it under his shirt and into his hair, John says, poured it all over him until he was soaked and his skin was burning. When that didn't cause him to flee, the manager got out a baseball bat. "I thought it was curtains for me," John says. "I really gave up the ghost when I saw him. I have never been so happy to see Chief Blake arrive as I was that night."

When Chief Blake came inside, John got up and went to the counter where the cash register was and sat down on the floor. Chief Blake asked him to get up and get out of the place. Chief Blake was bothered by the ammonia, and so were his men. "I wished he would leave," Chief Blake says. "But he wouldn't."

The six young people who had been doused with ammonia were taken to the hospital for treatment and to have their eyes checked. Quinton had his stomach pumped and was treated for first-degree burns. John was treated for second-degree burns. All six demonstrators were arrested, along with twelve others who sat down in front of the door of the grocery store, for trespass and resisting arrest.

Roland Giduz in the *News of Orange County* published another editorial criticizing the demonstrators. "They've proved unworthy," he said, and referred to their efforts the previous Sunday when, at the meeting at the church, John Dunne and Quinton Baker had "sanctimoniously defended their disruptive and harmful acts of violating laws they happen not to like," while their group was holding a sit-in at the Pines. "Incongruously, thus, while the Chapel Hill Police Chief, among others, sat at the same table with them in what was supposed to be a serious effort to work toward justice for all through orderly and lawful channels, they 'struck' again."

The demonstrators, even in the face of severe public condemnation, continued their demonstrations. On one night, Lou Calhoun and a group of demonstrators went to a segregated restaurant, one they had not previously visited; he and two Negro girls got inside the place before the doors were locked. A woman told them to leave, but they did not. Lou says she grabbed him and began to kick him.

"She was wearing tennis shoes, so she wasn't doing any harm," he says. "I balled up on the floor. Then I felt this stream coming down on me, and I thought, 'God, she's got ammonia.' I was holding my breath, trying to keep from breathing, and then she stopped, laughed and said, 'Anybody that'd let somebody piss on them.'"

The girls got up and went outside and sat down on the ground. "They were both high school sophomores or juniors, and they were very frightened," Lou told me. "Of course," he said, "it's a traumatic experience, I suppose, watching your spokesman and leader get urinated on."

Lou was dragged outside, and he and the other protestors formed a group of six sitting in the parking lot. He remembers thinking that surely he could not in his old age reflect on this experience without humor, yet he found precious little humor in it tonight. How far were the mighty fallen, he thought, publicly humiliated by a woman who straddled him in a public place. If his father and the people of Shelby had been concerned about his first arrest, they would really get excited about this. He had not, so far as he could recall, heard of anybody being urinated on in the civil rights movement before, anywhere in the country. "Freedom, freedom," he thought, wondering how he was going to explain this to John and Quinton.

"Water boy," he thought. "What a sacrifice, Lou," he told himself, "what a real personal sacrifice, to make for the movement. How low have the Golden Gloves champions fallen?"

He sat there on the stones on the cold ground and watched the police officers arrive. Chief Blake was one of them. He says a demonstrator told him a woman had urinated on Lou, and he says he and the other officer who carried Lou to the patrol car smelled urine and commented on it. All the demonstrators were arrested.

On January 3, a group of professors from Duke and the University of North Carolina decided to sit in, along with the young people. Five Duke professors and two University of North Carolina professors volunteered, and four young people, including John Dunne and Quinton Baker, were to accompany them. The group met in the Freedom Committee's office and listened to Lou Calhoun explain about his experience. They were much amused, but the incident had a macabre quality, too. It was perfectly apparent to them, as it was to Lou, that the reception would be different wherever this group went, for the men were mature, they were obviously educated, they were well dressed and eminently presentable; they could doubtless eat anywhere in the country.

"Well, where shall we go?" somebody asked.

"Watts Grill," somebody suggested, naming a nearby restaurant run by Mr. and Mrs. Austin Watts. The formal name of the place is Watts Motel and Restaurant.

Those from Duke were Peter Klopfer, a zoologist, David Smith, a mathematician, and three members of the Duke religion department, all ministers, Frederick Herzog, Robert Osborn and Harman Smith, a native of Mississippi. The University of North Carolina professors were William Wynn and Albert Amon, both of the psychology department. Professor Amon had been at all the demonstrations and had become accepted as the semiofficial photographer for the Freedom Committee. He had never been arrested. He had wanted to be arrested, he had tried to be arrested, but thus far Chief Blake had managed to pass him by, perhaps out of a sense of respect for his position in the university.

He was a small, kind, nervous man, rather sickly, and he frequently reported to the others that he would probably die soon, which was assumed to be another of his peculiar characteristics. He was admittedly a brilliant, almost a quaint person, whose presence earlier at the Raleigh demonstrations had stirred up the ire of some of the legislators at the Sir Walter Hotel; they had bombarded him with criticism and the next day had bombarded the university administration. Since then Professor Amon had persisted in the civil rights cause. He claimed that the intellectual in America ought to champion minority views, ought to be different from the standard society, and he said his chief fear was that the American intellectual was being made comfortable in an unfinished world. Tonight, at Watts Motel, he was determined to be arrested.

Quinton Baker, as was customary, dispatched the lead car. For the past few weeks, the police had been watching to see which direction the demonstrators would take. As a consequence, the demonstrators had sometimes found the doors locked before they arrived, or they had found the police there before they had a chance to present their requests to the owners. They had therefore started sending out decoy cars, so that the police couldn't very well know where they were going.

When the police spotters had dispersed, following the wrong car, John and the distinguished group went downstairs to two other cars and drove to Watts Motel. Lou Calhoun, who had been made spotter, took a third car. A spotter was usually sent to a sit-in, and if he saw that the demonstrators were in trouble and nobody had phoned the police, he phoned them himself. Lou said when he got to Watts he found that several others who had been at the CORE office were there, too, all watching as the two main cars stopped at the door.

The happenings of this night were later testified to during a trespass trial in Superior Court in Hillsboro, North Carolina, and both the version told by some of the demonstrators and that told by Mr. Austin Watts are quoted here from the court record.

Professor Albert Amon testified:

"We arrived in front of the two sets of swinging glass doors. As we got up, Mrs. Watts and a waitress were standing behind these doors, so in order to get in the restaurant we would have had to push past them. In order to be heard, I reached out and pulled. The doors swung both ways. I pulled one of them towards me and said, 'May we come in?'

And then in the background . . . someone in a chuckling voice said, 'Yes, let him come in.' Then he, Mr. Watts, reached past the waitress, took me by the coat, which is this coat, except I have new buttons on it. I lost the other ones that night. And pulled me forcibly into the restaurant. Then I stood for about twenty to thirty seconds, I would say, while they momentarily redirected their attention to those who were standing outside. Then they turned on me and Mr. Watts and Mr. Scott hit me. I fell to the floor, crawling around the inside glass door in such a fashion that my head was in the angle and thereby protected from their kicking as much as possible. Before I was able to do this, however, I received five blows, kicks to the head which were large enough to be medically detectable, three of which were severe, one of which opened my hair in a 3½ inch patch on the back of my head. I blacked out momentarily twice, then I got into the crevice of the door and in this way was somewhat protected, although my back, neck and genitals were targets for kicks. Mrs. Watts disappeared momentarily . . . and came back with a broom, then two people came in, first John Dunne, then Quinton Baker, not forcibly because no one was paying any attention to them, but walked in and fell on my body and received severe blows themselves. Shortly thereafter, meanwhile, spectators were saying 'Kill them, get the professors,' this kind of thing. Then we were lifted and thrown out, flying through the air, landing on top of the seated professors on the outside. While we were out there, we continued to be beaten with a broom and someone said, 'Get the fire hose.' There was no fire hose, but someone did get a garden hose, and it was a cold night and they used it quite effectively, aiming at mouths to stop breathing. . . . And several obscene statements were made as to where they suggested the water hose [was] being shoved. Eventually the police came and John Dunne said, 'Take care of that man, he is hurt badly,' and this was a surprise to me; previously I had thought I was well off. I was still conscious. But he said, 'He is bleeding from the back of his head.' This worried me even more. I had not been able to get my hand to the back of my head to check this, so I was taken to a waiting squad car."

Another witness from among the demonstrators was Harmon Lee Smith, assistant to the dean and assistant professor of Christian ethics at the School of Divinity of Duke University. Dr. Smith said:

"Dr. Amon pulled the door out, whereupon he was dragged into this little foyer between the two doors. He was immediately struck by Mr. Watts and fell to the floor, and was subsequently kicked and beaten by Mr. Watts and another man and Mrs. Watts, who were in the foyer together, and at this point John Dunne and Quinton Baker moved through the outer double doors into the foyer and fell upon Amon's body, and I sat down, as did others in the group outside the restaurant; that is, none of the others of us ever crossed the threshold of this place. I was pushed off to the right . . . the door pushed me over, somewhat isolated me from the main group. From this point on we were abused orally and physically, we were beaten with a broom, first with the sweeping end then with the handle, we were kicked—to my knowledge none of us was beaten [with fists] outside the restaurant. And we were very thoroughly hosed down by one of the waitresses with a garden hose, and we endured this—what shall I call it?—abuse for approximately 15 to 20 minutes, and then cars from the Sheriff's office and Chapel Hill police department came and we were taken away."

The description of the incident as given in the courtroom by Mr. Austin Watts is different from that of the demonstrators. Mr. Watts said that on the evening in question he had seen the demonstrators come to his restaurant. "I was behind the counter in the restaurant. I have two swinging doors that you come in, and there are two more about eight feet from it. I was behind the counter and there was a whole bunch of people swung both doors open and run in, and I seen them push my wife against the wall; they come on inside, and in front of the cash register they started laying down."

The solicitor, who serves as prosecutor in North Carolina Superior Courts, interrogated Mr. Watts as follows: "How many of them were there?"

"Ten or eleven. I think there was eleven."

"You say they came in and lay down in front of the cash register?"

"Yes, sir, all over the floor."

"Did they say anything to you, Mr. Watts?"

"No, sir, not that I remember."

"Did they ask you for any service?"

"Not that I recall."

"Did they say anything at all?"

"No, sir."

"Ask you for anything?"

"No, sir. Not that I remember."

"Tell you anything?"

"No, sir."

"Just lay down in the floor?"

"Yes, sir."

"What happened after that?"

"I told them to get out half a dozen times."

"Would you describe the words you used?"

"I told them, I said, 'What in the world is all this going on?' I said, 'You will have to get out. I am not going to have nobody laying in my floor.' Nobody could get in or out, or nothing else."

". . . What happened after you told them to leave. Did they leave?"

"No, they didn't. I called the law." Mr. Watts described the officers' arrival and the arrest of the demonstrators.

The defense attorney, Wade Penny, questioned Mr. Watts. "It is your testimony that they rushed in with such force and in such a hurry that they just kind of swept her [Mrs. Watts] aside, and went right into the foyer, past the foyer to right in front of the counter and that they just lay down in the floor without saying anything to you?"

"I don't think all went past the second door. Some of them stopped at the first set of doors, between the doors."

"And the ones who stopped between the doors, what were they doing?"

"They lay down. They are all laying down like a bunch of hogs."

". . . Did you see anyone assault anyone there that night?"

"No, sir."

"Do you deny anyone was assaulted?"

The solicitor objected to the question and was sustained.

"Did you yourself on this occasion strike any one of the demonstrators?"

The solicitor objected and was overruled.

"No, sir," Mr. Watts said.

"Did you see your wife on that occasion strike one of the demonstrators?"

The solicitor objected and was sustained.

". . . Do you see this gentleman with the glasses? Did you assault him yourself?" He was referring to Professor Amon.

"No, sir."

"Did you ever strike him?"

"No, sir."

"Did you ever have occasion to drag him out of the restaurant?"

"I don't think so."

On the night following the demonstration at Watts Grill, eleven demonstrators were arrested at the grocery store where ammonia had been used on them. On the night following that, five demonstrators were arrested at Watts Grill. In neither case was there violence; the proprietors simply phoned the police and told them to get all those sit-ins out of their places of business.

The two extreme forces in the town were now locked in a combat which neither one would abandon. If the town had worried about its segregated businesses being holdouts, it could now worry just as much about a group on the other side which showed not the slightest willingness to change its stance.

On Saturday night small hit-and-run parties also visited Brady's and Clarence's, and on Sunday night they visited Brady's again. In other action Saturday, picketing began at 10 A.M. and lasted throughout the day at Fowler's Food Store, as an objection to its employment practices.

On Sunday night, the staff of the Freedom Committee had a meeting. They had gone through a difficult, dangerous week, and they had held to the nonviolent oath required of each person before going out on a sit-in. Some of the segregationists had bungled their nonviolent resolves, but the demonstrators had not. The demonstrators were ready for more action, but they decided that night to call off sit-ins for the time being and await the second vote on the public accommodations ordinance, which was a few days away. If ever it had been shown in a town that only the intercession of the law could break a stalemate, they felt it had been shown here.

To help still further, the Freedom Committee had arranged for James Farmer, the National Director of CORE, to visit Chapel Hill at this time, to emphasize the importance of taking action. Floyd McKissick was to be with him. The staff also knew that during the week Pat Cusick, who had been granted several days' "good behavior" in the integrated prison to which, after Christmas Day, he had been sent, would be coming home. It was to be a week, they decided, of working with the aldermen and other influential citizens, to persuade them as best they could.

Many of the white liberals in town, and to some extent the Police Department, wanted the Chapel Hill Freedom Committee or its members to agree to press charges against any perpetrators of violence. It was a unique aspect of the Chapel Hill movement that this was against policy.

John Dunne says they "were deeply convinced that to ask the police and courts to retaliate for violence we had received was the same as retaliating ourselves, and would merely widen the schism between ourselves and the segregationists who assaulted us. For the Christians among us, it was inimical to Jesus' teachings, when he said, 'You have heard it said, an eye for an eye and a tooth for a tooth . . . but I say, Love your enemies,' etc., 'and if a man should sue you for your coat, give him your cloak also.' When the day of reconciliation comes, it is always much easier to become friends with someone who forgave you completely and did not seek harm for you in return for the harm you did to him."

Pat Cusick was released from prison on January 5. He had gone off his hunger strikes soon after Christmas, but he had lost over twenty pounds, even though he had gained three pounds in the last week or ten days, mostly from drinking milk, which he bought at the prison store near the cell block with the small amount of money he had. He had had a stomach ulcer for almost ten years, and the prison food irritated him, so he drank all the milk he could afford to buy.

He was driven to Chapel Hill by Professor Joe Straley, John Dunne and Quinton Baker. Pat was so glad to be out he wanted to stop everywhere along the road and experience simply the pleasure of being free. When finally they got to Chapel Hill, he was greeted like a returning hero. Whenever he went into a room, a chair was brought; whenever he wanted to write anything, a pen was supplied; whenever he wanted to talk, there were several people who wanted to talk with him. At the Chicken Box Number Two, he was received with a large dish of fried chicken and instructions not to go on a hunger strike on their premises. Everywhere he was asked to tell about prison, and he sensed a willingness, even an eagerness, on the part of some of the young people to be sent off to one, too. "It's a dull place," he told them. "You have the chance for action here. Prison isn't for you or me, either."

He went to work at once. Leaflets were mimeographed and sent to all the houses in the Negro section, telling about the approaching visit of James Farmer. He went through the stacks of newspapers and studied the press reaction, trying to assess in his own mind the bits and pieces which told the people of the town something of what was going on. He was distressed by what he found, for scant attention had been paid to the sit-ins in news stories, except by the *Daily Tar Heel*. The editorials in the *News of Orange County* and the Chapel Hill *Weekly* had been unfavorable, and the only time the Chapel Hill *Weekly* had criticized the segregationists was when the grocer threw ammonia and Clorox. Only the *Daily Tar Heel* was carrying full news stories and interviews, and pictures of the demonstrators being dragged, kicked and thrown out of places, and its editorials alone encouraged community action.

Also, the *Tar Heel* had been trying to get facts pertaining to segregation. By means of a telephone survey, they had found that Chapel Hill had much more segregation in its public businesses than the Merchants Association and the other newspaper had claimed. They wrote:

Three of Chapel Hill's five motels do not accept Negro lodgers. The other two are predominantly Negro, but do have some white patronage.

Thirty-two per cent of the local restaurants maintain discriminatory policies of some type. The discrimination ranges from stand-up or back-door service to complete refusal of Negro customers. One of these restaurants noted that they would only serve Negroes who are University students.

Of nine establishments listed in the Chapel Hill Telephone Directory to serve beer and ale, five do not have equal service. Two of the remaining four do not have seating facilities. One maintains the policy of standing service.

The *Tar Heel* also checked barbershops, almost all of which were segregated, billiard parlors, drugstores, grocers, hospital facilities, ice cream parlors and service stations, and found that "discrimination in service exists in one form or another at 25 per cent of the 116 service and accommodations facilities in Chapel Hill." The newspaper then listed all the segregated places by name, starting with Allen's Amoco Service Station and ending with Watts Motel and Restaurant. There were twenty-eight places on the list.

Joe Augustine, manager of the Chapel Hill Merchants Association, was asked by the *Tar Heel* for the particulars of the poll he had released earlier, indicating that 5 to 8 per cent of the places in town practiced segregation. Mr. Augustine said the Association had not kept records of its survey, which he said included categories of retail businesses not included in the *Tar Heel* survey, and which he said had been hurriedly made.

Pat put the newspaper back in the corner for Al Amon to clip.

Pat asked John how many reporters from the two local privately owned newspapers had been around the place to find out what the demonstrators were trying to achieve. The answer was that nobody had, not a single reporter, except that one night Roland Giduz himself had come by. John had been glad to see him and had told him the time hadn't come for the group to leave, but that he would be welcome if he wanted to go along to a sit-in. Giduz, however, saw a group get into a car and drive off. He followed them, not knowing they were a decoy, and ended up out in the country. He missed the sit-in and was angry about it. His had been the only visit to the place of a nonstudent local reporter.

John Dunne and Floyd McKissick met James Farmer at the Raleigh-Durham airport and drove him to the auditorium of North Carolina College. In the auditorium was to be gathered a group which included professors, housewives and other adult members of the Chapel Hill and Durham communities, as well as students from

North Carolina College and Duke, all of whom were to walk to Chapel Hill on a three-hour freedom march. As Farmer arrived, a freezing rain was falling, and as the three men went slipping and sliding up to the door of the auditorium, they supposed that ten or twenty people would be waiting for them. To their surprise, there were 170.

The group, carrying a banner which said "Walk for Freedom," marched toward Chapel Hill. They were met two miles outside of town by two hundred other demonstrators, and the combined group entered the town together and proceeded along Franklin Street to the Baptist Church, where Mr. Farmer was to speak. There another 200 or 250 people were waiting, so the combined audience filled the church and overflowed into the cold outdoors. The audience was chilled, some of them boisterously claimed to be frozen, and they were almost overjoyed with the success of the march. They began to clap their hands and sing, and when Farmer began to speak, they interrupted every sentence he uttered with prolonged applause.

This is a revolution, Mr. Farmer told them, the revolution of the 1960's, and seeks to include America's dark citizens in the American success and to fulfill the promise of the American Constitution. He also told the assembly that they were helping pass the Civil Rights Bill in the Federal Congress. This was greeted with prolonged applause. "They needn't think we've stopped caring," Farmer said. "We must continue."

When he got around to talking about the Chapel Hill public accommodations ordinance, the auditorium virtually shook with hand clapping and cheers.

He met with newsmen that evening and told them Chapel Hill was "a key to the South and the nation." He said, "This town has a nationwide reputation as a center of liberal thinking, but is only tokenly desegregated. It is on the verge of losing its reputation and its leadership. We believe the Board of Aldermen should adopt the anti-discrimination act, and we believe it must do so if Chapel Hill is to regain its leadership in the civil rights field."

He then made the challenge for which doubtless he had come to Chapel Hill. "If the aldermen fail to end discrimination in accommodations, the national office of CORE will throw its full support behind all efforts to eliminate segregation here.

"We will step up our activities, and Chapel Hill will become the central point of our work.

"All the stops to end discrimination will be pulled.

"If the aldermen pass the proposed legislation, we will shift our efforts to employment and housing."

So the matter rested.

On this same day, the Chapel Hill *Weekly* editorially opposed the passage of the ordinance, and recommended that the aldermen "direct those seeking redress of racial injustices to a somewhat higher level." This came as a disappointment to Gary Blanchard, who had asked the *Weekly*'s editor Jim Shumaker on Friday how the *Weekly* was going to view this issue. Shumaker had said he didn't know, that it looked like the vote of the aldermen might be unanimously in favor of it, and that the *Weekly* would, in that case, come out strongly for it. The meeting to decide on the vote was to be held that weekend, he said.

Evidently it had been held, and the decision had been made to oppose the ordinance. Who had been at the meeting, Gary wasn't able to find out. Of course, there's the possibility such a meeting never took place.

The same issue of the *Weekly* contained a petition of the Ministerial Association, signed by eighteen hundred local citizens, asking for passage of the ordinance. Certain of the state papers carried a report on the long freedom march from Durham and on Mr. Farmer's challenge to Chapel Hill at his Sunday news conference.

That night, three members of the Board of Aldermen met privately at Gene Strowd's house. Mr. Strowd had invited all the aldermen, but Mrs. Walters, Hubert Robinson and Roland Giduz didn't attend. The three members present, representing the more conservative half of the board, decided what the community needed was a mediation committee to try to bring about voluntary desegregation. They concluded that the reason for the failure of previous committees was that they had been too strongly integrationist in representation. Rather than support the public accommodations ordinance, the three aldermen decided to draw up a substitute motion, authorizing a new, more broadly based committee. Professor Wager agreed to draw up a statement for presentation at the meeting the following night. Their decision was confidential.

On Monday afternoon, the day of the critical Board of Aldermen's meeting, the Freedom Committee held another mass rally at a church. At about the same time, Alderman Giduz went to Alderman Wager's home and read the statement he was preparing. Wager suggested that Giduz present the actual motion, and Giduz, who was doubtless caught in a dilemma about the whole situation, agreed to consider doing so. He drove to see Mrs. Adelaide Walters, who had had much to do with his election to the board. He told her he hoped she would forgive him for what he was going to do that evening, that the matter was causing him moral qualms. She said that if morally he felt he ought to vote for the ordinance, he ought to do so, and if morally he felt, as no doubt Gene Strowd did, that he should not vote for it, then he should follow that course. If he had decided to vote against it because of the pressure of businessmen who advertised in the *News of Orange County* and his other publications, then she could understand that, too.

Mr. Giduz became angry and said the advertisers had nothing to do with it.

"Then why do you feel guilty?" she said.

He left, very much disturbed. Many other people had put pressure on him, too. Adelaide Walters was not the only one. And among the worst were the people who phoned his house and said, "I hate niggers, too," and people who had come up to him since the last vote on this ordinance and had patted him on the back and said they wanted to help him put the "niggers" back in their place. By nature, since his student days at Chapel Hill, Roland Giduz had been an outspoken liberal, usually a leader, but now as a leader he was caught in a vise. His friends on the whole were liberals, his business associates on the whole were conservative on this matter, and somewhere in between he was caught, wondering how practical this proposed law was, wondering about his political future, wondering about his responsibility to the town, to the Negroes, to himself.

Mrs. Walters wrote out a statement that she could read at the meeting that night, supporting the ordinance. She had dinner with her husband and drove to the meeting.

About this same time, Mayor McClamroch left his home, bringing with him a report he had received, which he and the aldermen had all seen, from the university Institute of Government. It stated in effect that the town had authority to pass a public accommodations ordinance under Section 5.41 of the town charter, but that such a law would contravene the state trespass law and the conflict would have to be resolved by the courts. Privately, the Institute had advised the mayor that the State Supreme Court would probably find the ordinance invalid. What the United States Supreme Court would find, they didn't know. The constitutional law professor of the university Law School, Dan Pollitt, said it was valid and proper for the Board of Aldermen to pass the ordinance.

The mayor also had with him the petition signed by eighteen hundred people which had appeared in the *Weekly,* supporting the ordinance, and had copies of a petition opposing the ordinance signed by seventy-one people. On the list were Austin Watts of Watts Motel; E. G. Merritt of Merritt's Service Station; John Carswell of the Colonial Drug Store; John S. Williams, who ran the Farmers Exchange; J. V. Lacock of Lacock Shoe Store; and W. D. Basnight, who ran a local hardware supply house. Their petition said, in part:

Whereas, public demonstrations are a mild form of mob violence carried out by a minority group and do not express the opinion of the majority of people, and Whereas, it is the right of an individual to operate a private enterprise as he may see fit within the limits of the law, and Whereas, it is unlawful according to the Constitution of North Carolina to have in effect a Public Accommodations Law; Be it resolved that the businessmen of Chapel Hill and Orange County go on record as recommending that the Chapel Hill Aldermen . . . do not pass any Public Accommodations Law that might be proposed.

The mayor also was aware of other influential people in town who were against the ordinance. The radio station telephone and the one at his house had been ringing often, and many of the people phoning to oppose the ordinance were advertisers on the radio station, which the mayor owned. So the pressure was severe.

Pat Cusick left the office of the Freedom Committee about the time the mayor was leaving his house. He and a number of others walked to the town hall, which is four blocks away, and were refused admittance to the building by a policeman. A few white citizens walked around the integrated group and were admitted. Pat objected to this, and the patrolman shut the door and returned a minute or so later to say that nobody else would be let in.

Pat assumed that the courtroom was full, and this was quite disappointing to him and to the Negro members of his party, who had for two days talked about little else than this meeting. There was nothing to be done, however, and he urged them to be quiet and wait for word about the hearing.

Inside about one hundred people were seated. They did not fill the hall. Among them were forty-five members and sympathizers of the Freedom Committee, including John Dunne. They listened as the meeting was called to order, and the mayor asked that nobody take part in the discussion except members of the Board of Aldermen.

As the meeting began, Alderman Robinson asked Mayor Mc-Clamroch to read one of the more important conclusions of the Institute of Government report.

"Only the Board of Aldermen," the mayor read to the gathering,

is in the position to determine whether passage of a public accommodations ordinance is necessary for the peace, good government and welfare of the city, or for the public health, welfare, order, or safety. The Institute of Government cannot comment on the merits of this issue, for this is a legislative function. If the members of the Board believe passage of the ordinance is necessary under existing conditions, they have the right to exercise this legislative authority. If they do not so believe, they have the discretion not to act. In any case, passage would probably be followed by a court test.

There followed a discussion of this opinion, and a dialogue between Alderman Giduz and the town attorney, Mr. John Q. LeGrand, which indicates the state of tension and confusion among the participants.

Mr. Giduz, referring to the Institute of Government report, said, "I wonder, Mr. Mayor, if we could have the town attorney's comments on this."

Mr. LeGrand said, "To what extent, Mr. Giduz, particularly?"

"Well, really only general comments."

"Well, I only received it last night, Mr. Giduz."

"As we all did, surely," Giduz said.

"And I've read it. It ends up with the, to some extent, same conclusion that the Attorney General of North Carolina had previously reached, and that is, the matter cannot be determined from the standpoint of the legality of an ordinance before the ordinance has been passed on by the Supreme Court of North Carolina. I think it's a question that cannot be determined, that's what you want me to . . ."

"Well, yes, sir," Giduz said.

". . . what you had in mind?"

"That was a general comment on it. Now . . ."

"The writers of this report say that it's a question that has not yet been decided and cannot be determined, the validity of such an ordinance, before the Supreme Court of North Carolina has passed on it. There's no precedent in North Carolina for or against it."

"Now I want to ask you also about when we have a proposal," Giduz said, "as I believe we will momentarily. I just wanted to ask you to comment on that also, in light of the report." Mr. Giduz evidently was referring to the motion which he believed Mrs. Walters would soon make.

Mr. LeGrand said, "You're going to ask my comment on the report?" he said.

"Well, when it comes. I say I can't ask it yet."

"Oh, oh, yes."

"That's all," Giduz said. "I mean, the question I'm going to put to you will just be in light, on the proposal in light of the report, see?"

The attorney made no reply.

"And so really the question had better be put later," Giduz said.

It was Alderman Walters' purpose to present the motion for a public accommodations ordinance. She took out her statement and read it in full.

The underlying idea of a Public Accommodations Law is so simple that it was expressed in one sentence by the President of the United States, Lyndon Johnson, in his State of the Union message on January 9: "All members of the public should be given equal access to facilities open to the public." This statement seems reasonable to most people in Chapel Hill, since this is a university town where freedom flavors the spirit of a great university.

It is likewise not surprising that Chapel Hillians are concerned that our Negro citizens often suffer personal embarrassment and shame from treatment received in some public places here.

We are aware that some 90 percent of our merchants subscribe to the principle of public accommodation. Indeed, the Merchants Association itself has gone on record in favor of open business for all citizens.

Why, then, is a Public Accommodations Law necessary? Why was the commandment "Thou shalt not kill" ever put into law? It seems regrettable that we need legislation to enforce a plain truth. But because the bigotry of a few is poisoning the peace and harmony of community relationships, we are impelled to take action.

The Human Relations Committee set up by the Board of Aldermen and appointed by the Mayor, the Ministerial Association, as well as many individuals, have urged us to pass a Public Accommodations ordinance.

Some say that such an ordinance is an invasion of private property rights. Others point out that such rights have always been subject to the laws of the land—laws of ownership, sale, inheritance, zoning, sanitation, eminent domain.

For these reasons and many more, it is my hope that the Board of Aldermen will pass a Public Accommodations ordinance and thus in part restore the damaged public image of what I believe is an enlightened community.

Mrs. Walters then introduced an ordinance based on a law adopted by the town of Rockville, Maryland. Included in it was provision for a local mediation board to consider all complaints. The board would be able by law to resolve conflicts by mediation within thirty days. She then moved that the town attorney be instructed to draft an ordinance along the lines of the one proposed.

Mayor McClamroch asked if there was a seconding of the motion. Alderman Robinson asked to be recognized. "The town has been witnessing something never seen before," he said, "an angry Negro, angry at himself because he has been hoodwinked. These demonstrations are an expression of distaste, of a realization that there has definitely been some behind-the-scenes maneuvering."

He continued, "Integration of schools, public facilities, playgrounds and so forth is not merely granting a special privilege to the minority group but aligning justice and fair play to take its rightful place in our American democracy. In a democracy in action, every man is free to move, to think, to go to school, to play without discrimination. This makes for a vigorous nation with high moral aspirations. If we are to have a working democracy, we must contribute to this cause. What better contribution could we make than to pass the public accommodations law now? I second the motion."

Alderman Strowd asked to be recognized. "I would certainly like to echo Mr. Robinson's remarks there, in saying that I think the Negro citizens' conduct in Chapel Hill has been praiseworthy through very trying conditions, and I think they in general deserve the commendation of this board. I do not agree with the proposal of the public accommodations ordinance, until we have exhausted all the means of effecting desegregation in our town, and I have not seen too much evidence that Chapel Hill wants a public accommodations ordinance."

The audience broke into laughter.

"It seems that has struck some people funny," Alderman Strowd said. "I went over the list that was in the paper, and I do not believe that more than 25 percent, 20 or 25 percent, of the electorate in Chapel Hill's names are on that petition. So I believe that the piece in the paper, from where I stand, would be more against a public accommodations ordinance than it would be in favor of it. So I would like to say that at this time I am not ready to vote for a public accommodations ordinance in Chapel Hill."

Alderman Giduz said, "I'd simply want to renew the question to the town attorney at this time. What if—"

"Well, my opinion, Mr. Giduz, is that until the courts pass on it, no one should have a real substantial and reliable opinion. I'm not—"

"You will not advise—"

"—prepared to tell you what way the Supreme Court will react if this matter were presented to them, and I think the Institute of Government report has made it very clear that it has not been decided."

Alderman Giduz said, "Mr. Mayor, I withdraw the question."

Mrs. Taylor, chairman of the Mayor's Human Relations Committee, came forward to address the board. "I want just to comment briefly upon the editorial in the Chapel Hill *Weekly*," she said. "The gist of this editorial was that this board was no place to consider a public accommodations law, with its constitutional and other ramifications. . . . I want to say that I think this is a terrible thing to say to you people and to the town. Because we have this problem here. We have the problem of segregated establishments who deny access to public places to minority groups. Reason will not touch them, and

I agree with you that reason will also not touch those who have been protesting. . . . The Human Relations Committee cannot do anything about this. . . . The Mayor's Businessmen Committee has done everything it can. And now it's only you who can help. The Supreme Court has passed on the constitutionality of public accommodations laws; you all know that there is good legal opinion that you have the authority to do so, and I don't believe that you all ought to bear the responsibility of *not* passing it."

Mayor McClamroch asked if there were other opinions. Alderman Joe Page said he didn't think the board should pass the law, "since the board had no authority to act."

Alderman Wager said he didn't think other remedies to the problem had been exhausted.

Alderman Giduz said he would like to make a statement concerning "how I have come to reach the position I have. I'm prepared to make this a very brief statement. My primary concern is the elimination of racial discrimination, not simply the passing of a law. There's no inherent value in a law as such. The list of names attached to the appeal that we have from the Ministerial Association has been thoughtfully read and very seriously considered by me, and I've discussed this matter with many of the persons who signed this particular petition sponsored by the Ministerial Association. But let me also say here and with absolute conviction that I shall not be affected in working toward this goal by acts of civil disobedience or by any and all extreme pressure tactics for the enactment of a public accommodations law. In short, I will not be intimidated or stampeded in any way to pass such a law. I'm very much concerned with the necessity to eliminate racial discrimination, but the threat that there will be renewed civil disobedience, that there will be demonstrations and mass pressure tactics that will force us to pass such a law will not affect me. The people of this community have always shown a tremendous concern for the elimination of racial discrimination, as evidenced so clearly, Mr. Mayor, in the Ministerial Association sponsored petition referred to. I grant to the good citizens of this town who have signed this statement complete integrity of their motives. I ask only that they grant to me the belief that I share their very deep concern and determination to resolve the situation and to make of this problem an opportunity. As a positive step toward the goal that this board is dedicated to seeking, I make a substitute motion at this time that the mayor head a committee composed of representatives of the Ministerial Association, the Merchants Association, the Chamber of Commerce and the university faculty, composed of two persons elected by each of these groups, to serve as a mediation committee to resolve racial differences that currently beset this town and to which complaints of racial discrimination could be brought."

Alderman Strowd seconded the motion.

Alderman Robinson said, "We've had hundreds of meetings. We go in 'em and come out just like when we went in there, not a thing being accomplished. And I think we've proven that we're not doing no good on the outside, and I think the only thing to do is to pass this public accommodations ordinance."

Mayor McClamroch said, "It's been of great concern on my part that some people might not know what my stand would be on various motions. I think it's all in fairness that before we take a vote I would declare what way I would vote. I think, from my personal experience as leader of this community in talking to all sides and weighing all issues, that the law, a public accommodations law, is not the feeling of the majority of the people in Chapel Hill and other community leaders in other communities. And I feel very strongly that at this time a public accommodations law for Chapel Hill will not benefit the community, it will not benefit the state; in fact, I think it would hinder what is being done voluntarily throughout the State of North Carolina. So I want to go on record, before any vote is taken, to—I think it's all in fairness to the people that elected me that I state my position. And I thank you for the opportunity to do so. Is there further discussion on the substitute motion, that this committee be set up?"

He said, after a moment, "Hearing no further discussion I'll call for the vote. All in favor of the substitute motion, please say 'Aye.' "

Four aldermen voted "Aye."

"All opposed," the mayor said.

There were two "No's," Mrs. Walters and Mr. Robinson.

"I declare that the motion carries, four to two. The substitute motion is in order."

"Mr. Mayor," Alderman Giduz said, "I'd like to express thanks to you for your willingness to work with us once again on this, and I trust that you will try to use the talents and the . . ."

The talking continued for a little while, but the news already had been made. The word went out. Pat Cusick and the demonstrators outside the door of the town hall were struck by it, and they simply sat down on the sidewalk and on the steps of the building where they had been standing.

Upstairs, about half the people began filing out, but forty-five, among them Joe Straley, a few other townspeople and members of the Freedom Committee, kept their seats. The mayor and the aldermen, and others who had attended the meeting, went down the stairs and left the building by a side door, one which permitted them to leave without going through the group of demonstrators at the main entrance.

The forty-five people sat in the courtroom upstairs, refusing to leave, planning to spend the night, even though they realized they might be arrested and thought they would be. Two of the girls began putting their hair in curlers. Outside, Pat and his group sat on the cold concrete. Some of the adult Negro and white citizens brought them blankets and coffee. They sat there for hours. Across the street there is a savings and loan association clock, which registers the time and the temperature. They watched the time go by as the temperature fell below freezing. The temperature went down to 15 degrees before morning came, yet nobody moved.

Chapter Eleven

ALONG ABOUT THIS TIME, the governor and Floyd McKissick openly differed on several matters. For one thing, Mr. McKissick insisted on continuing demonstrations in spite of the governor's objections. In spring of the preceding year, when Governor

Sanford had asked the demonstrators to get off the streets, he had invited to the state capital some two hundred young Negro leaders, and had said to them and to the state, "You are here at our invitation to find a better way to express your hopes, desires and aspirations. You must find a way not only which expresses the depth and breadth of your dissatisfaction, but which also encourages people to assist in opening up jobs and other opportunities. The device of the mass demonstrations has largely served its purpose in North Carolina. It got across your message and the urgency that had not been fully understood prior to then. The demonstrations have shown just how unhappy and discontented you are, how anxious you are to remove, and remove right now, the indignities and injustices which have been visited upon your parents and their parents. . . . The mass demonstrations awoke and jolted many people, but this method had reached the point of diminishing returns in its latter days, destroying goodwill, creating resentment, losing friends and not influencing people."

Since issuing that statement, the governor had worked to stop the demonstrations, at the same time seeking ways to improve educational and employment opportunities for Negroes. Floyd McKissick was well aware of this, but now he was planning the biggest demonstrations of all.

Another concern was that the Democratic gubernatorial campaign was starting soon, and the governor felt that the racial issue should be kept out of the way. Mr. McKissick might have agreed on this, but he was not willing to give up the demonstrations, which he said had proved to be the best technique the Negro had found in decades to gain progress. Also, he perhaps had political ambitions of his own. At this same time, the rumors started that he had been approached by several groups, who asked that he run for governor or lieutenant governor himself.

Mr. McKissick running for governor, or encouraging demonstrations in the home town of the state university, would certainly not help keep the race issue out of the campaign. All this is pertinent because of a statement issued by James Farmer the morning following the Board of Aldermen's meeting.

Mr. Farmer had planned to fly back to New York City, but the weather was bad and his flight was canceled. He stayed over in

Durham and the next morning held a press conference in Floyd Mc-Kissick's office.

John Dunne and Quinton Baker were there, and they made introductory statements. Quinton Baker said to the television cameras, "We do not want to demonstrate, we do not want to sit in any more than the people of Chapel Hill want us to. But we will use whatever means are necessary within the nonviolent philosophy to bring about desegregation in Chapel Hill."

John Dunne said, "The Freedom Committee welcomes the opportunity to meet and resolve differences with town leaders. I hope Chapel Hill will see the significance of its failure in not passing the public accommodations ordinance."

Both of these statements are basically conciliatory and were supposed to set the stage for Mr. Farmer's comments, but unhappily most television and newspaper editors paid no attention to them. (The Chapel Hill *Weekly* printed the second sentence of each statement and deleted the first, which made each statement sound more like a threat than an offer of conciliation.)

Mr. Farmer spoke next. He had spent the previous evening at Floyd McKissick's house talking about the problems of CORE, the shortage of staff and the need of more training programs in nonviolence. They had discussed the big-city attitudes of Harlem and Chicago. They had discussed the problems of their steering committee. McKissick had agreed to visit several areas within the next thirty days, and to try to set up workshops in nonviolence and the civil disobedience techniques of CORE. Their conversation had lasted until well into the night. They had also discussed the Chapel Hill situation with Quinton and John.

Now Mr. Farmer appeared before the television cameras. His normal conciliatory manner, which had characterized him when he arrived in Chapel Hill, when he met with Charlie Jones and other local white liberal leaders, and when he had spoken at the mass meeting, was suddenly gone. He spoke at the request of the Chapel Hill Freedom Committee, and what he was to say had been approved by them, even worked out in conference with them, but his statement carried the weight and importance of his national office as well, and it was emphatic.

"We mean business," he said. "I dislike ultimata and deadlines, but we will be forced to take action if Chapel Hill is not an open city by February 1. All our resources—staff, funds and nonviolent training— will be centered there after D-day."

He said national leaders of CORE had scheduled a steering committee meeting for January 24 in New York to decide on 1964 strategy plans, and that they would decide at that time on a plan centering their protest movement around Chapel Hill. A CORE legal meeting would be held in New York one week later, January 31. If no Chapel Hill action had been reported by that date, he said he would return with Attorney McKissick to direct the all-out offensive in Chapel Hill.

It was a point-blank challenge, and Governor Sanford happened to see it on television. Here during a gubernatorial primary campaign, from Floyd McKissick's office had come a racially oriented, explosive ultimatum, promising a series of events which very well could be perpetuated through the entire campaign.

At midnight the governor sent word to Mayor McClamroch and Roland Giduz that he wanted to meet with them next morning at breakfast. They began speculating about what he wanted.

Nearby at his home, Professor Joe Straley finished writing a letter, to an out-of-town friend, describing his feelings and those of people in Chapel Hill.

I could write this much more to tell you of the various shades and grades of opinion that are going around. This town is quite agog. When I was sitting down there at the town hall last night, I almost had to laugh at the idea that such a bunch . . . could put a community of scholars into such a frenzy. The really remarkable ingredient in the whole picture is John Dunne. I just can't get over the talent for organization that he has. His ragtag little army is completely at his command. How he can keep this thing going day in and day out without making a serious mistake, I cannot imagine. He will leave Chapel Hill either as a saint or in a police car. Time will tell.

On Monday morning, before Mr. Farmer had made his deadline statement, but after his statement of Sunday afternoon, Roland Giduz and Mayor McClamroch had come to the governor's office with a statement they had written, which they wanted the governor to release. "The mayor of the town has asked the help of the governor and of all the citizens of this state in an effort to restore order and to bring progress toward the goal of the elimination of racial discrimination in a lawful and orderly manner," the statement said, and continued for three more paragraphs. It was accompanied by a statement from Mayor McClamroch, who appealed to "all citizens truly concerned for the brotherhood of man to help us with their ideas, their support, and their prayers."

The governor had gone over the proposed statements, had heard his visitors report on the danger of violence in Chapel Hill, and had suggested that McClamroch and Giduz talk further with an aide, John Brooks. Mr. Brooks went over the statements and talked with the mayor and Roland Giduz about them. Later he talked with his immediate superior, Capus Waynick, a special consultant to the governor, and he talked with Governor Sanford. He then phoned Mayor McClamroch and said that the governor would not take part in the Chapel Hill situation.

Later that day, Mr. Brooks received a phone call from Mr. Giduz, who was anxious because of the decision and who arranged for a second conference in Raleigh with him. The conference, Mr. Brooks says, resulted in no change in his opinion. He said the governor's entry into the town's problems would be ill-advised.

Mayor McClamroch and Mr. Giduz were now coming to breakfast at the mansion, and they assumed their statements were once more to be discussed. They ate breakfast with the governor, with Dave Coltrane, who was director of the North Carolina Good Neighbor Council, with Joel Fleishman, the governor's legal assistant, and with Tom Lambeth, his administrative assistant. When they had finished eating, the governor took up a yellow pad on which he had written a strongly worded reply to Mr. Farmer, one much stronger than the statement Roland Giduz and Mayor McClamroch had left for him to review. The governor evidently had decided that if he was going to enter the dispute at all, he would enter it in such a way that he could not be misunderstood or ignored.

I am amazed that such brazen threats should be made against the Board of Aldermen of Chapel Hill. Here is a community which has led the way by many forward steps. Public places are generally open to all. Because of this very progress the officials are now threatened. Because there are a few holdouts who obviously do not reflect the community attitude, Chapel Hill is to be made the center of attention. Because they might decline to pass an ordinance to the exact liking of a particular organization, the entire community is to be subjected to possible violence.

The governor went on to repudiate this kind of approach. "Suppose a group of citizens opposed to the same ordinance should threaten violence if it passed?" he asked.

The town of Chapel Hill is part of the State of North Carolina. The sovereignty of the State will not bow to threats while I am Governor. Chapel Hill, of all places, should not be made a battleground. If it is, it will be because of the irresponsible action of CORE and in spite of all the town and State officials can do.

The statement was more militant than had been Mr. Farmer's. Its references to threats, violence and battlegrounds were unlike Governor Sanford and cannot easily be accounted for, unless the predictions from Chapel Hill leaders had been quite alarming.

He closed his statement by saying that the town officials were free to take whatever action they deemed proper. "They need not act in fear," he said, continuing his reference to imminent danger. "They will be given complete and absolute support by me with every resource at my command."

The mayor and Roland Giduz approved of the statement. John Brooks arrived about eight-thirty, and he read it. He said he felt it was not justified in the light of what he knew about the Chapel Hill situation and what Mr. Farmer had evidently intended. He said Farmer had not meant that Chapel Hill was to become a battleground.

This was the first contrary comment the governor had heard about his proposed action, and it did concern him. He told John Brooks to phone Capus Waynick, who for several months had been the governor's consultant on racial matters having to do with the state's mayors and city governments. Mr. Waynick knew the racial situation in the state very well; also, he knew politics and had been the campaign manager for Kerr Scott, the governor's own mentor, when he had run for the governorship.

Mr. Waynick, who was not in the best of health, didn't like to be phoned in the morning. He resented such intrusions deeply, and John Brooks knew this, but the governor had called a press conference for only an hour or two later. The general came on the phone gruffly, and John and Joel Fleishman, on two extensions, talked with him, then read him the governor's statement. General Waynick literally hit the ceiling of his High Point bedroom. He said if any such action was taken, he would have nothing to do with it.

This growling comment was reported to the governor, who attributed it to the general's illness. Doubtless, however, he now began to realize that there was a good deal more to the Chapel Hill situation than he had previously known. Even so, he decided it was time to call Floyd McKissick's hand, and having called a press conference to do so, he couldn't very well decide otherwise. If he didn't answer James Farmer, one of the gubernatorial candidates was likely to do so anyway.

The governor appeared before the television cameras that morning and read his statement, just as he had read it to Mayor McClamroch earlier. Before he went before the cameras, John Brooks phoned Floyd McKissick in Durham and told him what was about to take place. Mr. McKissick was instantly furious. "If the governor wants war, that's what he'll get," he said. John Brooks went on talking with him, and Mr. McKissick began to get his temper under control. John then phoned General Waynick, and tried to assure him that the governor was acting out of a sense of public safety and political reality. General Waynick remained unhappy. The Farmer statement had received little attention in the morning papers, he pointed out; now it would appear on the front pages; the governor was simply establishing the racial issue in the campaign, not the reverse.

It was too late to stop the action, John Brooks said.

I have talked with Governor Sanford and Mayor McClamroch about the governor's entry into the Chapel Hill situation. The mayor said it was his impression that the governor was worried about the possibility of violence; this, Mr. McClamroch said, was his concern, too. Governor Sanford does not, however, deny the involvement of politics in his thinking. "Let's say it this way," he told me. "I might have done it even if politics had not been involved." The politics the governor was referring to was not of a selfish sort, but was the struggle for control of the state between opposing forces, one of which seemed more willing than the other to move North Carolina ahead.

The matter was more one of statesmanship than of politics.

James Farmer in New York City, when he was told of the governor's statement, said, "The governor seems to imply that CORE has threatened to subject the community to violence." He said, "The opposite is the case. It is we who have been the victims of violence, not its perpetrators. We pledge continuation and, if necessary, an acceleration of our nonviolent efforts to achieve an open city in Chapel Hill."

In truth, he now had no choice about the matter. For CORE to back down in the face of a Southern governor, even Terry Sanford, would mean a major loss to the organization elsewhere.

Floyd McKissick issued a formal comment in Durham:

I did not expect such a statement from the "liberal" governor of North Carolina. It would be different if we lived in Alabama or Mississippi. The Negro will direct and chart his own course of conduct and his progress clock. This goes to prove again that the greatest friend the Negro has is himself. If the Negro is to be free, he will have to free himself.

Candidate Dan Moore, a corporation lawyer from the mountains, came out in support of the governor's statement. So did candidate L. Richardson Preyer, a Federal judge from Greensboro. I. Beverly Lake, the racist candidate, an articulate Harvard Law School graduate, said the governor was acting about three years late. He called Mr. Farmer's statement intolerable, and urged the quick dismissal of any faculty member, employee or student of state-supported institutions participating in demonstrations.

Editorial writers went to work at once, supporting the governor and the Chapel Hill Board of Aldermen, praising Chapel Hill for being integrated—95 percent according to the Raleigh *Times*, "90% or more" according to the Greensboro *Daily News*. Alderman Giduz, in addition to his other activities, was the local correspondent for both of these papers. The Chapel Hill *Weekly* came out with several articles and opinions, musically titled "Under the Gun Is No Time to Move," "The Town Won't Be Coerced" and "A Terrible and Sad Thing to Do." The *Daily Tar Heel,* in a front-page editorial, sought a compromise of the dispute, but they might as well have tossed a stone into the ocean.

While the state listened to comments about Chapel Hill, Father Clarence Parker was receiving coats through the mail. He received five, one of them from faraway New York City.

All of them fitted nicely. Two were black, and the others were blue. He made a choice of one, and returned the others.

He had lost his hat at the Pines, too, but nobody had given him one of those. Mrs. Parker bought him a beret, which he admitted was comfortable, though he guessed it would be some time before he felt at ease in it.

On the same day that he got the beret, January 18, a Saturday, there were three sidewalk marches through Chapel Hill by about eighty people, most of them Negroes. They carried a sign which said, "Black is not a vice, segregation is not a virtue; Chapel Hill's image is a fraud." The demonstrators also lay down in front of the doorway to the town hall, and after two hours of this twelve of them were arrested on charges of disorderly conduct and resisting arrest.

Roland Giduz had an editorial comment on that matter. "This action was tantamount to actual insurrection and rebellion," he said. "It is unbelievable by any sane logic that to prevent duly-constituted police from carrying out their normal duties of law enforcement can serve any cause whatsoever except that of absolute rebellion and insurrection. The words are deliberately repeated for emphasis."

He concluded his piece with a brief summary: "Perhaps Chapel Hill has been too tolerant."

There were many other personal struggles and official and semiofficial stands being made and announced in Chapel Hill now, in a spasm of activity and wonder, not all of it logical or controlled. Perhaps the loneliest statement of all was that of Miss Rosemary Ezra. Since the Board of Aldermen's meeting, she had lived in the courtroom, silently dramatizing her personal protest and in this way requesting the aldermen to pass a public accommodations ordinance.

Born of English parents in France in 1938, Rosemary had grown up in California as an American citizen. In her early twenties, she had worked in a nursery school and had done some work in the office of the CORE chapter in Los Angeles. She had moved to Durham in 1962, after attending two-week CORE workshops in Texas and

Ohio, where she met several North Carolina people. She came to North Carolina and was active in the picketing and other forms of demonstrations in Durham, but once Mayor Grabarek and the other Durham leaders got the situation in hand there, she moved to Chapel Hill, hoping to retire from civil rights activity. She had arrived about the time the Chapel Hill chapter of CORE was started; she was invited to the first meeting, and from that time on she had been involved in the work of CORE and the Freedom Committee. Now, sometimes at the front upstairs window of the Chapel Hill town hall, her black hair, red sweater and red plaid skirt could be seen from half a block away, as her presence dramatized her continuing protest.

There was not much of a view from there, she says. There were the time and temperature figures on the savings and loan association building, and there were people going in and out of the segregated Tar Heel Sandwich Shop across Columbia Street. That was about all she could see. Sometimes she felt a compulsion, almost overwhelming in its suddenness and intensity, to leave, to go outside. The worst day, she says, was the fourth.

She looked forward to the town court sessions on Tuesdays and Fridays. When the court was not in session, she read books and talked with people who dropped by. At night she put a sleeping bag on the floor and went to sleep, and she was usually awakened by the noise made at eight o'clock by workmen who were renovating the old Fire Department area of the building.

While Miss Ezra kept her solitary watch, which was to last fifteen days in all, the ministers in town, who had been asked by the Chapel Hill *Weekly* to reconsider their position, were, indeed, trying to do so. They came together and wrote a statement which twenty-one of them signed and sent as a letter to the local press. They said they would not themselves break the law, but that they remained concerned over the continuing problem of discrimination in certain of the community's public eating establishments. They asked that these places cease discrimination, and called upon all those

of our citizens who share this concern to express their concern to these establishments in their own way. We will act in our way to call the community to decision.

While the religious and moral imperatives of our position should be evident to the community, we are compelled at this time to bear witness to the need for serious moral decisions on the part of the proprietors and customers of these discriminatory establishments.

While the ministers were defining, perhaps modifying, their position, the members of the Mayor's Human Relations Committee were trying to define theirs. A new mayor's committee was being formed, and Margaret Taylor didn't know to what degree her committee had been superseded. She asked her committee to meet and talk it all over. They did so and agreed that they were unhappy about the statement from CORE. They also said they believed they had failed in their mission. Finally, they said they were disappointed by the failure of the aldermen to enact a public accommodations ordinance.

The university administration also was seeking to declare its position. When Chancellor Aycock had taken office in 1957, the university had been much involved in local government, from the mayor's office down; it also ran the largest public laundry, the water department, the power company and the telephone system. The chancellor for eight years had been drawing away from much of this involvement, and it seemed unfair now for a situation to be developing which involved the university staff and students more than any others in recent history. He issued a statement, characteristically brief, in which he said that the university's own facilities were integrated, but that he wasn't going to get involved trying to force somebody else to integrate theirs. "Such a policy," he said, in what was surely an historic understatement, "would be fraught with dangers and pitfalls too numerous to discuss at this time."

Mrs. T. Franklin Williams, who had been active in civil rights work for years and was a leader of the white liberal forces, had been asked to explain why the Ministerial Association petition she had got up in support of the public accommodations ordinance had on it the names of dead people and children. She said she had, on checking, found one dead person's name and one child's, and she admitted these two errors. To another charge, that of an irate citizen who claimed he had been asked at three o'clock in the morning to support the petition, she said that she had checked the cards, and that "such a call was not made by any of our volunteers."

The university hospital issued a statement, in reply to charges made by John Dunne that the hospital was operated on a segregated basis. John claimed that Negroes were not employed in the hospital's admitting, maintenance, business and personnel offices, or as ward clerks. He had said that among janitorial workers all sweepers were Negro, all scrubbers were white, and that the scrubbers received higher wages. He had said that in male nursing all junior assistants were white, and that Negroes hired as nursing assistants performed menial tasks. He had said that a Negro could not get a semiprivate room until he supplied another Negro to share it with him.

The director of the hospital, Eugene Crawford, sensing danger at close hand, said racial discrimination was not a policy of the hospital. He said male and female patients were separated; children and adults were assigned to different areas; a patient undergoing heart surgery didn't room with a patient with pneumonia, and patients with contagious diseases were isolated from other patients. In addition, he said, coming to the heart of the matter, the cultural backgrounds and emotional attitudes of patients were considered individually as a factor in their proper medical care and in the assignment of room accommodations. He said that patients of different races were not assigned to the same room, but said the hospital would permit a white patient and a Negro patient to share a room if the arrangement were requested by both patients and if their type and degree of illnesses would safely permit it.

The hospital was, of course, required by terms of Federal grants not to discriminate or segregate; at the same time one assumes from a careful reading of this statement that it did so.

If Mr. Crawford had problems, the manager of the segregated grocery store where the ammonia had been used and his wife had none, for they solved theirs by means of a personal declaration of conscience. Reading that a new mediation committee was being formed by the mayor, knowing that their grocery store would doubtless be visited by this new group, the manager and his wife wrote out their views. They invited two members of the mayor's new committee, the only two members they said they were interested in talking to, and Chief Blake to come to their grocery and hear the wife read the paper aloud.

We would like to thank you for coming by. We feel certain that you, like us, have very little time, yet many things to do. But I know you, like us, are grateful and thankful to have the health to do the things we do. . . .

We have spent much time in prayer, thought, and discussion between ourselves and our family in this matter. We feel there is absolutely nothing immoral or un-Christian to run your business the best way you see fit, so as to make the best living for your family as you can, so long as you are not breaking any laws. We don't feel that we have broken any laws. We surely don't feel we are using any rights for ourselves others don't likewise have. They have the same privilege as we to open up a place of business, to work hard, and I do mean hard, because you don't have a paying business without doing so, as we all know. In running a business of theirs, they have the right to serve colored only, white only, or whom they please, as long as they run a lawful place. So you see, we can't take away a right from them they have, are entitled to and can use the same as we, if they care to at any time.

We would like for it to be known we have no hate in our hearts for anyone. We do feel CORE has dealt us a grave injustice. But we refuse to let groups such as CORE and NAACP to cause hate to grow in our hearts for anyone.

They, and they alone, are the reason for the white-only sign on our door at this time. [We had] already decided, about two weeks before the visits of CORE began, to remove the white-only sign from our door, not that we were going to solicit the Negro business or encourage their business, neither were we going to refuse their business. The reason we felt we would be able to do this was due to the fact we had made such a complete change in our store. . . .

About two days before the sign would have been removed, was when we were paid our first visit by the demonstrators, thus causing us to take the faded sign off and have a brand new one painted on. All I can see that is being accomplished from all this is the demonstrations are causing the scars to go so deep they will never have a chance to even begin to heal. If the relationship between the two races is ever to get better, the first thing to do, in my opinion, is to rid the town of any group that is making bad matters worse. . . .

Now we'd like only to say, we are law-abiding, Christian people. All we ask is not to be molested by any group, this includes not only the groups the demonstrators belong to or follow, but to all the race committees and different groups which we truly feel are only causing the two races to draw further apart instead of closer together. . . .

We would like to thank you again for taking this time to meet with us this afternoon. We also hope this has helped to enlighten you on our true, sincere, and heartfelt feelings on the situation.

We thank you.

The two members of the new mediation committee noticeably shook themselves. Chief Blake, who stood nearby, stared self-consciously at a display of canned goods. After a while, he went on over to the door, being careful, one suspects, not to knock over any bottles of ammonia which had been left lying about.

On Tuesday night, the twenty-eighth, only a few days before CORE's D-day deadline, the demonstrators held a sit-in at the Pines Restaurant. Ten were arrested. They were taken to Hillsboro rather than to the local jail, in order to spare the Chapel Hill police yet another all-night round of freedom songs.

Later in the week a large sit-in was held at the Colonial Drug Store. John Carswell and his son threw most of the demonstrators out the door before the police arrived; a few of them were still in there, however, trying to sit in the booths. The others were sitting on the sidewalk. Nearby, a group of singing demonstrators was on hand, and, of course, many curious spectators gathered. Tempers were at the danger point, both those of the demonstrators and those of the police, who were getting tired of hauling bodies around and who weren't getting paid overtime for all this work. They hauled several bodies to the police cars, in the process splitting Pat Cusick's lip, Pat says. The officers came for the others, and this time some of them, while picking up the men, grabbed hold of their genitals, or so the men say. They reportedly grabbed Charles Foushee, the younger brother of James Foushee, by his genitals, and it hurt so badly he started to squirm. John Dunne says the officers then struck Charlie in the face and, using him as a ramrod, charged the demonstrators.

"They scattered everybody," John told me, "knocked a few girls over. Well, I swear, the kids were so angry—that's the closest we had come to a riot. The people began to scatter, and I was telling them to come back, because I didn't know what they might do. I was calling to them to come back and get back in line. Panic and a riot were what I was afraid of. Lieutenant Herman Stone came up to me, whirled me around and told me I'd better get out of there as fast as I could or I'd be under arrest. But I didn't leave. I was doing everything I could to keep this crowd under control. There were a lot of onlookers, a lot of adults, and a few people were kind of tight, standing around, and people were getting mad. Some of the Negro parents were there, and you don't like to watch your kid getting beat up and not do anything about it. A couple of other cops came up and grabbed me, and I thought we were about to have a full-scale riot there against the police. The kids were boiling. I told Stone he had better watch it or he was going to start a riot out there. Quinton grabbed me and pulled me away from Stone, and we both worked as hard as we could to get the kids up the street and into the church basement. And, my Lord, they were mad!"

Many Negroes who didn't believe in nonviolence, and therefore couldn't take part in the demonstrations, had seen the action at the Colonial Drug Store and were now out on the street outside the church, ready for retaliation. The Negro section boiled with anger and resentment, and John and Quinton walked many of the young people home, seeing the more aggressive ones to the very doors of their houses. It was eleven o'clock before they felt they had the situation safely under control.

At the police station Pat Cusick says he was being beaten by police in the hallway of the main floor of the building. Officers began kicking him, he tells me, even as they carried him inside the building. He says he looked up and saw that they were about to ram his head into a steel post at the corner of the stairway. "I struggled to try to keep my head out of the way, and supposedly when I did that, I kicked one of the policemen. They put me down on the floor, sat on my back and started kicking my ribs, and they put the wrist clamps on my wrists and started bending my wrists. In fact, I'm still numb in here, in my side." He told me about this at Sandy Ridge Prison in June. "And it was almost ironical, because then Chief Blake came on the scene, and they stopped and they took me down to the cell, and one came down about a half-hour later and read out a warrant on me for assaulting a policeman with a deadly weapon, the weapon being my shoe, and I had to listen to that. Then they took me over to the hospital and X-rayed me."

Later Lieutenant Creel visited him in his cell and talked with him for about an hour. He said he was sorry about what had happened and was worried about "our town."

This was the attitude, the stormy atmosphere, as the town prepared for the opening of CORE's new campaign. In both the Negro and white communities tempers were short. But most citizens didn't know this. Except in the student newspaper, there were no pictures or feature articles, and the news items were matter-of-fact, given over to casual statement, as in this account:

> Officers carried the demonstrators, who went limp on the sidewalk in front of the Colonial Drug Store, to waiting police cars and hauled them to jail where some 285 civil rights workers have been booked since the sit-ins began here December 13th.
>
> Observers said there was some scuffling between police and demonstrators inside the police station and a photographer charged that one officer threatened to break his camera if he was seen at another demonstration.
>
> Meanwhile, the director of N. C. Memorial Hospital here said that racial discrimination was not a policy of the medical faculty.

I have talked with Chief Blake about the charge of police brutality. He had investigated the charge when it was first made. He says he was at the Colonial Drug Store that night, and that he understands when the police arrived Pat Cusick already had blood on his mouth. The Carswells had treated the demonstrators quite rough, he said, and they had created an atmosphere of tension, one conducive to violence; he thinks the attitude of the demonstrators toward the police was shaded by their attitude toward the Carswells. Beyond that there was, he says, an unfriendly disposition on the part of Pat Cusick, Charlie Foushee and some of the others, and he told Pat later on that same night that he knew police brutality was the easiest charge to make and as one which would gain national publicity, but that he hoped the demonstrators would not seek publicity through this means in Chapel Hill.

It was very hard to carry Pat that night, Chief Blake tells me. "He was adept at going limp. He could manage to get his legs wrapped around any post he came near, and he weighed over two hundred pounds." Charles Foushee resisted arrest all the way to the police station, Chief Blake says. "He kicked and squirmed and fought. When the officers got him downstairs to the jail level, I told them to let him go. I had known him since a kid. I talked to him, and he got up and came on into a cell. Then I went upstairs and Pat was hand-cuffed and was lying on the floor. He said he had been kicked. We sent him over to the hospital for examination, as we always do whenever anybody makes a charge like that."

The demonstrators, Pat among them, have only the highest regard for Chief Blake, but they maintain that his officers were getting tired of the restrictions he had imposed, and that often officers could be heard to say, "Blake's gone. Let's get 'em."

Chief Blake told me, "If any of my men got nervous, if they couldn't take any more of it, they would come to see me and I'd send them to the Glen Lennox patrol, and in a day or two they would come back into the office and say they were all right again." Glen Lennox is a suburb of Chapel Hill which had no demonstrations.

Chief Blake has studied pictures of the demonstrations—those Professor Amon took and those made by Howard Pendergraph, a detective on the police force. He has seen the picture Al Amon took which ostensibly shows an officer picking up a demonstrator by his testicles. Chief Blake says Amon himself said he wouldn't say the picture showed any such thing. Chief Blake says, "I think the policeman was reaching for the demonstrator's belt."

Chief Blake says the demonstrators had an observer beside every police car. "They always did that, to watch what went on. And most of the demonstrators conducted themselves well. Only when they brought that bunch in from Sanford, they were rough—I think they weren't trained. The women here were particularly well conducted. Rosemary was a problem in that she always wore nylon slips, and if you didn't watch it, her coat and dress and everything else went to the top of her head. I did strongly object to one thing, to the use of juveniles. I felt some of these young people were going to prison, and they kept using these kids, some of them twelve or thirteen times. Then when they were arrested, the juveniles would lie about their age, because they wanted to be locked up with the others, so a Negro officer would go down each night and identify the juveniles. They'd known them and knew they weren't sixteen. We'd take them out and phone their parents and ask them to come and get them. Sometimes the parents would tell us they didn't think it was wrong to demonstrate; sometimes they would say they didn't know where the child was, that he simply hadn't come home from school that day; and sometimes they would say they didn't want the child to demonstrate. One mother talked with Pat right out on the steps of the town hall. She said, 'Pat, I don't want my boy to be part of these things any more.' Pat said if the boy wanted to, he could take part. The mother said, 'If he does it again, I'll get you for contributing to the delinquency of a minor.' Pat said he would understand that. 'Yes, you'll understand why I did it,' she said, 'and I'll understand, but what will my race think?' "

As Chief Blake prepared for the February 1 date, he told his officers to be on the lookout for any sign of what tactics were likely to be followed and to work their contacts, seeking information. "We never did tap their telephone," he says, "though they claimed we did, but we had many ways of finding out what they would do and we often knew where they were going. The only time we didn't know were the two times at the Rock Pile. After that first night they promised to phone and let us know when they planned to go back out there. Ben Spaulding was supposed to phone, but the call never came through. Usually we could tell what they were about. You could tell a great deal just by watching what they wore: they had their demonstration clothes and their regular clothes."

He had contact with police departments elsewhere, and he had pictures of civil rights leaders. He and his men also noticed that many of the white segregationist leaders, some of them from the rural areas near Chapel Hill, some of them from Rowan County and other places, were showing up in town. Phone calls increased, with people saying, "If you don't get those damn niggers off the street, we will." Chief Blake says he never worried so much about handling the Chapel Hill people, but that no small town can take care of the integrationist leaders and segregationist leaders arriving from all over a state or region. "The State Patrol offered fifty officers," he said, "and I appreciated it, and I asked Burlington if they could let us have fifteen or twenty officers to use for crowd control."

Chief Blake admits that his men were really weary now. "We never complained outside the office here," he said, "but you take a man who comes on at 7 A.M., and about six-thirty there's a street march and he has to be kept on duty to watch after that, and then if you aren't careful, they'll start another one right after that one, or they'll use worrying tactics—they'll put a few demonstrators near a segregated place and you don't know whether they're going to sit in or not. Then there will be a sit-in somewhere, and officers are needed there to make arrests, others to control the crowd, and others to watch that the white segregationists don't cause trouble, to break up their groups wherever they appear around town. So about 2 A.M. the booking is finished and the warrants are drawn up. The officer can go home then, but he has to be back at 7 A.M. After three months of that, I don't see how they stood it. And I don't think there is a group of twenty-four men anywhere who could have stood it any better."

Chief Blake was aware that in Chapel Hill there were now no fewer than thirteen workers paid by civil rights organizations. Eight of them spent most of their time there. In addition, Rev. Fred Shuttlesworth, national president of the Southern Conference Education Fund, said he expected to visit Chapel Hill during the first week in February.

Rev. Martin Luther King, commenting at this time on the Chapel Hill situation, said that James Farmer had talked with him about his statement after it had been issued, and that he hoped civil rights demonstrations in Chapel Hill would continue to be of a nonviolent nature.

That, of course, was one of the chief worries of Chief Blake and everyone else who knew the actual situation.

Chapter Twelve

THERE WAS a new civil rights group now existing in Chapel Hill, formed in the main by university professors and their wives, who sensed that a catastrophe might be shaping up and who were anxious for the town to settle its problems in legal ways. About fifty of them met on the evening of the day of Governor Sanford's reply to Mr. Farmer. About 175 people came to the second meeting, which was held on January 18.

At that time, after a lengthy discussion, they authorized the steering committee of five people to draft a letter to the mayor, asking that his new mediation committee be formed promptly and try assiduously to desegregate the holdout segregated places. Further, they asked that the city attorney be asked to draft a proposed public accommodations ordinance for public comment and discussion; that the town's prosecuting attorney, Roy Cole, be directed to consent to all requests for postponement of trespass trials until the United States Supreme Court had had opportunity to pass on these issues as represented in cases the Court was then considering; that the prosecuting attorney be instructed to consent to bail bond in civil rights trespass cases which was not higher than that usually required for trespass cases; and that all town employees be required to practice courtesy and diplomacy toward all citizens in the halls of justice. "We feel that these proposals will form the basis for intelligent discussion," the letter said, "and thereby avert the impending collision which can only hurt everyone."

The executive committee of the group, which came to be called the Committee of Concerned Citizens, tried to implement their program, to arrange a compromise acceptable to CORE and to the town. There was nothing in the list of points they drew up in their letter which the mayor and aldermen could not do, and at the same time they constituted a partial achievement for CORE.

Therefore the executive committee invited the mayor and Alderman Giduz to the meeting, to which they also invited John Dunne and Quinton Baker. "We worked awfully hard to find a time when everybody could meet," Joe Straley says. "We wanted time enough to talk the situation over and try to reach a compromise." Dan Pollitt met with Floyd McKissick and obtained from him a promise to try to persuade Chapel Hill CORE to accept as a compromise the points enumerated in the letter. Dan Pollitt says the main one was that Mr. Cole be asked to treat Negroes as politely as he treated white citizens in the town court.

The meeting was held at the Community Church. Joe Straley was secretary, Dan Okun was chairman. I have gone over the minutes of the meeting and find a general discussion of the problems of the community, without much persuasive effort to compromise the existing, dangerous situation. Roland Giduz, near the opening of the discussion, said everything should be channeled through the mayor's new committee. "We can't settle anything here," he said.

Mayor McClamroch said he had appointed Rev. Vance Barron and Mr. W. T. Thompson of a local bank to the committee and hoped to make the other appointments by the following Monday. He said the new committee "does not supersede the Human Relations Committee. I hope they will keep up the good work."

John Dunne said the James Farmer deadline "is not rigid. We can expect CORE to hold off as long as we see action. CORE has to succeed to maintain itself; the Negroes have a new courage and determination. From our, CORE's, standpoint, we must continue until a moment comes when we will never be needed again. Promise to stop segregation and kill the movement; we are anxious to go out of business."

An hour after it began, without any indication from the town that a compromise was possible, the meeting broke up. Roland Giduz had said at the start he could stay one hour only, because of other appointments which could not be changed.

One further effort to bring about reconciliation was made. Bob Brown, who had been out of the center of things, on January 15 came running up the steps to the Freedom Committee office and told John Dunne and Pat Cusick that he had been sent by the Chapel Hill *Weekly,* but that he wasn't permitted to say who there had sent him. He said a painful editorial was going to press in half an hour, on the front page of the newspaper, and that it would surely destroy the movement. Bob could stop the printing of the editorial; that was part of the deal. The rest of the deal was that four places would be integrated at once, and that about twelve were to come along right after.

"Those four places," John Dunne told me at Sandy Ridge, "were the Pines, the Rock Pile, Brady's and the Tar Heel Sandwich Shop. The first three of those were the toughest rocks in the whole city. If we would merely recant the statement about the February 1 deadline, say that we did not intend it to mean what it said it meant, Bob said all this would be done."

"Of course, we couldn't accept this," Pat Cusick told me at Sandy Ridge. "For one thing, we couldn't make a deal without knowing whom we were dealing with."

"That would be selling out the Negro community," John said.

"So many promises have been broken," Pat said, "dating all the way back to the summer, that we were very skeptical that it would be carried out. We couldn't lay ourselves on the line to these unknown people."

John and Pat did write out a news release, saying they would like to negotiate the matter and would call off all civil disobedience in response to a gesture of good faith. They sent this back with Bob Brown and mailed copies to the mayor and others, but it was not printed and they got no reply.

The *Weekly* editorial did appear. It was simply titled "CORE Invasion." Its last paragraph stated the heartfelt, hurt feelings of many of the residents of the town as they faced a showdown with forces from outside and within. It went as follows:

We are deeply saddened by what has been done and is being done to this town, but we know at the same time that this too will pass. Chapel Hill will endure it and recover. We are more saddened by what the leaders of a once inspiring freedom movement are doing to themselves and to their cause. At best, they will leave here with a taste of ashes, and a self-inflicted wound that will carry a permanent scar.

John Dunne was having housing problems again. Professor and Mrs. Reckford were fond of him and were anxious to help him, but John had become increasingly withdrawn and somewhat careless about their sensitivities. He was not rude, Mrs. Reckford says, but he had become busier and busier, and they were growing weary of having him and his many visitors around all the time.

"It was lovely at first," Mrs. Reckford says. "One day in mid-September he came by, and he had no place to stay. We kept him for dinner and phoned all our friends. One of them, I recall, wouldn't take him, not because of his involvement with the race situation, but because he had been so much in favor of world peace. We kept him in our house, finally, on provision that he emphasize his studies."

John had not done so, of course, and his general attitude toward life and his friends had grown more sullen. He was generally in rebellion against almost everything now. When the Reckfords went away at Christmas, they had asked that he not fill the house with visitors. When they returned, they found evidence that he had done so. So they asked him to leave at the close of the semester, in mid-January, and on January 17 they set his chair and table out in the yard as an additional reminder. "It was," Mrs. Reckford says, "better than scolding him, for he no longer listened to what was said to him."

Quinton had been spending much of his time in John's room. Both boys now went out to find a place to live, and, of course, they encountered enormous problems. John was essentially now dispossessed from the white community of the Southern town, and the Negro section had nothing available that either of them would live in. Finally, they found a house in the Negro section of Durham.

At this same difficult period, John was receiving a great many threatening phone calls. The phone at CORE was tapped, or so he believed, and he arranged codes for his official conversations. One night he was working late at the CORE office, trying to complete plans for the series of demonstrations ahead, and he thought of calling a Negro woman about the use of an automobile. He was talking with her when he heard on the phone the sound of water running. She heard it, too, and neither knew where it was coming from. Then they heard the sound of somebody breathing into the phone.

John says he was conscious of being alone, there over the funeral parlor in this dead-of-night place, and a chill went through him which seemed to bring into his body all in one moment his utter loneliness.

The breathing stopped. He heard a deep-voiced chuckle; it became a laugh, and then a deep voice, speaking each word in a grossly exaggerated manner, said, "White . . . man . . . talk . . . ing . . . to . . . a . . . nig . . . ger . . . wo . . . man." The man laughed deeply, ominously. John says he was scared to death. "White . . . man . . . talk . . . ing . . ." the voice repeated, and John slammed down the phone.

His parents in Ohio also had been receiving ominous calls from strangers each time John's name appeared in the newspapers of the nearby city. One man told Mrs. Dunne he had police dogs and was going to go to Chapel Hill with them and have some fun with John. "I knew he wouldn't," she said, "but I was frightened anyway."

John mentioned this when on January 24 he wrote his parents:

DEAREST FOLKS,

Just a note to let you know that I'm still well and functioning. The struggle continues here, and preparations for a real confrontation are in full swing and we hope, but have little reason to hope, that it can be avoided. All national press will be here on February 1st and that day or soon thereafter we will be exploding. It's tragic that Chapel Hill leaders refuse to take us seriously. They could solve the whole mess and without anyone losing face.

I still haven't found permanent lodging, but will be checking on some possibilities in Durham later this afternoon. Unfortunately certain realtors show their real "liberal" colors when something like a movement is going on.

How are you at home? Hope the job is going well, and that you aren't being plagued with telephone calls, etc. We're getting a number of them here. There is also so much work that I begin to truly understand why great bureaucracies come into being, even in those organizations which are fighting them.

It makes me ache to see how high the walls of ivory are around the academic community here. They're almost all liberal, which serves one purpose, really, and that's to assuage each other's consciences. But liberalism which is in the area of talk and writing books and reading papers and being distressed that people are beaten in Birmingham, and does not get translated into action in the other part of their home town, doesn't help the Negro one bit. In fact, it is a source of deep bitterness. Until the white liberals of this town stop patting each other on the back for abstract political and moral views, and start realizing the facts of suffering as being the issue, we will see very little progress anywhere in this country. In order to correct social ills which were created by the white man, and which have caused great suffering for the Negro, which continues at this very moment, it's going to be necessary that the white man suffer some inconvenience, and this is just what he cannot understand.

Was on TV the other night in a most frustrating position, but it got some good reactions. But once again in Chapel Hill, a panel was set up to discuss what the Negro wants and why he wants it, and the panel was all-white. Intellectual positions are obsolete in this area—the white man just cannot experience or understand this suffering or this urgency.

Well, must go to Durham to check on housing. Hope I can get away to see you all soon. Until then, know that I love you, as always,

JOHN

February 1 was a clear, bright day, one of the winter days in Chapel Hill which remind the citizenry of spring and make them long for it. Nobody wears overcoats on such days, and most people seek to shuck their worries as well. No doubt many did, but others were cautiously aware of the contingent of State Patrolmen who arrived in the morning, and the other contingents from the sheriff's office and the Burlington, North Carolina, Police Department, fifteen officers who had been sent for training, all of them wearing riot helmets. The town also was host to hundreds of visitors, among them many reporters and television cameramen who had come to see what sort of tactics CORE and the Chapel Hill Freedom Committee would unveil.

About two o'clock, Leon Rooke, the writer who had helped Bob Brown prepare the posters for the first parade, and I went downtown to see what was happening. Leon had recently taken a job with the North Carolina Fund, the agency Governor Sanford had established that past fall to work on the cycle of poverty in our state, the pilot statewide antipoverty program for our country. We went down to the Negro church where the demonstrators usually gathered, and they were inside, all right. We could hear them singing. Their singing was far different and far better than the singing on that first march the summer before, when Leon had marched with them.

The singing seemed to be going on and on, so Leon and I went up the street to the Dairy Bar, which two years before had bowed before eight months of picketing. We had an ice cream cone apiece, and stood there watching the people come and go on the sidewalk outside, jockeying for places. We walked on down to Leo's Restaurant, across from the Colonial Drug Store; there were perhaps two hundred people waiting there. Maybe they had concluded that the new wave of action would center on these two places.

I went into Leo's and looked around to see if he was ready for the protest. There were several nervous customers inside sitting at the counter, each of them attentive to every sudden sound from the street.

When I got back outside, many film and television cameramen had arrived, one of them rather outlandishly dressed, wearing sandals on his feet and a towel around his head. "He's not one of us, is he?" a photographer for the Durham newspaper said to me hopefully. There were quite a few photographers about, most of them men who were seen often at the Capitol.

At about one o'clock, the crowd broke from the church and came out onto the lawn. A few minutes later, the demonstrators took to the streets, carrying a huge poster and singing, filling the air with music. All their posters, I noticed, were critical of Chapel Hill. They didn't say anything about Leo's or Clarence's or the Colonial Drug Store; they were critical of the town itself—not the town government, you understand, but the town. They were critical of Leon and me as citizens, I suppose, though we didn't look at it that way that afternoon. The throng of marchers moved past Leo's and the Colonial, giving John Carswell no more than the last verse of a freedom song, dismissing him with that. They swarmed on down Franklin Street toward the main block of town.

Leon and I quickly drove up Cameron Avenue and parked on the university campus. We went running down an alley to the center of the main block, arriving as the marchers were walking past. The sidewalks were jammed with people, and the number of marchers was certainly impressive—the newspapers later reported there were 350. As the marchers moved past, I noticed a new, strange sight.

Ranged across the street was a line of demonstrators, each demonstrator sitting on the pavement, and each holding a poster critical of Chapel Hill. There they sat, seven or eight young people of college age, staring before them, unattentive to the astonished voices all around. They sat there as if they belonged there, as if they were determined to make their protest heard there, and about them was a sense of fulfilled dedication that did not reveal itself in nervousness, but only in the concentrated way they looked before them, evidently not noticing what their eyes were seeing, hearing nothing, concentrating only on what it was they were peacefully representing, forgetting perhaps even the inevitable approach of the police and the inevitability of arrest and jailing.

All of them, as I said, were young people, and the girls were unusually beautiful, yet so incongruously out of place there in the middle of the street. One instinctively wanted to go to them all and say, "Look now, come on away from here and we'll talk this over and surely find some easier way to work this thing out, some way closer to the heart of the matter you protest." But nobody touched them; they were removed from us by a moat of belief which only through months of commitment had they managed to attain with such a complete sense of self-sacrifice.

The police arrived, and a shudder went through all of us watching. We accepted the inevitability of the police, but it was all out of kilter with the society each of us represented. Society's men were in uniform; they represented society militaristically. The police were powerful; the accused were limp. The police were armed; the accused were unarmed. Society today was aggressive; the accused were yielding. Society was irritated; the accused were calm. It was all backward, somehow, and was deeply moving, as perhaps the arrest of young people who are representing a cause they feel is right and good must always be moving, and that was the point of it all.

This was my first view of the new Chapel Hill paddy wagon. I had heard that the town had got an old bread truck and had painted it white. It was an awkward, square creation, with solid metal sides and a metal roof; two doors opened at the back, and through these the police now stuffed the bodies of the demonstrators. Each one, still clutching his sign, was pushed into the bread truck, which then rolled on down Franklin Street to the post office, where another group was blocking the street.

Leon and I didn't go to see the rest of it. We turned and started back to our car, and we came upon Bill Scarborough, one of the *Weekly*'s two main reporters. Evidently he was as disturbed by the event as we had been. Bill had recently announced that he was going on leave from the newspaper in order to become press aide to Dan Moore, who was then running a poor third in the race for the Democratic nomination for governor. I asked Bill something, wondering aloud what Mr. Moore was going to say about the race issue, and Bill murmured that he thought he would say nothing. Leon and I walked up the alley past the Porthole Restaurant, trying to adjust our minds to what we had seen and could not yet evaluate.

Chief Blake had about a hundred officers in town and over thirty patrol cars. From early morning he and his men had been on the move, watching and listening, trying to find out what to expect, identifying the civil rights leaders and the segregationist leaders, who had flooded into town as the morning progressed. Once the march started, some of his police moved out in front, and others followed. Whenever they approached a group of known, militant segregationists, two or three officers were dropped off to watch them.

About the time the demonstrators got to the bus station, Chief Blake says, "Two or three white men went into the Western Auto Store across the street and picked up shovels. They came outside and one of them began to hit every Negro he could get to before we arrested him. He was the same man who drove his car through a march back in July, drove right through a march of two hundred demonstrators. This was pretty serious to us, all of it was. I'm not sure all the demonstrators knew how serious it really was."

That night a large sit-in was held at Brady's. Forty-four people were arrested there. Down the road, another nine were arrested at the Rock Pile. The total arrested for the day was seventy-five, and they filled the Hillsboro jail.

This was the start of the new wave of action, and was a mild start, when one considers the climax a week away. Or even when one considers the statements made the next day by a CORE leader, Rev. B. Elton Cox of High Point, who came to Chapel Hill to talk to the demonstrators and urge them on. He succeeded only in confusing everybody. Certainly he confused Quinton, Pat and John, who had no idea a Negro leader would get up before a large congregation and say he might burn himself to death for the cause of integration. For his efforts, Rev. Cox won from the demonstrators the title "fireball" and got a quick ride out of town. Later he decided he couldn't very well burn his body under any circumstances, since it was the temple of the Holy Spirit.

A somewhat more consistent leader, Rev. Fred Shuttlesworth, the president of the Southern Conference Education Fund, came to town that week, too, and spoke more moderately of his personal intentions. He said that people all over the country had volunteered to come to Chapel Hill and help. He said that integration was nearer completion in Chapel Hill than anywhere else in the South, and that "we want to finish it so it can be used as an example."

After his talk about 175 people held a silent march through the streets. This was on Friday night.

On Saturday everything happened which could happen in civil rights demonstrations in a small town. It was the day of the UNC-

Wake Forest basketball game, the biggest of the season, so hundreds of visitors were crowded into the city. They mingled with the Highway Patrolmen, sheriff's deputies and the Burlington and Chapel Hill police. It was also the winter social weekend, sponsored by the fraternities, and girls had been brought in from home towns and campuses far and wide for the festivities.

Early in the afternoon, Floyd McKissick led a march of over 350 people from one of the Negro churches down the main street and back again. They went inside the church, where a meeting was held. At the end of the meeting, those who didn't want to get arrested were asked to leave. About 150 remained. Of these, five groups were formed, four of them small and one of them consisting of about 110 people. All five groups left the church at the same time.

The largest group walked uptown and, at the main intersection, that of Franklin and Columbia streets, formed a long spiral which kept closing in on its center, until they were tightly packed into the intersection itself. Everybody then sat down, blocking the intersection to traffic. At the same time, the smaller groups sat down on the four main highways serving Chapel Hill, blocking all of them.

On the Durham highway three Negroes and two whites sat down several hundred feet from the Eastgate Shopping Center. Astonished drivers pulled to a stop and stared in bewilderment. One driver inched forward until his bumper touched two of the prone young men. They didn't move. The driver turned off the car motor and sat there, exasperated. Soon cars were backed up for half a mile, two abreast. Even the police cars couldn't get through.

The Pittsboro highway was blocked near Merritt's Service Station and Grocery. Men who came over from the service station and from stopped cars roughly dragged the eleven demonstrators off the highway, but they jumped back into the road as soon as they could. Signs were torn from their hands. Their clothing was torn. An instructor at the university, Robert Sitton, who had driven some of the demonstrators to this place, says he stood nearby and in agony watched his wife being beaten by the men. Dr. Robert M. Miller, a history professor at the university, stepped into the middle of the affair and tried to restore order, to hold down the tempers of the white men and to modify the determination of the demonstrators. At one point the men dragged the demonstrators off the road and a car started through. Another demonstrator threw herself onto the street and was almost struck.

The police arrived twenty minutes after the sit-down had started and arrested all the demonstrators. The white men then began to strike a cameraman from Station WSOC in Charlotte; the police managed to stop that. Lieutenant Creel, murmuring, "It's almost too wet to plow out here," went from one person to another, trying to bring about order.

The Hillsboro highway was blocked by seven demonstrators, who were arrested and hauled away. The Raleigh highway was blocked at the Country Club Road intersection. James Foushee was there. "The policemen wouldn't arrest us," he says. "They were campus police. They dragged us off the street, and we just walked back on and lay down again. A student came up with his Corvair, a Monza, came up the street at about seventy miles an hour, and he got right on us and saw we weren't going to move, so he hit his brake and stopped his car about that close, about an inch, from me. So the policemen pulled us off the road again, and we got back on. That went on for about half an hour, with them dragging us off and we would get back on."

At about the same time, just before the afternoon basketball game let out, these same demonstrators went to Woollen Gym and lay down in the road leading out of the parking lot. The campus police dragged them off to the side; they crawled back. Several drivers got out of their cars and pleaded with them to move. One lady said she had to take her little boy to a birthday party. They wouldn't move.

At the main intersection of town, the chief of police asked the demonstrators to leave. They did so. But soon five Negro and three white demonstrators returned and lay down. Several cars wove their way between them at high speeds. They continued to lie there in the road even so.

The paddy wagon, which was being driven by the fire chief, kept hauling people away, until at last, some say, it broke down, blocking a road itself.

That night sixty more demonstrators marched to the main intersection and sprawled on the pavement. James Foushee says he was lying there in the street when a woman drove her car up to him. He lay there. She came forward until her wheel hit him. He lay there. Five policemen came up, dragged him out of the way and said they were arresting him on the charge of attempted suicide, Jim says.

In all, that day ninety-eight people were arrested.

Whatever complacency might have existed in the town that morning was gone by now. Never before had the town arrested so many people; not in many decades had it been so mightily interfered with. Many citizens were enraged. The homes of the aldermen and policemen were busy with telephone calls. Mayor McClamroch, who had spent the entire day at the Police Department, wondered if the town had gone crazy.

And nobody knew what could be done to stop further actions by these masses of young people, who were evidently so skillfully led, so sure of their cause, that they would put their bodies down on the public roads and lie in the path of oncoming traffic, who were undaunted in the face of police, who could be piled into a paddy wagon until the paddy wagon itself expired. But the young people did not expire, did not relent, did not break, did not show any sign at all of giving one inch in the struggle they had aroused and which they insisted must take place, the confrontation decades in the making.

Negro parents knelt in prayer in the churches and in their homes. Whatever belief had been promoted by segregationists that the Negro community was itself disinterested was dispelled now. The Negroes had offered up in one day scores of their young people. In spite of their fears of jails and policemen and authority, they had sent the best young people they had into the very jaws of civil authority, and their only appeal, the one many of them made all that night through, was in the form of prayer to the only Higher Authority they knew.

Sunday night the personal assistant to James Farmer, Mr. Robert Gore, spoke to a congregation of demonstrators and told the hundreds of people assembled that CORE would support them "200 per cent." He said, "We are going to change the status quo here." He criticized the university for not taking, as he put it, an official stand against segregation. "It's past time for discussion," he said. "The university and its faculty ought to take the lead in the desegregation movement." He criticized the Democratic Party for allowing Southerners to hold up passage of the Civil Rights Bill then before Congress, and criticized state politicans "who think they have my vote in their pocket. My vote is too big for anybody's pocket."

After his talk almost two hundred members of the audience marched in single file down the sidewalks of Franklin Street to the main intersection of town and crisscrossed the middle of the intersection, stopping traffic. Wearily the police asked them to cut it out. Their paddy wagon was broken, and they were tired to death of all this. The demonstrators left the intersection and went on down the street, walking in silent lines through the nearly deserted streets.

Monday night the worried Board of Aldermen met and tried to avoid the issue so acutely at hand. They ignored the subject of the Freedom Committee and discussed, instead, the pickets of the new Committee of Concerned Citizens who had recently appeared at Clarence's, the Colonial Drug Store and elsewhere. Injuries to pickets had been reported on Saturday night.

While the board discussed this, fifty demonstrators spiraled back into the main intersection of town, which is only a block from the town hall, and sat down, blocking traffic.

Chief Blake wearily told the aldermen that two of his men had resigned from the force, so there were now only twenty-two men and himself, and when these were divided into three eight-hour shifts, seven days a week, the police force wasn't large enough for the duties it now had. Also, three or four of his men had checked into the hospital and weren't currently available for duty.

The aldermen got to talking about putting a curfew on picketing. Some of the members wondered if they might limit the picketing hours to 7 A.M. to 7 P.M., in order to reduce the police duties, since the pickets had to be protected now from violence. Some of the aldermen said such a rule would be unconstitutional; others thought it was the best thing, considering the limitations of the police force. Favoring the restriction were Aldermen Page, Giduz and Strowd. There was a three-three vote cast, so the mayor had to vote, and he voted in favor of the curfew.

Mrs. Susie H. Weaver, a Negro, approached the board and asked them to pass a public accommodations ordinance, and Professor T. Franklin Williams approached the board and asked for the same thing. Alderman Giduz read a statement reiterating his support of the Mayor's Mediation Committee. The mayor made a report, saying that the Mayor's Mediation Committee hadn't been able to accomplish anything as yet.

The besieged alderman moved on now to discuss the plan of Section 4 of the Ridgefield Heights subdivision. A block away fifty demonstrators were being dragged off the streets to the sidewalks and arrested. They were being pushed into police cars while other demonstrators threw themselves under the wheels of the cars, both behind and in front of the wheels, so they couldn't be moved. The police dragged these demonstrators out and arrested them, only to have other demonstrators take their places. The police cars were jammed full and immobile. A girl demonstrator was struck by a car driven by a civilian. The demonstrators wouldn't move.

The sweating policemen carried and dragged them toward the town hall, while the aldermen talked about rezoning Sections 2 and 3 of Colony Woods from agriculture to RA-15 and RA-10. The desk sergeant downstairs in the building began to book the demonstrators into the town jail.

The aldermen went on to discuss retaining a section in the parking ordinance concerning private parking on highway right-of-ways, and a Section 5 of Farrington Hills subdivision, while the music of the freedom songs started in the jail in the building where they met.

John Dunne and Pat Cusick came to the town hall and stood at the door, watching their friends being carried inside. A man came downstairs and told them what the aldermen were discussing, and John says he felt a limpness come over his spirits as complete as the limpness of the bodies of the young people being carried past him to the cells. He says he was too weary even to sit down on the steps of the little colonial building. He was deathly tired as he watched the deathly-looking bodies carried past him through the propped-open doorway of the town hall.

They had challenged the town. Now they found that the town was deaf to them. They could go on to yet another stage, could disrupt even more completely the order of the place. Or they could stop now and be the ones who after all would save the town from violence. The aldermen were indeed asking them to save the town from violence;

the aldermen were counting on the sense of citizenship of the young people who had defied the citizens and the citizens' sense of citizenship to save the town.

Quinton, John and Pat say they decided they could not again send the young people against what to them was an unfeeling wall. They had come to the end of the ten-day plan of action, and now they would wait a while, then draw up another plan, perhaps of a different type altogether.

* * *

A few days later, Rev. Charlie Jones decided to test the ordinance limiting picketing. Picketing had had a great deal to do with Charlie Jones' life for several years and had advanced his cause considerably. "One morning I phoned Dan Pollitt," he says, "and asked him if a curfew on picketing was unconstitutional. 'Of course it is,' Dan said —you know Dan. So the two of us went to call on the mayor, and we told him we would have to challenge the ordinance in the courts, unless it was withdrawn. Mayor McClamroch checked with a few people and reported that he thought he could get the time limit changed, so that pickets could picket until 9 P.M. I said that wouldn't do."

Charlie Jones decided that four people would picket that night and establish a court case. The chosen four were Mrs. Isabelle Carter, Mrs. Barbara Cleveland, Rev. Tom Davis and himself. Mrs. Carter had been the Sunday school teacher of the Recorders Court judge, Bill Stewart, and it was believed this fact would help all four of them stay out of jail when they came before the bar of justice. Dan Pollitt was not included, in order that he could arrange for legal defense. Joe Straley was to be the observer.

Charlie Jones says, "I phoned Chief Blake and told him we were going to be arrested that night and we could come to the town hall and picket there, in order to make it convenient for him, and we could appear at any time he set. Chief Blake asked if he might call us back. I'm sure he didn't really want to arrest us."

Another group of white liberals had organized to oppose the restriction on picketing. Professor Sitton, J. Allen Reddick, a recently arrived citizen of the town, Professor Straley and about forty others were part of it. This group had wanted to go on down and picket at once, but Charlie Jones had urged them to consent to planning. He also hinted, Professor Sitton tells me, that his group, which at this time was named the Committee of One Hundred, might be able to get legal defense money from the Civil Liberties Union.

A compromise had been reached, which called for Charlie Jones' group to come to Al Reddick's apartment, where the two groups would, at the proper time, march together to the town hall and share the honor of the occasion, though it was agreed that only Charlie Jones' group would do the actual picketing.

On the assigned night, the four who were prepared for arrest, along with several of their advisers, met at the Community Church. They were getting ready to leave for Mr. Reddick's apartment when Chief Blake came huffing and puffing to the door. He said he didn't know whether he had good news or not, but that he had been told that a state law requires a town ordinance pass by a two-thirds vote, or, failing that, be passed at the next meeting of the aldermen by a majority vote. So there is no picketing ordinance to worry about, he said.

The four people were disappointed; they had steeled themselves for the experience. Rev. Davis evidently was particularly upset. He had refused to become involved in the arrests generated by the freedom committee because he didn't approve of their general approach, and he was now being deprived of an arrest which he could justify to himself and everybody else.

The four people and their companions went along to Mr. Reddick's apartment anyway, and from there the entire group walked to the town hall, Father Parker and Professor Straley leading the march along Franklin Street. When they arrived, they picketed for a while, then asked that a representative of the town come outside to meet with them. Chief Blake dutifully came to the door and stepped onto the stoop. Professor Robert Sitton, who had been wondering for an hour what in the world the new organizations might do to justify this extraordinary display of power and energy, came forward and, by the light of a flashlight, read to him in a loud voice the First Amendment to the United States Constitution, which Chief Blake silently took in.

So ends what can be described as a baffling experience involving some bewildered American citizens. I suspect they were somewhat shocked by all the action which had been going on around them, so they decided to create some action of their own.

The ordinance was not taken up at the next meeting of the Board of Aldermen, so it never was passed into law.

Hate literature, signed by the American Nazi Party, with an Arlington, Virginia, address, began to appear in town. The literature had recipes for "instant nigger mix," which told how to make one's own Negro slave out of garbage and the like. Two men, both North Carolinians, came into town with the literature, and one of them, perhaps both, left it at Harry's Grill and other restaurants. They attended a party held by some of the demonstrators and distributed it there, and one of them late in the evening, affected by his anger at the demonstrators and the whisky he had consumed, had to be dragged away from a young blond demonstrator, a student at the university, whom he had choked almost into unconsciousness.

The next day the student's apartment was broken into.

There were other reports of forced entry and assault on demonstrators, but none of them was seriously injured.

Chapter Thirteen

A UNIVERSITY CAMPUS is itself a community with its own government and laws. As is true of most all universities, the campus at Chapel Hill operates on student, faculty and administrative levels, each having semi-autonomous courts, administrators and spokesmen.

All three levels had been participating in the civil rights struggle, though the students were by far the most active, just as they also were the least vulnerable.

Mike Lawler, the president of the student body, and Bob Spearman, the vice-president, came out in favor of a student boycott of those businesses which would not serve all students. The student legislature voted to support this position. The *Daily Tar Heel* supported it, too. When the Chi Omega sorority and the ATO fraternity held banquets at the Pines Restaurant, they found themselves picketed by their fellow students, most of them members of the Wesley Foundation, and they were royally trounced in an editorial in the *Daily Tar Heel,* which considered their explanation, that it would have been inconvenient to go elsewhere, to be close to insulting. The Chapel Hill *Weekly* commented on the matter as follows:

> The Brothers and Sisters might look on this sort of criticism as somewhat unhinged, since they are themselves rigidly segregated, and patronizing segregated establishments is simply a matter of doing what comes naturally. . . . Perhaps for the first time since the struggle began, the pot is being taken to task for NOT calling the kettle black.

About fifteen hundred students signed a petition supporting the boycott; those who objected to the boycott said they had a petition, too, with about fifteen hundred signatures on it, but they would not let it be published.

In the student courts, the charge was brought against student demonstrators that their conduct broke the honor code, that it was essentially ungentlemanly, and that they should therefore receive punishment, which could be expulsion or suspension from the university. A test case was brought before the all-student board of judges, the Honor Council. Speaking for the defendant was Robert Sitton of the philosophy department, who argued that "It is not the breaking of a law per se that matters; it is which law you break and why you break it."

Concerning the matter of "going limp," the graceless matter of flopping around in police cars like rag dolls, he said, "Here, I grant you, it looks pretty silly. Yet it seems to me that a gentleman is the kind of person who is man enough to look silly when there is good reason to do so. If looking silly will help bring respect, liberty and fair play into the lives of colored citizens, then I say there is good reason for looking silly."

Professor Sitton said the Negro had every right to go onto the street to demand his citizen's rights. "The United States of America, in the past, has actually gone to war for less reason than the Negro has right now for simply sitting in at lunch counters, or, when necessary, lying in the street. The blood of Americans, both black and white, has been shed for the sake of preserving the rights of Poles and Czechs, and yet we fail to see the immoral and illegitimate enslavement of a substantial portion of our own people within the borders of our country. . . .

"But the Negro does not fight; that is the important thing. He does not openly retaliate. . . . In this I say he is not only gentlemanly, he is superhuman. And this student on trial here tonight for acting in the same manner is equally due our respect, for how many of us would have the courage to act likewise? How many of us would not strike back when flagrantly attacked and beaten as we have seen demonstrators attacked and beaten in recent days in Chapel Hill? How many of us would contain our hatred upon being suffocated and burned with ammonia by a man not worthy of the property sold him by the state? How many of us would not have struck viciously back at the unspeakable action of a woman so despicable as to relieve her very body over another human being? Or who would not have exploded with rage at the twelve men who beat, kicked and tore the clothes off demonstrators on the Pittsboro Road this past Saturday? I say to you in all honesty that a person who can undergo these horrors and emerge saying, as I heard one demonstrator say recently, 'I love them and I forgive them for their ignorance,' is truly a gentleman. He is a gentleman in precisely the same sense that Jesus Christ was a gentleman."

Professor Sitton concluded by asking the youthful judges to consider their action in terms of their place in the history of the country. "I want you to look upon the decision you are about to make from the perspective of ten years hence. Ten years from now, should Providence permit that we are still alive . . . what will you say when you are asked where you were in 1964 and what you were doing in this struggle? What will you say when you remember this night and the action you are about to take? Will you say that you found your fellow student guilty of 'ungentlemanly conduct' because he subjected himself to brutality and embarrassment for taking part in what some people are already calling the American Revolution of 1963?"

Professor Daniel Pollitt of the university Law School also spoke in defense of this same demonstrator, discussing the legal matter involved, using as reference the code of standards of the American Association of University Professors. Then, with what the *Daily Tar Heel* described as "a significant and historical step in freeing us from an outdated definition of gentlemanly conduct," the Honor Council decided that Thomas Bynum, the defendant, was not guilty of ungentlemanly conduct because of his actions, even though he had broken the laws of Chapel Hill.

The *Tar Heel* editors said:

> We feel the decision was not only just, but courageous. There seems little doubt that much invective will be hurled at the Council members for having reached their decision. It is unprecedented in any university in the South, and this is particularly fitting since Carolina has been a leader in the past and should return to that position. The Honor Council has helped us reach for that leadership.

The faculty was not nearly so actively involved as the students in civil rights matters, but they were a long way from being aloof. About 150 faculty members signed a statement supporting the student boycott, and the local and state chapters of the American Association of University Professors voted their support of any professor's right to join in demonstrations; the local chapter further appointed a committee to see if discrimination in hiring practices was being employed on the Chapel Hill campus, and a committee on student academic freedom. The committees never did anything, evidently, but they were established.

By no means did all these professors, or even most of them, like the type of civil disobedience tactics being employed. "Nobody had to carry Jesus limp to the cross," one professor, at one of the AAUP meetings, growled. But they did almost unanimously approve freedom of action.

A meeting of the Faculty Council took up a pertinent question during this period. It pertained to a recommendation of the television committee that a series of programs dealing with the subject of segregation not be carried. The series, "Dynamics of Desegregation," had been produced by a Harvard professor and was distributed by National Educational Television. The local committee had voted not to broadcast the series, and Professor Wesley Wallace, chairman of the department which teaches television courses, objected to this action, pointing out that the educational television station owned by the university had never before refused a series of the national educational network.

History Professor James Godfrey, the dean of faculty, said the chancellor was responsible for what was broadcast and had a perfect right to refuse a series if he wanted to. Dean Godfrey said that in his opinion the fact that a program had been produced by a Harvard professor didn't mean that it was necessarily educational. To which a professor replied that he tended to agree, but thought it wise to mention that the professor in question had earned his degree at the University of North Carolina.

The chairman of the meeting, Chancellor Aycock, managed to get the matter returned to a committee, which action effectively killed the effort to have the series broadcast. The issue never came to a vote of the Faculty Council.

Some of the faculty members and their wives picketed segregated establishments. Others wrote letters to the newspapers and to public officials. Dean of the Law School Henry Brandis wrote an open letter to Senator Sam Ervin which criticized the senator's apparent effort to keep the Civil Rights Bill from coming to a vote. Their exchange of letters was published in the *Weekly* and elsewhere.

"The pending civil rights proposals," Senator Ervin wrote, "are the most monstrous blueprint for governmental tyranny presented to an American Congress since George Washington took his oath of office." He said the pending civil rights proposals attempted to transfer from the states to the Federal Government power to prescribe the qualifications for voting in Federal elections; attempted to "confer upon all departments and agencies administering any program involving the use of federal funds the power to use untold billions of dollars of federal appropriations to bribe or browbeat States, political subdivisions of States, charitable institutions, industry, and individuals into an acceptance of their views in matters relating to race"; undertook to regulate the use of privately owned property and the "rendition of personal services within the States"; and undertook to give the Attorney General and other Federal officials vast discretionary powers. Senator Ervin objected to what he believed were invasions of the rights of the states. "I cannot be silent upon these matters as long as the rules of the Senate permit me to speak," he wrote.

Dean Brandis replied that the ultimate authority on the constitutionality of legislation is the Supreme Court, not a minority of senators, and he said, further, "You are greatly perturbed by the effect of legislation restricting an individual's freedom of choice. I do not recall that you have ever been similarly exercised over numerous state statutes, enforced for so many years, not only restricting freedom of choice, but also denying equality of privileges and rights, by requiring segregation." Concerning the argument that the proposed law invaded rights of the states, he said:

> The same contention made with reference to human slavery led to secession and the Civil War. Yet who now, looking back over the intervening century, seriously believes that slavery was not a national problem? I believe that today the issue of human rights is still a national problem, rather than one to be inconsistently dealt with or neglected by the states. If it ever should have been regarded as merely a local issue, then it has nevertheless been forced on to the national stage by the refusal of our southern states to face it realistically.

The individual rights guaranteed by our Constitution should, he said, be made true and meaningful for all our citizens.

Dean Brandis had also written a letter critical of the Chapel Hill demonstrators and their street-blocking tactics.

> It is not more saintly to engage in criminal activity because one disapproves the law being violated than, as in the case of the traffic-blocking, to engage in such activity because one disapproves some other law or some general condition in the community. At least, if this is saintly, then Barnett, Wallace and General Walker are equally entitled to canonization. . . . There is no possibility that more complete equal justice can be achieved for the Negro through the destruction of public order.

This came closer to pleasing Senator Ervin, who wrote in his open letter to the *Weekly:*

> While I do not agree with the observations made by you in your letter to me, I do approve what you had to say in your previous letter to the Chapel Hill *Weekly*. You rightly condemned the demonstrations which have recently occurred in Chapel Hill in which the demonstrators by the sheer force of numbers denied the general public its undoubted legal right to the free use of public streets and public sidewalks, and the private

owners of property their undoubted legal right to use their own property for their own purposes. . . . Since the coercion inherent in a multitude of demonstrators is equivalent to the use of actual violence, it is wholly erroneous to describe demonstrations of this nature as "peaceful and non-violent."

Dean Brandis made his views known to lawyers of the state, too, and in one talk to them said, "It's very much more dangerous for a small minority in the Senate to block votes on the Civil Rights Bill," than for "young fanatics" to lie down in the street. He also took ministers to task, those "who, in defining the ideology of the demonstrations, are attempting to depict lawbreaking as a moral and Christian activity. I call this 'scofflaw Christianity.' It is much more dangerous than the ordinary variety of hoodlumism. The idea that it is all right to break the law if your conscience tells you to is uncontrollable when placed in the minds of people already disposed to fanaticism."

Among other professors who made talks at this time was one of Dean Brandis' friends and associates, Dan Pollitt, who spoke in defense of the demonstrator brought before the Honor Council, and spoke often in the community, explaining the provisions of the Civil Rights Bill then before Congress. On one occasion he spoke before the Women's Republican Club, which is itself something of a minority group in Democratic Party-controlled Chapel Hill.

Other professors took part in civil rights activities by teaching Negro students when some seventy high school students, exasperated by the poor conditions they found in the Negro high school and motivated by a general sense of rebellion and protest, bolted from the place and attended a makeshift school established for them by the Freedom Committee. Nobody was quite sure what purpose this boycott was to serve. Each bulletin from the Freedom Committee seemed to contradict the one of the day before, and nobody felt the boycott was either well planned or likely to achieve much.

Pat Cusick says the leaders of the Negro students came to him and said they were going to leave school and wanted the Freedom Committee to set up a school for them. He says he had been encouraging them to represent their rights and to exert leadership; now he felt obligated to go along with them. He persuaded the local Church of

God to provide classroom space, and he asked several university professors to teach, which they did, even though doing so held them up more to ridicule than to praise. The teachers found the students woefully lacking in formal knowledge and pitifully eager to learn. The school lasted for only eight or nine days, until an uneasy truce was made with the public school system. The student leader of the revolt was refused readmittance by the superintendent of schools, Howard Thompson, who told the School Board he would resign rather than readmit him.

Another professor, Maynard Adams of the philosophy department, devised what he hoped would be a permanent system for dealing with community social problems, a new agency supported by the main city and county governmental bodies, one empowered to carry out research and action programs to alleviate injustices and create opportunities. He appeared in support of his plan before the Mayor's Human Relations Committee, the Board of Aldermen, the County Commissioners, the town School Board and the university administration, and he won their agreement of support. How the programs were to be financed was yet to be determined.

The Committee of Concerned Citizens was another faculty-dominated civil rights venture. It had evolved out of the picketing ordinance groups and had formed a comprehensive program with committees assigned to work on housing, education, employment, voter registration and picketing. The CCC, which was now the chief haven of the nonmilitant Chapel Hill liberals, had two hundred members, and these members formed groups of lobbyists to travel to Washington and work in favor of the Civil Rights Bill, and to find out how best to implement the law once it was passed. James W. Prothro, a political science professor, wrote a twelve-page statement for Congress, summarizing the efforts made in Chapel Hill to abolish segregation, and he concluded that

the only solution to Chapel Hill's difficulties lies in the passage of the Civil Rights Bill now before the Senate. Voluntary action can achieve much, as it has in Chapel Hill, but it cannot achieve a community-wide policy in which a Negro can feel certain that he will be treated as an individual rather than as a member of a race. In some respects, the plight of the Negro is worse under partial integration than under complete segregation, because he must constantly wonder when he will be accepted as a customer and when he will be rejected.

Chapel Hill has come a long way on its own. It cannot manage the final step that is so desperately needed without the help of a Civil Rights Act.

The Prothro statement, supported by groups of professors of the university and by the weight of evidence assembled by the various committees and demonstrations in Chapel Hill, constituted one of the most emphatic pieces of evidence to enter the Senate's discussion.

The university administration had to keep an eye on both the students and the faculty, and at the same time steer a course for the university which would not let the ship end up on the reefs. In charge of university policy was the chancellor, who had control of the local campus, and the president, who had general administrative control of the campuses at Chapel Hill, Raleigh and Greensboro.

The Chancellor was William Aycock, a law professor, who had already announced that he was returning to teaching in September and was giving up administrative responsibility. He was a tough-minded man, eminently fair, who worried about each of the university's problems as it appeared, and they appeared these days by the score.

He dealt with the subject of discrimination at length in a public statement, pointing out that the hiring offices of the university were open to all applicants and were used by both Negroes and whites. He said that Negroes on the whole were less qualified and when offered a job usually decided not to take it. He could not explain all this, and he admitted the fact remained that none of the members of his 750-professor faculty was a Negro, and that, except at the hospital, few Negroes were found in white-collar or supervisory positions.

When Professor Sitton said publicly that the chancellor had discouraged him from taking part in the demonstrations, using as grounds the ire of the legislature, the chancellor denied this. Four days later he replied in detail, saying, "I don't think anyone connected with the university should participate in civil disobedience. I think it injures the university. It's not on the grounds of what might or might not happen in the legislature. It's on much broader issues." He discussed the public image of the university, and also the effect arrests of faculty members might have on students. The rest of their lives, he said, "they may not know which laws to violate and which to obey."

Professor Sitton maintained that the free exercise of one's conscience can never, under any circumstances, harm an educational institution, "whereas the refusal to take a stand would certainly sooner or later hurt our university."

The chancellor defended the right of any member of the faculty, including Professor Sitton, to state his opinion and to follow the dictates of his conscience. The chancellor was essentially a man of law. One of the laws he recognized and which was most dear to him was the law of academic freedom; he considered it very close to being supreme. He did not, however, dismiss all other laws. He was quite evidently willing to enforce the laws which fell to him to enforce, and he obviously refused to become involved with the enforcement by others of laws which fell to them to enforce, even if faculty members and students were involved.

The president of the university, William C. Friday, also a lawyer by training, was the official who worked most closely with the legislature and the governor. He was a buffer between political pressures and the right of the university to determine its proper role in the society of which it was a part. No university in the South, and perhaps none in the country, had a closer orientation historically to its society than had the university at Chapel Hill, and no university was part of a society more subject to change and retaliation.

In terms of political pressure, three chief ingredients needed to be watched most carefully at this time: one was the governor, another was the legislature, and the third was the public, which eventually would change both governor and legislature as it chose to. At this time the governor, who was also chairman of the university Board of Trustees, was openly dedicated to fairness, as he defined it, in the race issue. His position was clear. In one recent speech he had said, "A lack of good will between races does no good at all. There is nothing we have to do, no task which we have to undertake, which cannot be better undertaken in a spirit of good will." He also said, "As we hold down any group of citizens, we hold down the whole state. North Carolina is coming through with a show of conscience never before felt in its history."

He had recently invited the Negro college student leaders to meet with him in Raleigh, and he had proposed that they stop all sit-ins and marches and put their minds to work on the production of a series of television documentaries which would represent their grievances. In return for their cooperation, he would seek to get for them production and broadcast facilities, and would ask the people of the state to watch the programs they produced. The young leaders present agreed, and now those programs were being produced in Raleigh. The governor also had Good Neighbor Councils operating in over thirty communities, and he had mediators at work with the mayors in the state. In terms of the Civil Rights Bill, he had called it extreme, but was the only Southern governor who had not testified in Congress against it. By his words and actions, the governor's position could be clearly interpreted.

The legislature did not, however, speak with a single voice, and some of the members were openly antagonistic to the governor's position, which they felt favored the Negro against the white citizen. In the last session of the General Assembly, the state legislature, which had supported the governor's program in all other respects, in its closing hours pushed through a speaker-ban law which made it unlawful to use facilities of a state-supported college or university for speaking purposes if the speaker was a known member of the Communist Party, was known to advocate the overthrow of the Constitution of the United States or the State of North Carolina, or had pleaded the Fifth Amendment of the Constitution of the United States when asked about such possible connections or views.

The bill was characterized by the president of the State Senate, Clarence Stone, a venerable lawmaker of North Carolina, as an effort to get revenge on the civil rights demonstrators. The university had not been given a chance to comment on the matter, and now it was saddled with the law, since there was no veto permitted a North Carolina governor. The law was anathema to the officials, in that it closed down the university campuses to the free exchange of ideas. President Friday and the chancellors publicly had gone on record against it; Mr. Friday had met with any number of editors and citizens groups, explaining his objections to it. As of the moment, all three Democratic candidates for governor had taken stands on it, Candidate Lake being in support of the measure with minor adjustments and the other two candidates favoring amendments to it. Not a one of the candidates had come out against it.

This was an indication of the feeling of the people in the state as a whole. The entire trend of the current gubernatorial election was an indicator of the popular sentiments of the state. Yet complicating any accurate forecast of the outcome of the campaign then going on was the position of the Negro leaders themselves. Floyd McKissick, speaking in Misenheimer, North Carolina, had recently said, "What's the difference, in the eyes of a Negro, between a so-called liberal candidate and a candidate favoring segregation who admittedly would do nothing? Many Negro people feel they have no real gubernatorial candidate they can vote for, and many Negro people are considering formulating their own slate of candidates."

Civil rights leaders in Chapel Hill tended to follow his train of thought. "To the average Negro, Sanford and Lake are little different —both simply 'white governors in Raleigh.' " That was how one reporter, Ed Yoder of the Greensboro *Daily News,* summarized the views of John Dunne, Quinton Baker and Pat Cusick after an interview with them in Chapel Hill.

When one considers the views of the governor, the views of the legislature and the completely undefined views of the populace, the position President Bill Friday found himself in at this time can be viewed with sympathy, especially when one recalls that at his very doorstep fifteen hundred charges had been brought against demonstrators, many of them students of the university at Chapel Hill. At this critical time in the gubernatorial campaign, at a time of dangerously mixed emotions among the people, all these cases were due to come up for trial. Several hundred charges had already been given the Orange County Grand Jury, and almost certainly the jury would report indictments. It was clearly a time for battening down the hatches.

So the comments of the president and chancellor of the university at this particular time must be judged in terms of this condition around them and around the university. Evidently they had decided that all they could responsibly do was maintain an atmosphere in which the students and faculty members could work out, each with his own conscience, his responsibility and actions. By the same token, if they ran afoul of the law, they would need to represent themselves.

As of this time, therefore, the people, including the governor and the leaders of Chapel Hill, who might in normal times have intervened in favor of moderation in the trials of the demonstrators, were unable or unwilling to do so.

There was, however, one final effort made to resolve the differences. It was organized, at the suggestion of David Coltrane, head of Governor Sanford's Good Neighbor Council, by Anne Queen of the university YMCA-YWCA; James C. Wallace, a Chapel Hill businessman; Mrs. Margaret Taylor; and others, among them Mr. Allard Lowenstein, who attended Chapel Hill as an undergraduate, then went on to Yale. Since then he had become involved in civil rights activities in Spain, the Union of South Africa, and the United States.

It was Al's habit to turn up at moments of crisis, and so he came to Chapel Hill. One night he went to a meeting at Anne Queen's house, where the members of the newly formed group were seeking to find a compromise position which would be acceptable to both sides and would advance the town. The members of this new, unnamed group had been visiting various local leaders, asking what compromise would be acceptable to them. The reports were brought to the meeting, where they were reviewed and discussed. Late that night a plan was agreed upon. It proposed that the Chapel Hill Freedom Committee stop all illegal demonstrations and drop its demand for a local public accommodations ordinance until after the Federal Congress had disposed of the Civil Rights Bill; the town was to agree to a new mayor's committee with membership representing the Freedom Committee, the community leaders, and those working to form the anti-poverty program. This committee was to review the situation in housing, employment and other aspects of life in the Negro community and was to report recommendations for an action program which might involve the combined effort of the community.

Al Lowenstein was asked to talk with the Freedom Committee

about the plan, and Dave Coltrane was to talk with the mayor.

Al talked with John Dunne first, and John admitted that the Freedom Committee didn't have money or supporters left to mount another massive effort. Al asked John to accept the compromise position. A few days later the two of them, along with Professor Amon and some of the other local leaders, went to a reception being given for James Farmer at the home of Floyd McKissick. The reception was delayed, because the host and his guest had been given an appointment with the governor, and they were at the governor's mansion.

Al while he waited brought up the subject of the Chapel Hill compromise. Professor Amon roundly denounced any compromise; he said he knew of white leaders who were now ready to join the movement for the first time, that the movement was going to win in Chapel Hill. This was, of course, what most of the people present wanted to hear, and Al Lowenstein, as so often happens on such occasions, found himself in the uncomfortable position of being an Uncle Tom at a civil rights gathering, and a white Uncle Tom at that.

When Farmer and McKissick arrived, huffing and puffing from their drive from Raleigh, talking about having had their bowl of porridge at the governor's house and being disappointed with the terms he had then presented to them, they also became part of the discussion about Chapel Hill. James Farmer was the first to pay attention to what Al Lowenstein was saying, and he led the way to an acceptance that night by leaders of the Chapel Hill Freedom Committee of the compromise position.

Mr. Coltrane reported to Anne Queen and the others that the conversations with Mayor McClamroch had also been satisfactory. The Chapel Hill Freedom Committee waited hopefully to see what would come of all this, whether the community could be brought together again.

What came of it were the trials and the prison sentences and nothing else at all.

PART II

THE TRIALS

Chapter Fourteen

Dᴜʀɪɴɢ ᴅᴇᴄᴇᴍʙᴇʀ ᴀɴᴅ ᴊᴀɴᴜᴀʀʏ, after the arrests were made, most of the defendants had appeared in Chapel Hill Recorders Court and requested jury trials. Their cases would therefore be carried over to the Orange County Superior Court, a state court, which meets every few months in Hillsboro. Many defendants made no such request, but asked for trial in the Recorders Court; their cases were sent to Hillsboro anyway.

Hillsboro, the county seat of Orange County, is the oldest town in this part of piedmont North Carolina. It once served for a few years as the state capital, and in colonial days it was the center of revolt against the British governors, the people of the area then feeling that the governor and the lowlanders were discriminating against them. The Orange County people, finally, proudly revolted against English Governor Tryon, who met them with an army at a place called Alamance. This was several years before the battles of Concord and Lexington, and, to some people, the Battle of Alamance is the first battle of the American Revolution.

The Regulators defeated Governor Tryon's army and were on their way home when the governor, who saw them walking off from the field, attacked for a second time and defeated them. He hanged their nine leaders in Hillsboro.

This onetime center of civil disobedience was now the place for the trials of the demonstrators.

Hillsboro is dominated by an old and a new courthouse. About the biggest activity in the small town is the court sessions. The old courthouse, which houses a clock sent to Hillsboro as a gift of an English king, is now used as a museum. The new one has a large courtroom, as well as modern offices for the county officials. The town is divided between East and West Hillsboro, the eastern residents being devoted to the historic lore of the place and to genteel residential living. The West Hillsboro residents, being workers in the textile mill, the farm-

215

ers exchange, the stockyard and other businesses, live in clapboard houses which line hilly streets. The town is split down the middle by a main street, which accommodates about three blocks of stores, drug-stores and filling stations.

Generally to be sensed here is the languid attitude sometimes attributed to the entire South; there is a slumbering feeling, as if the town has been left behind in the wake of other places.

The County Commissioners met and appropriated about $18,000 to pay for a three-week special session of court. This was all they could easily afford. They hoped the next regular session could take care of some of the cases, and that the three-week special session would take up the others, or many of the others.

The regular session opened in February, and Judge C. W. Hall was able to try one civil rights case only. This was the case of the Duke math professor, David Smith. Professor Smith had originally been charged by the police with trespass and with assault on a female. The female was Mrs. Austin Watts. The Grand Jury, in reviewing the charges, dismissed the charge of assault, but cited him for trespass.

In the Orange County Superior Court, the solicitor was Thomas (Dick) Cooper, a native of the area, a colorful speaker who could be counted on to represent the state's side of a legal argument in a hard-hitting, partisan manner, using many rural idioms. He had attended prep school in Virginia with Mayor McClamroch, and received his legal training at Chapel Hill, graduating in 1952. He had served as assistant solicitor elsewhere in the state, and he liked the job so much he had run for solicitor when the post became open in his home area. He had been sworn into office in January, 1964, and the trials of the demonstrators were his first real challenge. Politicians in Orange County believed that Cooper was politically ambitious, that the role of solicitor was the first of several he envisioned for himself, and that this first assignment was the first major test he had faced in his career.

On the cold, wintry morning in question, Mr. Cooper began the trial by putting onto the stand Austin Watts himself, the six-foot-one, 280-pound proprietor of Watts Motel and Restaurant. As quoted earlier in the book, Mr. Watts testified as to what he saw that evening, stating that he did not see or take part in any violence. Mr. Wade Penny, the defense attorney, then cross-examined him further. "Have you ever been convicted of any criminal offense in the State of North Carolina?"

"For fighting only," Mr. Watts, according to the court record, answered.

"Do you recall when that was?"

"Twelve or fifteen years ago."

"Only one conviction?"

"Two or three, I don't recall."

"Have you had any recent ones?"

"Yes, sir."

"How recent?"

"About two weeks ago."

"What was it for, fighting?"

"Yes, sir."

"Were those the only criminal offenses you have been convicted of?"

"All I can remember."

"I will ask you if you yourself on one occasion have not been convicted of trespass?"

"No, sir."

"I will ask you if in the year 1937 in Chapel Hill Recorders Court you were not convicted of trespass?"

"Not that I recall."

"It is my understanding you do not recall, you don't know for certain?"

"I don't think I was convicted of trespass."

"You do not remember back that far?"

"Yes, I can remember that far."

"Do you deny you were convicted of trespass in 1937?"

"Me and my wife has had some trouble. She might have had me up for trespass, I don't know. I have not been convicted of it that I know of."

"Did any of these assault charges involve your wife as prosecuting witness?"

"No, sir."

"You say she has not been the prosecuting witness?"

"No, sir."

"I will ask you in reference to an assault, were you not convicted of assault on or about October 20, 1947?"

"Not that I recall. I believe I was in 1948."

"Was the prosecuting witness in that case Mrs. Jeffrey Duke?"

"I don't recall, not that I remember."

"Was your wife's last name Duke?"

"Yes, it was."

"You don't remember who the prosecuting witness was at that occasion in 1947?"

"I don't remember any case called."

"Judgment was continued on condition you not molest Mrs. Duke, and be of good behavior?"

"In 1947 she was my wife."

"You were married to her at that time?"

"Yes."

"Is Duke her maiden name?"

"Yes, sir."

"The most recent assault charge is the one two weeks ago?"

"Yes, sir."

"Do you have some difficulty controlling your emotions?"

"No, sir."

Following Mr. Watts' testimony, W. E. Clark, a deputy sheriff, testified that he had heard Mr. Watts ask the members of the group to leave, and that he had "told them they would be arrested for trespass if they didn't leave. I told them they would be arrested for resisting arrest if they didn't get up and . . . walk."

Mr. Penny asked him if the demonstrators he found out in the parking lot of the restaurant "had been soaked with water?"

"They were wet," Mr. Clark said. He said they were huddled together in a group, sitting on the ground just outside the door of Watts Motel and Restaurant.

These two, Mr. Watts and Mr. Clark, were the witnesses for the state's case. The two Negro policemen who were the first police officers on the scene were not called to testify.

The defense first put on the stand Professor Robert T. Osborn, the thirty-eight-year-old associate professor of religion at Duke. He testified that as the group of eleven people approached the restaurant "the doors were being closed in front of us, and just as they were about to be closed, so we could not come in, the door was opened again and Dr. Amon was identified by the group, they recognized him and drew him in, and I was standing at that time right outside of the door, and they drew him into the vestibule between the two doors, and he was immediately knocked down and they began to kick him. . . ."

Dr. Osborn testified that the group outside the building was hosed down with water. "I can remember very vividly the back of my shirt being pulled from my neck so the hose nozzle could be tucked under. There was, I believe, Mrs. Watts with a broom, systematically beating, hitting members of the group."

Mr. Penny asked Professor Osborn "whether or not Mr. Watts made any statement to you upon your arrival at the restaurant?"

"No, he made no statement to me."

" . . . At that time that you were present on that occasion as a member of the group at Watts Restaurant, did Mr. Watts ever address you individually?"

"No."

"Did you ever hear Mr. Watts address you collectively as a group?"

"No."

"I ask you now, did you ever have any conversation with Mr. Clark, the deputy?"

"No, no conversation."

"Did you hear him address you personally?"

"A deputy addressed me personally. I cannot honestly say that it was Mr. Clark. There were other deputies there. But a deputy did address me personally."

"Tell the jury what was stated."

"He put his hand on my arm and told me that I was under arrest on a charge of trespass."

"Did any person ever address you individually and tell you to leave the premises?"

"No."

Under cross-examination, Dr. Osborn said he had been invited to dinner that night by an ex-student, Joseph (Buddy) Tieger, a CORE field representative. He said the purpose was to go to a restaurant, request service, and if refused, to "make a cause of it, a demonstration."

"You were going to be arrested?" Solicitor Cooper asked.

"If necessary," Dr. Osborn said.

"Did you and Buddy Tieger talk about this?"

"It was understood that we would probably eat at a place that is not likely to serve us, and if not served we were going to protest not being served by not leaving if asked to leave."

"By being arrested if it took that?"

"That is right." Dr. Osborn said the matter had been discussed with the others who had gone to the restaurant that night.

"Where was this agreement, when all of you were present there, agreeing together?" the solicitor asked.

"I can't give you the address. It is in Chapel Hill, a place where the civil rights movement in Chapel Hill meets." He said that they had decided to go to Watts' Restaurant. "We understood there had been violence there, but our understanding was, and we believed it, that we were professors, and that this might make a difference, and we were not there to create violence but to see if we could not be served and help integrate this restaurant, but we did not expect violence, possibly naïvely, but we didn't."

"You considered the possibility of violence?"

"All things are possible."

"And you were prepared to meet it if it occurred with your nonviolent technique?"

"If it occurred."

"You said that you thought being college professors made a difference. May I ask you, sir, if you feel that college professors have more right to deliberately violate the law than other people?"

"No more right, no."

"Actually, shouldn't they be more concerned with other people's rights?"

"That is why we were there."

"They have the greater advantage of education and knowledge?"

"Yes, and we felt our responsibility as responsible persons to be there."

"To violate the law?"

"A law that we feel violates the higher law."

"You don't like that law, do you?"

"I don't object to the trespass law, that is not my objection."

"You don't like it applied to you?"

"No, I am not really protesting that, either."

"You say you feel you have an obligation to violate the law?"

"This is not to say that I object to the law; I am willing to accept the consequences of the law."

"You are?"

"That is why I am here."

Dr. Osborn was asked about his statements that Dr. Amon had been pulled into the restaurant and beaten, and he testified that Quinton Baker and John Dunne had gone inside and had tried to protect Amon with their bodies, and that all three were beaten. "It was a shocking moment," he said.

"Quite a bit of confusion?" the solicitor asked.

"Yes."

"It was easy for a person's mind to be confused about details?"

"I believe my testimony evidences that."

"I agree. You were confused and probably some of the others were?"

"I have never experienced this kind of violence in my life. I was very much confused."

"Your intention was to go through with what you had to do to make your point about who Austin Watts would serve in his restaurant?"

"I am not certain that I would want those exact words to interpret my actions."

"You had planned to undergo any pain, peril or torture to make your point that night?"

"No, this I won't agree to. I wasn't undergoing pain, peril and torture to make a point."

"It wasn't pain to have a hose stuffed down your back?"

"I wasn't doing this to make a point. This is the part I object to."

"But you did not leave?"

"No."

"You just sat there?"

"I didn't want to run. It seemed to me the only thing to do."

"To run or sit there?"

"To sit there."

"To sit there and let somebody put a hose down your back in the middle of January? It was cold that night, wasn't it?"

"It was very cold, yes."

"I expect that shirt got to feeling sort of bad, didn't it?"

"Mr. Amon had been detained, one of our group was held and beaten. I had either the choice of sitting, running or fighting. I felt that sitting was the most reasonable approach to the situation."

"You didn't feel it was reasonable to get away from there?"

"Not and leave one of our group to the mercy of the beatings he was suffering."

"You made no effort to help him?"

"No, this is a nonviolent protest. This is the best we can do. We can witness, we can stand by, but we do not fight back."

"You felt the better part of valor was to sit—"

"Not the better part of valor; the better part of truth and wisdom."

Solicitor Cooper ended his cross-examination, and Osborn was asked by Mr. Penny about the position of the Methodist Church, in which he is a minister, in regard to matters of discrimination. He said the Methodist Church expressly forbids segregation of membership in its church and that the bishops had expressly condemned discrimination in public accommodations and had supported the civil rights movement. "This is the official position of the Methodist Church," he said.

Solicitor Cooper asked him if the church advocated the deliberate violation of the trespass law.

"I will answer that, if I may," Dr. Osborn said, "by saying that the Methodist Church acknowledges the right of obedience of the law of God and conscience above the law of the state, if necessary, or the principle and the right of civil disobedience, if you are willing to suffer the consequences."

"Let me ask you again, Doctor, does the Methodist Church advocate the deliberate violation of the trespass law?"

"Not in so many words, no."

"In any case?"

"No."

The next defense witness was Professor Amon, who testified that he did research in thought processes and other complex processes, and also in decision-making under stress, watching people make up their minds in situations which are like military situations. "In this case I work on contract for the Air Force," he said. He testified concerning his experiences that evening, as quoted earlier, and said he had been driven away from the restaurant by the police and taken to the emergency room of the hospital, where he was treated, then had been taken to the police station, "where I said that I was as guilty as anyone, if anyone were guilty, and we called Hillsboro to see if charges had been filed. They had not, so I called my wife and she came and picked me up and took me home."

"At the moment you were confronted at the door, did anyone make a statement to you to leave the premises?" Mr. Penny asked.

"No. I felt unwelcome, however." Then he added sincerely, in a quiet voice, "There was something about the expressions of the people confronting me which made me feel that I probably would not be served dinner."

The next witness for the defense was Harmon Lee Smith, assistant to the dean of the School of Divinity at Duke. He testified much as the others had, indicating that the defendant, Mr. David Smith, who is not his relative, had not entered the restaurant, and nobody to his knowledge had ever been asked to leave. He said, "The deputy came to me and pointed and said, 'How about this one?' And Mr. Watts said, 'Oh, just leave him with me; I will take care of him.' And then there was a pause. It seemed like a rather long pause. I was rather hoping the deputy would like to take me with him. And after this pause, Mr. Watts said, with no other words being injected in the conversation, 'Trespass and assault.' The deputy said, 'Come with me,' and I got up and went with him."

When Solicitor Cooper approached the witness for cross-examination, he said, "You and I are old friends, are we not?"

Professor Smith, who had been a Methodist pastor in Burlington, the solicitor's home town, and who had been a member of the Junior Chamber of Commerce with him, said, "That is right, Dick."

"We have had many debates together in the past?"

"Not to say who won or lost."

"Harmon, you went over to Watts that night with the intention of violating the trespass law if necessary and getting arrested if necessary, to do what you felt was your obligation to the civil rights movement?"

"I am not sure now, Dick, are we talking like friends or—"

"You are testifying."

"I was prepared to risk civil disobedience."

"What do you term civil disobedience?"

"Breaking the law."

"You don't term that criminal disobedience?"

"Well, in this case, is that what you call it?"

"I am just wondering what you call it. You intended if necessary to break the trespass law if necessary, and get arrested if necessary, is that correct?"

"Yes, I just wasn't sure whether my intention was relevant to what I actually did."

"Now, to use the vernacular, you all resent the treatment you say you got that night with the hose and the broom?"

"No, I can't say that."

"You have all been very fond of describing in detail what happened. You didn't like it, did you?"

"No, I won't say that I liked it, but I won't say either that I terribly resented it."

"Have you ever in the innermost recesses of your mind, to use the vernacular, ever even considered, even a little bit, that you may have asked for it?"

"Yes, I have considered whether we may have asked for it, and I have considered we did not."

A final witness was Professor Joseph Straley of the University of North Carolina physics department, who corroborated that part of the other defense witnesses' testimony which he had knowledge of. After cross-examination, Deputy Sheriff Clark was recalled to the witness stand, and he once more testified that he had asked the defendant, David Smith, to leave and he had not, and as a consequence he had been arrested for trespass. After brief cross-examination, the state and the defense rested their cases.

Judge Hall, a fatherly type of man, took about half an hour to review the testimony and the laws pertaining to trespass, then the jury withdrew. The jury consisted of nine white men, one Negro man and two white women. They were out of the courtroom ten minutes and returned to deliver a verdict of guilty. The verdict, I'm told by Professor Osborn and Professor Harmon Smith, came as a shock.

Judge Hall asked Professor David Smith, who had not taken the witness stand himself, to come forward. He talked with him for a few minutes. "You have to respect the law or you don't have any society," he said. He quoted William Pitt's statement, "Where law ceases, tyranny begins." He said he was disturbed by the case, even though, as he said, the offense was not so serious. "You are a man of learning, and of all people ought to set an example for others."

Before pronouncing sentence, he asked Professor Smith if he had anything to say. Professor Smith said simply, "I do not believe that I have the disrespect for law and order that is implied."

The judge worried about that for a moment, then sentenced him to sixty days of hard labor on the state roads, which sentence was appealed.

This was the first trial, and the only one to be tried under Judge Hall. The others would be tried in a special session of Superior Court. I have reported on this trial in some detail because it more or less establishes the pattern for the others involving the professors of Duke and the University of North Carolina. The excerpts of testimony come from the record of the trial obtained from the court stenographer, Mrs. Faye Hulet.

The young people, John Dunne, Pat, Quinton and the others, were not involved with this trial and most of them did not attend. Their turn came the following Monday morning. Almost a hundred of them drove in many borrowed cars to Hillsboro and found parking places; they swarmed up the cracked walks of the old, distinguished town and entered the new courthouse. Some of them admit to being star-

226

tled when they entered the courtroom, for it is painted in green and salmon colors and has all the antiseptic cleanliness, including a white acoustical-tile ceiling, of an operating room. They retreated at once to the outdoors and the more friendly winter scenes of the cluttered street.

The judge of this session of the court was Mr. Raymond Mallard of Tabor City, best known in state legal circles for his trial a few years ago of labor organizers at Henderson, during which he criticized the idea of outside agitators coming into the South to stir up labor, heavily involved the SBI (State Bureau of Investigation) and made extensive use of the conspiracy charge. He is famous for his strict courtroom discipline. In 1960, while serving as judge in a previous civil rights trial in Durham, he found no fewer than six coeds in contempt of court. A gray-haired man, somewhat short—he once ordered that several books be removed from his bench because "the Court is short of stature"—he has a whiplike way of speaking and moving, and he demands absolute attention of everybody in the courtroom. Whenever he leaves the courtroom, the aisles are cleared for his departure.

Roland Giduz tells me that some years ago when he first began reporting on the trials in Hillsboro, he was unable to talk with Judge Mallard or get information from him, and on more than one occasion he was threatened with contempt of court. However, after being around for a while and being careful of what he said, he was accepted by the judge and they were friendly at last.

On this Monday morning Judge Mallard opened court promptly at ten. He made it clear that certain rules would be followed strictly, all of them enforced by the sheriff and his deputies. There was to be no reading ("This is not a reading room"), no eating or drinking ("This is not a lunchroom"), no talking or laughing ("This is a court of law"). Later he was to enforce rules against writing and knitting as well. The rules were for everybody, not only the civil rights defendants; they were for visitors, for law enforcement officers, for lawyers, for everybody within his sight, inside the courtroom and in the hallway outside the courtroom as far as he could see to the front door of the courthouse.

Having established the attitude of decorum and respect he wanted, he went to the first order of business, which was to discuss with the

Grand Jury its responsibilities to bring in charges. He called the jury's special attention to one crime, that of criminal conspiracy, which he said was "an unlawful concurring of two or more persons in a scheme to do an unlawful act or a lawful act by unlawful means." He said the jury could bring in any such charges to the solicitor if they felt this crime also was involved in the civil rights cases.

That being done he was about to move on into the bulk of cases when he came upon a mimeographed statement which had been filed that morning at nine-thirty with the Orange County clerk of court by the four Negro attorneys representing all of the defendants except the five Duke professors. The document had been presented by attorneys C. C. Malone, Moses H. Burt, Jr., W. A. Marsh and Floyd McKissick. The mimeographed document declared that the defendants were being held for trial solely and because of their being Negroes or because of their association with Negroes, and that the arrest, trial, prosecution and any judgment against these defendants by virtue of the warrants and/or indictments was unconstitutional and invalid by reason of the privileges or immunities, equal protection and due process clauses of the Federal Constitution, and that for these reasons the defendants were asking the Federal courts to assume jurisdiction over the trials.

Judge Mallard described the statement as "a scurrilous attack on all of the courts of North Carolina, including the Supreme Court." He called one of the young defendants before the bench, read his charges in full, and asked him if these four men were indeed his lawyers. The defendant said they were. Judge Mallard asked if indeed he did want to be tried in a Federal court? The defendant answered yes.

Judge Mallard dismissed him. He called another of the defendants before him. In answer to questions, the defendant said the four Negro lawyers were indeed his attorneys and that he wanted a Federal trial.

Judge Mallard called another defendant, and so on, right through the entire day.

When adjournment time came, he still had thirty or so defendants left. He told all the defendants to report back the following morning.

They did so, getting rides as best they could to Hillsboro. That morning he continued the process of the day before with those thirty people. Finally, having found agreement among the defendants, he ordered the transfer of the case to the Federal court, to be considered there in terms of whether the Federal court would accept the cases in spite of the objections of Judge Mallard and the state.

When asked by a reporter of the *Daily Tar Heel* why he had gone through the long list of defendants, Judge Mallard refused to answer.

This action left, at least for the moment, only a few cases in court, those of the professors who had been at Watts Motel. The Duke professors' attorney, Mr. Penny, had not wanted to appeal to the Federal court. The Chapel Hill professors' attorneys, Mr. Malone and Mr. Burt, felt Penny's actions reduced the effectiveness of their appeal. However, they had no choice but to leave Chapel Hill Professor William Wynn's case in the state court, since he was involved in the same action as the Duke professors.

Professor William Wynn is a thirty-five-year-old, slight and bespectacled psychology professor at Chapel Hill. His case, Judge Mallard or the solicitor decided, would be tried first. A jury was chosen, one composed of four white women, six white men and two Negro men. On the jury were two of Professor Wynn's colleagues at the university and one instructor from Duke.

The questioning of witnesses had just begun when in midmorning Judge Mallard, for reasons not explained, adjourned the court for the day.

The next day the trial was resumed. Mr. Austin Watts told his story. Deputy Sheriff Clark told his. A new prosecuting witness, Detective Howard Pendergraph of Chapel Hill, took the stand and said he, too, had heard Mr. Watts ask the defendant to leave his parking lot.

On Thursday Professor Wynn took the stand in his own defense, and on Friday the jury was given the case. They left the courtroom and were gone an hour or so without a report. Judge Mallard was reading and writing at the bench. The solicitor and various reporters and lawyers were clustered in conversation. Professor Wynn absent-mindedly picked up a newspaper, glanced at it briefly and let it drop back to its place. Judge Mallard saw him do this, and called him before the bench, where he reproved him for "contumaciously interrupting the Court by his insolent reading of a newspaper in defiance of the Court's express orders." He issued an order for Professor

Wynn to appear before him on Monday to show cause why he should
not be held in contempt.

A short time later, a woman who was new to the court entered the
courtroom, took a seat and began to unwrap a candy bar. She took
one bite, then another, chewing away in a relaxed manner, mildly
annoyed that people were staring at her. Judge Mallard stopped writing at his bench and gazed out over the courtroom. He saw her.

He called her forward and criticized her for "defying the Court,"
and she returned to her seat, astonished at the marvels she had wit-
nessed here on her very first visit to a courtroom.

Later, while the Wynn jury was still deliberating, Judge Mallard
decided to go on to something else. Solicitor Cooper introduced a
Grand Jury indictment against six of the Chapel Hill demonstrators
for conspiracy to commit a misdemeanor. This indictment was based
on the testimony of Professor Osborn in the trial of Professor David
Smith during the regular session two weeks earlier. The Grand Jury
had charged six men with "inducing and procuring" Professor Osborn
to trespass. The six named were John Dunne, Albert Amon, Buddy
Tieger, Quinton Baker, Thomas Bynum and Ben Spaulding. They
were ordered to appear the following Monday for trial, and Judge
Mallard ordered their immediate arrest and detention until each one
had put up $500 bond.

In addition, Ben Spaulding was indicted on a charge of issuing a
worthless check to the court for eighty dollars. The check had been
written during the regular session, when Judge Hall was presiding, to
pay court expenses levied against several demonstrators. Five hundred dollars' bond was required on this charge, also.

At ten-thirty o'clock at night Judge Mallard asked that Professor
Wynn's jury come into the courtroom. When they were seated, he
asked if they had reached a verdict.

David P. Schorr, Jr., the retired army general who was their
spokesman, said that they had not, that they were divided eleven to
one.

Judge Mallard told them to go home, but to return on Monday
morning.

On Monday morning he sent them out again to deliberate, and all day they did so. At five o'clock they reported that they were still deadlocked eleven to one.

Judge Mallard asked if they believed they had exhausted every way of reaching a verdict.

"I believe we have exhausted every conceivable means toward reaching a verdict," Mr. Schorr said.

Judge Mallard asked the jurors who agreed with that opinion to raise their hands. All of them raised their hands.

Judge Mallard then dismissed the jury, announced a mistrial in the case and announced that the case would be scheduled for the following Monday. He told Professor Wynn his contempt charge would be taken up at that time, too.

There was no announcement made as to whether the eleven jurymen had stood for conviction or acquittal, but it was soon learned that they had stood for conviction and that the lone dissenter was Mr. Otha Thompson, a Negro who lived in Cedar Grove, a nearby farm community. He was a member of the NAACP and had so stated during earlier examination as a juror. In the jury room he had held out, refusing to agree with the other eleven, for about seventeen hours of closed session. Later, when a reporter asked him what his views were, he said, "I ain't going to discuss it no more. We've been through that over and over in the jury room." The reporter asked if he had been put under undue pressure during the deliberations. "Was I!" he exclaimed.

On Tuesday of this second week, the court tried Professor Herzog, a thirty-two-year-old, tall, scholarly-looking man, the associate professor of systematic theology at Duke University. Each day since the special session began, he had been required to be present in the courtroom; now his time had come at last.

Dr. Herzog decided to represent his case alone. He was sworn in and in a low, halting voice tried to explain what he had done and why he had done it. He said he was "trying to bear witness to the love of Christ." He said he joined the demonstrations "because of Christ, who, although He was accused of breaking the law, didn't feel He really was."

Solicitor Cooper's arguments against the defendant, who was, of course, a Methodist minister, had much to do with the Bible. He said the defendant didn't love his neighbor as himself, since he had used pressure against Austin Watts. He said he ought to consider "the mote in his own eye before examining the beam in another's." He said that the Bible taught that "not one jot or tittle of the law shall pass away."

The arguments were presented seriously and no doubt were attentively considered by the jurors.

The next morning, Wednesday, Professor Herzog's jury reported that he was guilty of trespass. Judge Mallard, left with the first conviction of the special session, said he would sentence Professor Herzog after the other cases connected with the January 3 incident were concluded.

He went immediately into the trial of Professor Peter Klopfer of the Duke zoology department. Witnesses were heard, and the next day, Thursday, while Professor Klopfer's jury considered the case, Judge Mallard went on to select a jury for Professor Osborn. Counsel for the defense, Mr. Penny, began to question one of the prospective jurors closely, a man who had sat on the Herzog jury, which had returned a guilty verdict. The juror said that the other trial wouldn't prejudice him, but Mr. Penny knew that the evidence and witnesses for the prosecution were identical in the cases involving the professors. He therefore moved that the Court excuse this juror for cause, that being the impossibility of his considering this case without prejudice.

Judge Mallard ordered all jurors to leave the room and then reproved the young lawyer, saying that the lawyer had been asked on the previous day if he wanted additional jurors, that he had said no, that he was now seeking to impede and embarrass the Court. Mr. Penny tried to speak, but Judge Mallard loudly interrupted. He then granted the motion of dismissal of the juror for cause, and said he would deal with the attorney after the trial.

When the jurors returned, Mr. Penny removed four other jurors peremptorily, whereupon Judge Mallard again ordered the jurors to leave the room. Once they were gone he accused the lawyer of seeking to create causes for appeal and of impeding the court. He then ordered the case of Professor Osborn continued until the following Monday, this being a Thursday, and the defense counsel was given notice that he would be dealt with later. Mr. Penny tried to make a comment concerning the matter, but he was not allowed to do so.

On Friday, the last day of the second week, the Klopfer jury was deliberating its decision, and Professor Klopfer left the courtroom and went to the clerk's office, in order to make a few notes. While he was absent, Judge Mallard ordered his bond forfeited.

The stunned defendant returned at once to the courtroom. Judge Mallard summoned him to the bench and criticized him for having been absent from the courtroom without permission.

Professor Klopfer said that the judge himself had on the previous day given him permission to work in the clerk's office, and that he had assumed this permission still held. Judge Mallard denied this, but did order the forfeiture of bond stricken.

When the jury finally did return to the courtroom, it announced that it was finally and hopelessly deadlocked.

Judge Mallard declared a mistrial and continued the Klopfer case until Monday. The defendant's lawyer, Mr. Penny, asked Judge Mallard if Professor Klopfer might leave the courtroom. Judge Mallard said he had continued the Klopfer case for retrial on Monday, and why had the lawyer interrupted the Court to ask this permission? Mr. Penny said he wanted to be sure that his client was not again absent without permission. Judge Mallard angrily asked whether counsel's behavior was not impertinent.

The lawyer and his client withdrew.

On the Sunday which introduced the final week of the special session, the *Daily Tar Heel* revealed that for several days the State Bureau of Investigation had been investigating two of the defense attorneys, Mr. McKissick and one other, not named. Gary Blanchard, the young co-editor of the *Tar Heel,* had heard rumors of this, which he considered to be a possible means of intimidation of defense counsel, and he had phoned Solicitor Cooper at his home in Burlington. Mr. Cooper said yes, that the question had been raised as to whether or not two of the lawyers had been involved in the planning of the street sit-ins, and the result of the investigation would determine whether or not a bill of indictment against them would be sent to the Grand Jury.

This needs to be considered alongside the fact that the solicitor already had introduced the charge of conspiracy, which involved six men at this point and could conceivably be enlarged, even to include those who drove cars for the demonstrators or worked at the CORE office or belonged to the Freedom Committee (although Mr. Cooper had told a reporter he didn't think it would go so far). The degree of possible pressure being held in bargaining position by the solicitor needs to be mentioned here.

Roland Giduz covered the trials for papers all over the state, as well as for his own paper, and his reports were the ones often used, even by the Chapel Hill *Weekly*. Except for him, there were few reporters around. There had been three editorial comments. Jonathan Daniels, in the *News and Observer,* had said the sentence given Professor Smith was unnecessarily harsh and put Chapel Hill in the same league with Birmingham and Mississippi. The Chapel Hill *Weekly* replied with an editorial titled "Into Each Strife Some Tears Must Fall," which criticized the idea that Chapel Hill was thought in Raleigh to be responsible for what took place in Hillsboro. The third voice was that of the *Daily Tar Heel,* which published an editorial critical of Judge Mallard. It was written by Jim Shumaker. Mr. Shumaker had visited the courtroom one day, and he had been asked by the student editors to write down his impressions.

The piece was titled "Tip-Toeing on the Scales of Justice," and went, in part:

In Hillsboro Monday morning, you would have thought the court house was standing on crates of eggs. Sheriff's deputies soft-shoed around, wall-eyed and jumpy. Anyone standing in the corridor outside the courtroom was enough to throw the deputies into trauma. The judge required an unobstructed view.

A student sitting in the courtroom with an open book on his lap was hustled outside forthwith. . . . The student insisted he hadn't been reading. The deputy said he would have to face the Judge's wrath.

At one point, one of the defense attorneys forgot to stand when he said Yes Sir to the Judge. Judge Mallard reminded him pointedly to be on his feet when addressing the bench. The defense attorney didn't forget again.

There were long, seemingly purposeless pauses in the Mallard court on Monday, some of them lasting for minutes. At times you began to wonder if the wheels of justice had run off the axle and become lost in aimless wandering.

234

After several hours of this iron-hand courtroom discipline, you begin to get an idiotic urge to stand, stretch, yawn, and say to Judge Mallard something like, "Well, I've had enough of this nonsense. I'm going home." Having seen that stern, forbidding gentleman in action, you realize, of course, that only one thing could happen: North Carolina, if not most of the Eastern Seaboard, would break off from the Continent and slip gently beneath the Bounding Main, with not even an oil slick to mark its passing. . . .

On Monday the cycle started again with the retrial of Professor Wynn. There was one variation, however, in that the co-editors of the *Daily Tar Heel* appeared as defense witnesses. One of them, David Ethridge, took the stand and testified that as a reporter he had been at Watts Motel on the night in question and that he hadn't heard Mr. Watts ask the demonstrators to leave.

Solicitor Cooper, in cross-examination, asked Mr. Ethridge if he had written the editorial in his newspaper which had referred to the procedures of the court as being nonsense.

The defense objected to the question, and the judge sustained the objection.

Solicitor Cooper asked Mr. Ethridge if he had written editorials advocating boycotts of establishments which did not serve people of all races. Mr. Ethridge said that he and Gary Blanchard often collaborated on writing editorials and that, in that respect, he had written such editorials.

Gary Blanchard was next called to the stand. After he had testified that he hadn't heard Austin Watts ask anybody to leave, Mr. Cooper in his cross-examination asked him about the editorial criticizing Judge Mallard in the *Daily Tar Heel*. Mr. Blanchard did not admit writing "Tip-Toeing on the Scales of Justice," evading that by saying that he as co-editor was responsible for it.

Judge Mallard ordered that the jury leave the room, and he then addressed the courtroom. "This Court is not on trial," he said. "They [the witnesses] are entitled according to the Constitution to say whatever they want to about the Court . . . unless it gets to be a violation of the contempt statute."

Mr. Cooper said the jury really had a right to know if the witness felt any of the proceedings of the court were to be regarded as nonsense. The jury could use it to "weigh the credibility of the testimony offered by the witness," he said. "I'd like to ask the witness if he feels this Court is nonsense."

Mr. Malone and Mr. Burt said they would not object to such a question, even seemed to want it asked. Judge Mallard called the jury back into the courtroom, and, when they were seated, Mr. Cooper once more approached Mr. Blanchard, who was sitting in the witness chair. "Do you feel the proceedings of this court are nonsense?" Mr. Cooper said.

"No," Mr. Blanchard said.

"Do you feel this Court's action in attempting to keep the court quiet and to keep it in order for its business is nonsense?"

There was a long pause. Mr. Blanchard said, "Some of the means I have felt to be arbitrary."

"Do you feel them to be nonsense?"

"What do you mean by nonsense?"

Mr. Cooper said he meant what the editorial meant by nonsense.

"I feel that some of the restrictions imposed to insure the administration of orderly justice, in which all of us agree, to be nonsensical," Gary Blanchard said.

"Excused," Solicitor Cooper said, and Mr. Blanchard left the stand.

That afternoon, however, when Judge Mallard dismissed the jury for lunch, he asked Gary Blanchard to step before the bench. He told him sternly, "You will come back to this Court to be dealt with in a proper manner when the trial is over and the jury is in." In effect, he was citing Blanchard for contempt of court.

On Wednesday Professor Wynn's second jury went out to consider its verdict and came back forty minutes later to tell the quiet, still courtroom that Professor Wynn was guilty of trespass. Judge Mallard said he would sentence Professor Wynn on Friday, but at this time he would consider the contempt citation against him.

Defense Counsel Moses Burt came at once before the judge and explained that his client by looking at the newspaper had not meant any offense. The judge listened, then held that the defendant was in "willful contempt" in that he "insolently and contemptuously began reading a newspaper in the presence of the Court, which condition tended to impair the respect due the authority of the Court and interrupt its proceedings." He set a fine of ten dollars.

Mr. Blanchard was called before the Court. He had got a young Chapel Hill attorney, Barry Winston, to represent him. Also present in the courtroom were several reporters from the major newspapers of the state. The word had evidently gone out that a newspaperman was in trouble in Hillsboro.

Attorney Winston moved that the contempt charge be dismissed on grounds that his client had "no intent to insult your honor or be contemptuous," but was merely giving an honest opinion asked by the solicitor while on the witness stand.

Judge Mallard looked out over the courtroom. Doubtless he noticed the dozen or more reporters, sent by four major dailies, three television stations, and some other news outlets.

Attorney Winston said he didn't think his client had had any choice but to say he thought Judge Mallard's restrictions were nonsensical. If he refused to answer, he could be held in contempt. If he lied, he would make himself guilty of perjury and contempt. If he admitted his opinion, which he did, he was charged with contempt.

Judge Mallard began to write something on a piece of paper.

Attorney Winston said that his client had felt that the rule against reading, for example, placed a hardship on a number of students, who had to appear in court every day to answer charges.

Judge Mallard went on writing.

Attorney Winston pleaded that Mr. Blanchard meant that some of the procedures "made no sense to him." He said Mr. Blanchard didn't feel that students who were defendants in the court were "obstructing justice" by studying while they were in court, and that he simply stated an honest opinion in reply to a court official's question.

Judge Mallard went on writing.

Attorney Winston said that if the defendant were found in contempt, "it is done so for his holding an opinion."

Judge Mallard looked up and read what he had written: "Although what the respondent said was contemptuous of the Court and in violation of general statutes . . . in that such statement did tend to impair the respect due to the Court, however, due to the fact that the respondent was answering the question of the solicitor and due to the fact that the respondent had denied any intent to be contemptuous and due to the apparent immaturity of the respondent, the Court takes no further action in the matter and the respondent is discharged."

The news went out to the state papers, and many editorials were written, all of them supporting the wisdom of the judge in not taking further action in this matter. The state papers gave more editorial attention to this hearing than to all the other Chapel Hill civil rights trials combined.

By Friday, the last day of the special sessions, not all of the six professors had yet been tried, but three of them were awaiting sentence. All six had had to be present every day of the three weeks, and for the trial of Professor David Smith during the previous regular sessions as well, so they had spent almost a month in the courtroom.

Before sentencing them, Judge Mallard called for the case of the bad eighty-dollar check, which had been given the clerk of the court by Ben Spaulding.

Ben Spaulding says he was baffled by the incident. His records had shown that money was in the account to cover the check, and the bank had not notified him that a check on the CORE account had arrived and that funds were not available to meet it. Such notice is customary in Chapel Hill, and seems all the more likely when one realizes that the account was actually short by two dollars.

On the advice of counsel, Ben Spaulding now entered a plea of *nolo contendere,* which means in effect that the defendant pleads no contest to the charge and places himself at the mercy of the Court.

His attorney, C. C. Malone, explained the circumstances to the judge. He said somebody had taken the CORE checkbook out of the car used by Mr. Spaulding and had written a check which had depleted the account.

Ben Spaulding told the judge he had not intentionally given a bad check, that extenuating circumstances accounted for the lack of funds when the check was sent to the bank, and that he had deposited well over $100 worth of checks in the CORE account when he had been told by the bank that it had returned the check to the clerk of the court. He presented several character affidavits, all quite favorable.

Judge Mallard considered the whole matter and sentenced Mr. Spaulding to pay court costs and serve four months at hard labor on the state roads. The sentence would begin at once or, if Mr. Spaulding preferred, it could be activated at the Court's discretion any time within the next five years.

The sentence came as a shock to Ben; evidently even his attorneys were stunned. They conferred with him as to whether to accept the five years of probation or the active sentence. Judge Mallard told them when one minute was up, then, since Ben was unable to reach a decision, he put him under five years' probation.

Judge Mallard then went on to the three professors, two from Duke and one from Chapel Hill, who had been found guilty and who awaited sentencing. They were Professor Wynn of the University of North Carolina and Professors Herzog and Osborn of Duke. Judge Mallard told them that he would hear anything any of them had to say before the Court passed sentence.

Professor Wynn said, "Your Honor, I realize I am not on trial for my attitude, but rather for my actions, and yet at one point or another some statements have been made concerning my attitude. From the implications made, which I do not feel correct, I would like to clarify. In the action for which I have been tried, I feel I not only have acted according to my conscience, but that I have also exercised the best judgment of which I am capable. I have shunned no responsibility to the ideal that we have in our tradition of Christians and good citizens. I have shunned no responsibility to my fellow men and to my society. If I have broken the law, I have not done so lightly or capriciously, or without careful consideration of the consequences of my act, nor have I done so without the highest regard for the law, for law is absolutely essential for social harmony, if society is to be preserved. If I have broken the law, I have done so with the intent to call attention to grave and widespread and long-standing social injustices. . . ."

Judge Mallard said, "You still hold to that position?"

"What I have said I believe to be true," Professor Wynn said.

Judge Mallard asked if Professors Herzog or Osborn had any comment.

Professor Herzog said, "Your Honor, I acted on January 3 in obedience to God, as God gave me light to understand this obedience at that time. I wanted to bear witness to the equality of all men before their Maker and their fellow men. I wish to pay my highest respect to the laws of the state and our nation, which you in your high office represent. I appeal to no other laws, but I wish that these laws could so be interpreted that according to their divine essence all men could in all respects see themselves, regard themselves, as equal before God and their fellow men. Thank you."

Judge Mallard said, "Is there anything further for either Dr. Herzog or Dr. Osborn?"

Professor Osborn said, "Your Honor, I, too, would like to express my respect for the Court, and for the laws of this land, feeling that they derive their law-enforcing value and dignity to serve justice. For this reason I do feel that when it is used to enforce and uphold segregation of public accommodations, it does not actually serve justice, which it is called to serve, and therefore loses a measure of its dignity. For this reason I was involved in the misdemeanors. I was also involved because I believe I should serve the Lord who involved himself in the affairs of men and I thought to involve myself in this particular type of activity for the same Lord who said, 'Inasmuch as ye have done it unto the least of these . . . ye have done it unto Me,' and I feel that in our society it still is true that the Negro remains the least among us, and I took this particular point of action because I felt the need is urgent and acute, not only for the Negro, but for all of us in our country and especially here in North Carolina. Thank you."

Judge Mallard said, "Dr. Herzog, do you still think you have the right to violate the trespass law?"

Professor Herzog considered that. "I have done it once, and I have seen the consequences. I cannot again do the same."

"Dr. Osborn, do you still think you have the right to violate the trespass law?"

Professor Osborn said, "Your Honor, the question is difficult to answer. I would say first, if I may, when I did violate it, I didn't feel I had the right before the law to violate it. I knew I was violating the law in the sense I didn't have the right to. On the other hand, I was obliged by what I understood to be the dictates of my own conscience at that time. In answer to your question, I would have to say if the circumstances arose again in which my conscience before God conflicted with the law of the state—"

"With the trespass law?" Judge Mallard said.

"With the trespass law, and I felt that a case would arise again—I don't foresee it—and I felt before God that I had the obligation and the responsibility, I don't think, before God, I could do otherwise."

"Gentlemen, this will probably appear as a lecture," Judge Mallard said. "It is not a lecture. I would like all three of you gentlemen to stand, if you will, so I can see all of you. I want you gentlemen to know, all three of you, that I worship the same Christ that you do. I have been taught from my youth until now that a Christian, and all Christians in a democracy such as we have, are the best citizens, and should so conduct themselves.

"It is a fact that crime is on the increase in this country. It is a fact that crime is on the increase in North Carolina. Not many weeks ago I read in the Durham *Herald* where crimes of a certain type had increased 19 percent in the year 1963 over the year 1962. You gentlemen, instead of being as you probably should, and as the place of responsibility that you occupy require, the answer, or one of the answers, to such problems, are not; but instead of that, we have spent three weeks here in this county—and how many thousands of dollars it cost the county I do not know—and you have become a part of the problem, instead of the answer to it.

"One of you, a Doctor of Philosophy, teaches modern Christian thought; Dr. Herzog is a Doctor of Theology; Mr. Wynn also teaches the youth of our country. If everyone took it upon themselves to determine the law that they would obey, then we would have anarchy."

He called attention to a comment made earlier by Professor Herzog, that for violating a law in Nazi Germany his father had later been praised by a Federal judge in this country. Judge Mallard said, "I repeat, the Christian should be the best citizen in it. We not only do not have that attitude here, gentlemen, but two of you still reserve the right to violate the law, still inform the Court that should you feel

that some law should be violated, that you have the legal right to do
it. The inference is there, whether the wording is there or not. I saw
you shaking your head, Dr. Osborn. The inference is plain. You used
a lot of language. The Court will not attempt to debate theology with
either of you. I have a simple faith and believe in Jesus Christ as my
savior, as you, Dr. Herzog, believe, and I believe Mr. Malone said
that Mr. Malone and all of us are Christians. I believe also in a
democracy where we abide by the laws, and as they are interpreted by
judicial process. . . .

"I have been entrusted with a portion of the power of the State of
North Carolina as judge, and it becomes my duty, and I assure you,
Dr. Herzog, in imposing the sentence that I am imposing, that I have
uttered many a prayer that I might do justice in these cases. I have
thought of the words that Mr. Burt has said, that come from Micah,
'What doth the Lord require of thee, but to do justice, and to love
mercy, and to walk humbly with thy God.' Isn't that what you
quoted?

"I don't mind telling you, Dr. Herzog, I have shed a tear or two
over you. I am not going to send you to prison. Not because you
didn't do the same that these others have, but in my opinion your
motive and your attitude are different from theirs. I am going to send
both of them to prison, but I am not going to send you."

Then he said, "Dr. Osborn, if you feel that the Negro is the least
among the people in this country, I will take issue with you. If you
will come to my area of the country, I will show you just as many of
the other color. When you say that the Negro does not have the
opportunity of the whites—there" (pointing at Mr. Burt) "Mr. Burt
is a Negro, is as good a lawyer as there is in North Carolina. He came
up in North Carolina. He became and is a product of our state, he
behaves himself with dignity, he treats others with respect and is
treated with respect, and when you said a while ago—I wrote it
down—that the Lord said, 'As you have done it unto the least of
these,' I take issue with you, sir, that this man" (pointing at Mr.
Burt) "has not had equal opportunity. You are entitled to your belief.

"Before I do sentence you, I want to call particularly to the attention of Dr. Osborn and Dr. Wynn, I want to read you what civil

liberty means. I am not undertaking to tell you, you who hold doctorate degrees. I hold no such degree, but this is what civil liberties means." He then quoted the definition of civil liberties which is found in Black's *Law Dictionary*. He followed this by quoting Dean Henry Brandis' letter to the Chapel Hill *Weekly,* the letter of February 19, 1964, in which Dean Brandis criticized the demonstrators for breaking the law. Judge Mallard commented that he did not know Dean Brandis as well as he would like to.

He then sentenced Professor Wynn to ninety days of hard labor, Professor Osborn to ninety days, and Professor Herzog to pay a fine of fifty dollars and court cost. "Anything you gentlemen want to say?" Judge Mallard asked.

Apparently the three men had nothing more to say.

Later, outside the courtroom, Professor Herzog wept. He felt he had been badly misunderstood, John Dunne says. He had evidently intended by his last answer in the courtroom to indicate that he had suffered so much hardship detrimental to his work and emotional well-being from the many weeks in court that he probably would never disobey another law. But Judge Mallard, as did the news media the next morning, had interpreted his statement as a recantation.

When he got home, Professor Osborn found his three children upset and crying. None of them understood that sentencing didn't mean jail, that their father and the other two professors had appealed their sentences to a higher court and might get them reversed. "They sensed the ambiguity that the adult community senses in terms of civil disobedience," he says. "They were having a hard time adjusting to my not being wrong, even though guilty in the judgment of the Court."

He admits that it's not easy for him to figure it all out, either. "It would be wonderful to be as right as Mallard," he told me, "and suffer no moral qualms. I know I have more moral qualms than Mallard appeared to have. When I was considering taking part in a demonstration, there were many valid reasons I entertained for not participating, but there is no ethical position which is wholly justified. I have moral reservations about civil disobedience. I certainly wouldn't want to generalize on it. I can only say that for me, in this action at this moment, it was right."

This ended the first of the special sessions. Austin Watts had testified six times. Everybody involved, including the attorneys, had for weeks spent just about every waking minute getting to, being in or getting home from the Hillsboro courtroom. Now most of them were either engaged in appeal cases, or had not yet been tried, or were involved in the conspiracy trial yet to be heard; none of them was through. Except, of course, for Judge Mallard, who went home to Tabor City.

The editors of the *Daily Tar Heel* wrote a farewell editorial:

His mind through ignorance is shuttered by the laws he is sworn to uphold, and the law cannot ever legitimize its own disobedience. But that is not to say that such disobedience is never justified. We believe it is justified under certain circumstances and when done in a non-violent, submissive manner—which, Dean Brandis, is the difference between Martin Luther King and Gov. George Wallace. Then civil disobedience is not only justified but desirable, in that it serves as a safety valve for frustration and prevents frustration from deteriorating into despair, with all its accompanying implications of desperate acts. . . .

In the years to come, when all of this is behind us, UNC instructors William Wynn and Albert Amon, and Duke instructors Frederick Herzog, Robert Osborn, David Smith, Peter Klopfer and Harmon Smith, will be seen in their true light: Men who braved the winds of near universal disapproval to be true to the ideals of their God and their country, and in so doing, helped the rest of us to ultimately do likewise.

On Thursday, the day before the sentences were passed out, the Federal court in Greensboro refused to accept jurisdiction over the hundreds of Chapel Hill civil rights cases.

The cases were, therefore, remanded to Orange County Superior Court, and another special session would need to be called. Any one of a number of eight Superior Court judges could be appointed by the State Supreme Court to that special session; it would not necessarily be Judge Mallard.

Judge Mallard's participation in this first special session obviously had stirred up deep wells of feeling in him. Not long after this, he appeared at a Baptist Church in Durham to speak. In the audience were some of the professors he had recently sentenced; they had discussed bringing newspapers which they could read while he spoke, but of course they had not done so. They listened as he presented his text: "I . . . beseech you that ye walk worthy of the vocation wherewith ye are called," which is from the fourth chapter of Ephesians.

In the course of his talk, Judge Mallard said, "I have tried people who teach others and who in the name of Christ are advocating the breaking of the laws of our land. . . . Of all this disturbance that we have seen in the name of religion . . . the greater portion of it is a prostitution of religion, and we are being duped by that kind of people."

A week or two earlier, President Johnson had appealed to leaders of the Southern Baptist Convention to use their influence in the cause of civil rights, "encouraging elected officials to do what is right."

Judge Mallard told his audience, "Do not let anyone tell you as Baptists that you should do anything which would give up the freedom you have as Baptists—be he the President of the United States or anyone else. . . . This cause, too, this cause of human dignity, this cause of human rights, demands prophets in our time, men of compassion and truth, unafraid of the consequences of fulfilling their faith."

Chapter Fifteen

In THE ARGUMENT concerning whether respect for law or conscience ought to have the greater authority in the good citizen, we will need to consider this three-week session as partial evidence of the manner in which the laws are left to be enforced. Those who support the superiority of conscience often have the embarrassment of explaining how their system is to work on a practical level; those who support the superiority of laws have the embarrassment of the way their system does work, day in and day out, at the working level.

The law is one thing if studied in the law school, where one is able to see it related to the centuries of progress of man; it is a second type of thing when most citizens come to deal with it, for they can afford lawyers who can get continuances from the judges and can generally work around or through the maze of the system, so that most people never actually go to court; it is still another thing when studied in terms of the people who cannot afford influential lawyers and who must enter into the system itself.

One of the noteworthy aspects of the special session was that professors experienced what usually is denied professors and other men of influence at all: they had been tried in a courtroom. They were offended by it, by the manner in which justice was dispensed to them and in which their own testimony and rights were treated. They had the reactions members of minority groups who come before the courts habitually have had: they didn't think justice had been dispensed to them at all. Rather than be persuaded to favor law over conscience, they were propelled just the other way.

For John Dunne, in any case, the matter already had been decided. With the quick judgment of youth, with the ability young men have to sweep across a complex argument and bury the details under an impression they receive, he had come to believe that the courts were unjust to such men as he and that the work to be done by him had to be done through new demonstrations.

It is part of the nature of the advocate of conscience over law that he is always trying to reach the consciences of others. As James Foushee expressed it to me recently, "You have to reach the heart, man. You don't do nothing if you don't reach the heart." One way to do this is through agitation, but irritants without emotional results are of partial value, and it was not clear to John Dunne, Pat Cusick, Quinton Baker and the others that they had gone about as far as they could go along the paths of irritation.

At first they had simply started picketing a small café; that had stirred up animosities. Later they had started street marches, and people who had been agitated by picketing now said, "Look, why don't you picket and stop these infernal marches?" Later they had gone to the sit-in, and they were told, "Why don't you picket and march and stop these sit-ins?" Later they had gone to street blocking, and they were told that it wasn't difficult to see the validity of sit-ins in segregated restaurants, but what did they mean by these outrageous street blockings?

They decided what they needed now was a new tack entirely.

While the special session had been in progress, they had worried in their various evening meetings at Harry's, at the Chicken Box Number Two and at the Freedom Committee office about what they were going to do. They did not discuss the matter with Mr. McKissick, who was busy all the time anyway, trying to get the Federal court to take charge of their civil rights cases. LaVert Taylor did talk about the matter with Rev. Martin Luther King, and LaVert and Pat Cusick talked with C. T. Vivian and other leaders of the civil rights movement.

The idea they discussed most had been suggested in a sermon on prayer and fasting preached one Sunday by the Rev. Foushee. His main thesis was that "We shall overcome, but not overcome unless we fast and pray." Praying alone was not enough, he said; the people must both fast and pray, for fasting is, he said, a form of prayer, involving sacrifice. Pat Cusick, who had often encountered fasting when he was a Catholic, particularly when he lived in the monastery boarding school, became interested in this concept. He found that Rev. Foushee often fasted with members of his church who had personal problems. Evidently there was a tradition of fasting among the Negro Methodists, although the traditionalized fasting days of the Catholics and Episcopalians were not observed.

The idea of prayer and fasting appealed to Pat. Perhaps Rev. Foushee was right, that more could be done now with prayer and fasting than in any other way.

If there was to be a fast, where should it take place? In a church? In the homes of the people? Pat said the fast could easily be ignored by the public if held only there. He suggested the lawn of the post office, on the main street, in the main block of town.

Should the fast be publicized? If not, it might be misunderstood; if so, it would be called a publicity stunt.

Should a date for its termination be announced? Some felt the fast should continue until the town passed a public accommodations ordinance; others thought this would be called coercion of public officials and would lose effectiveness.

When should it take place? Why not Holy Week, Pat said, starting with Palm Sunday, the week that was approaching?

John Dunne received a letter from a friend in the North who had been on a public fast, and he suggested that the young men not shave, that this made the length of their fast all the more evident and illustrated their desperateness. This advice was discussed, and it was decided that such a device was hypocritical.

Somebody said the group should dress up. Somebody else pointed out that lying on the ground for a week was not an occasion for formality and that the men would end up looking worse than if they wore informal clothes. This latter view carried.

Having made these plans, the members were asked which ones of them wanted to take part. Pat Cusick, John Dunne, LaVert Taylor and James Foushee did. Lou Calhoun didn't want to display himself night and day before the people of the town; he said he would go on a fast, too, but at his home. Quinton Baker, who was working on an NAACP conference, said he would fast at his Durham office and home. Some of the others said they would like to come together in a church each day and spend the afternoon and evening in prayer and fasting; for their use the Baptist Church in the Negro section was made available by its pastor.

This having been planned, the four young people went to the post office lawn to look at the place they had chosen. It was a small plot, indeed, no more than fifteen feet on a side. They went to a nearby church to see if there was a toilet there which they might use. There was. They brought clothes to Mr. Allen Reddick's apartment nearby and left them there. They talked with Roland Giduz and other town leaders, ministers and reporters, and told them what they planned, for an hour explaining the nature of it, and assured them that this was an act of reconciliation, not a new tactic of pressure.

Pat also sought out Captain Blake and Lieutenant Creel and asked them if he could talk with them a few minutes. Both men doubtless had all sorts of worries, wondering what next would be done by the Freedom Committee. Captain Blake could remember distinctly the time John Dunne had come by the office, less than a year ago, to announce the picketing at the College Café, and when Bob Brown had come by a few months later to talk about the first street march. He had had many meetings with them since then, each one dealing with some further advance toward danger. Now they were back, and what the next wave of action would be he could not bring himself to guess.

He thought he was prepared for anything, but he was not able to believe what he heard. A fast? A prayer and fast? On the main street? On the post office lawn? Near the flagpole? During Holy Week?

"Oh, I wouldn't do that, Pat," he said. It didn't matter to him so much from a policeman's point of view, though that was involved, but it was going to be physically damaging to the young people; at any rate, it certainly was going to be physically painful. "I wouldn't do that, Pat," he and Lieutenant Creel both said.

It was rather touching, Pat says, to find that the two chief police officers in town were concerned about four of the demonstrators after all the work they had been put to. "We really have to do this," he told them. "It's right that we do it."

Just before Palm Sunday arrived, Pat decided that a leaflet explaining why the four were fasting ought to be mimeographed, so that it could be handed out to individuals who expressed interest. It would not be a press release; it would be a statement of testimony which might allay some misunderstanding. He, LaVert and John wrote the statement and mimeographed it.

HOLY WEEK FAST

Beginning Palm Sunday, and continuing through Easter Sunday, several persons will participate in a Holy Week fast. The participants will remain in front of the Post Office and will take only water for the eight-day period. The fast is in keeping with the philosophy of Satyagraha (nonviolence) advocated by M. K. Gandhi. Holy Week, which commemorates the suffering of Christ, could have been alleviated if (1) Pontius Pilate had not "washed his hands" and refused to make a decision or if (2) the people of Jerusalem had demanded that Jesus be released. Our fast calls to attention the daily sufferings of the Negro citizens of Chapel Hill. . . .

We believe that a fast is the highest form of prayer, and look upon this Holy Week fast as a prayer that the city will live up to its responsibilities —and of course the "city" is not a vague and abstract concept; it is the duly elected officials and each person who resides in Chapel Hill. We hope that by fasting publicly, we can remind each person that we have not solved this problem and we hope that each of us, as we observe the final week of Lent, will ask ourselves the question, "Have I honestly and sincerely done all in my power to eliminate racial discrimination in Chapel Hill?"

On the back of the leaflet they printed the names, addresses and telephone numbers of the town aldermen and the names of twenty-nine segregated businesses in the town area.

On the night before the fast was to start, Miss Melody Dickinson, twenty-four, a native of Tennessee and evidently a student of Duke University, got in touch with John and asked if she could join the fast. On Palm Sunday morning, well before dawn, John drove by for her, and the two of them went to Pat Cusick's room behind the Chicken Box Number Two, where James Foushee and LaVert Taylor had spent the night.

"We arrived at five-thirty," John says, "and rousted them out of bed. Soon after, we were on our way to the Carolina Cab stand on East Franklin Street, carrying our sleeping bags, books, clothes and personal articles as best we could. What a sight we must have been. The cab took us to the post office, where we unloaded, put down our tarp, piled up our stuff and resolutely sat down, looking or trying to look for all the world as though we had been performing this strange ritual since time immemorial."

The five people sat there and talked, watching the sunrise spread out over the campus, which was directly across the street, and over the Methodist Church. A few curious people walked by, but they didn't seem to notice the five people sitting on the lawn.

A few friends from the Freedom Committee came by and stood about, some of them rather awkwardly, not knowing whether to sit down and thus become part of the demonstration or to stand on the sidewalk and look on.

The man who ran up the flag each morning came to the flagpole and stared at the group. He fastened the flag onto the rope, raised it to the top of the pole, then left.

About eight o'clock, Mrs. Otelia Conner, a featured citizen of town who has a policy of criticizing those who don't abide by the courtesies she was reared to respect, stopped and stared with some surprise at the group. They told her what they were about. Her reaction was to criticize them for not wearing hats. She said they ought to wear hats in the open, for it was the proper thing to do. She also said they were likely to catch cold if they didn't do as she said.

As the day went on, a few segregationists, known as such from the days past, stopped and gave the young people to understand that they were certainly doing the wrong thing. They advised them to go home. Quite a few people stopped nearby and laughed. John and Pat and the others felt no less awkward because of that.

Whenever anybody stopped nearby, John Dunne would be on his feet at once and would go over to him and hold out his hand. "Excuse me, but I don't believe we've met. My name is John Dunne," he would say, and sometimes people would not want to shake hands with him. "We are fasting here," John would say to the astonished new acquaintance. "We believe that a fast is the highest form of prayer, and that the time has come to stop arguing about abstract issues and start searching our consciences in terms of what Jesus believed."

The poor fellow, who perhaps had only been going to the post office to mail a letter, would, as often as not, stare wordlessly with astonishment.

"We believe," John would continue, "that Chapel Hill people need to fast and to think about their responsibilities toward the Negro, don't you?"

Some did and some didn't, and the whole thing was a bit hard for most people to believe.

Roy Armstrong, the director of the Morehead Foundation, came by, choosing when he saw the group of demonstrators to go up the side steps to the post office lawn. He had almost got inside the building when he heard a youthful voice call out to him, "Mr. Armstrong, I've been meaning to drop by to see you."

It was, of course, John Dunne. Nothing deterred John from any opportunity to talk about the need for change in Chapel Hill. That day he had no dinner or supper, either, but his energy was as bouncy and his resourcefulness as strong as ever. He talked a good deal, listened more attentively than usual, met arguments with gentle persuasion, and by nightfall had got quite a large group gathered around, listening, wondering, arguing, discussing the plight of the South and the need in Chapel Hill to do something about discrimination.

John talked to me at Sandy Ridge about his feeling concerning this type of demonstration as contrasted with the earlier ones. "Some demonstrations are not conciliatory at all," he said. "You try to keep down the hostility part of it, and you hold to nonviolence and keep out retaliation, but at the same time they are intended to create a certain amount of tension. They are intended to push, to create what Mr. Giduz calls a nuisance, something which builds tension to the point of urgency in the white community equal to the urgency of the Negro community to rid itself of segregation. Then there are other demonstrations such as the fast, which are intended to reconcile differences, to get people back together. In using the two types of demonstrations, what you try to do is balance them out, using one to help make the other more effective. You play them against each other, so that you never create firm barriers."

Pat Cusick talked about this at Sandy Ridge, too. "Gandhi said never to fast against your opponents, but only against your friends. I didn't see the sense in that until we began our fast. Its greatest effect was on our friends, or people who had once been our friends."

John was on his feet most of the time. "I figured I was out there for a purpose," he says, "and I didn't want to go hungry for a week for nothing." He admits now that he felt out of place. "You felt damn stupid sitting out in front of the post office, people coming by and ogling at you. We almost had a few wrecks—you know, people driving by. You felt stupid. But then I decided that I had done some other stupid things in my life, and brazened them out."

Pat told me, "The first time I ever picketed I felt foolish, and it was the same situation, except the College Café is near one end of the main block of Franklin Street, and the post office is at the other."

Leaflets were given out, not only by Pat and the other demonstrators, but also by members of the Committee of Concerned Citizens, who mimeographed their own. Since the inception of their group, they had avoided any connection with the aggressive Freedom Committee, but now their members were standing near the fasters, supporting this specific demonstration and keeping watch, actually standing guard from 9 P.M. to 6 A.M. daily.

One of their leaflets was a quotation from George F. MacLeod of Scotland, and it was used to answer the criticism that the post office was not the proper place to hold a religious fast:

> Jesus was not crucified in a cathedral between two candles but on a hill between two thieves, at a crossroads so cosmopolitan that they had to write His title in Hebrew, and in Latin, and in Greek, at the kind of place where cynics talk and thieves curse and soldiers gamble, because that is where he died, and that is what he died about, and that is where churchmen should be and what churchmen should be about.

Roland Giduz came by every day and told the demonstrators what the weather forecast was. He came to be known as their weatherman. Also, he told them they were making the mistake of still further polarizing the forces of the community, undercutting the moderate, middle ground. They felt they were doing just the opposite, and they decided he had become the friend in court who now had no friendly advice to give. They sensed his disappointment in them, all right, but they felt none too pleased with him, and they sensed uneasily his own disappointment in himself. He kept discussing his own actions and explaining his motivations long after the reasons for his actions had lost importance to them.

Paul Green, the dramatist, who had been in the thick of Chapel Hill protests for forty years, came by and spoke to the group encouragingly. Novelist-in-residence John Knowles and other writers came by and spoke encouragingly.

Students came by at all hours. One young man, perhaps a student, wearing the insignia of the American Nazi Party, stepped back a ways from the group one day and studied them critically. He went on off, but soon came back again and surveyed them darkly, as before. He went away, but came back a third time and this time came somewhat closer, at which point John Dunne was on his feet at once and approached him, his hand out. "Excuse me, my friend," he said, "do you have a minute? I'd like to talk with you."

"About what?" the young man said.

"About anything you want to talk about."

"But I'm a Nazi," the man said.

John grasped his hand, shook it and began to talk earnestly with him about the psychological evils of segregation on the minds of both white and Negro children. After a while the Nazi got away and walked off dazedly.

"But I doubt very much that he will be thinking of the civil rights cause in the simple terms he had been thinking of it before," John told me.

Monday morning the demonstrators awoke to a clear sky and a pleasantly promising day. "It's strange to wake up and see two strangers staring at you," Pat Cusick told me. "You feel like you ought to be able to wake up privately." Then he saw a most remarkable sight, he said. He saw Father Parker nearby on his knees. He saw him lean over and pick something up. Soon it became evident that he was cleaning up the property, the patch of lawn and the walks near the lawn.

"Father, what in the world are you doing?" Pat said.

Father Parker said he was cleaning up a bit, so people wouldn't have cause to criticize the way the place was left by those who stopped to talk. "There's not much more I can do these days," he said.

Chapel Hill Postmaster J. P. Cheek had a unique problem on his hands, all right, for he had no idea what the Post Office Department would say about this use of Federal property. He wrote a letter, explaining the situation, and asked for instructions. "The only thing I will do," he said to reporters, "will be to make certain that the entrances and walkways do not become blocked."

Chief Blake of the Police Department said the matter "is entirely in the hands of the Post Office Department. It is Federal Government property, and we have no jurisdiction."

On the second night, some of the town's more militant segregationists began what was to be a frequent feature of the fast. They would stand behind the bushes on the campus, or get down in back of the post office, and throw eggs. James Foushee and the others would hear a splattering noise, and would draw down deeper into their sleeping rolls. Sometimes a firecracker would explode near them.

During the daytime, reporters were coming by constantly. "A television station would set up its cameras, tape recorders, the whole works," John Dunne told me. "A crowd would gather around and everybody would be thinking, 'Well, they're getting what they came for.' And it was a difficult decision to determine whether we ought to give interviews, but we decided this would be misunderstood, what we were doing, if we didn't try to get the message out."

One of the most interesting surprises of the Easter fast pertained to Miss Dickinson. As the week's fast progressed, it became more and more apparent that one of her main interests in fasting was to lose weight. The men became annoyed whenever a reporter came around, for dieting was what she wanted to talk about. They found out soon enough that Miss Dickinson was not a student at Duke University, but had recently been on a rice diet at Duke University Hospital. Having found that diet not to her liking, she had joined the public fast, with good intentions pertaining to civil rights and civil liberties, but also to lose as many pounds as she could.

She lost quite a few.

Another person, Harry Muir, a white student at the university who came originally from Goldsboro, North Carolina, had also joined the fasters. He walked up one morning and asked if he could join the others. He and one other student had been responsible for the fifteen-hundred-name student petitions calling for a boycott of segregated business. A white engineer from the university's educational television station also joined the fast each night and worked days without eating. A native of Baltimore, he too was a stranger to the others.

People would bring the fasters blankets if the weather appeared to be getting colder. One lady brought a vase of flowers. What was in her mind or why she did this, nobody asked and nobody seemed to know. Pat Cusick set the flowers at the base of the flagpole. Soon there were many vases of daffodils and other spring flowers there, filling the concrete platform.

The Chapel Hill Local 1217 of the United Federation of Postal Clerks made a poll of its twenty-four members and said the local unanimously objected to the presence of the demonstrators. John says a few letter carriers stopped by to say this wasn't their view, but they had gone along with the majority because they hadn't wanted to make an issue of it. The president of the local, Fred Conner, also said the fast was a degradation to the flag of the United States, and a discredit to the clerks and the postmaster.

There were, during this period, many other annoyances, of course: The demonstrators felt dizzy from time to time.

Another annoyance was sunburn. All the fasters suffered from it, LaVert the worst.

Somebody left a sign which said, "Please Don't Feed the Animals," which the fasters left in place on the lawn.

They read an item in the *News of Orange County* reporting that "a rumor" had it that the fasters were eating food on the sly.

The ground seemed to get harder every day, and now was as hard as a jail floor.

Sometimes people would come by and would stop and begin eating something with exaggerated relish.

They were called all manner of names, and were cursed at times.

But there were even more signs of courtesy and good feeling, the fasters said. "One girl brought me an Easter egg," John Dunne told me. "I thought she was trying to annoy me, and I said to her that I couldn't eat it because of the fast. She said there was a note with it. There was, I saw, and I opened it. The note said, 'It's harder to give a gift like this than it is to throw one; take this as a token of my appreciation.' When I looked up, she was disappearing into the crowd."

One has hunger pains when he fasts, and often has headaches, but the process clarifies one's thinking, Pat says. At least, he had found it so in prison and to some extent here on the street.

John Dunne found it harder to concentrate for long periods at a stretch. He says, however, that hunger itself ceased to be a problem. He reached the point where it was surprising to him to see people go into the restaurant to eat.

James Foushee had severe headaches. He was by nature an action type of man, and he felt closed in by the inactivity here. There was a lot of talking, in a sense a lot of speechmaking to one another, and his emotions would get to throbbing and his head would ache. He would rather be in jail, to tell the truth, he said.

LaVert Taylor, who is from Shreveport, Louisiana, was sick at his stomach for a while, and he reached the point where he wasn't hungry any more, unless he smelled food cooking next door at Harry's Delicatessen or heard somebody talking about food.

Melody Dickinson said she dreamed of food every night. "It's very vivid," she said. "I can even smell it."

She says that one night a young man came down to where they were and stood back a ways and watched them for about fifteen minutes; he made a few comments, and his face was contorted with some emotion. Suddenly he came toward them and put his hand in his pocket. They were not at all sure what he would bring out, a knife, a gun or what. It was a flower, and he put it in the girl's lap and hurried away, crying.

"It rained one night," Pat Cusick told me. "It really rained hard, and people came down and hung canvas over us and were solicitous for our welfare. We had never seen most of these people before."

It was on Friday that they first heard about the meeting of the North Carolina Klan, planned for the following night. James R. Jones, the head of the Klan, said the members would discuss candidates for governor and burn crosses in a big field next to a filling station on the Durham-Chapel Hill highway, three miles out of town.

No meeting of the Klan had been held near Chapel Hill in many years, and the situation required special watching for that reason and because several people, all known integrationists, were vulnerably exposed on the post office lawn.

I didn't attend that night, but I understand from James Clotfelter, a reporter for the Durham *Herald,* that the Klan meeting had about six hundred curious people present, including many interested members of the local civil rights movement. They stood under a full moon, sharing the light from the television remote truck and from a twenty-five-foot kerosene-soaked cross which burned against the sky while a record player played "The Old Rugged Cross."

There were only forty robed Klansmen in attendance, each wearing a peaked hood but no mask, and a dozen helmeted and black-booted Security Guard troops. The Ku Klux Klan was put on the United States Attorney General's list of subversive organizations years ago. The North Carolina Klan disclaims affiliation with that organization and, nominally at least, has disavowed violence and in some instances has employed certain techniques of the civil rights movement in furthering its mission, which is to retain segregation in the South. There are observers, however, who feel that the inclination of the Klan to violence isn't going to be thwarted by decree, any more than it was thwarted in the old days by laws passed against it.

Grand Klokard Mrs. John R. Jones, head of the Women's Auxiliary, assured the crowd that the Klan was not a hate organization. One of the other speakers, Calvin Craig, Grand Dragon of the Georgia Realm, the Invisible Empire, the Knights of the Ku Klux Klan, Inc., from the back of a flatbed truck discussed the future by saying, "Before the inauguration in 1965, more blood will be shed in America than in the past ten years." He was particularly distressed about the Federal Civil Rights Bill, then before Congress.

North Carolina's own Grand Dragon, Mr. Jones, wore blue and green robes for the occasion. He roundly criticized gubernatorial candidate Richardson Preyer. "Federal judges belong in Washington," he said. "Federal judges don't belong in the statehouse of North Carolina. And thank God for the law that governors of North Carolina can't succeed themselves. Four years is plenty to put up with Terry Sanford."

People warmed their hands near the broken pieces of the cross, which now lay burning on the ground. They listened to Rev. George Dorsett of Georgia tell the young men, "We've gone to the dogs. Young boys, when you look for a wife, you want to find a thoroughbred. You don't want a mongrel, part white and part nigger. You want to find one that's got papers. If things keep going like this, you'll need papers to know who's pure."

A hound dog began baying. Ignoring the interruption, Rev. Dorsett blasted local post office officials for allowing a group of antisegregation fasters to camp on the Chapel Hill Post Office lawn. "The people of this city should move them," he said.

He said he expected "Malcolm X to take over the reins of the civil rights movement from Martin Luther King. The only thing the Negroes want today is violence on the streets. That is the only thing that will bring Federal troops."

When Rev. Dorsett was done, Grand Dragon Jones gave a call to action: "If you're for integration, I say go over and join the niggers. But do something in this fight."

Mr. Jones was interviewed by Jim Srodes of the Durham *Herald*. Mr. Jones is thirty-six, has a wife and a nine-year-old child, and makes a living as a salesman for a Salisbury manufacturing firm. He has reorganized the North Carolina Klan, which became so emaciated that it fell apart in this state around 1958 when it was routed during a meeting by a group of Indians. Mr. Jones does not consider himself to be a racist or hatemonger, but he does believe that the Negroes "have been, are now and always will be inferior to the white man. Now I want you to understand, if a person wants to associate with a Negro, Japanese or Chinaman, I feel that's his business. But I don't believe a person should be ordered to associate, eat or do anything with anybody he doesn't want to."

He feels that the integrationist movement in this country "is a Communist plot. The Communists are using the Negro, just like a farmer uses a plow." He feels that the leaders of the integrationist movement are Jews, "the most segregated people on earth."

Mr. Jones was convinced that the country would rally to the segregationist point of view and kill the Civil Rights Bill. If they did pass it, he said, "they will have to make one out of every three men in the country a Federal marshal to enforce it."

Mr. Jones says it's "hard to be a white man in times like these."

His immediate program in the North Carolina Klan was to organize a unit, or "klavern," in every county. The klaverns are supposed to "counteract Communist teaching that is going on in our schools," and to organize a voter registration program among the whites to counteract "the Negro bloc vote."

This was in late March. The first primary to choose the Democratic candidate for governor would come in late May. If a runoff were needed, the runoff would come in late June. Both dates were in the thinking of Mr. Jones.

That night after the Klan meeting, a group of about 150 people came together at the Chapel Hill Post Office to protect the fasters. Several professors of the university who had not allied themselves with the demonstrators before and many Negroes who had come out of the beer halls in the Negro section, men who weren't part of the civil rights movement, were there.

Meanwhile Klansmen ate dinner quietly at Watts Restaurant. Then some of them, not wearing robes, and others who had attended the Klan rally as spectators began to arrive at the post office. Austin Watts arrived and immediately came under police surveillance. Another man evidently threatened to strike Lou Calhoun, whom he called a nigger lover. He did strike Lou, some say, and he was arrested and charged by the police with assault and battery. The other segregationists vented their anger with heckling and not much else. By this time, most of the Chapel Hill Police Department was on hand, the patrolmen dressed in riot helmets, and the paddy wagon was cruising up and down Franklin Street. Alderman Adelaide Walters and perhaps others of influence had asked that police protection be given the fasters, whether they were on Federal property or not.

About ten-thirty, an old Navy cyanide bomb was discovered on the grass beside the demonstrators' encampment. Lieutenant Creel put it in the back of the paddy wagon, where it was left all night. (Later it was found not to be active.) By midnight most of the people began to drift away to their homes, but fifty or sixty stayed. About one o'clock, Father Parker asked the group if he might speak. He stood on the sidewalk, facing the post office, and talked about the meaning of Easter. He delivered a brief sermon, gently spoken, and he handled the comments of hecklers very well.

The Chapel Hill *Weekly* was unhappy about the Klan meeting and about the formation in Orange County of a klavern. In an editorial titled "Ku Klux Klan Comes to Chapel Hill, for Comic Relief Among Other Things," it concluded that the Klan had grown as a consequence of the activities of the Chapel Hill Freedom Committee.

In the next issue of the *Weekly* there was a long letter to the editor, facetiously thanking the newspaper for recognizing that the Klan did now exist in Orange County. "If ever a city needed the services of the Klan, it is this cesspool of Communism and antagonism called Chapel Hill," the letter said. It continued:

Our great little metropolis has a city government that has tried to solve racial problems by giving everything possible to the "Negro" (with a little *n*), and of course the poor mistreated individuals of the minority will not accept their good intentions, and resort back to demonstrations to harass every person afoot. The Chapel Hill Police Department on Saturday night even broke their seemingly binding statement of a week earlier and "trespassed" on federal property to protect a hand-full of diet-determined demonstrators from the big bad Klan which, however, had no intention, does not have now, and never will have any intentions of aggressively assaulting any opponent physically. Self-defense is another matter. . . .

Well, sir, this little town is going to get our assistance, like it or not. After all, we live here also. We are all honest, upright citizens and taxpayers that have lived here all our lives and it is time we expressed our views and do something toward ending this "unnecessary" period of unrest. The integration "fanatics" have hypnotized some of our citizens into a feeling of guilt toward the "negro," who in reality has more benefits than any member of the White Race in Chapel Hill today.

The writer said that space would not permit him to go into details. The letter was signed, "Yours for God and Country, Klavern No. 9, Orange County."

There were a few other letters to the editor concerning the Post Office Fast. These asked that citizens consider their responsibilities anew in this Easter season, the time which commemorates the resurrection of Christ. One letter said:

I am writing this on the Saturday that falls between Good Friday and Easter Sunday, that moment of suspension between despair and hope. It seems to me that Chapel Hill is now existing in such a moment. Have we now the opportunity to move from the one to the other? Can we not contribute to our ultimate salvation?

On Easter Sunday Alderman Adelaide Walters brought her Sunday School class of nine- and ten-year-old children by to see the demonstrators, and she explained to the children why the young men and the woman were sitting on the ground at the post office.

That morning hundreds of friends came by, and at 12:45 a large group gathered at the flagpole. There was a service, somewhat like a religious service. Professor Joe Straley, the physicist, as head of the Committee of Concerned Citizens, spoke first. Then LaVert Taylor led the group in prayer, an eloquent prayer many called it. Finally, John Dunne spoke briefly about the purpose of the fast.

At 1 P.M. it was over, and friends gathered with bowls of warm chicken soup and crackers, and fruit juices. The fasters ate what they wanted. Melody Dickinson tasted the soup tentatively, then drank it down. "I still feel a little dizzy," she said.

Professor Walter Spearman was there. Later he wrote John's parents that he thought

John looked wonderfully well, seemed strong and very much in command of the situation. As they were breaking the fast and getting up, a little Negro boy about 2, dressed beautifully in white shirt and blue trousers, came up to John. John picked him up in his arms and smiled down at him, and it made a beautiful picture. John's magnificent spirit transcends everything he does.

The fasters were taken from the post office to various homes in the community, where they had dinner. That afternoon they held a mass meeting at the Baptist Church, one which had as guests fifty visitors from Williamston, the other most troubled town in the state. The Williamston leader was Mr. Golden Frinks, an official of the Southern Christian Leadership Conference; he had been trying to make Williamston the model town of the South, achieving for Martin Luther King what the Chapel Hill effort had intended to achieve for CORE.

The efforts in Williamston, in spite of the help of many Massachusetts clergymen, some of whom had been arrested there, had not been successful, and Golden Frinks, a young, often arrested, dedicated man, told the rally at the Baptist Church that the Klan had taken over Williamston, that brutal attitudes now prevailed, and that physical violence was not uncommonly encountered. He warned the rally not to fall easily into voting for any of the gubernatorial candidates. He said he aimed his remarks particularly at Judge Preyer, who, though more liberal than the others, had not come out in favor of integration. He demanded that Governor Sanford do more, too, that he appoint Negro judges and more Negro members to the State Board of Education. He roundly criticized Governor Sanford for being much too conservative in his attitudes.

Mr. Frinks and the demonstrators led a street march, at the end of which he and his group went driving off to Raleigh to try to see the governor, to ask for protection in Williamston.

On the march, LaVert Taylor became quite ill and was taken to the hospital. The doctors were worried, for none of them had had any experience with illnesses arising out of fasting. One of them asked Pat Cusick to advise him. "You do this all the time, don't you?" he said.

LaVert, who was in severe pain, was hospitalized, and three days of treatment began.

That night at dinner, John and Quinton were guests of Duke graduate students, friends of theirs. They talked about the fast and many other things, including the way the police had tried to protect them on Saturday night. Maybe now, the fasters decided, they had become the property of the town, a prized possession to be guarded, as a man might become rather fond of an affliction if it is distinctly his own and if nobody has one nearly so bothersome.

As they talked about the police, they got to talking about the court trials coming up. The judge had been appointed for the new two-week special session, they were told.

John braced himself as he listened for the name to be announced. Yes, Judge Raymond Mallard was to preside.

Chapter Sixteen

IN LATE MARCH, before the second special court session started, a resident of Chapel Hill, Professor William F. Goodykoontz, wrote the Durham *Morning Herald* a letter urging better press coverage of the Superior Court sessions in Hillsboro.

I write as a former member of the District of Columbia and West Virginia bars who practiced law for a time and who, before that, was a reporter several years in Washington, D.C., where I covered the courts—from police court to the United States Supreme Court. I have never before been in any court room in the United States where everyone but the bailiffs and prosecuting attorney (and I am not sure, even, about the solicitor) appeared to be intimidated. . . .

I hope you will forgive me for saying that an alert, a full reporting of the news by the press of North Carolina (shall we say by the "mature" newspapers of our great urban centers?)—in short a free press functioning as such could, I think, have prevented the excesses taking place in the Hillsboro court room, perhaps even have forestalled the occasion for them.

Now the second session was to begin. As before, the *Daily Tar Heel* reporters were often tied up in classes, and the only other newspaperman who showed a consistent interest in reporting the events was Roland Giduz. Mr. Giduz, who had said in his own newspaper that the demonstrators were guilty of insurrection, and who had been involved in the Chapel Hill civil rights action as an alderman, was the reporter used by AP, UPI, the Greensboro and Durham papers, and the Raleigh *Times*. Even the Chapel Hill *Weekly,* his competitor, reprinted his stories. The defendants were annoyed because of this, especially when, as the special session started, they noticed he ate lunch each day in the Hillsboro Inn with the judge and the solicitor. Since the dining room was segregated, the defendants could not go into the place themselves.

There were 217 defendants now involved in all these cases which would appear before the two-week special session, or, at least, which were docketed. Of these, 117 had taken part in street blocking. The total number of Grand Jury indictments would mount to twelve hundred, and, before it was over, to something like fifteen hundred, of which about a thousand had already been reported out. The cases were not scheduled, and the defendants felt bad about this, because it meant that all 217 of them had to be present every single day and sit in Judge Mallard's nonconversing, nonreading, noneating courtroom for the entire time, missing school and work. The matter of getting car transportation to Hillsboro became one of the big problems Pat, Quinton, John and their associates had; it was the task they turned to each night when all else was done.

At the same time, it was rather unfair to expect the solicitor to schedule one thousand cases in a two-week session of court, for that simply couldn't be done. Assuming a forty-hour court week, this would mean that a jury would have to be selected and sworn, witnesses heard and cross-examined, the jury charged by the judge, the jury reach and report its verdict, and sentence be passed at an average rate of five minutes per case. If we can learn anything from the three-week special session recently completed, about five days were actually required for a case, even when all the cases to be heard dealt with the same incident and had the same prosecuting witnesses.

Of course, trying all these individual cases was close to impossible anyway. Buying that much court time would pretty well bankrupt the County Board of Commissioners. It was admitted that the county would have to have a special bond issue or raise taxes.

This was the situation facing the court. The defendants' tactics were to ask for a complete hearing of each case, and then to appeal each decision to the North Carolina Supreme Court. They did have conscience pangs at this, they admit today, for they were certainly guilty of many offenses, and some of the defendants wanted to go ahead and say so, but they were wary of Judge Mallard. They had decided that what they were being tried for was not only their crimes, but also their beliefs, and, to hear some of them tell it, their lives.

The strength of the defendants' position was offset somewhat by the fact that Floyd McKissick, the most experienced civil rights lawyer in the state, was not available to represent their cases. McKissick is one of the few lawyers in North Carolina who has managed to get one of Judge Mallard's rulings reversed; this came about in a civil rights case which McKissick carried to the U. S. Supreme Court.

Mr. McKissick says that he tried to get a continuance from Solicitor Cooper, so that he could represent the students, but the solicitor refused to continue the cases or to delay the opening of the special session by four days. McKissick, who spends about half his time out of state and the rest of his time on a tight schedule, says he was unable to participate, as he wanted to.

One might also imagine that he was aware that the SBI was investigating him, that the possibility of a conspiracy charge was hanging over him, and that the prospects for a contempt citation in Judge Mallard's court were pretty good. Such a citation might be a source of embarrassment to national CORE. In any event, he left the trial of the young people to two other Negro attorneys, Mr. Burt and Mr. Malone, and he worked out with them the strategy that was to be followed.

Mr. Burt and Mr. Malone were relatively inexperienced, but their attitude in court was professional. They were not defiant, and they did apologize for the actions of the demonstrators. This caused dismay among some of their more fiery, proud clients. James Foushee told me he much preferred Floyd McKissick's courtroom manner, that he didn't want anybody to be subservient to another man on his account. "Don't beg the man for me," Jim said.

John Dunne was so disturbed by the apologetic manner of the attorneys that he appealed to Floyd McKissick and James Farmer for their reconsideration of the appointments. James Farmer said the defendants ought to have the best attorneys in the country, and that he would help supply them, but McKissick felt that this was unwise and unnecessary.

Roland Giduz was the one who announced through several newspapers that the trials were about to begin. On April 13, Thomas E. Gibbons, a nineteen-year-old freshman at Duke University, was called as the first defendant. His charge was blocking the Pittsboro highway on February 8. The hearing on Mr. Gibbons' case proceeded through the day.

That night in Chapel Hill a meeting was called of all the defendants who had blocked the streets or highways. They gathered in the Freedom Committee office, sat on the floor, admitting to being almost as crowded as they had been when twenty-four of them had been put in a four-man cell in the Chapel Hill jail one night. At this meeting, the impression was left in the minds of the defendants by their attorneys that Judge Mallard and the solicitor would be pleased to get all these cases tried with something less time-consuming than the present process. Of course, deals between attorneys and judges are never made, are illegal, and nobody was going to get disbarred by talking about such a thing. It was simply believed that if all the accused would plead *nolo contendere,* one after another very quickly, there would be active sentences for only Pat and John, and all others would go free. This was rejected unanimously.

The next evening there was another meeting, and Mr. Malone insisted that the arrangement was as lenient as the solicitor and judge could accept. Only two or three would receive active sentences, perhaps ninety days; there were to be no apologies or promises not to resume activities; and there would be no fines in addition to court costs. No doubt Judge Mallard would appear to be harsh, he would talk a great deal about how wrong their actions had been, but all cases except the street-blocking cases would be nol-prossed terminally, and the street-blocking cases would receive suspended sentences. The demonstrators voted to accept.

John says today that had he and Quinton been in town, they would have "continued to oppose accepting or prostituting our cause with any deal put forth by the solicitor or the judge or anyone. This is inimical to any movement philosophy."

Floyd McKissick now says much the same thing, but he was present at the meeting on this Tuesday night.

In other respects this day had been disappointing. The Duke freshman had been found guilty by his jury, which consisted of nine white men, two white women and one aged Negro woman. Judge Mallard said he would sentence the young man later. He had then gone on to the next case, which turned out to be that of Professor Harmon L. Smith of Duke. The courtroom sat back to listen once again to Austin Watts tell about what happened at his restaurant on December 3.

On Thursday afternoon the *News of Orange County,* Mr. Giduz' newspaper, is distributed free to the townspeople of Chapel Hill and Hillsboro. His report on the trial said: "The slow course of the Chapel Hill civil rights cases through Orange County Superior Court was resumed this week as one more of the more than 1200 cases yet pending trial was disposed of." He then referred to a possible compromise. "It is known that discussions are going on at a decision-making level as to the possibility of speedier disposition of some cases before the court. But precisely what this will mean as compared to the present status of the huge backlog of cases cannot now be ascertained at this time."

Cars were arranged for transportation of all defendants to the trial, and the worried, somewhat frightened and harassed band arrived on Thursday at the courtroom, where they discussed Professor Harmon Smith's trial, which ended with his conviction. Now at long last the young demonstrators were to be tried.

Moses Burt and C. C. Malone told Judge Mallard that several of the young people were prepared to enter a no-contest plea on the blocking of the Pittsboro highway south of Chapel Hill. This was, of course, the first sign that the high-level conferences which Roland Giduz had referred to in his newspaper had borne fruit.

Judge Mallard instructed the several defendants to come forward. He talked with them, asking if each had made a free choice not to contest the charge, if each had done so without any promise or concession having been offered, and if any undue pressure or coercion had been brought on them while making their decision. "The question jolted me," Pat says. "At first I thought we would be lying if we answered no. But then I saw that the phrase 'undue coercion' meant we could truthfully say yes, because there had been no undue coercion. But the whole thing made me sick, because for several months we had been listening to lectures on the integrity of the law and I thought, 'Here we are discussing deals at night in the back room and having to listen to how pure the law is in the daytime.'" Judge Mallard explained to each that if convicted he could be imprisoned and fined.

The defendants were then asked in effect if they would at any time anywhere ever again break any law of the United States for any reason whatsoever, a question they were not prepared for and which none of them was willing to answer in the way expected of them.

Prosecuting witnesses have to be heard in a case in which the defendant has pleaded *nolo contendere* in order that the judge may be able more properly to set the sentence. This was done, starting on Thursday afternoon with the case of the Pittsboro highway sit-ins. By Friday morning, Judge Mallard was able to declare sentences on the nine young people, and also on Professor Smith.

He called Professor Smith forward first and gave him a sentence of ninety days at hard labor on the state roads. Professor Smith appealed and posted $900 bond.

The nine young people were then told to come forward. Judge Mallard consolidated the charges of obstructing the highway and resisting arrest for six of them and sentenced each to sixty days on the road, the sentence, however, being suspended on payment of court costs, and on condition that they "not engage in or be a part of or physically assist in demonstrations or physically accompany any person or persons engaged in any demonstrations for any cause on any public street, highway, or sidewalk or at any public place," for the period of the suspension, three years in some cases, four in others.

As for the other three defendants, the judge said, he would delay their sentencing until Thursday of the following week.

Professor Sitton was called to Hillsboro that day by several worried students, who felt that his wife's reply to Judge Mallard would result in her being sent to jail. He drove from his classes to the courtroom, and found out that Sherry Sitton, when asked if she would break a law again, had asked Judge Mallard if he was referring to the moral or the legal law. This, evidently, had irritated him.

Her sentencing, of course, had been delayed, and she rode back to Chapel Hill with her husband. They went to the office of the Freedom Committee, where attorney Malone came, too. He sat down wearily in the old dentist-office chair and sighed deeply; he began to talk to Bob Sitton about being a Negro lawyer in a court, wondering what he could safely do that he didn't do, wondering how far he could go in what he said. He and Judge Mallard and the solicitor had evidently discussed the disposition of these cases informally, and Judge Mallard had invited him to come to lunch with him sometime, Malone said. "I told him unfortunately I couldn't go to lunch with him in Hillsboro," he said, "that I was a Negro." Other than that, Malone said, he hadn't talked about being a Negro with Judge Mallard. "I sit there fat and black and stupid, and I smile and say 'Yes, sir.' What else can I do?"

Bob Sitton says it was strangely moving to listen to him talk, to see him let go of the tensions of the courtroom and to vent some of the hurt and worry he had. He was defending young people who had broken the law, he said. Everybody knew they had. What was the defense?

Bob Sitton mentioned that protest was a basic right of citizens, that Carry Nation did not sit in at saloons when she was fighting alcohol, but she did go inside them with an ax and destroy them. And that Susan B. Anthony had led hundreds of followers to Pennsylvania Avenue in Washington, where they lay down in the street to protest for woman's suffrage. He said it had been sixteen years since Bayard Rustin had been arrested in the Chapel Hill bus station for refusing to leave the white waiting room, and in that sixteen years the town had refused to end segregation, and that a street sit-in was justified as a rightful protest.

But, according to Bob Sitton, Mr. Malone didn't trust himself to come out with an open defense of the sit-ins; he suspected that if he did, the sentences would be worse than if he didn't.

A stormy session followed that afternoon, at which the defendants objected to the conditions of the suspended sentences. They thought they had understood the terms suggested to them, they had accepted those terms, but the conditions of suspension were contrary to what they had been willing to agree to. Their young attorneys mollified them somewhat by saying that the condition imposed by Judge Mallard was unconstitutional, in their opinion, and that it could not therefore be enforced.

The attorneys were asked, also, why three of the nine had not been given their suspended sentences. They were not among the "two or three leaders" of the movement. John Dunne and Pat Cusick were to go to prison, everybody knew that, but why had these other three people not been sentenced that day?

I'm told the attorneys didn't know the answer, but that they did feel Judge Mallard wanted the young people to act more humble when they appeared before him. Also, he evidently wanted them to say they were sorry for what they had done and that they wouldn't do anything like that again; if the defendants would say that, the judge would go much lighter on them. If they would not say that, perhaps more people were going to jail than had previously been thought.

Saturday morning, Quinton and John returned from New York City, where Quinton had talked with the national leaders of the NAACP and John with the national leaders of CORE. While there Quinton received the Louis M. Weintraub Award for the youth who had contributed most nationally with the greatest personal sacrifice to the field of civil rights and civil liberties. Meanwhile, the discussion continued in Chapel Hill, intermingled with efforts in the office of the Freedom Committee to get the money to pay court costs for the ones already given suspended sentences. On Sunday night another meeting was held, and this time the attorneys advised the group that two conditions had been added: each defendant must tell the Court he was sorry for his actions, and each defendant must assure the Court that he would not break the law again. Anybody who did not comply would probably receive an active prison sentence.

A quiet followed. Everyone began thinking about what this meant to him. One of the demonstrators says he decided, "Tell the truth and you go to jail, tell a lie and you go free." Most of the young people felt they couldn't go along with these new conditions, that they didn't want to lie and they didn't want to say anything that would hurt the movement.

John Dunne spoke to the group and told them that each person would need to make his own decision about this. If a person wanted to tell Judge Mallard he recanted, that was all right, it was his business. Each of them needed to consider the fact that he might have to go to jail if he did not.

"I played the devil's advocate that night," Pat says. "I painted a very grim picture of jail, of the road camps. I told them what it was like. Everybody realized that if they remained silent, did not speak out and say they were sorry and would not break the law again, there was a chance they would get sent to prison."

The two attorneys asked if everybody was willing to say he was sorry and wouldn't break the law again.

The young people said they would not. They stated that they had already agreed to a compromise and they would stay by their commitment to it and believed the Court would do the same. Only two or three defendants were wavering on the matter of the apology, because in truth they were sorry they had got into all this legal mess, but they decided to stand with the others.

"Well, will you plead *nolo contendere?*" the lawyers asked.

The young people said they would do exactly as they had promised earlier. By now, with many of the young people having already made a *nolo contendere* plea and being more or less at the mercy of the Court, they felt they had no alternative anyway.

On Monday Pat Cusick pleaded *nolo contendere* in court, and opened the way for the entire group to do so.

That night, Monday, Judge Mallard spoke at Chadbourn, North Carolina. The Greensboro *Daily News* next morning reported on the speech, as follows:

The alien in North Carolina is feeding the minds of young Tar Heels a "bill of goods" and "Yankee money" is coming into the state to "enlighten the sinful South," Superior Court Judge Raymond Mallard of Tabor City told the Chadbourn Future Farmers of America at their annual banquet tonight.

The jurist, who has just finished a week of hearings in Hillsboro, mainly of cases stemming from charges connected with civil rights demonstrations, said some people say religion gives them the right to violate the law and these people are destroying the minds of young people.

"I tell you these things because it is time for young people to become informed of what is going on here and elsewhere in the world," the judge said.

The local future farmers listened intently as Judge Mallard spoke "straight from the hip."

"We must not let anyone come along and destroy our minds and sell us a bill of goods that it is all right to violate the law. This circumstance is getting closer to us every day."

He told of demonstrators lying down in Chapel Hill streets some weeks ago, saying these people were sent there to help enlighten the sinful south and that they were paid $6 per day from northern funds. He said the demonstrators were sent there by higher-ups to violate the law in the name of religion.

On Tuesday in court, the defendants who had seen the news item could understand better why he persisted in asking certain questions, and why whenever a defendant from outside the South appeared, Judge Mallard would pay particular attention. "It's more than strange," he would say, contemplating the presence in North Carolina of people from other places. "It's more than passing strange."

The questioning progressed on Tuesday and Wednesday, as Judge Mallard sought to identify everybody, pin down motivations, locate suspicious manipulators and generally to survey the operations of the Chapel Hill Freedom Committee. When Rosemary Ezra appeared before the bench, for example, the evidence which the solicitor felt was pertinent to the charge of blocking traffic included the comments that she had come into the state from California, that she had fed demonstrators in her home, that her neighbors said she had had interracial parties, that she had been a financier of the Chapel Hill Freedom Committee, and that she had held a legal sit-in in the Chapel Hill courtroom after a meeting of the Board of Aldermen.

As he went along, Judge Mallard would give some defendants

suspended sentences, always with a condition that they not demonstrate legally or illegally for three or four years; in the case of others he would defer giving the sentence until Thursday. One series of sentences went as follows:

Quinton Baker, docketed for fourteen counts, was known to be a leader. His sentence was deferred until Thursday.

Miss Alice Faye Boyd, twenty-one, of Roxboro, North Carolina, a college sophomore, was known not to have been a leader, and she was given sixty days, suspended for three years.

Ronald Boyd, sixteen, a high school student of Durham, up for seven counts, was given a six-month term, suspended conditionally for five years.

Miss Laura E. Burnette, a Negro high school student of Chapel Hill, was up for two counts only and was given sixty days, suspended conditionally for four years.

Miss Patricia Davis, twenty, of South Carolina had six counts against her, and she was given a six-month term in the Women's Prison in Raleigh, suspended conditionally for three years.

Miss Gerald Dean Duncan, twenty, of Asheville, North Carolina, a sophomore at North Carolina College, had two counts against her, and she was given sixty days, suspended conditionally for three years.

James Foushee, twenty-two, of Chapel Hill had thirteen counts against him, and his sentencing was deferred until Thursday.

Mrs. Doris Nickerson was given sixty days, suspended for five years; Miss Lucile Balor was given a six-month sentence, suspended conditionally for three years; and Miss Vynetta Ward was given a sixty-day sentence, suspended conditionally for four years.

In his afternoon newspaper Roland Giduz reported on Judge Mallard's actions in this way: "In the cases of defendants having four or more and as many as 28 civil rights law violation cases pending before the court, the Judge continued prayer for judgment on sentencing."

Actually, it wasn't quite that simple, but it would appear that Mr. Giduz realized that the defendants were not being tried for the specific charges brought against them, to which they had pleaded *nolo contendere,* but were being tried in a sense for all the charges brought against them in the civil rights movement in Chapel Hill, and for the degree of their participation in that movement.

On Thursday afternoon the cases remaining were those Judge Mallard had deferred sentencing. Late in the afternoon he began calling these young people before him one by one. He would ask them if they had anything to say. It was their last chance to admit they had done wrong and that they intended no further demonstrating, but not a one of them had anything to say. Judge Mallard sentenced each one, then suspended the sentence conditionally.

At about four-thirty he called Quinton Baker forward. Judge Mallard asked the solicitor if Quinton was "a leader or a follower."

The solicitor, according to the court record, replied, "If this were a TV Western they would call him ramrod."

"You gentlemen have heard what the solicitor has to say," Judge Mallard told the defense attorneys. "I take it he is informing me he is one of the leaders."

"I did not mean to be facetious," Solicitor Cooper said. "He was, from my information, one of the planning leaders and one of the acting leaders, engaged in any demonstrations for any cause on any public highway or any other public place or private business establishment."

Mr. Burt said he hoped the Court would consider Quinton's need to complete his college education, "and that the Court also take into consideration the motives of this particular defendant, however much in disagreement his motives appear with established law."

"His motive for blocking a road cannot be for any purpose other than to terrorize the community," Judge Mallard said.

Mr. Burt said the aim in the defendant's judgment "was to call the attention of the nation to the plight of the people in whose behalf he was making his effort."

Judge Mallard said, "Mr. Baker, is there anything you want to say or any witnesses you want me to hear or any other evidence you want me to consider before I impose judgment?"

Quinton said, "No, Your Honor."

Judge Mallard then sentenced him on one count to serve six months in prison and pay a fine of $150 and court costs, "and upon the failure to pay the fine and cost he shall remain in the prison after the expiration of the fixed time for his imprisonment until the cost shall be paid or until he shall be otherwise discharged according to law." He further ordered that he be returned under $1,000 bond at the August term of court to be sentenced on his second count, prayer for judgment continued until then.

An instant shock had gone through the courtroom, for many of the demonstrators had held to the notion that nobody would go to prison except John and Pat.

Quinton returned to his seat, admittedly dazed, not at all sure about what the judge had meant about waiting until August to find out what his second sentence was to be. Six months, the first sentence, loomed before him now, and evidently another sentence was to be given him later.

Pat Cusick was called up next. The judge asked if he had anything further to say. He had nothing to say, he said. He stood there awaiting his sentence, which now he suspected would be six months.

Judge Mallard said that there were two counts against him at the moment, and he would sentence him on the first to serve one year of hard labor on the state roads. On the second count, he would sentence him to two years of hard labor on the state roads. As to the second sentence, he said he was willing to suspend sentence conditionally for five years if the defendant requested it.

"I started talking with my attorneys," Pat told me later. "It couldn't have been over two minutes and might have been no more than forty seconds. All of a sudden Judge Mallard said something to the effect that if I couldn't make up my mind he would make it up for me, and he suspended the sentence and put me under probation for a period of five years."

The usual terms of probation were, according to the court record, to be imposed, and the additional provision Judge Mallard attached was that Pat "not engage in or be a part of, or physically accompany any person or persons engaged in any demonstrations for any cause, on any public street, highway or sidewalk, or any other public place in North Carolina." Judge Mallard then said, "Let the record show that he did not answer me when I asked him about suspending the sentence to a conditional type judgment. Thereupon the Court placed him on probation."

At five o'clock Judge Mallard adjourned court for the day, but not before he had arranged for deputies to put under arrest many of the defendants who had not yet been sentenced. They were to be held in Hillsboro jail until sentencing.

John says that this was one of the saddest nights he remembers. There was quiet talking, almost sighing sounds, as in mourning. They had been put in six-man cells; seven men were in John's cell. Everybody was depressed. Somebody started to sing, somebody down the hall, and that helped some, but it was not really a time for singing, either, not a time for claiming "We Shall Overcome Someday." Tonight was a time for sadness, unrelieved even by hope. They had a real problem on their minds tonight and tomorrow, and after that, the state roads.

Somebody began slowly and without much emphasis to sing a ballad, perhaps of his own creation.

> Some sat in and went to jail,
> Trusting CORE to pay their bail.
> Some got Clorox and ammonia in their face.
> Some wrote protests quite discreet,
> Others sat down in the street,
> While the *News of Orange County* cried "Disgrace!"
>
> Mister Wager, Mister Giduz,
> How can you hope to rid us
> Of public business power to segregate
> With another weak committee
> Meant to pacify the city
> By some unofficial chats to mediate?
>
> When the disappointed crowd
> Heard McClamroch side with Strowd,
> They could see the vote would still be four to two.
> You could see the people grieve
> As they got their coats to leave
> While they wondered how much more they'd have to do.

The next morning the young people were taken one at a time, each under guard, to the courtroom for sentencing. Judge Mallard asked John Dunne if there was anything further he wanted to tell him, or any other witnesses or evidence he wanted to produce, and John said there was not. Judge Mallard then sentenced him on the first count to one year in prison and a fine of $150 and court costs. On the second count he sentenced him to two years to begin at the expiration of the first sentence, the commitment "to issue upon further orders of this Court and in the Court's discretion and at any time within five years from the date hereof."

Joseph (Buddy) Tieger, the Angier B. Duke Scholar at Duke, was brought under guard to the courtroom. Buddy Tieger said he had nothing to say beyond what had been said, but his attorney, Mr. Burt, said he had talked with Buddy Tieger and that Buddy planned to resign his position in CORE and wished to accept a fellowship for study at Brandeis University in Massachusetts, and further that he planned to be married and move his residence to Massachusetts. "I recall when several of the other persons were being sentenced earlier in one of the earlier cases, one of the questions asked by Your Honor was whether or not a person felt differently about his involvement in this movement. I am thoroughly convinced this is one individual who does."

Judge Mallard asked Buddy Tieger if he had anything to say, and Buddy said he did not. Judge Mallard, according to the court record, then said, "Mr. Burt, when a person or group of persons terrorizes a whole county and almost a whole state, I would be derelict in my duty if I did not imprison those who were the leaders thereof. This man has the dubious distinction of having the most arrests in Orange County. While he lives in Durham and is from East Orange, New Jersey, he had the dubious distinction, if it is a distinction, of having twenty-three cases against him. I am not assuming in punishing him that he is guilty in any of these cases, but from the information that was given me by you, that he was an official of the Congress of Racial Equality, that he graduated from Duke in June, 1963, and that he has been a field worker. Now a field worker is one who goes out into the field and works up details as to when and where and how the obstructing of the highways was to be set up, and he led all this. Those of us who have the greater opportunity have the greater responsibility. The Court will have to send him to prison."

Judge Mallard said further, "A graduate of one of our best universities in the country, he continues to live here in the South where he came for an education, and continues to stir up strife and be a leader in the violation of the laws upon which he demands protection from and from which he gets his protection. . . . He may be one of the ones that are being used by the international conspiracy who would destroy this country. He may be one or he may not be one. His conduct certainly serves their cause, whether he is one of them, or associates with them, or even knows of their existence. His conduct has served their cause and served it well. Again I would violate the oath of my office if I did not send him to prison."

Judge Mallard then sentenced him on one count to one year in prison, a $250 fine and court costs, and on the other to two years in prison, the sentence to begin at the expiration of the first sentence and "to issue upon further orders of this Court and in the Court's discretion and at any time within five years from the date hereof."

Buddy was stunned, partly by what Mr. Burt had said. He had told Mr. Burt he was hoping to go to college and to get married; if he were to get a six-month sentence, he could, with good behavior, be out of prison in four and a half months, which would make it possible for him to reach the campus barely in time to register. So he had hoped to avoid a one-year sentence, but he had not meant to recant anything. "I was sentenced and led out of the courtroom," he says. "Ginny [his fiancée] had left her seat and was standing in the hallway. I dropped something I was holding as I got near her so that in pausing to pick it up, I could say something to her. I didn't say, 'I love you' or kiss her. I said, 'I didn't tell Burt to say all those things.' "

Judge Mallard went on to sentence J. V. Henry of Asheville to a twelve-month term and a $150 fine which had to be paid before he could leave prison. J. V. had tried to withdraw his *nolo contendere* plea, but Judge Mallard refused to permit him to do so.

Arthur Crisp of Reidsville was given a four-month term; then, in a change of heart, the judge reduced his sentence to ten days with a strict probationary term. Mr. Crisp said he couldn't accept the probationary conditions, which required him to leave Chapel Hill. Judge Mallard then sentenced him to eight months.

Rosemary Ezra was given six months in Women's Prison, a one-year sentence to begin at the discretion of the Court any time during the next five years and a $500 fine which she must pay before she could leave prison.

Lou Calhoun was given a six-month term to begin on June 1 and was told to put up $2,500 bond; sentence on the second count was to be given at the August term of court.

Joyce Ware of New York City was given a twelve-month term to ensue at any time in the Court's discretion during the next five years. Five other young people were found guilty and were told that they would be sentenced at the Court's discretion any time during the next two years. There were several terms of twelve months, suspended conditionally for five years; there were five or more terms of eight months, suspended conditionally for five years. There were terms of six months, suspended conditionally. And so forth, down a long list of over forty individuals.

Then the other charges which the Grand Jury had passed on to the Court, which had been brought against these same individuals, except the charges of conspiracy, were nol-prossed with leave to reopen, which meant that the individual indictments against any one of the defendants concerned could be tried at a later date if the Court desired.

Some of the prisoners returning to the cell came back sadly, others less sadly, but nobody joyfully. Eleven had active jail sentences, and everybody was under the Court's control. The understanding that had been suggested, which they had agreed to, had not been followed, and though they didn't know who was responsible, they felt cheated, lied to, mistreated by society. Society always claimed to be proper; the law always was represented as honorable. Was this the law? Chapel Hill had said that they were doing wrong in what they did. Well, they thought, what they had done was done out in the open. They had not worked in secret, nor had they worked for selfish reasons or for personal gain.

They had cooperated with the Court, and now they had their reply; it came in the form of jail cells, the road camps, the years of restrictive probation.

John Dunne's letter to his parents, written on a long strip of toilet paper and smuggled out of the jail on Saturday, contains his impressions as of that moment.

DEAREST FOLKS:

Well, here we are!! In February, 117 Americans made a protest and in doing so chose to disobey the laws. Now, as responsible citizens we are paying the legitimate cost of that action. Great injustices were common fare during the trials, but the injustice to the demonstrators was the least of these! The fact that we were sentenced on the basis of charges which had never even come to trial, much less conviction, is a minor tragedy. The source of my sorrow is the cruel lie which this court and the system it serves continues to perpetrate upon the unfortunate masses of white people: as long as the white people of this country are allowed to believe that this revolution is anything but a result of the legitimate anger and frustration of the oppressed people of this country, violence and tragedy will continue to grow. Judge Mallard bears great responsibility for everyone who dies or is hurt in the coming months of racial violence—for everyone whose soul is further frozen with hatred. He did not lecture us about our lack of responsibility as citizens, nor about the wrongness of civil disobedience as a method to attain our just goals. Instead, he spoke in the incredibly ignorant and guilt-ridden words of the Klan, that we are all pawns or malicious agents of "the international conspiracy," that we were all paid $6.00 a day by Northern funds to come into the South, warping young people's minds to think that Christianity permits you to break the law with impunity, that we were all alien forces of an alien power being supported by alien funds, and so on and on. I am afraid— afraid that I will be forced to see the disintegration of America and the dream it once symbolized, the light it once gave the world.

John put into the letter the list of active sentences received by everybody, expressing his utter dismay. Then he went on.

Also the judge claims for the record that we were sentenced solely on the basis of the two charges, blocking traffic and resisting arrest, for which we were tried, which is an absolute and bold-faced lie. This is one of the most corrupt systems of justice I've seen, the worse because of its ability to remain barely within the letter of legal procedures and still act unjustly and violate the essence of those procedures. . . .

I am in no way ashamed of what I have done, nor have I in any way altered my views concerning my actions or my commitment. Those views have merely been further substantiated and bolstered by increased awareness of the extent of evil in our world. I worry that cynicism will overtake the soul of many of the people most committed to love today. It is one of the greatest problems facing the movement today.

He then referred to his determination, and that of the others, not to cooperate if put in a segregated prison camp. He said there were three prison camps in the state which were integrated, and that he hoped to be put into one of those. He concluded with an effort to convey confidence and good spirits:

This should be a good experience for me—educationally and from the standpoint of self-discipline during the more unpleasant days. There is some question as to who may write to us, but I think everyone can as long as they do not criticize the government, prison, judge, law, etc. All mail is censored!!! We have no legal privacy, so beware!!! It's about time for lights out, so I'd better sign off. If a section of a letter seems sort of irrelevant and includes some crazy references, check every tenth word for a message. Keep in touch through Quinton, who is my Power of Attorney and may be able to see me occasionally. If you receive a letter which is addressed to Mr. and Mrs. J. Dunne, please forward it to Harold [Harold Anderson at Choate]. We are only allowed to write our immediate family. This is probably the last uncensored letter I'll be able to smuggle out.

I know that this will not be an easy time for y'all, and I will be thinking of you often. But try not to worry. I'm in good company with some wonderful friends, and we must approach this together as another chapter in a richly varied and very fortunate life. Without this experience, how- ever unpleasant, certain depths of my being might never be plumbed or fulfilled. I love you all, and my visit home and yours here, Mother, was a wonderful thing for me before going to jail. If you ever get down, do check before with Quinton as to visiting regulations etc. I'll keep you posted from week to week, and will look for your letters. Much love as always from your devoted son,

JOHN

The Hillsboro Jail
April 25, 1964

A few days later the prison cage rolled down the road, transporting the demonstrators to prison. Buddy Tieger, J. V. Henry, Pat, John, Arthur Crisp and Roosevelt Atwater were transported together. They huddled in the back of the small truck and agreed that upon their eventual release each would contact Floyd McKissick's office to find out the others' addresses.

Buddy found two pieces of bread in his jacket pocket. They shared the bread, for they were hungry, and someone pointed out that it was similar to a final communion together before they were sent to the various prisons. For several minutes there was a reverent silence as each ate his bread.

Chapter Seventeen

IT's INTERESTING TO SPECULATE on this trial, as on any trial. The results were decisive, in that the leaders of the Chapel Hill civil rights movements were sent to prison and were, beyond that, under probationary sentences that severely restricted their activities for many years to come. Their followers were also restricted. The powerful position the defendants had held a week earlier had been lost, and they had not got so much as they had hoped for their *nolo contendere* pleas.

The sentences themselves created some polite talk among legal circles. Professor Pollitt of the university Law School says he has not found their equal in American jurisprudence; at least, this is so, he says, in terms of some of them. For example, John Dunne, Rosemary Ezra, Lou Calhoun, Pat Cusick and Quinton Baker had been given fines which had to be paid before they could leave prison. If Rosemary Ezra, while serving her six-month term in the Women's Prison, could not get together $500 to pay her fine, she would have to remain in prison until she did so. She was, therefore, in a spot not unlike that of the people who centuries ago were put in debtors' prisons.

Giving six-month and one-year active prison sentences on misdemeanor charges is unusual, especially for first offenders.

Four- and five-year suspended sentences for first offenders on misdemeanor charges is equally unusual. Quite a few confining regulations and requirements go with being under probation. (Three months after being put on probation, Keith Payne was called back to court on the charge of violating probation by writing Judge Mallard a personal letter which was critical of the judge. He was given a prison term to be activated at the Court's discretion during the next four years. Five months after being put on probation, Walter M. Mitchell tore the probation papers into pieces, saying he would rather be in prison; he was taken before Judge Mallard and was accommodated with a one-year active prison sentence. In other words, being on probation is not necessarily a friendly situation, and a lengthy probation period for a trespass violation or something of that sort is not customary.)

The method of sentencing a prisoner and saying that his term will start at the discretion of the Court, any time within the next several years, is unique. This gives a solicitor and judge almost complete authority over the actions of citizens. It is referred to by Judge Mallard as "one of my special types of sentences."

Further, it appears that Pat Cusick, Lou Calhoun and some of the others were charged with a violation of a Chapel Hill street obstruction ordinance, for which the maximum penalty is thirty days in jail or a fifty-dollar fine. Yet on this specific charge Pat had been sentenced to a year and John to two years, suspended at the Court's discretion for five years. The wording of the charge is the wording of the Chapel Hill ordinance, and the number of the ordinance is listed as part of the charge, and there is no reference to any other law or ordinance in the charge. If the defendants were charged with violating the state statute pertaining to blocking a highway, under which evidently they were sentenced, though not charged, then one must look at that statute. One finds that it was passed long ago and pertains only to those who block a road in order to keep people from going to church or to a well used by a church. Certainly nobody going to or away from Chapel Hill on Saturday, February 8, could convincingly claim he was on his way to church or to a church well.

Also of concern was whether or not "going limp" constitutes resisting arrest. There is no precedent for this, either. Normally in North Carolina, as elsewhere, one who resists arrest uses force against or attempts to flee from the arresting officer. These defendants did neither. They submitted; believing their arrests to be morally unjust, though legally authorized, they refused to assist in the arrest itself, although they had in some cases gone out with the express purpose of being arrested. It's interesting to note that they would be charged in one case with purposefully trying to be arrested and in the companion case with resisting arrest.

As to the charge of conspiracy, the pertinent question here is whether or not conspiracy laws were formulated with the idea of protecting society from those who conspire to commit a misdemeanor.

There was, too, the speculation concerning whether or not Judge Mallard, because of his public statements, ought to have disqualified himself from acting as judge, and a few people wondered if the court was using its power in an effort to abolish legitimate moral persuasions and legal activities of American citizens, in effect to control an unpopular political movement.

All these points merit attention, but the fact is that the young people were in prison, and appeals are expensive and time-consuming, even if successful. If unfair measures are ever taken in a court, one's best immediate defense lies in the opinion of the public and the press, which can often be counted upon to raise the dickens. The public, however, knew nothing of these questions of law, and there were no suggestions in the press that any of the defendants were surprised or unhappy about the outcome of the trials.

The Chapel Hill *Weekly* had an editorial about the trials; its only concern was why the parents of the accused had not appeared to request mercy from Judge Mallard. Why had the parents of the defendants not cared about them? it asked. The *Daily Tar Heel,* which now had newly elected student editors, accepted the action of the court in a brief, pleasant editorial, until the following Tuesday, when they printed an angry editorial written by James Shumaker, the editor of the *Weekly,* who had given it to them on Sunday, I suppose when he found he could not get it printed in his own paper.

"It is said that all men are equal before the law," the editorial concluded, "but the handling of these 12 cases leads us to believe they were no more equal than a Negro in Mississippi. The very severity of the sentences Judge Mallard handed down is Mississippi law, not North Carolina law."

The editorial also called attention to the fact that Judge Mallard, before sentencing Buddy Tieger, suggested he might be a "member of an international conspiracy that is threatening to destroy America." "In no way can this be construed as a judge's lecture—it is an accusation, pure and simple," the editorial said. "And accusations are meant to be backed up by fact. We have seen no evidence of any 'international conspiracy,' and we seriously doubt Judge Mallard has either."

In the earlier mass trial of the labor organizers in Henderson,

North Carolina, the severity of the sentences Judge Mallard handed down could be related to the position in the union which the defendants held: the higher their position in the union, the stiffer was their sentence. The same policy seems to underlie the sentencing in the Chapel Hill civil rights cases, and motivated the further charge made in the *Daily Tar Heel* editorial that "Judge Mallard has accomplished his purpose—to destroy the civil rights movement in Chapel Hill—and he has gone to every extent to do so."

Except for this belated editorial in the student newspaper, there was no critical comment concerning the sentencing and imprisonment of the young people. So far as I can discover, there was no public comment, pro or con, from the Law School, the mayor's office, the Orange County Bar Association, the Ministerial Association, the university or any other group. Solicitor Cooper tells me he received two complimentary notices from Chapel Hill, both of them perhaps prompted more by personal friendship than by any knowledge or appreciation of his work: Mayor McClamroch congratulated him for what he had done, and Dean Henry Brandis wrote him, saying he had received requests to intercede during the trials on behalf of the demonstrators, but that he knew Dick Cooper was doing his job.

Solicitor Cooper did receive several critical letters from demonstrators and their friends, and there was a street march held soon after the sentencing. The demonstrators walked down Franklin Street to the post office, where Professor Straley, standing at the flagpole, made a brief talk. There were thirty-five demonstrators in the march.

I have heard three explanations for the lack of public notice.

One is that people thought the price paid by the demonstrators was legal and therefore fair or necessary.

Another is that the liberal leaders of Chapel Hill were worn out. They had for months been troubled by hard-core conservatives, irritated moderates and overly active young liberals who did not seek advice and did not follow it when it was offered.

The third explanation was made many years ago by Paul Green, the dramatist, who told a reporter: The university is like a lighthouse which throws a beam out to the far horizons of the South, yet is dark at its own base. I interpret that to mean here that the university preferred to avoid local matters if it could possibly avoid them, and usually it could.

Except, of course, when they come inside the university's own walls, as they did at this time in a trial before the student Honor Council of Mr. Keith Payne, a philosophy major. Mr. Payne was brought before the student court for ungentlemanly conduct in breaking a law, that of blocking traffic. His case was called abruptly, and when Professor Sitton got word, he had only the briefest time to help prepare a defense. He, Professor Pollitt and others prepared what they could, and at the trial they appealed to the student judges to consider Mr. Payne's motivation in breaking the law.

"Every possible means of petition seemed to have failed—boycotts, letters, phone calls, committees," Professor Sitton said. "Still Negroes were being insulted, spat upon, doused with ammonia, urinated upon. The community and its elected officials had steadfastly turned a deaf ear to the crucial needs of the Negro. There was no alternative but to appeal to the community in a more shaking, more shocking, more dramatic way, hoping that the people of Chapel Hill would thereby move to correct age-old injustices. In a final act of desperation, the protest moved to the streets and highways in an attempt to tell the people that the race problem was their problem, that they were going to have to stop in the midst of their complacent, carefree lives and start meeting the needs of their fellow men. That was what Mr. Payne did. There was a reason for his being on that road. The reason was sixteen years of asking, waiting, pleading with the community and still being refused the rights and privileges that rightfully belong to every citizen of the United States."

Professor Sitton said we in this country understand whenever young people go to war to protect the Constitution and our freedom; we have not yet come to understand so well when nonviolently they go out to try to support the Constitution and our freedom here at home. He made a half-hour, forceful speech, and others spoke. The Honor Council deliberated and found student Payne not guilty of ungentlemanly conduct and dropped the other similar civil rights cases.

The decision surprised many people. Certainly it surprised and irritated Solicitor Cooper, with whom I talked later. He couldn't understand how a student could be found guilty in Superior Court of breaking a law, yet be found innocent of ungentlemanly conduct in a student court in a university.

Charliese Cotton jumped bail. The young girl was probably frightened to death, and she decided it was high time to join the mass migration of Negroes away from North Carolina. She had no money. She had no job, either, and the only person who had ever offered her a job was a man in charge of a carnival. She decided that was her only opportunity for success in life, and for escape at the moment. So she ran off and joined the carnival.

Her bondsman found her, and had her arrested and returned to the Hillsboro jail, to the cell where during the previous Christmas season she had spent a few unhappy days.

At first nobody would let her phone a lawyer or her mother, she says. When she did make a phone call, she discovered that her lawyer, C. C. Malone, wasn't at all pleased by what she had done, and neither was her mother. Both came to visit her finally, but neither would bail her out of jail, and maybe neither could, for Judge Mallard had set her bond at $7,500.

After a few weeks she asked if she might write a letter, and the jailor brought her a piece of paper. She wrote Judge Mallard and asked him how he would like to be separated from the ones he loved. She asked him to please reduce her bond, so that she might get it paid.

Judge Mallard reduced it to $4,000, then later to $2,000, and Professor Straley and Rev. Jones got a bondsman for her. After thirty days in jail, she was released and went home to listen to her mother fuss about her having gone off to the carnival.

There are many other personal stories that might be told. Pat Cusick's mother in Georgia is old and sick. She is a segregationist, and Pat didn't write her about everything he did, or about the trials and the prison. Even so, she was quite upset because of him.

John Dunne's parents were worried. Mrs. Dunne often phoned the Director of State Prisons and sometimes she couldn't help but weep when she talked with him. In one letter she told me that what worried her most was that in the evening, which was the time of day John liked so much, she realized they were locking him up for the night.

287 : THE FREE MEN

Lou Calhoun's father received no word from Lou. Lou says he didn't know what to write him. Once he had served his sentence, as well as the other sentence which was to be set in August, he planned to approach him and try for a reconciliation.

Rosemary Ezra's father came in from California to find Rosemary in the Women's Prison, the first Jewess ever to be locked up there. He found that her house was mortgaged and so was her car; she had evidently spent the money to help finance the civil rights movement. She was serving a six-month term, and after that she had a two-year term which could be activated at any time the Court pleased. Her father asked her if she would go to Europe, take a trip around the world, when she got free from the six-month sentence. She was reluctant to agree to leave, to abandon the cause which had for so long controlled her.

Quinton Baker's family had recently moved to New York City. All his life Quinton had wanted them to move out of North Carolina. Now they had, but he was left. His mother, of course, was distraught to have a son go to prison, but she reasoned that Quinton had not been acting selfishly. She reasoned that if a man goes out and breaks a law for his own gain, or due to thoughtlessness or malice, that's one thing, but selflessly to break a law is another. She wept a good deal and tried not to talk about the matter. She had a job as a maid in a home in New York City, and her husband had a job as a janitor.

Buddy Tieger's father came in from New Jersey with a lawyer from the Civil Liberties Union, and the lawyer had Buddy out of prison in twenty-four hours on an appeal. Buddy didn't want to leave the state, but Mr. Tieger insisted that he do so in order to see his sick mother. His father concluded that a young person is like a pair of scissors, one blade, that of the intellect, being sharp and the companion blade, that of judgment, being dull.

For whatever reason, the attorneys representing the other prisoners did not get them out on the same basis Buddy Tieger had gained release.

In Chapel Hill itself, most of the Negro adults were distressed. There had been a time when the Odd Fellows Hall was the control center of their protest. They had chipped in from their savings to pay hospital bills for demonstrators and to help raise bond money for them; they had come to support the demonstrators fully.

Now they were crushed, too. They spent their evenings on the side-walks or in their homes, discussing wrongs that had been done in other years, telling stories about beatings, rapes, murders, land thefts, disappearances in the night, the stories of their own experience or those their parents and grandparents had passed on to them.

There was much bitterness. One Negro maid was asked by her mistress what was going to be done, now that the demonstrations were over, and the maid replied, "We have a plan and we have even begun to pick out the houses in the white section we want to live in. Yours is the first one on the list." The comment achieved nothing, except that the maid was fired.

Many of the white people were troubled, too. Bob Brown ran into Father Parker at the post office one night, and Father Parker told him he was getting ready now, that he had told Mrs. Parker that his time had about come. He said he was moving all the furniture she would need into a single room, so that she could more easily care for her-self. Their son was to come by every day and see her, and she had rented out a front room to two students, so that people would be nearby at night.

Bob assumed he meant he was dying, and he sensed keenly the tragedy of this elderly couple being separated after decades of living together.

I went by Father Parker's house a few days later and sat down in the parlor, where he had stored many of the effects of his travels and of his lifetime of being a pastor. He told me about his going away. I asked him what he meant. He was preparing to go away to prison, he said.

"Oh, I don't think so," I said.

"Oh, yes, I'm going to prison along with the others, once my trial is called," he said.

"Father, an Episcopal priest doesn't go to prison in this country," I told him. "Only occasionally does a Methodist pastor get to go."

"I only hope I'll be strong enough when the time comes," he said. "There was a period when Christian pastors often went to prison."

I saw Mrs. Parker peeping out from the room where he had put her. "Father, I'm sorry," I said, "but it's not going to take place, you won't be sent to prison."

He would not accept that. He was going, as certain as the sun was going to rise, as soon as his case was called at the next session of Superior Court in Hillsboro. "I never did take part in the street blockings," he said. "Some people say the young people went too far, but I'll not say that about them. I know why they did what they did. The only reason I never did lie down in the streets myself was that I wasn't sure I could get up."

He suddenly groaned and made a sour face. "I was in a meeting last week, and an alderman was talking about Maynard Adams' proposal to start an agency to help integrate the community, and this alderman said, 'Now I'm for this new proposal, and you people go on and do what you want to do to bring about integration, so long as you don't stir up things.' Can you imagine such a comment? The devil, the devil, the devil had his tongue. But he was safe, you see. He was for the plan ostensibly. It's only that the plan won't work that way."

He talked about trips to Washington to lobby for the Civil Rights Bill, which was still in the Senate. He talked again about getting ready to go to prison, and I left him alone after an hour, not having shaken in the slightest his intention to spend a few months or years of his old age behind bars.

In May Judge Mallard was the speaker at the annual spring convention of the Eastern North Carolina Law Enforcement Association. Approximately one hundred officers of the law assembled to hear him.

"We must not give up the freedoms we enjoy under our rule of law for a false, though attractive, promise of Utopian security under an all-powerful state," he said.

"We must not take for granted that our system of law and order will continue by itself, because there are those among us who are trying to or being used to destroy this free society of ours, through strife, mob action, and what is called by some civil disobedience."

The last Saturday in May the Democrats went to the polls and voted for their gubernatorial choice. In that vote, Judge Preyer, the moderate candidate, got the highest vote, followed closely by Dan Moore. Dr. Lake, who had appealed to the segregationist vote, was last, but each of the three candidates polled over 200,000 of the 750,000 votes, and since no candidate had a majority, a runoff was called for one month later.

A few weeks prior to that first vote, deciding that an account of the Chapel Hill situation needed to be written, I resigned my job at the governor's office and the faculty appointment at the University of North Carolina which I had held for ten years. I rented an apartment in New York City and sought to isolate myself from the activities which had been my day-and-night consideration.

I arrived back in North Carolina in June in time to vote in the runoff, and in time to attend a meeting of the Board of the Learning Institute of North Carolina, another of the special projects of Governor Sanford, this one bringing into partnership resources of the University of North Carolina, Duke University, the teacher-training institutions and the public schools in an effort to find ways to make education effective for the children who weren't learning much, most of them poor children, white and Negro. A day or so after that meeting, on Thursday afternoon, Governor Sanford asked me to come to the mansion. I found him and four members of his staff in the library upstairs. He told me that Judge Preyer's headquarters had just asked him to support Preyer publicly.

What evidently had happened was that Dr. Lake, the segregationist, had turned his support to Mr. Moore, and Moore had accepted it. On the previous evening, Lake had gone on television and had told his supporters that he didn't trust Moore's backers, but that Moore had assured him of the cooperation of the new administration, and that he would keep Moore honest. He also made several damning criticisms of the governor and of Chapel Hill, where, he said, "The liberals are a red, festering sore on the body of a great university."

It now appeared that Dr. Lake's instruction to his followers was going to be heeded by them. Reports coming in from across the state indicated that the segregationists were likely to bloc-vote for Moore, which would mean that Moore would win by a margin of about two to one, unless many of Moore's supporters defected because of the deal he had made with a racist candidate. Preyer had asked the governor to join him in Charlotte on the next day, to appear with him on television and to ask the people of moderate feeling in the state to continue to support the moderate course which for years the state had followed.

We had dinner that evening at the mansion, and each person at the table—there were four or five of us—suggested what the governor ought to say on his television appearance. After our discussion, he summed it up pretty well by saying, "I realize now that I've jumped out of a plane and don't have a parachute."

We spent the evening talking and writing, each one trying to construct a draft of a ten-minute speech. At 2 A.M., I left what I had written and went to a motel and slept until six, when Hugh Cannon, the director of the Department of Administration, came by for me. We flew to Charlotte. The governor was going to drive in his chauffeur-driven car and try to put together the talk on the way.

When the governor arrived at the Heart of Charlotte Motel in Charlotte, he had a talk which he had written in the car. He had put his typewriter on the jump seat of the limousine and typed away. He had used none of the material left for him, which was just as well. What he had was good, and Hugh and I retyped it.

In another room in the motel Judge Preyer worked on his speech.

At the television station Governor Sanford asked that North Carolina voters reject a course that would aggravate the racial problem. He spoke of the Learning Institute of North Carolina as being the type of project we needed to support in our state. He mentioned the Chapel Hill civil rights matter and his participation there as evidence that he was not soft toward racial demonstrators. He maintained that the Good Neighbor Councils were useful and ought to be encouraged, and that the state needed to pay attention to the needs of the Negro citizens.

After the broadcast, I rode back to Chapel Hill with the governor. At one point he told me that he thought Judge Preyer would win, that he was confident the moderate citizens in the state would, in spite of their anger about the civil rights matters, assert themselves, as they had so often in the state's history. He said if he could place a secret bet he would bet on Preyer's victory.

He talked that way, but he knew very well Preyer would lose. Every poll that had been made had indicated a landslide vote against him. If in the first primary the segregationist candidate, Lake, had

292

come in second, the businessman's candidate, Moore, would not have thrown his support to him and Preyer would doubtless have carried the election. As matters had worked out, however, Preyer was facing the votes of them both.

As we rode along the governor talked hopefully, with a deep sense of calmness, which is typical of him. The next morning he and his wife voted, then with their two children drove to Blowing Rock, North Carolina. On the way he told them Preyer would lose and asked them not to talk about it.

That day, the people of the state went to the polls, and Preyer lost by two to one.

The defeat of Judge Preyer had a big influence on the thinking of John Dunne and Pat Cusick. It dramatized for them the Southerner's resentment toward whatever challenges his existing way of life. Pat and John had thought they could knock down the wall of segregation by picketing, sit-ins and so forth; they had not succeeded. Now they could study the fate of a political candidate who was, by their standards, hopelessly conservative. It came as a revelation to them that even Judge Preyer couldn't win.

Pat Cusick told me in prison that before this he had always been unwilling to accept the lesser of two evils; to him a decision had to be made between right and wrong. Now he had come to believe that one needed to support the lesser of two evils, since that is the sort of choice life usually gives us.

I believe both Pat and John felt that what they had done in Chapel Hill had contributed to the powerful emergence of Mr. Moore and the defeat of Judge Preyer. No doubt it had. The demonstrations had aroused a sea of anger. People everywhere were incensed, and they went to the polls and protested the activities of the demonstrators, as well as the Federal Civil Rights Bill and the dead Massachusetts man who had for three years been President of the United States, who had sponsored that bill, and whose nomination at the Democratic convention Terry Sanford had seconded.

Mayor McClamroch supported Moore. Most of the businessmen in town seemed to support him, too. One of his chief backers was George Watts Hill. Moore's candidacy also was supported by Orville

Campbell, the publisher of the *Weekly;* Moore's press aide was Bill Scarborough, a reporter on the *Weekly;* one of Moore's speech writers was James Shumaker, editor of the *Weekly.*

Pat Cusick and John Dunne got only one smile out of the campaign. They read in the Greensboro newspaper that Mr. Moore, while campaigning, was asked what he would do in handling the racial situation that Governor Sanford hadn't done. He replied that he would deal more harshly with the demonstrators and might even allow them to be sent to prison.

A week after the election, Charlie Jones and some others in Chapel Hill got ready to implement the Federal Civil Rights Law, since its passage seemed to be imminent. They had a meeting at the Community Church and divided into teams.

The teams were to go out on the morning of July 4. However, President Johnson signed the bill on the night of July 2, and on the night of July 3 Pete Leake and one or two friends formed an integrated group and entered Brady's Restaurant. They were served. Carried aloft by their success, they went to Watts Motel and Restaurant, where they were told to leave.

"You aren't going to comply with the law?" Pete asked.

"If you want to get served here, you've got to get that small-assed President of yours to serve you," a man said.

"Why, aren't you going to comply with the law?" Pete said, at which point he says Austin Watts hit him hard in the jaw with his fist. Pete believes he was hit a second time before falling down to the floor. "By this time there were fifteen or twenty people there," Pete says, "and they started slugging others of our group. We went for our cars, and a woman stuck a butcher knife into the window of the car I was in and said, 'I'm going to kill all you niggers and nigger lovers.' "

On July 4, Rev. Jones' groups, composed on the whole of more mature citizens, went into the previously segregated restaurants, including Watts Restaurant, asked to be served and were. The food was all right, the service was prompt. By noon they could report the integration of just about all the public accommodations in Chapel Hill. After four years of trying to do so, a Negro could even sit down in one of John Carswell's soda fountain booths.

Pete Leake tried for days to get the Chapel Hill clerk of the court to issue a warrant for Austin Watts' arrest. Finally this was done. The Chapel Hill Recorders Court tried the case, found Mr. Watts guilty of assault and battery and Judge Jim Phipps laid upon him the penalty of $10.40 court costs.

In the first street march, Charlie Jones, standing on the steps of the town hall, with the mayor listening inside the building, had asked for a public accommodations ordinance for Chapel Hill. Now there was one, and Charlie Jones, reflecting on the matter in his study, concluded that if one had been passed in Chapel Hill earlier, the waste of human effort could have been avoided.

Chapter Eighteen

In JUNE I received word from John Dunne's father that John was in trouble at Sandy Ridge, and that for his own safety he had been taken to another prison. From New York I phoned George Randall, the Director of the State Prisons, and asked him what was happening. He said John Dunne evidently had been trying to start a movement inside the prison, and that the whole thing had come to a boiling point when an integrated group of visitors had come to see him and the other demonstrators. Randall said there had been rumors of unrest at Sandy Ridge for some time, and although he suspected some of the rumors were exaggerated, there was too much smoke for him to conclude there was no fire.

John Dunne was all right now, Randall said. He had been sent to the Burke County Prison Unit near Morganton, and Lou Calhoun had been sent there with him. John was working on the road, and seemed to prefer this to the type of work he had been doing at Sandy Ridge.

The next day John's parents received a letter from him, saying he was all right, that he liked the new camp, and was in no danger. Even so, I was apprehensive, and I suggested to John's father that he write John and ask him to refrain from agitation.

In mid-July I received word from Randall that John Dunne was in trouble at the Burke County Camp, and that he had, because of agitation, been sentenced to three to thirty days in the hole. Lou Calhoun and Quinton Baker, when they were told about John's sentence, had gone on a fast and a work strike, so they were in isolation now, too. I told Mr. Randall I would come to North Carolina and talk with the three boys and ask them to stop agitating, that I understood his problem and regretted it as much as he did.

I prepared at once to fly to North Carolina, and a spirit of despondency which I had never known when going home came over me. I know North Carolina very well. I have written about it in historical plays, in books, in outdoor dramas, in documentary films, in short stories, in articles, even in proposals to foundations. Yet there was no feeling of elation now that I was returning.

I don't know quite why. Perhaps a writer learns to identify with people, and now for the Negro citizens of the state I felt a special uneasiness. The election had denied them their right to hope for improvement, I felt. Negroes who had been in danger before were in greater danger now—those living back in the deep places, in the shallow farms, in the shadowed towns, in the poverty pockets, where the white men could come sometimes now and do whatever they dared, for the Negroes had even less appeal than before to police or courts. As for the white child, I suspected this recent election would help teach him hatred and mischief. To a degree the Old South had been reaffirmed in North Carolina. My forefathers owned slaves and were planters, but I doubt if they would choose the old days over the new, and certainly I wouldn't.

When I got to Raleigh, I obtained from the Prison Department permission to talk with Lou, Quinton and John, who had just been let out of the hole. I drove to Morganton. This was Saturday, July 18, and I arrived at the Burke County Prison about four o'clock. In appearance the prison is much like the one at Sandy Ridge, except that Morganton is in the foothills of the mountains. The prison had been set in a valley beneath the green hills and looked very much like a toy a child had made and dropped there. Nobody was moving about anywhere. On Saturday afternoon the men sit around in the cell block, watching television and talking.

In preparation for this visit, I had bought a tiny battery-powered tape recorder, which I slipped into a briefcase. I had recorded my conversations with John and Pat earlier, and was prepared to do so here.

Usually a reporter isn't permitted to see prisoners, but the guards knew of my previous association with state government and made no issue of this. The sergeant went to find John, whom I asked to see first, and he appeared, walking with a jaunty step. He was dressed in a prison work uniform, which was a faded blue color. He was as powerfully built as ever, and he seemed to be not at all dejected or beaten down. He smiled now on seeing me. There is something eternally undefeated about him, and youthful. We sat down under a big tree, on a wooden bench, and talked at random until suppertime. After supper, which consisted of spaghetti and meat sauce, green beans cooked in fatback, corn bread and hot coffee, I talked with John, Lou and Quinton together.

In the conversations of this afternoon and evening at Burke County Prison, and in my conversation next morning at Sandy Ridge Prison with Pat Cusick, I gathered quite a lot of information about how life in prison is for civil rights offenders in the South, or at least in North Carolina. They are part of a world of undereducated, castoff people, almost all of them segregationists, and almost all of them opposed to civil rights demonstrators.

I asked Quinton what the other men were in prison for.

"I sort of steer away from asking people that," he said.

"We all do," Lou said. "Once you ask them, they ask you."

John said, "I'm right now in the midst of a difficult situation. A fellow came in, very nice guy. We were friendly, getting along fine. 'What are you in for?' he asked me. I avoided replying, but obviously he has found out by now, for everyone in here knows. So today the subject came up, and he went off on his views of the racial situation. Well, I was trying to avoid it, and I kept avoiding it, and I still haven't discussed it with him, and I'm not going to discuss it with him, but it gets on one's nerves.

"I must do anything possible to keep that conversation from coming up. So I don't say anything, but the other men begin to come back, begin to gather around, and they begin asking piercing questions, and if you are sitting there and they ask you point-blank, do you think 'niggers' should marry whites, you have your choice about answering it, and my answer is not a very smashing, shocking answer, but it's an answer I believe and it's one they would disagree with. Consequently I can't answer that, for I would be charged with agitating. I'm not whining, I hope, but it's a very awkward situation.

"Also, they have very often, in fact all the time, such erroneous concepts, misunderstandings of why the demonstrators were in the streets, why we are going to prison proudly instead of ashamed, why we believe in nonviolence, and I have the feeling that if we could only blot out these misunderstandings, so that they would know the facts, then maybe someday the light would come through. This may be the only contact they will have with somebody who can explain. But we can't talk here. Outside of prison you can take certain passages in the Bible which talk about love and about equality before God, and so forth, and after somebody has preached to you about how the Bible says the earth is flat and how the Bible says the sun goes around the earth because when Joshua fit the battle he told God to make the sun stand still, then you can go to the next chapter and say, 'All right, if you believe that, what about this?' And you can get into some interesting discussions. But you can't do that here, and you can't do it anywhere in the state prison system, because we are the point of contention."

Lou said word had got out in the prison that he was an expert on Southeast Asia. At this time Vietnam was much in the news, and one of the men approached him with his ideas. "We tried to have a logical conversation," Lou told me. "He was avid for Goldwater for President and he finally ended the conversation with the belief that Goldwater should send 'all them niggers' to Vietnam and sick 'em to it, let the Chinese Communists kill them all. As soon as he finished that, he went up to a man named Wolf, who is a tall, very belligerent, aggressive Negro, a very bitter person, and asked him to play checkers and give him a light, and began talking, and it was not the Southern paternalism, it was the all-purpose thing, real friendship. He was really coming on strong, it was just like it was another white guy he was talking to, as if he had no racial prejudice. But later he would sit back there and talk about the niggers in the South. You get really scared about him. You wonder."

Quinton, being a Negro, had a somewhat different problem. Most of his acquaintances in the prison were Negroes. "They don't talk with me about civil rights. The only thing they will do is, if there is an article concerning civil rights, they will call me over and show it to me. Of course, it can become a point of contention, because if I start talking with them about it, then the small minority of whites who are on my side of the cell block will get furious. So I have to avoid conversations. There is a man on the bunk next to mine who tries to talk about nonviolence, who can't understand it, but if I were to get into the philosophy of nonviolence, or my own belief in it, then I'd be called a coward, or I'd be less than, you know, less than a man, and you get into a difficult problem in the Negro circle if you get the brand of being less than a man. You're in hell. So I steer clear. I just make jokes about television, and that's about it."

Quinton brought a New Testament to prison with him, but he didn't bring the King James translation, and that's another thing which makes him different from the other prisoners and suspect.

"Something I've noticed repeatedly is the effect of the inmates on each other in terms of trust and interpersonal relationships," John told me. "The inmates cannot know they are trusted, therefore they cannot trust others. And the guards—I get this feeling—believe they cannot trust the inmates. So gradually it becomes impossible for anybody to trust anybody, and at the same time, in order to get along, you've got always to put up a front. In other words, an inmate in here may treat you on the surface constantly with a smile and a pat on the back, and when he pats you on the back, that means your back is turned and that's the biggest mistake you ever made, because the next moment a knife will be in it. This has occurred time and time again.

"With the guards at Sandy Ridge, every single one of them would make a joke with you, make some kind of crack, but then you'd get a report from somebody who worked in the office, who is a friend of yours and was listening around the corner rather than dusting off the table. He would tell you about the comments being made about you and the lies being told about you, and when this would happen you began to realize that no one had any basis for trust."

Pat Cusick, when I visited him at Sandy Ridge Prison next morning, told me something of the same thing. "In the usual prison camp people will beat the hell out of somebody," he said. "They don't here, because everybody has a good deal, and they don't want to lose it. So I operate on a principle which is that I can't trust anybody here in terms of talk, and so I don't. That's kind of a reversal for me, for I've always operated under the theory that you can trust everybody. So I get along pretty well; nobody bothers me. John had a harder time than I did because, first of all, he's a Yankee, and also because he's more open and friendly. He meets everybody halfway, and if they want to be friends, they're his friends, that's all."

I talked with Pat a good deal about why John had been transferred from Sandy Ridge Prison. Pat said he hadn't known why until after the transfer. He said the transfer was actually the culmination of a great many charges, of a lot of talk in the office among the guards and some of the prisoners. Pat said it was apparent from the first that some of the guards had been waiting for John. The second day he was in the camp, Pat said, the lieutenant called him to the office.

"He said, 'Pat, what the hell's wrong with Dunne? I'm calling you out here because I know you from the time you were in here before, and I don't know him.' I said, 'Why?' He said, 'He's not funny, is he?' I said of course not. He said, 'Well, someone just came in here and complained that he's in bed with a colored boy in the cell block.' Well, I laughed and said, 'That's absurd. I've just come from there. We were sitting talking. If I'm not mistaken, both of us were sitting on the bed with our feet on the floor, both upright in the middle of the room with forty-five other people there.' And he said, 'Well, you know a lot of people are probably out to get him on something like this. You better wise him up.' So I went to the cell block and on some pretext called John out, and I told him, 'This is absurd,' but I told him what had been said."

There were other rumors and innuendoes, Pat says, many of them about John, and all of them false. The same guards and prisoners kept coming in with them, reporting that the civil rights people were trying to convince the Negro prisoners to join demonstrations, or the white prisoners to believe in intermarriage, or whatever. Lou went through something of the same experience, Pat said, even though Lou was a Southerner and on that basis somewhat less objectionable to the group. On his arrival at the prison it was noticed that his hair needed cutting. Word went out at once that Lou was a homosexual. Pat says there is no homosexual activity at Sandy Ridge, or any place for it. The men live and sleep in a single large room, the light is left on all night, and a guard is stationed outside the door. Be that as it may, the subject of homosexuality is a favorite one, and Lou, once he heard he was being discussed, decided he would have to prove his masculinity in some way.

The way he chose was to put on his boxing gloves again. The man who was to box against him was a 240-pound Negro, the man who serves as boxing coach for the prison. The boxing match took place, and Lou by no means defeated the Negro, but he was not defeated either, and by the time the bout was over, the prisoners had decided Lou was not a homosexual.

Buddy Tieger had arrived at the prison needing a haircut, and immediately the rumor was started that he was a homosexual. When the girl to whom he was engaged, also a demonstrator, came to see him on visitors' day, the rumor was scotched when the prisoners noticed the warmth of their greeting. One of the guards then started the rumor that he had seen Buddy and the girl having sexual intercourse behind a bus, there in the daylight in a public place.

There were, Pat told me, basically two types of rumors which were passed around, one of them having to do with sexual activities which could not very well take place and which, he says, did not take place, and the other having to do with "agitation," which is a Prison Department term referring to efforts to cause trouble in prison. The charges of agitation had to do, in the case of Pat, John and the others, with their discussion of civil rights, their efforts, according to the charges, to start a movement in the prison at Sandy Ridge. Pat says that they did not discuss civil rights issues very much, and never discussed them with prisoners except when asked a question. "We believe in nonviolence," Pat told me. "These other prisoners believe in violence, or at least practice violence. Converting them would, in most cases, be next to impossible. We turned away men in Chapel Hill who wanted to take part in the demonstrations but who believed in violence. So we weren't trying to start a new movement. We did hope the men who expressed an interest in the matter would think well of us and think better of what we had been doing, so we did answer questions when we were asked them by people we believed were sincerely interested."

Pat feels that two specific incidents led directly to John's being sent away from Sandy Ridge. One concerned visitors to the prison, who had come to see him as well as Lou and Pat. The prison has a visiting Sunday for Negroes, then another for whites, and never before had the prison had to define whether the regulation indicated the race of the prisoner or of the visitors. The civil rights prisoners had visitors of both colors, of course, and it was decided that the regulation referred to the race of the prisoner. This meant that integrated groups of visitors began to arrive for the first time in the history of Sandy Ridge.

On this particular Sunday, a group of visitors were present talking with the demonstrators when LaVert Taylor, the Negro minister, arrived. Rev. Taylor had been in St. Augustine, Florida, with Martin Luther King, and rumor had it that he had been shot at several times and wounded. Everybody was surprised to see him at Sandy Ridge and pleased to find him well. The Sittons, who were present, welcomed him, and Mrs. Sitton embraced him, or he embraced Mrs. Sitton. Nobody is quite sure about that, but the embrace set off all sorts of smoldering resentments among the prisoners. People in High Point, ten miles away, by nightfall were angrily discussing the situation and seeking a way to see to it that nothing like that ever happened again in Guilford County. Mrs. Sitton happens to be blond and attractive, and many of the prisoners, isolated for months and even years, were beside themselves with hurt and anger, and evidently some of the guards were, too.

The other incident happened the next morning in the office, where John had worked for about a week, doing typing. Another inmate worked in the office, too, and he told John that he didn't see how John could shake hands with Negroes and be friendly with them, that John had lost all his self-respect. John said he didn't think so, that he accepted Negroes on the same basis as he accepted white people. The inmate became more and more agitated, until finally he said John was a yellow-bellied son of a bitch, and "If you don't like my saying that, stand up."

John went back to his typing, and the inmate stormed out of the office and into the next room, the guards' room, where he explained his predicament, that of being required to work in the same place with a "yellow-bellied son of a bitch who wouldn't even fight."

That same day Captain Muncy called John and Lou to the office and said he was transferring them to another prison "because of all the things that have been going on." Captain Muncy told John that he was not new to this business. "I know what's been going on," John quotes him as saying. "I know more than you think I do."

John asked him what the things were that had been going on, but Captain Muncy wouldn't say. At one point, he did say that had he been at the prison the day before, and that a lot of things that went on out there he just wouldn't have stood for. "That Rev. Taylor won't be visiting anybody any more."

Pat Cusick was distressed because of the transfer and tried to investigate the matter. He talked with Captain Muncy, and was told that John had created a scene in the office, which was like the other agitating that had been going on. He said John had once been reported for being in bed with a colored boy, and so forth. Pat says he was astounded. Captain Muncy intimated that he had shipped one man out of the prison because he was becoming involved with the demonstrators. This man, Pat found out later, was a huge Negro who was in prison for murder, and had let it be known early that if anybody physically assaulted any of the demonstrators, they would have to deal later with him. This evidently had resulted in rumors being started about him, too.

Pat wrote the Director of State Prisons a long letter, about six pages, trying to explain the nature of the charges against John, which he said were universally unfair. "I told Mr. Randall that it was one of Gandhi's main points that it is even more important to adhere to the philosophy of nonviolence and the search after truth while you're in prison than it is when you're outside of prison. It's the most important part of your witness in civil disobedience, even more so than getting arrested. From this standpoint, we very much wanted to have a good record while we were in here, both as individuals and as far as the movement went."

Mr. Randall talked with Pat on his next visit to Sandy Ridge and assured him John's transfer was not punitive, and that John preferred the other prison.

I have gone through John's prison record in Raleigh. There are three papers pertaining to the matter at Sandy Ridge. One is a letter of July 5, 1964, from John to Mr. Randall, in which he says he has begun hearing rumors about why he was transferred to Burke County. "Having learned something of these allegations responsible for my transfer, I am utterly astonished that such fallacious, and I must say, ridiculous, accusations, would be believed, particularly without my ever having been questioned in the matter. . . . I am dismayed that charges such as these made against me remain in the background of my prison record." John asked that he be told what charges had been made in order that he might "subsequently clarify them to the best of my ability." This was never done.

Another paper in the file is a memorandum dated June 15, 1964, to Mr. Randall from Captain Muncy, who explained that on their arrival he had talked with both John Dunne and Lou Calhoun for about an hour, explaining to them the rules and regulations and what he expected of them.

However from the first day, they kept the Unit in a state of confusion, and resentment. It appeared that they had very little respect for anyone, except the Negro Race. On Visiting Sundays, their conduct while Visiting was very unbecoming, as they would embrace and become intimate with Negroes. Inmate Dunne would watch his chances to get into seclusion with our Negro inmates. On one occasion he was caught sleeping with another Negro inmate, and at another time was caught in bed with another Negro inmate. Inmate Dunne would also if opportunity arose, try to coax Negro inmates into his cell in the Yard Help Building.

As for inmate Calhoun, while he was somewhat cautious about it, he operated quite like Dunne. They were very careless and unsanitary with their personal appearance and toilet habits. They tried to incite trouble concerning the manner in which our White and Negro inmates slept. They used Self Abuse to the extent that they disturbed other inmates around them sleeping.

A third paper in the file is a Social Attitude Report, dated April 29, 1964, signed by Captain Muncy. The report indicates the following: that John Dunne's daily attitude toward rules and work was "very good"; that his trend of daily conversation was "sports and current events"; that he "gets along good with other inmates"; that no weaknesses have been observed in the prisoner; and that the "inmate is polite to prison personnel." There is no indication of any dissatisfaction with him.

On one occasion I was present during visiting hours while Negro visitors met with John. I noticed at the time that one of the guards was wary, doubtless because of the interracial nature of the visiting group, but there was no effort on John's part to irritate any guard or inmate. I have visited him unexpectedly at other times and have found him on all occasions to be clean and neat. I have twice talked privately with some of the officers at Sandy Ridge Prison about him, and all reports made to me, all of them volunteered, were that he was a model prisoner.

It's true that John and Lou liked the Burke County Unit better than Sandy Ridge. John apparently likes to do road work. Anything which gets him out close to nature, and which gives him a chance to do physical labor, appeals to him. Lou, who didn't like the road work, didn't object to the change, either, though he was irritated by the reasons for the transfer. Quinton, who had spent a day in Sandy Ridge before being sent to Burke County, had told them what Pat had managed to find out (it was subsequent to this that John wrote Mr. Randall, asking to be confronted with the charges).

There were aspects of the Burke County Unit which Lou, John and Quinton didn't like, boredom being the most oppressive of them, and their fears being second, fears that arose from being helpless in a system they didn't trust that held almost life-and-death power over them.

The food was not very good, they decided, and it was not the type of food they were accustomed to. Also, there were no books. The efforts of their friends to provide them with books were unsuccessful. Another objection was that there was only one television set, and a majority vote decided what show was to appear on it. Rarely did a public affairs program win in the vote. At first, they wouldn't watch the popularly selected broadcasts at all. After a while, they would

watch them with disdain. Eventually, however, they would sit attentively before the set and watch the parade of crimes and pillage,
violence and horror. Occasionally they would see a pleasant comedy
about American family life in middle-class, white suburbs.

All the men found prison to be mentally depressing. "Whenever
I'm separated from John and Lou, I'm left in a mental vacuum here,"
Quinton told me. "And I think if I had a little more yard, a little
more freedom of movement, prison would be different. Everywhere
you move around here, there's somebody already there. There's no
place to get off to yourself, there's absolutely no privacy."

Mail was another problem they worried about. Each one could
correspond only with authorized individuals. Letters could be written
only on Sunday at the Burke County Unit, and no more than three
letters could be written in any week. Each must be on a single piece
of paper supplied by the Prison Department. All mail was censored,
and no criticism of the Prison Department, a judge or a court was
permitted, except in letters to the Prison Department itself.

The incident at Burke County Prison Unit which resulted in John's
being sentenced to spend three to thirty days in the hole had to do
with the guard in charge of John's squad. John, Quinton and Lou say
this man was the least popular guard at the prison.

"When I got out there on the road," John says, "I could easily see
why. He is constantly gouging at the prisoners, degrading them, making derogatory comments. There were several who bucked during the
time I was on the squad. On one occasion, four bucked because we
were forced on a hot day to drink water that had come through a hose
that had grease running through it the day before. The water, you
couldn't see through it and it tasted very bad and was extremely
warm. He wouldn't let us go get spring water, have a water boy like
the other squads do. When the boys came to me and asked if I would
go with them and get up on the truck and refuse to work for the rest
of the day, I said no. I said, 'The best way to handle this is to finish
out the day's work so that you don't get into trouble. You can do
without water for a day, and then go see the captain about it, and he'll
probably work it out.' This wasn't the way they wanted to do it, so
they went on and got on the truck, and I went on working.

"On other occasions, boys have got into arguments with the guard.

After he has goaded long enough, they start to talk back. And as soon as they were out of earshot of him, and they were swearing how they were going to kill the son of a bitch and use the bush ax on him, I tried to calm them down.

"Then on the Friday before the Fourth of July it started to rain, so our squad went over and got in the truck. The guard got in the front of the truck with the other white inmate who is on our squad, and I was in the back of the truck. The rest of the inmates back there were Negroes. We sat around, talking about this and that, and one fellow who had, at a time previous, challenged me to a fight, which is sort of a tradition with some of the younger convicts who are trying to be what's known as a 'stag'—well, I had explained to him at that time that I didn't believe in fighting. He brought this up while we were sitting in the back of the truck. He made some comments about how he thought not fighting back was pretty dumb, and I said to him that there had been many times in recent months when I had been beaten up, and I hadn't fought back and was glad I hadn't, because had I fought back I would probably be dead by now.

"He said, 'Well, if one of those white sons of bitches ever hit me, or laid a hand on me, I'd try to kill him.' And I said, 'Well, I suspect if it ever did come to fighting, most of the Negroes would be killed, but many whites would die also, that's true, and that's the tragedy of it.' I was cut off before I could finish by the guard calling back from the front of the truck, 'If that's all you have to talk about, shut up, because I don't want to hear it.'

"We heard nothing more from him. We said nothing more, and soon after the rain stopped he came out of the truck, all in a huff, and with a tremendous amount of verbal abuse, cursing and so forth, saying that all I had been doing since I'd been out there was agitating, that I had been trying to stir up trouble, that the only reason I was in North Carolina was to try to get the Negroes and the whites fighting, and that once the fighting started, I'd leave and wouldn't suffer any.

"He went on to call a couple of the Negroes to one side. I was working at some distance, but I could hear what he was saying. He was trying to persuade them that they should dislike me and stay away from me, for I was trying to make them think I was their friend, but actually I was down here, he said, working for the Communists, trying to get Negroes in trouble and people shooting at Negroes, and then I would step out and watch the goings-on, and the Communists would come in and take over the country.

"On Tuesday, when I was ready to go out to work, I was put in the sickroom, and Captain Johns came in and told me I was to be tried that day by the major, because the guard had written me up for agitating the other inmates against working. I was surprised, for the only criticism he had ever made of my work was how I held my bush ax the first several days.

"The major came out and read the charge, and the captain verified the fact that all reports on my work had been good, and I asked the major if he would like to talk with some of the other inmates. I also said that another foreman had also been with our squad for most of that Friday, and he could verify that the squad had been working. The major shook his head and said, 'You know, we just can't tolerate anything like this. All I know is three to thirty days in punitive segregation, and I'll check back with you in a week or ten days.' "

There are no punitive isolation cells at Burke County Prison, so John was taken to Hudson Prison and was put in a bare cell which he had time to measure repeatedly and which he has reported to me was about 7 x 8 x 10 feet in size. He was offered food, a liver-base, sustenance diet, twice a day. He refused to eat. He objected to the sentence he had been given, and he objected further to the fact that the cell he was in was in a segregated prison unit.

After nine days, the major came by to see him and found him in good health and good spirits. The major released him, and he was returned to the Burke County Prison, arriving the day before my visit.

After talking with other prisoners, as well as with the captain and the lieutenant, Lou Calhoun and Quinton Baker decided that John was not guilty of an offense, so they went on a fast and refused to cooperate with the Prison Department. They were sent to still a third prison and were put in punitive segregation, where for nine days they remained. They were also returned to the camp on Friday, the day before my visit.

The following Monday they went out to work. On Thursday Quinton collapsed, and returned to work the following Monday.

I made a report of my findings, and such conclusions as I was able to make, to the State Prison Department in Raleigh, and I went over the written charge the guard had made, as well as statements from four prisoners who supported some of his contentions. The first part of the charge has to do with John hindering the performance of work of the other prisoners, and the last part has to do with John's alleged efforts to start a violent struggle in the South between Negroes and whites, which the guard said John would escape at the first shot by putting six states between himself and the insurrection. The guard said he told the squad that "they would be killed and I would be, too. I further stated that nobody would make a statement like Dunne made unless he was a Communist."

I concluded that the last half of the guard's charge is false. I doubt if anybody who knows John Dunne would believe that he had changed from a pacifist to a militant insurrectionist. Also, he is not a Communist. I have concluded, therefore, that the first half of the charge, since it was written by the same man and at the same time, might be in error also. I hope this conclusion on my part does the guard no injustice, and I admit the possibility of error on my part, as I trust he does on his. I believe that a guard who feels that a prisoner is trying to start a violent struggle within the South, who is trying to subvert the country, is likely to go to any extreme to stop that individual, and that he would be acting out of a sense of moral obligation. I don't deny that the guard is acting out of a sense of moral obligation, but I suspect that his premise is faulty.

I find the letters of the four prisoners who also complained of John Dunne somewhat more meaningful. These four people also were embarrassed by having John Dunne and the other demonstrators in prison with them, were annoyed by their presence and by what they said and did. One of them wrote the following letter, which was considered by the major in sentencing John to the hole:

I have been at unit 084 for 4 months. I was here when John Dunne come here. At first he seem like a good boy but it didn't take long for the rest of us to fine out what he was. He try to turn the other boy into hate. Well the white didn't like it so about 4 of us come to the office to talk to the cap. Dunne had the coler boy wave at the white women on the road. He thought that we didn't care. But if my wife was on the road and one would wave at her I would stop him somehow. The camp was alright before he come and brought the other two with him if they hadn't got him away from here there was going to be troble. And we all saw it coming and for my part I dont want nothing to do with him for I was not rise up to like people like him I am here try to make my time. but people like him wont let me and I would not like to get more time because of him and I would like very very much if you can do something about it.

This plea for help is almost as pitiful as the predicament John and Lou and Quinton were in. This prisoner was up against it; his moral standards were being challenged, perhaps by what John and Lou and Quinton said and did, but certainly by the fact that they were there in that prison; his personal morality was being questioned by men who had a better education than he, who were friendly and unafraid, and who might very well win out in the end. Yet what could he do?

I felt as sorry for him as I felt for John Dunne, and I told George Randall as much. I reminded him that I had gone to the prison to ask the demonstrators to stop causing trouble, and I had come away believing that the trouble being caused was not due to their actions so much as to their presence. I had no doubt that they did testify to what they believed, but that was all right and was to be expected. Quinton Baker in this regard had reminded me of a verse in I Peter, the third chapter: "Be ready at any time to give a quiet and reverent answer to any man who wants a reason for the hope you have within you."

I told Mr. Randall that both John Dunne and Pat Cusick had told me they would gladly submit to a lie-detector test concerning every charge which had been brought against them while they were prisoners of the state, including all suggestions or claims or rumors about them of any sort whatsoever, and that they felt it would be a good idea for this test to be made. Their instant willingness to take such tests was itself significant, I felt.

I suggested he consider isolating civil rights prisoners from the others in his system, treating them in much the same way that political prisoners are treated in Europe. I told him under the present circumstance I doubted if the Prison Department could handle the situation with its usual standard of fairness.

Because of this difficult situation, which I judged Mr. Randall had no alternative but to continue, I began to work to get a parole for each of the civil rights prisoners. This turned out to be quite a chore, but in time I had a job offer and a place of residence for each of them, and the Parole Board had been convinced that they could safely be set free. In August, on various dates, they were released.

John Dunne was paroled to Connecticut. He had an offer of a job in a Wallingford hospital, and he had a place to live near the campus of Choate School.

Pat Cusick was paroled to Massachusetts. Professor Walter Spearman went to Sandy Ridge one afternoon at 4 P.M., drove him to the nearby airport, and Pat was put on a 5:40 jet plane to New York City. He arrived at my apartment, stunned by the shock of prison and the even greater shock of suddenly being out of prison, more shaken by it all than John had been. The two men met at my apartment and talked the night through, John leaving on an early train for Wallingford in order to be at work on time. His job was in the physical therapy laboratory of Gaylord Hospital, helping the patients exercise and regain the use of their limbs.

Rosemary Ezra was paroled to North Carolina. She said she didn't want to leave Chapel Hill.

Quinton Baker was returned to court in August for sentencing on his second count, and he was asked by Judge Mallard if he felt he had the right to break any law in the country, to which he answered no, meaning he did not think he had the right to break *any* law. Judge Mallard said prison had evidently had a salutory effect on him and did not sentence him to serve a second active sentence. Quinton was soon thereafter paroled to New York State, where his parents live, and he got a job as a clerk in a Lexington Avenue office.

Lou Calhoun was returned to court in August for sentencing on his second count, and the question asked him by Judge Mallard did not permit a satisfactory answer. Judge Mallard sentenced him to serve an additional year in prison. He was soon thereafter given a temporary parole to Pennsylvania, where he had worked in previous summers at a camp, in order that he could do useful work and could resume his college studies in September under parole supervision. He was employed by the Christian Association in Philadelphia.

Joseph (Buddy) Tieger was still out on his appeal, and he prepared to enter Brandeis University on a scholarship.

In Boston Pat Cusick was offered interviews at several computation centers, but he selected instead a job in a poverty program where he worked as a clerk for two dollars an hour. He tells me that his first interview with his parole office was of special interest to him, for the officer began by complimenting him on the work he had done in the South. The Southern Negroes needed help, the officer said, for they had been subjugated for years, were hard-working and reliable. The officer said that Pat would soon discover, however, that the Negroes in Boston were shiftless, lacked ambition, committed crimes and were not dependable. He instructed Pat not to associate with Negroes in Boston or go into a Negro section of town.

Pat felt rather much at home, he says, with that sort of start.

In mid-August John Dunne talked with me about his chances of being admitted to Harvard. It seemed to be a distant chance but worth trying. He made application, explaining that the lateness of the application was due to his having been in a prison in North Carolina for several months. Once Quinton was free, he asked me what chance he would have to be admitted to the University of Wisconsin, the school he most wanted to attend. He applied, explaining his reason for being late with the application and giving his reasons for wanting to attend Wisconsin. Both these universities were kind enough to give the men consideration. After a series of letters and interviews, both were admitted on scholarships, John to Harvard and Quinton to Wisconsin, and they began their classwork in September. I have not seen two more surprised and pleased individuals in some time.

The physical placement of the students was due to many influences, and it interests me that Pat, John and Buddy Tieger have all ended up in Boston. Pat isn't working for a computation center, but in other respects their situation is similar to the earlier one in North Carolina. This causes me to say a small prayer for Boston, Massachusetts.

Pat, John and Quinton talk often of Chapel Hill and North Carolina, and speak fondly of the people there. I have sensed no bitterness in them. None of them wanted to leave the state, and none of them would have left except for the belief that they would not be able to live reasonably free lives if they stayed. All of them think of themselves now as Southerners, and like most Southerners they are critical of the situations they've encountered in the North. All of them very likely will return sometime to North Carolina.

Only Al Amon will not be back. He died during the summer, during the night, at his home. He left sixteen hundred pictures of the Chapel Hill civil rights struggle, and he had never been arrested.

Subsequent to all this moving about, after the people were out of prison I went through the prison records of each and found, except for the reports already made, little of consequence in them. There is a guard's notation that Quinton ate one meal while on his fast at Burke County Prison; Quinton denies this. There is also a notation that Pat Cusick ate one meal while on his Christmas fast at Central Prison; Pat denies this. Evidently Rosemary, while at the Women's Prison (which Jim Foushee in conversation refers to a "the Ladies' Prison"), showed little interest in the life going on around her, and it was thought best to have a psychiatrist talk with her—not an unusual occurrence in North Carolina prisons. His conclusions were that the interview

did not reveal any startling information with reference to the likelihood of a psychiatric disorder. The fact that she has been active in the CORE organization does not necessarily imply that she is mentally sick or suffering from a psychiatric disorder, inasmuch as many people nowadays are engaged in such activities—perhaps they are not obstructing traffic as was done in Chapel Hill, but there are many other ways of furthering the cause of integration which is engaged in by people who are interested in this phase of life.

There was one folk hero I discovered in my prison visits, a Negro man who escaped from Sandy Ridge in order to attend the New York World's Fair. He saw the fair, all right, then went to a police station near Times Square and turned himself in. The desk sergeant indicated that he wouldn't think of sending a Negro back to a Southern prison and for him to get on out of there, but the Negro held to his rights and insisted on being arrested. Other police officers tried to dissuade him, but to no avail, so he was packed home at last and settled down to telling the other prisoners about the wonders he had seen.

PART III

THE CONCLUSIONS

Chapter Nineteen

October 11, 1964

I HAVE SPENT THE last two months here in Chapel Hill, trying to find out what the outcome of all this has been. A town gets ripped up when a revolution strikes, and it has trouble getting put back together. I talked recently with Professor Emeritus of Journalism Phillips Russell, who has written biographies of Jefferson, Franklin and other statesmen of the American Revolution. He said a revolution always starts with disorder. "Where else can it start?" he said. "Its leaders try to deploy it, but they might as well try to deploy a lightning bolt."

Lightning struck in Chapel Hill in 1963 and 1964, and the reactions of the town have to be evaluated in terms of that. The effort to return to normalcy also ought to be considered sympathetically.

I have talked with Bob Brown about this. A few days before our meeting, a milk truck had backed into his car, and in other ways, too, his personal affairs were in disorder, no doubt contributing to his discouragement.

"Since I've been in Chapel Hill, my actions have been discursive," he told me, "completely useless, and this society is crumbling everywhere, man. The Roland Giduzes and McClamrochs and Wagers and people like that, they have the authority and they corrupt society. So you see guys with sandals and beards, and they are like that because what do they see ahead? Three days ago, I decided to start a political action group. Jesus! Yeah, you know, Jesus Christ. You can go around here like a madman trying to get something done, trying in this community to find somebody doing something in politics, working toward solving this town's troubles. Dad, it's not happening.

"You take the last time the aldermen ran for aldermen. Joe Nagelschmidt ran and got beat. Nagelschmidt came out strong for what underlies our society. He worked like a son of a gun for that job. He went everywhere. He knocked on doors on every street in town, except in the Negro section. He knew the Negroes were for equal rights. So he got defeated, and we end up with Page and the furniture man. At some point it seems that's about the thing. One has to do something about politics. In that north precinct is where most of the Negroes vote. In that precinct Page came in first and that furniture man second, so they beat Nagelschmidt. He lost the Board of Aldermen in the north precinct. Reverend Manley bought his church pews through the furniture man, and he got up in church, he told his people to vote for him. Meanwhile Page was down at the Negro schools giving away pen and pencil sets, things like that, with his office supply company's name on them." Bob groaned and grumbled. "It's a disgrace, this politics is a disgrace, and I'm going to start a write-in campaign, or something."

Except for Bob Brown, who has little political influence, the prevailing political climate in Chapel Hill is caution. There is the feeling that the liberals got the town into trouble and must now be guarded against, that the businessmen are willing to open their purses to stop them. And the liberals have been torn asunder, are in many different groups, and the groups are inactive.

When Solicitor Cooper and Judge Mallard announced that a special term of court, to meet August 17-28, would try Charliese Cotton, Charles Foushee, David McReynolds (the *Village Voice* writer who was arrested at the Pines), and a dozen or so other civil rights offenders, there was no complaint. Several of these persons were given jury trials during the session (David McReynolds' case was not heard), and the sentences handed out were, on the whole, tougher than those given out to John Dunne's group earlier. Charliese Cotton, for example, the seventeen-year-old daughter of a domestic, was given six months in the Women's Prison, an eighteen-month term to begin during the next five years at the discretion of the court, and a fine of $1,500. A professor at Bennett College in Greensboro, Elizabeth Laizner, a white woman born in Germany who had taken part in one Chapel Hill demonstration, was given similar sentences. The town was quiet; there was no protest.

"I can't conceive of this in New York City, Washington or other places I've been," Professor William Goodykoontz says. "I can conceive of injustice, but not public apathy. The problem clearly is not that of the judge and solicitor, but of the whole people; that's the great problem here. There is positive sadism in the sentences, as I see it; Mallard had to make it impossible for them to continue their loyalty to their principles. But complacency, the response from the public, is the greater concern. Complacency is what strikes me now about Chapel Hill, since I've returned, as contrasted with the old Frank Graham spirit of the university community."

He lays much of the blame at the doorstep of the press. "If there had been a free press, operating as a free press ought to operate, many of the abuses would have been corrected. I love Chapel Hill, but I'm appalled that these sentences could go on with so little protest."

Except from this professor, I have heard little said about the trials. I have heard Judge Mallard mentioned only one other time; that was at a party following a football game, when two liberal women, wives of leading liberals of the community, said they admired the fair way in which he had handled the cases of the civil rights demonstrators.

I talked with Solicitor Cooper about future trials, and he said he hadn't decided whether to bring other cases to trial or not. I tried to talk with Judge Mallard, too, but he would not see me.

The Chapel Hill Freedom Committee has ceased its protests and has been occupied almost exclusively with trying to raise money for bondsmen's fees, fines and court costs. The individuals who have been left to do this are Professor Joe Straley and Mrs. Joan Drake. She, a white mother of two children, only recently moved to Chapel Hill. She was not engaged in the Freedom Committee prior to the trials, and neither she nor Professor Straley encouraged or partici- pated in civil disobedience activities. They are, however, the ones who beg the money needed. In September I was told a debt of $3,000 was outstanding to one bondsman, there were debts to Professor Straley and others, one of the lawyers told me he hadn't been paid, and a massive series of new fines was ahead, unless the appeals made by Charliese Cotton and Mrs. Laizner were upheld by a higher court. National CORE, other than making a single donation of about $4,000, has shown little disposition to help. The total amount of money involved thus far in fines and fees and costs is about $20,000.

No demonstrations are being planned. During the summer Floyd McKissick wanted them to resume, and he approached John, Pat and

Quinton to ask them to lead the action, if he could get them out of prison on appeals. They were willing to do so. However, the young people went back to school, and the demonstrations, in McKissick's opinion, are over.

Few Negroes are found in the previously segregated restaurants. None has been in the College Café in months. Segregation is gone, but integration has not yet taken place.

There are two small liberal forces at work in Chapel Hill, both motivated in part by the demonstrations. The adult Negro leaders are more determined and active than they used to be. Rev. Manley, Rev. Foushee and Hilliard Caldwell are leading the opposition to the town's placing a Federal housing project in a Negro neighborhood, maintaining that it ought to be put where it can be integrated. There is in the Negro community a heightened awareness of importance, of their rights as human beings and citizens. Many Negroes have recently gone to their bosses and asked for wages equal to those of the white employees and they've got them without a word. That they dared do this is in itself significant.

The other effort by a liberal group is being made by Professors Maynard Adams and James Wicker, who seek to establish an anti-poverty program for Chapel Hill and Orange County. The program lists as one of its chief purposes the integration of the communities, but some of its chief supporters are the ones who oppose integration of the proposed housing project.

Mildred Ringwalt, who was sympathetic with the demonstrators, says the local conservatives haven't changed much. For example, she says in April she saw her druggist's picture in the paper attending a club meeting at Watts Restaurant. "I felt I should talk with him about it, and I found him very evasive. I told him I would take my business to another place, and he said all right then. Once the Civil Rights Bill had passed, I went back and told him I was sorry we had had the difference of opinion and that I was resuming trading with him, but he didn't say anything revealing about any change which might have taken place inside himself."

This is fairly typical of the general state of affairs in town. Many people aren't speaking to certain other people, and there is much resentment.

The ultrasegregationists seem to be baffled and worried, as well as angry. They are committed to a way of life which, largely because of national pressure, is being disrupted and made illegal. An elderly lady with whom I always have Sunday dinner when I'm in town has little use for Negroes. She tells me that one of the worst periods of her life came when two Negroes were found drowned in the university lake, the town water supply. "I could taste them for months whenever I drank water," she said. "I said to my daughters, 'Do you taste them two niggers in this water?' " She gave me the devil every week I remained on "terrible Terry's" staff. Not long ago, however, she suddenly looked up exasperated from her dinner plate and demanded of me, "Well, what *do* the niggers want?" a question at least indicating a new interest on her part, which I took to be a sign of change in her.

The relationship between segregationists and integrationists is more tense than ever. An extreme example of this took place on Saturday night, September 19, when about one hundred people attending an integrated party at a private home a mile or so outside the town limits were harassed by gunfire. The hosts phoned the Sheriff's Department, and Deputy Sheriff Clark, whom we met in connection with the trials of the Watts Motel sit-ins, came to the scene, told the eight or ten segregationists to stop disturbing the party, helped escort the women and the Negroes out of the area, then left. There was more gunfire.

At 3 A.M. a few men attacked the house, and a fight began which resulted in one of the intruders having his head bashed by an oak table leg.

This was, of course, a most unusual occurrence, and one doubts if it will be repeated. The more customary form of abuse is insults and other minor irritations. For example, a lady visiting Chapel Hill in September was refused a room at a motel because she was the mother of one of the demonstrators.

Such small and large signs of resentment supply evidence that John Dunne and his colleagues, by stomping about in the Southern society, have broken open a box of passions. The personality of the ultrasegregationist has been challenged, and now it asserts itself dangerously. The chief problem of the South is, as Professor Henry Brandis told me, the hate these people have, "which corrodes all that it touches." It might be that this intensification of hatred is part of a healing process; sometimes people when pressed will reaffirm their old doctrines and, having paid a final obeisance to them, will yield to their extinction, even insist on their going. But whether this stage is what we have in the South or whether we are simply inflicting deeper wounds on each other can't yet be known. That the South, as well as the North, has more than its share of sadists is evidently so. Hitler had to train his sadists; ours are produced by our society as a matter of course. Hitler had to create places for his sadists to operate in, but ours have plenty of places in the society itself.

The mind of the community is dulled by the civil rights struggle. People seek reasons not to be liberals, to avoid the new, more demanding requirements made of liberals locally. One resident told me she had supported the Civil Rights Bill, but now she wasn't sure it was a good thing. When asked why she had changed, she said the Negroes were getting hair oil on the back of the bus seats she used going on weekends to Roanoke Rapids.

I talked with dramatist Paul Green about the Chapel Hill situation. He said there was something about it which eluded him, and there was, he suggested, something elusive about Southerners as a people, too. Of all people in this country, they are the most kindly, friendly and hospitable, he said, yet they are also the most sadistic at times, and the most violent.

Mr. Green said he recalls as a boy in Harnet County, North Carolina, a handsome young sawmill man boarding at his family's little four-room house. He was a friendly person, admirable in all ways, as the boy Paul saw him. "One night we were having supper, and he said, 'I'm going out and help hang a nigger tonight.' When supper was over, he went out; sometime later he came back, and he was as friendly and kindly a human being as he had been during the past days.

"I've seen Negroes beaten," Mr. Green said. "I saw a little Negro boy beaten once. The problem is some kind of ignorance, ignorance of the known and fear of the unknown. 'They know not what they do.' And the town is like that now in a way; the community isn't informed, and that's where some of the ignorance comes in."

The failure of the journalists in the Chapel Hill story is generally admitted, even by the journalists I've talked with. Interestingly enough, the Chapel Hill *Weekly* in August and September published a series of excellent articles on the civil rights situation in Williamston, North Carolina. Bill Scarborough wrote the series. That same attention to the Chapel Hill problem had not been possible, evidently, for him or others on the staff. The failure of the national press to notice the events in Chapel Hill is also significant; there seems to have been a news blackout on the Chapel Hill crisis. The over-all lack of concern evidenced in the public press over what was going on helps to explain the apathy of the townspeople.

Another partial explanation lies in the failure of the town's leaders to lead. It would be fair to put the blame here on the mayor, and since the mayor tells me he reached his decisions only after conferring with Alderman Giduz, and since Giduz confirms this, some of the responsibility rests on him, too. A statement Roland Giduz made in December, after the dangerous series of sit-ins began, is helpful in this regard. Concerning the demonstrators, he said, "I will consider their opinion, along with what seems to me to be the facts, the needs, the entire logic of the situation and, in particular, in consideration of what the legal authority of the town is and then the merits of the issue. So all of this weighs in together."

It's a solid statement, fair and clearly put, but nobody can do all that, and at a time when lightning is striking, one hopefully does what he can to attain the ends he has said are desirable for the community. A leader uses the forces available to him to serve the needs of social progress. In Chapel Hill there was plenty of force released, there was much confusion, and out of it came no progress that one can see. This failure has to be partly attributed to the men in power, to their withdrawal at the critical moments of the contest. It's not quite enough for them to say they would not respond to pressure. Actually, they did respond; they had to. They had their policemen work hundreds of extra hours without pay, they brought in policemen from Burlington, they brought in the State Highway Patrol and the governor, they bought a paddy wagon, they filled their jail cells and clogged their courts. These are responses to pressure, but they don't constitute progressive action.

A better approach was used in Durham, by a mayor who didn't campaign on a liberal platform. When a crisis came, he waded into the thick of things and took hold, exerted leadership and saved the city the danger of massive demonstrations, while at the same time solving some of its problems.

I sense in talking with Mayor McClamroch and Alderman Giduz that they feel no real compulsion to work for integration in Chapel Hill, that they feel no pressing need for moving along in this area. They have not yet really seen the Negro's painful predicament. Jim Foushee tells me that once somebody asked him, "How does it feel to be black?" Jim says he replied, "How does it feel to be white?" That's fair enough.

For us to feel the need of the other race or sense its apprehensions requires a certain sympathy and ability, to be sure. I don't mean here to criticize any official for not having this ability. The more critical point is that at a time of crisis in the community the officials, because of this reason or some other, withdrew from the field of action. The appointment of another committee does not constitute leadership. It appears that, except for Chief Blake, they left the town close to leaderless.

The apathy of the citizens, the inadequacy of the press and the withdrawal of key town leaders all make a single pattern. One thread goes with the other two and they are woven together. They represent a Southern town proud of its reputation as a liberal community, which is so afraid of tarnishing that reputation that it draws back from being a genuinely liberal community. It suggests a town that wants peace more than it wants achievement, as Professor John Clayton has suggested to me. Afraid something ugly might take place, they just wanted all the trouble to go away; they didn't want to use the trouble as a basis for corrective action. They responded to the revolutionaries by saying the revolutionaries were not neat and tidy; they did not take this opportunity to see themselves and study their problems. Peace was what they seemed to want, a withdrawal from a commitment or from any action or change; and what they are left with, now that the challenge is over, is not peace, really, but apathy, and at least a temporary inability to act on their own.

This situation can conceivably come about in any town. There is a fourth aspect to the local problem, however, which is unique, and that is the aloofness of its main institution, the university, which also wanted to avoid action.

Pat Cusick tells me that, should the whole thing be done over, the demonstrators ought to press their energies not on the merchants or the town officials, but on the university itself, which has enough power over merchants and officials to bring about change. He feels that by sparing the university the demonstrators permitted it to advise caution and moderation.

There is a considerable dissatisfaction on the part of the demonstrators with the university. I'm not sure why that is so, and I'm not sure the demonstrators are, either, but in addition to their affection for it, they have a certain amount of distrust. Young people reach decisions not on the basis of what is told them, but on the basis of what they feel is so. It was all very well for the university hospital to say it was not segregated, but it was. It was all very well for the chancellor to say the university did not practice segregation, but in some ways it did, and in other ways, one feels, it wanted to but could not because of laws. An institution which deals with young people needs to ring true to young people, and certainly an educational institution needs to.

A university also might properly have somebody in the administration capable of understanding students like John Dunne and Pat Cusick. If these students are not accommodated within the university, then they will very likely leave, and their actions outside the institution can result in considerable expense to society as a whole. There was nobody in the administration at Chapel Hill these young people felt they could go to and talk with and learn from, in terms of the issues which concerned them at this time in their lives.

I asked carefully about this, and I even went so far as to play for Pat, John and Quinton a tape recording of a talk made by Frank Porter Graham. I asked them, after they had heard it, if they would have left the university if this man had been an administrator there. Pat Cusick said he thought he would not have left. John Dunne thought about the matter for several days, and then reported that he agreed with Pat. Quinton wasn't a student at Chapel Hill, but his opinion was that Pat and John had reached the conclusion he would have reached.

It is one thing for a state institution to be realistic about politics; it is another for it to have a wavering voice which means nothing to anybody. To advise faculty members not to speak out in order not to irritate the legislature is to suggest that the way to preserve academic freedom is to discourage its use. This isn't likely to make much sense either in Raleigh or in Chapel Hill. If the university cowers and is afraid, it is likely to be ineffective. In the 1930's and 1940's, as an official of the university Frank Porter Graham used to get himself and the university into a lot of trouble, maybe too much trouble, but he did keep many young people from street demonstrations and jailings, I believe. He went into action with them if the action was legal and responsible. He voiced with them the hopes they had for a better society. He helped them, and by some means or other he usually kept them within bounds. And when he spoke out, there was considerable clarity.

I am told that in the 1940's an assistant went into his office and told him a newspaper editor had phoned to say he had a rumor that at the concert that night Negroes were going to be admitted as part of the audience. "I have checked on this," the assistant told Dr. Graham, "and have found that the man in charge is indeed admitting Negroes but is seating them in the balcony. Is it all right if I phone the editor and get the story straight before he writes his editorial?"

Dr. Graham could have nodded. Or he could have made some sort of evasive statement or tried to stop the newspaper story. What he did was this: He said to the young assistant, "Do two things. First, find out who is planning to seat the Negroes in the balcony and ask him to let them sit where they please; second, phone the newspaper and tell them that at Chapel Hill we do not distinguish."

Students in a university, whether they are liberals or conservatives, can respond to that sort of action, because they see honesty in it and they respect leadership. And, of course, liberals like John Dunne accept that type of action readily; it doesn't drive them from the institution, it draws them into it, closer into the web of society itself, which helps make what they do productive and revitalizing to society.

In this respect, it is right to mention that a new chancellor arrived at the university in September, 1964. His name was Paul Sharp, and he was from the Midwest. About the first problem that came up was a rule instituted in 1963, that Negro students would be segregated from white students in the dormitories. It had been instituted by Chancellor Aycock on the advice of an advisory council of unnamed faculty members. Chancellor Sharp, when he encountered this rule, could have nodded and let it alone, but he did not. He announced that the university was discarding the rule, not because of a law or Federal contract, but because it was morally wrong. He said he was taking the action on his own authority without consulting any committee.

I have mentioned the apathy of the people, and have commented on a few other problems which led to a failure in Chapel Hill. There is one other component, at least, that is to be blamed, and that is the demonstrators themselves. There were severe faults in them. John, Pat and Quinton, after the action was over, were not at all certain that what they did in Chapel Hill was always sensible, and they realize it wasn't always fruitful. They were aware that they didn't seek advice and that they rarely took it, and that they had many shortcomings.

This is concurred in by most of the white liberals in town. Charlie Jones says the demonstrators managed to put a wall between themselves and these white liberals. "It got to the point," he says, "where they would say, 'Are you with us or are you not?' To be with them meant you did what they did, you know. And my secretary, Mrs. Marian Davis, is the only person I know who stayed close to them and never did get arrested. Up until the last, John and Quinton would come around the church here, talking about what they were planning to do and saying, 'What do you think of it?' But what you thought of it didn't have anything to do with what they were going to do."

Joe Straley feels that the young people did not realize their own strength. "With only a little effort the activities of CORE and its associated organizations could have commanded the enormous liberal sentiment of the community, and for the young people to go it alone was quite foolish," he told me.

Charlie Jones says, "To some of them it seemed almost a psychological necessity; it was almost a compulsion of their entire beings to go the whole way. John was willing to die, you know. I don't think Pat had quite that necessity. I think Pat had to struggle to do it. John would just go right on. Quinton would go right on. Quinton's motivation came out of aggression. John's was halfway spiritual. And Pat was working out of a sense of obligation and a sense of guilt. John didn't have a sense of guilt. The three of them in a way form a Father, Son and Holy Ghost."

They were a self-contained leadership committee. Made up of one man from outside the South and one white man and one Negro from the South, they composed a total unit with considerable versatility and force, and certainly with a world of dedication. But they were, no doubt, jealous of their new-found authority and didn't much want to share it with others, particularly older people, and it's true, too, that they had good cause to be disappointed with the leaders of the town and university, particularly those who considered themselves to be liberals. They respected Charlie Jones and Joe Straley, but not the leaders inside the institutions.

There was one other fault, not entirely their own. They had found themselves mounted on a runaway horse, and they didn't know how to stop it or get off. Activities had started slowly, quietly, with a couple of students making picket signs one night and picketing a small café at dawn; then they began going faster and faster. "I think there was nothing to stop the street sit-ins except desegregation," Charlie Jones says. "Once you try something and it fails, you have to try something more advanced." They went from one tactic to another, each more advanced than the other, each taking them further away from the main body of the liberal community, which could have been their chief source of strength.

Floyd McKissick doesn't see it this way, however. He says the fault lies with the white liberals themselves. "I wish they would keep their mouths shut and send in their contributions," he told me. "To hell with their curiosity. They ought to stick with us, right or wrong, like your child. 'You have gone one step too much,' they say. To hell with that. They either support me or they don't. I'm about to abolish 'white liberal' from my vocabulary. Either they're for total citizenship now for the Negro or they are not. If you ask me what is the main cause of the Chapel Hill plight, I'd put my finger on the white liberal."

Mr. McKissick and the white liberals agree on one thing: that the most fortuitous action taken by anybody during this critical period was the passage of the Civil Rights Bill in Congress. I know of few leaders in Chapel Hill, in either the liberal or conservative camps, who don't admit privately that the passage of the bill was helpful. The alternative was more negotiation committees, more demonstrations; and the consequences of such a series of assaults on our institutions, in places all over this country, is beyond the mind's power to consider.

Mrs. Agnes Merritt and her husband run the Pines, and she said recently she was certainly grateful for that law, for she now had her old friends and customers back. Soon after the bill was passed, as a matter of fact, the white liberals flooded to her restaurant again. They were anxious to go back, and it was almost like old home week, they say, for they all seemed to arrive together to reclaim their long-lost territory.

The Chapel Hill story has meaning in terms of other national matters. For example, what do we Americans mean by law? Do we mean the local law or do we mean the Constitution of the country? When we speak of law, do we also need to speak of justice? I talked with Solicitor Cooper about this in terms of the trial of Ben Spaulding for writing a worthless check. After talking with Ben, I believe he was honestly in error and did not mean to deprive the Court of the eighty dollars. The solicitor simply says Ben was given a trial according to law. Perhaps so, but what about justice? To what extent is the law obligated to justice? To what extent is a solicitor obligated to justice in enforcing the law? We have often said that justice is blind; what the Ben Spaulding incident indicates is that the law can be blind to justice. And this is only one court case, of course, among many which might be mentioned here.

Walter Lippmann in *Drift and Mastery* wrote: "If the courts made law that dealt with modern necessities, the people would, I believe, never question their power. It is the bad sociology of judges and their class prejudices that are destroying the prestige of the bench."

The question of law and morality was discussed by Robert E. Cushman, dean of the Duke University Divinity School, on April 19, 1964, in the Duke Chapel. "Are all laws, at all times, equally to be honored whether they serve human good and civil justice or not?" he asked his congregation. "It may surprise you when I say that Jesus did not so believe respecting the law of his day and did not so act, that is, if we may trust the New Testament record. He subordinated particular laws to the standard of the Great Commandment: 'Thou shalt love the Lord thy God with all thy heart and with all thy soul and with all thy mind . . . and thy neighbor as thyself.' "

Jesus, Dean Cushman said, ignored the rules pertaining to the Sabbath day and did healing and traveling on the Sabbath; he ignored the ceremonial rules of diet and cleanliness; he fraternized and dined with publicans and sinners; he preached that human well-being and the love of one's neighbor, even of the despised Samaritans, have prior claims to men's loyalty, exceeding in urgency many others of the Law of Moses.

"For Christians the sovereign rule of life is the Great Commandment," Dean Cushman said. "By fidelity to it, Christ was reckoned with transgressors. . . . For America, the sovereign law is the word of the Great Declaration that men are endowed by their Creator with the inalienable right to life, liberty and the pursuit of happiness or life fulfillment. To frustrate the realization of these commanding principles by misapplication of laws or willful failure to enact laws is the nation's self-stultification. It is the real and most perilous form of civil disobedience.

"But it was Christ who was reckoned with transgressors in those callous and ugly days, not the Pharisees and the lawyers. He was, in fact, crucified for theocratic disobedience. For some time now we have regarded this reckoning as a case of mistaken identity. Indeed, we have reversed the verdict and long since convicted his jury. But we are blind about ourselves."

Writing in the Spring, 1964, issue of the *Duke Divinity School Review,* Dean Cushman said:

For the Christian, no positive law is an absolute, and among other reasons, because it is always an imperfect vehicle of Divine Justice. Judged by the New Testament, the Christian cannot, therefore, always evade the dilemma implied in the Perine resolution: "We must obey God rather than man."

This highlights the dilemma of both the professors and the court at Hillsboro. Neither, I think, really believes that the trespass law is an absolute if its application abridges fundamental human rights. So the professors are committed to a "higher law" that presently does not exist, and the court to a law that *exists* but is a wholly deficient vehicle of justice. Neither professors nor judge really has any alternative and no resolution of their dilemma because the existing legal structure is inadequate as a vehicle for the justice that is sought by both but is presently outraged.

The Chapel Hill story might help in the study of other national matters, as well. By looking at this town and its experiences, we can begin to evaluate how our various institutions and groups are participating. For example, consider the churches. The freedom songs of the movement are essentially spirituals; the emotion-filled talks to demonstrators are sermons; the meeting places usually are church buildings; the moral values of the movement are essentially the moral values of the church. All of this combines to give the civil rights movement a foundation. (In some of our major Northern cities the churches are less effective, and the consequence might very well be riots rather than demonstrations.)

Also, in terms of the national scene, the Chapel Hill situation helps tell us what the young people of America are up to. Of course, most of them are involved with courtship and trying to find enough money to live on and so forth, but there is a distinctive character, a difference from one generation to another, which it is helpful to consider. Several decades ago we had the Lost Generation, many members of which went to Europe and wrote about each other and America from a distant place. My own generation served in the war with Germany and Japan, and we felt we had saved America, so we didn't feel obligated to reconstruct its institutions. We were followed by the Beat Generation, which seemed to repudiate society, then withdraw from it. Now we come to this new group. John Dunne is not going to leave the country, nor does he have a military war to fight, nor is he willing to disassociate himself from the problems. He, Pat, Quinton, Lou, Rosemary and the others are part of a free generation which seeks to bring about in our country a society based on the principles we have always claimed were ours.

Few people up to now have really expected our national moral commitments to be translated fully into action; we have not believed that we could achieve in our society what is envisioned for it by our political saints, any more than in our lives we believe we can fulfill our spiritual aspirations. These young people, however, insist that we do. They are not hesitant in making their demands, either. They are presumptuous in them, they are confident of them, and they are confident, as was neither the Beat nor Lost Generation, of America's ability to deliver on its promises.

Frank Porter Graham is unhappy about the breaking of laws; he feels the massive assault on the society which the young people got themselves into is wrong. But before they got into so much trouble, and got the country into so much trouble, he did talk about them in a way which seems meaningful to me now. He said the Southern youth movement was "part of the unfolding American Revolution in its modern phase." He said:

It started in a college supported by the State, a Negro college, in Greensboro, North Carolina, in 1960, and its further headwaters were in Carpenter's Hall, Philadelphia, where was declared the first universal declaration of human rights on the 4th of July, and its farther headwaters were in the Judean hills some 2000 years away where the carpenter's son . . . taught and lived and died for freedom and dignity and opportunity for all people.

The present-day American youth movement, he feels, is our native response to the world revolution of colonial, colored and oppressed people, a revolution which also was planted by the American Revolution.

As viewed in terms of the Chapel Hill contingent, the members of this disorganized American youth movement are not ragged individuals. They are not lost or beat. They proclaim themselves to be found, and they claim to be victorious even in defeat. They are willing to sacrifice in order to improve our society, all of this to be achieved, one gathers, not eventually, but now, and they mean right now.

I suspect it was this new youth movement which struck Chapel Hill. It was not a bolt of lightning from alien lands; it was native American, actually native Southern, and whether we like it or not (and we are not asked) it is ours.

I do not know how many of these young people there are in the South or the country. In Chapel Hill over two hundred different individuals have been arrested in civil rights demonstrations. In North Carolina perhaps two thousand different students were arrested in civil rights activities during 1963 and 1964. Beyond that, the state had many young people who volunteered for the Peace Corps and other public service programs. For example, the North Carolina Fund in the spring of 1964 announced that it wanted one hundred college students to go into poverty pockets of the state and work for subsistence wages during the summer months; 750 college students applied.

I meet the same types of young people in the North, and I suspect they are all over this country. The characteristics the Chapel Hill group has in common are these:

1. They are confident of our country's ability to achieve its stated goals, if it really wants to.

2. They are critical of leaders who aren't as confident of this as they are, and they generally are dissatisfied with the standards most people set for themselves and their institutions.

3. They are morally, not politically motivated; therefore they are serious, dedicated, self-sacrificing, uncompromising, but they are politically naïve.

4. Tactically, they are nonviolent but tough. Many of them are dedicated to nonviolence as a responsible philosophy for individuals, and some of them believe it is a proper policy for nations as well.

5. They are interested in self-improvement and take readily to books and learning. Their saints seem to be Jesus and Gandhi, among others, but they have no set code.

6. Their social habits are moderate and controlled. Some of them enter a given commitment as if entering a religious order.

7. They commit themselves to a mission for a limited period of time—one summer or one year, something of that sort. All this seems

to be parenthetical to their life plans. In effect, they say they will spend a certain time working in this special work, then resume their plans where they were left off.

8. They come from the lower or middle economic class; if one does appear from the upper class, he or she most likely has repudiated its more artificial standards.

9. They are almost always late for an appointment.

10. They are always broke.

Our country for years has said it needed a sense of mission. We now have a new group of citizens with a sense of mission, and they tell us it's time to move ahead toward the fulfillment of the American democracy. They present a puzzling problem to our country, one which might grow even more puzzling as we come to see them for what they are, and to realize that the newcomer in our midst is demanding institutional changes of a revolutionary sort, at a revolutionary speed, and with revolutionary doctrines which come from our own American Revolution and from our own churches, synagogues and cathedrals.

To me this group was the most important discovery I made in my study of the Chapel Hill activities. In meeting it, I came to have a sense of excitement about the next twenty years in our country.

When I was a boy in Asheville, one of my earliest recollections is riding on a bus. I got up to give a Negro woman my seat, and my father instinctively slapped me, a light, abrupt gesture of surprise and irritation. My father is not a deeply prejudiced man; I believe it was not the Negro problem which concerned him, but that he realized he ought to uphold the ways of the society in which he lived. He was trying to help me learn to conform, as all of us must, to the social system.

I have since, quite on my own, learned to get into trouble on my own, and to evaluate social rules as well as the inevitability of social change. In writing about these young people, I have come closer to identifying myself with the new social order, the one that is ahead, and because of them I do so with considerable confidence. Somebody once said that the only freedom we have is freedom to select our own form of bondage. The form of bondage I have selected, in part because of them, is the bondage of the American white man who believes not only that the Negro should be equal and free, but that he can be. This is the added dimension these young people have helped supply, and is needed in order for one to be a free man and at the same time to be responsible as a citizen of the country.

I believe not only that the Negro can be admitted to citizenship, but that all our people can be admitted to a fuller, better life in a better country, one which does manage to afford each man and woman and child fairness and a chance for decency and productivity and goodness in their lives. I don't see all this accomplished in a few years; I don't see it, either, in terms of civil rights or integration, so much as in terms of solutions to poverty and the cycle of poverty, and the cycle of ignorance—yes, and the cycles of fear and injustice and hate and violence and apathy.

The question for our country now is whether we are going to accept this considerable task of self-improvement, of giving new chances to the lower one-third of our people, white and Negro, and improving the lot of us all. That is the basic question in Chapel Hill, too, one it has avoided meeting. Today for the first time in man's history, we have the techniques and wealth to create the needed changes; perhaps now we have the people, too, the young people, who are the key to any effort we would make. The next step would be an upheaval of social and educational forces.

It was particularly fitting that on May 22, 1964, President Johnson made his Great Society address on the campus of a university. "For half a century," he told students at the University of Michigan,

we called upon unbounded invention and untiring industry to create an order of plenty for all our people. The challenge of the next half-century is whether we have the wisdom to use that wealth to enrich and elevate our national life, and to advance the quality of American civilization. Your imagination, your initiative and your indignation will determine whether we build a society where progress is the servant of our needs or a society where old values and new visions are buried under unbridled growth. For in your time we have the opportunity to move not only toward the rich society and the powerful society, but upward to the Great Society. The Great Society rests on abundance and liberty for all. It demands an end to poverty and racial injustice, to which we are totally committed in our time.

President Johnson asked the young people:

Will you join in the battle to give every citizen the full equality which God enjoins and the law requires, whatever his belief, or race, or the color of his skin? Will you join in the battle to give every citizen an escape from the crushing weight of poverty? Will you join in the battle to make it possible for all nations to live in enduring peace as neighbors and not as mortal enemies? Will you join in the battle to build the Great Society . . . ?

The answer of the young people might be yes. A great many of them appear to be prepared to make it in terms of a full commitment, more self-sacrificing than any peacetime commitment our country has previously known. Now we need to hear from the leaders in our states and communities and universities, from the McClamrochs and Wagers and Sharps and Fridays, for this work cannot be done from a central office in Washington. It must be done where the people are, in our own streets and other places. The question to us is the question President Johnson has raised: Do we want to build here the Great Society?

The best understanding of America begins, or so it seems to me, with the realization that this nation is young yet, that she is still new and unfinished, that even now America is man's greatest adventure in time and space. And the call which we hear is our own call from our own people, new pioneers in a way, not of the wilderness roads, not of the clearing of land and the building of cities and factories, but of the other effort we have been making in this country from the first, the companion effort to build here a society in which democracy can exist without vulgarity, and all men can fulfill the best that is in them as free and productive citizens.

The full achievement of this is yet to be attained; it is the promise of our country and the question of our time. I have come to see of late that the young people are more ready for the work at hand than are most of the rest of us.

I set out months ago to find out why John Dunne got sent to prison. Out of this have come certain discoveries about him, "the so-called Negro white leader," as Jim Foushee tells me some people refer to him now ("Oh, man," Jim told me, "you ought to hear what they call John"). I believe I know now what led to that prison sentence, and maybe I know him better, too, although the full definition of himself is not yet made by him and will doubtless take a few more years to finish up. In this study I have also come to see him as part of a larger group. That group almost wrecked Chapel Hill, but if the schools and other institutions across our country come to understand them, the prospects for good are immense. I believe they offer us our greatest opportunity in several generations.

I won't weigh them down by trying to compare them with Jesus or other saints, or with the early American patriots; such comparisons aren't usefully applied to individuals on the present-day scene. But I must say that it is too bad they were imprisoned. It didn't hurt them so much, of course; perhaps it only made them stronger in what they believed and in their sense of dedication. But what a pity it is for a town, and a university town at that, to lock up or unconcernedly look on while others lock up young people who are among the best leaders of the new generation.

Postscript

On December 5, 1964, Governor Sanford commuted the sentences and fines of fifteen of the demonstrators but let their convictions stand. Included were the professors from Duke, Bennett College, and the University of North Carolina, as well as several students, among them Joseph Tieger and Charliese Cotton. (The Chapel Hill *Weekly,* with a tone more fatherly than usual, said Governor Sanford "understood as well as anyone that these demonstrators, convicted though they stood, were not criminals in the ordinary sense, and although their proper place was not lying in the streets, neither was it moldering in a jail.")

Later in December the Governor commuted the sentence of Walter Mitchell, and the United States Supreme Court ruled that the public accommodations section of the Civil Rights Act of 1964 was effective retroactively. This did away with hundreds of charges against Chapel Hill demonstrators and complicated to near-distraction the debate about who all along had indeed been on the side of law and who against it.

* * *

Quinton Baker is still at the University of Wisconsin, Lou Calhoun still has his job in Philadelphia. John Dunne wrote his parents from Harvard at Christmas: "This place is wonderfully free and stimulating. . . . It almost overwhelms me to think that scarcely three months ago I was behind bars, and eight months ago at 20, I was passing judgment on the acts and beliefs of my elders with no more thought of my age and relative inexperience than of reticence or fear."

Ben Spaulding is working in New York City, saving money so that he can return to the University of North Carolina next summer.

Pat Cusick is still working in Boston. Just recently he received word that his probation papers were being transferred from North Carolina to Massachusetts, which he was glad of until he read them and found that he must sign a statement agreeing to obey for five years all the special requirements Judge Mallard had imposed. Pat refused, and the NAACP Legal Defense Fund has agreed to represent him in court action against the state of North Carolina. The Massachusetts probation officers supported the North Carolina demands, which gives Pat one more reason to wonder how Boston can continue to call itself "the cradle of liberty." Many other young people in Chapel Hill are under probation and will be affected by any decision in this case.

* * *

In December, 1964, the Orange County Board of Commissioners passed a resolution. "We . . . do hereby commend Judge Raymond B. Mallard for his devotion to his judicial duties and for [his] learned and impartial manner . . . and for his deep knowledge of humanity as shown by judgments rendered, all in the highest tradition of the administration of justice in the state of North Carolina."

* * *

During late fall of 1964 trial was held in Chapel Hill Recorders Court of three men charged with harassing an integrated party attended by about one hundred people; one was found guilty of forcible trespass and was fined $25 and court costs; two others were found guilty of simple assault on a constable and were fined $15 and one-half court costs each. To what extent a violent attack on a party of one hundred people is more dangerous than a street blocking or a sit-in was not discussed by the court. These charges are misdemeanors as were the charges against John Dunne, Pat Cusick, Quinton Baker and the others.

* * *

Alderman Adelaide Walters early in 1965 wrote Gary Blanchard, who is studying at Princeton:

The pain and worry of a year ago was absent from our Christmas season in Chapel Hill. At least there were no young people in jail. In a way, it seems a little sad that we can see so little in the way of changes from our experiences. Unless we can channel that tension and dedication and con-

cern into a continuing attack on our problems of training and employment and use of resources, it will seem in vain. There is a residue of
distrust among the Negroes which is unpleasant at times. I don't like it
even if I do understand it. We are slowly making progress toward using
some anti-poverty funds for pre-school integrated classes, etc., but it is
a limping program at this point. I think our experience has been meaningful in that it gave new purpose and resolution to the Negroes and
shattered the white illusion of "good race relationships." I think it also
helped a great deal to make our adjustment to the Civil Rights bill easier
and enabled whites to accept the social changes as they never thought
they could.

I have been trying to follow the evolution of the new generation
as it shows up in different places and forms. The University of California at Berkeley has been having a series of student demonstrations,
including marches and sit-ins, much like Chapel Hill's. Governor Pat
Brown called them "anarchy," and President Clark Kerr denounced
what he supposed was a Communist uprising. The Chancellor resigned.

The Berkeley revolt differed from Chapel Hill's in that the students
were from a single, almost all-white institution and were all of college
age; also in that the students did not attack civil rights problems in
the community but attacked the university itself in order to protect
their own civil rights as students and to help create a campus climate
responsive to student needs.

Significantly, students on thirty other campuses at once voted support of the Berkeley students, and many worried administrators sat
down to try to figure out if their crusty institutions could be better
adapted to student use.

I have recently visited Berkeley and have also visited with young
people who have left both school and community to go into full-time
service in the deep South. After eight or ten months they take on the
look of war veterans; they begin to be as cyncial and courageous too,
and like veterans try to see the whole country from the perspective of
their own place of action, which is apt to be distorting, and the entire
movement in terms of their own group. All this is to be expected, I
know, and it points up the need for a behind-the-lines center to which
they can come once in a while, to congregate and share ideas and ex-

periences, to read, and perhaps to meet with teachers who can supply information they want about preschool, adult-illiteracy and other community programs.

*   *   *

I have written about my own town, friends and acquaintances in this book, and there are going to be hurt feelings. I'm sorry about that.

But I stand with the book. I appreciate deeply the help scores of people have given, but the conclusions are my own and I am accountable for them.

I go along with the italicized statement which is published in each issue of the Chapel Hill *Weekly:*

"If the matter is important and you're sure of your ground, never fear to be in the minority."

February 3, 1965

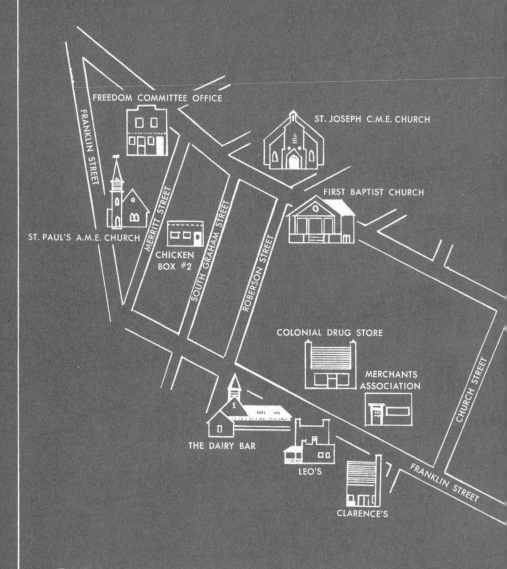

FREEDOM COMMITTEE OFFICE

ST. JOSEPH C.M.E. CHURCH

FRANKLIN STREET

FIRST BAPTIST CHURCH

MERRITT STREET

ST. PAUL'S A.M.E. CHURCH

CHICKEN BOX #2

SOUTH GRAHAM STREET

ROBERSON STREET

COLONIAL DRUG STORE

MERCHANTS ASSOCIATION

CHURCH STREET

THE DAIRY BAR

LEO'S

CLARENCE'S

FRANKLIN STREET

CHAPEL HILL, North Carolina
1963-1964

TO WATTS
MOTEL AND
THE PINES